PRINCIPLES OF ECONOMICS

Saifedean Ammous

PRINCIPLES OF ECONOMICS

ISBN 979-8-9879755-1-0 *Hardcover*
979-8-9879755-4-1 *Paperback*
979-8-9879755-7-2 *Ebook*
979-8-9879755-0-3 *Audiobook*

To my father, who taught me the most important lesson of this book before I could read, and to my son, so he too may learn it.

Table of Contents

About the Author xiii
Introduction 1

PART I. FUNDAMENTALS **9**

Chapter 1 Human Action **11**
Action, Purpose, and Reason 12
Economic Analysis 14
Quantitative Analysis 15
A Contrast of Approaches 22

Chapter 2 Value **27**
Utility and Value 28
Valuation: Ordinal and Cardinal 31
Value and Price 34
Free Exchange 34
Determinants of Value 35
Marginalism 36
Marginal Utility 37

	Law of Diminishing Marginal Utility	38
	Valuation by the Least Valuable Use	39
	Water-Diamond Paradox	42
Chapter 3	**Time**	**45**
	The Ultimate Resource	45
	Opportunity Cost	47
	Material Abundance	48
	Simon's Bet	56
	Time Preference	58
	Economizing Time	59
	Economizing Action	61
PART II. ECONOMY		**63**
Chapter 4	**Labor**	**65**
	Labor and Leisure	65
	Production	68
	Productivity of Labor	69
	Unemployment	71
	Will Work Ever End?	74
	Is Labor Exploitation?	76
Chapter 5	**Property**	**79**
	Scarcity and Property	79
	Types of Property	82
	Self-Ownership	83
	Importance of Property Rights	85
Chapter 6	**Capital**	**89**
	Lengthening Structure of Production	90
	Saving	92
	Higher Productivity	93
	The High Cost of Capital	98
	Capital and Time Preference	103
	Saving Fallacies	105
	Limits to Capital	108

Chapter 7 Technology **111**
Technology and Labor 113
Technology and Productivity 120
Technological Innovation and Entrepreneurship 123
Software 125
Property in Ideas 128

Chapter 8 Energy and Power **135**
Energy in Human History 138
Energy Abundance 139
Power Scarcity 142
Power of Hydrocarbon Alternatives 154
Energy and Freedom 156

PART III. THE MARKET ORDER **159**

Chapter 9 Trade **161**
Subjective Valuation 164
Absolute Advantage 166
Comparative Advantage 168
Specialization and the Division of Labor 172
Extent of the Market 174

Chapter 10 Money **181**
The Problem Money Solves 181
Salability 184
Salability across Time 189
Why One Money? 195
Money and the State 197
Value of Money 199
Money's Uniqueness 202
How Much Money Should There Be? 203

Chapter 11 Markets **209**
Consumer Good Markets 211
Equilibrium 220
Producer Good Markets 224

	Economizing in the Market Order	225
	Consumer Sovereignty	226
	A Contrast of Approaches	228
Chapter 12	**Capitalism**	**231**
	Capital Markets	234
	Capitalism Is Entrepreneurial, Not Managerial	236
	Profit and Loss	238
	The Economic Calculation Problem	240
	Modern Economics and Calculation	244
	The Effects of Entrepreneurial Investment	247
PART IV. MONETARY ECONOMICS		**249**
Chapter 13	**Time Preference**	**251**
	Time Preference and Money	255
	Time Preference and Saving	257
	Time Preference and Civilization	261
	Time Preference and Bitcoin	268
Chapter 14	**Credit and Banking**	**271**
	Banking	271
	Credit	272
	Commodity Credit	274
	Interest Rates	275
	Can Interest Be Eliminated?	281
Chapter 15	**Monetary Expansion**	**289**
	Circulation Credit	289
	Mises' Typology of Money	292
	Business Cycles	297
	The Business Cycle Graphically	301
	Capital Market Central Planning	309

PART V. CIVILIZATION **313**

Chapter 16 Violence **315**
Non-Aggression Principle 316
Government Coercion 318
Rationales for Government Violence 325
Rationality in Economics 336

Chapter 17 Defense **341**
The Market for Defense 342
The Market for Law and Order 347
State Monopoly of Defense and Law 349
State Monopoly Failure Modes 354
A Free Market in Defense 359

Chapter 18 Civilization **367**
The Cost of Civilization 371
The Case for Civilization 374
The Fiat Slavery Alternative to Civilization 379
The Triumph of Reason 386

Appendix 1 391
Bibliography 395
Index 397

About the Author

Saifedean Ammous is an internationally best-selling economist and author. In 2018, Ammous authored *The Bitcoin Standard: The Decentralized Alternative to Central Banking*, the best-selling book on bitcoin, published in 36 languages. In 2021, he published *The Fiat Standard: The Debt Slavery Alternative to Human Civilization*, available in 12 languages. Saifedean teaches courses on the economics of bitcoin, and economics in the Austrian school tradition, on his online learning platform Saifedean.com, and also hosts *The Bitcoin Standard Podcast*.

Saifedean was a professor of Economics at the Lebanese American University from 2009 to 2019. He holds a PhD in Sustainable Development from Columbia University, a Masters in Development Management from the London School of Economics, and a Bachelor in Mechanical Engineering from the American University of Beirut.

Introduction

The vast majority of textbooks taught in universities today are in the mainstream Keynesian-Samuelsonian economic tradition, which confuses students more than it informs them. I have taught these university textbooks for years and witnessed droves of intelligent students leave class with more questions than they entered it with, struggling to understand the significance of the obscure equations they studied, or to see any convincing reason to believe their outputs. Over the years, I have spoken to dozens of highly intelligent students and graduates who report a similar experience: They did what they had to do to get the grade they wanted, but none of the material made sense to them. They incredulously try to convince themselves to undertake the astounding leaps of logic necessary to make sense out of the irrelevant equations in order to pass exams, never to consider the ideas of the course again. If students learn from the mainstream textbook, they learn to understand theoretical models with only a tenuous link to reality. Success in the courses consists of understanding the models, not reality.

While teaching economics, I would include insights from the Austrian school of economics. Students invariably found these to be the most practically and intellectually interesting parts of the course, and the one that provided them lasting value beyond securing a degree. Austrian ideas are almost entirely ignored in most of today's universities. Modern textbooks rarely ever mention the Austrian school, let alone elaborate their ideas. I had to constantly resort to a variety of readings on various topics. The most prominent Austrian textbooks and treatises, such as Mises' *Human Action* and Rothbard's *Man, Economy, and State*, are difficult for most modern readers to digest, and, sadly, they spend far too much time attempting to argue with mainstream thinking, which after a point impedes clarifying the Austrian perspective.

I always wanted a clear, concise, and readable treatment of the main economic ideas in the Austrian tradition, culminating in an understanding of the civilizational importance of the extended monetary market order. I began developing the outlines of such a textbook for graduate and senior courses I taught at the Lebanese American University. After publishing *The Bitcoin Standard* and finding a receptive readership that appreciated my writing on economics, I decided to turn my attention extensively to writing the textbook that I had always wanted to teach. In 2019, I decided to leave my university job and start teaching and publishing independently, on my website saifedean.com. In 2019 and 2020, I developed two Principles of Economics courses, ECO11 and ECO12, which further developed the ideas that would grow into this book.

Teaching and interacting with hundreds of students from around the world, and being liberated from the academic publication mill's increasingly arcane and esoteric journals and publishers, I could now focus on writing for the reader, not committees of academics. After two decades of studying and learning economics at university level, this book represents the knowledge of economics I would like to have had when I was 17. It is what I hope my children will read when they become curious about economics.

This book forms an introduction to the principles of economics, and the economic way of thinking—a powerful tool of mental planning useful for everyone to understand. In a university, I would teach this book over two semesters, to introduce students to a broad view of the topic of economics and the economic way of thinking. More than just a university textbook, this is a book written for a general audience of anyone interested in economic ideas. Even if you are not studying economics at a university, you are making economic decisions every day of your life. For this reader, I hope this book offers a concise and actionable summary of the most useful insights of the economic way of thinking, which would be helpful in personal and business decision-making.

This book is unapologetically Austrian in its approach. It uses the plain written word to explain what many economists throughout history have found to be the most powerful methods of understanding economic phenomena. It applies the human action approach to explaining the most important concepts and topics in economics, building on the work of the economists of the Austrian school. It tackles major economic concepts and topics independently, but in a logical sequence aimed at delivering the reader an understanding of economics at an individual and societal level, and the widespread implications of economics as a topic. The first part of the book introduces the foundational concepts in economics and the Austrian method of this book. The second part of the book, Economy, introduces the actions that individual humans perform to economize. Part III, The Market Order, examines economizing in the social context, why the capitalist economy develops, and the role of money. Part IV, Monetary Economics, examines time, interest, and monetary and financial economics. Part V, Civilization, examines the economics of violence and security, and what they imply for the possibility of advancing human civilization.

Each chapter of this book discusses an important economic concept, and can be read as a standalone essay on the topic. But the book is also structured as a monograph narrative, laying out these concepts in a logical sequence. The first chapter introduces the Austrian methodological approach to economics, and provides an example, as well as a comparison with the methodological approach of the natural sciences. Chapter 2 introduces the foundational concept of value, and explains its subjective nature, as well as the concepts of utility and marginal analysis, based on the work of Carl Menger, father of the Austrian school. Chapter 3 introduces the importance of time in economics, the unique nature of economizing time, and how all economizing acts can be understood as attempts to increase the quantity and subjective value of our time on earth. This chapter also introduces the pivotal concepts of opportunity cost and time preference.

The second section of the book introduces the main actions humans carry out to economize individually. In each of the chapters of this section, a key concept is introduced and analyzed in terms of the reasons humans engage in it, the problem it solves, and how it helps them economize on time. The first and most basic concept is labor, the topic of Chapter 4. Chapter 5 explains the economics of property, why it emerges and the problem it solves, and the concept of self-ownership. Chapter 6 introduces a particular type of property, capital, which consists of goods used for the production of other goods, and discusses the cost of capital, its productivity, and its connection to time preference.

Chapter 7 discusses technology as an economic concept, why it increases labor productivity, and its unique status as a non-material economic good that is non-scarce. The chapter concludes with a discussion of the concept of intellectual property, and how the non-scarce nature of information makes it differ from other productive goods.

Energy, the topic of Chapter 8, is not a conventional topic in most economic textbooks. However, I believe that understanding the economics of energy is essential to understanding economics, particularly as the modern capital-intensive and technologically advanced market economy would not be possible without substantial increases in modern humans' power—the ability to wield large amounts of energy in short periods of time. Moreover, approaching economics through the Austrian method, through marginal analysis, is essential to understanding the realities of energy production in the world today.

Whereas the second section of the book examines individual economizing acts, the third part of the book looks at economizing in a social context, introducing other people into the analysis and exploring the implications. As soon as another person is present, trade becomes possible, and both parties have an incentive to engage in it, as it benefits them both. Chapter 9 explains the rationale of trade, its benefits, and the implications of the growth of the market in which the division of labor takes place.

Chapter 10 introduces the concept of money, explaining the problems it solves, how these problems shape the characteristics that are desirable in money, and how money helps humans economize and increase the value and productivity of their time. The chapter explains how money is a product of the market, and not the state, as is commonly but erroneously taught in economic textbooks. While this chapter introduces money, the broader discussion of monetary economics will be left to Part IV, so it can follow the discussion of capital markets, an essential topic in monetary economics.

The social order in which individuals peacefully engage in all the aforementioned economizing acts is called a market order. Chapter 11 examines how individual preferences and economizing acts result in the formation of prices, whose essential significance to the market process is explained. Chapter 12 explains the term capitalism in the Misesean tradition, and how it is an entrepreneurial system inseparable from private property and economic calculation. We examine Mises' litmus test for determining whether a society has a market economy, and how it can help us understand economic history.

Part IV, Monetary Economics, approaches the topic of money from an Austrian perspective, and so Chapter 13 begins with time preference, and its relationship with saving, money, and capital accumulation, which is what makes credit and banking possible, the topics of Chapter 14, which also explains interest rates and whether they can be eliminated. Chapter 15 examines the Austrian understanding of the business cycle by examining its underlying cause, monetary expansion via circulation credit issuance.

As the earlier parts illustrate the function and form of a capitalist market economy, and how it can only work in a system of respect for private property, the fifth and final part of the book, Civilization, examines the viability of capitalist civilization against the threat of violent aggression. Chapter 16 examines the economics of violence, in both its private and governmental forms, while Chapter 17 examines the economics of defense, and shows how this is just another market good, which today is predominantly provided on the market.

The book's final chapter discusses the concept of civilization from an economic perspective. Civilization is viewed as an order that emerges when a society can remain peaceful, productive, low time preference, cooperative, and innovative enough to sustain intergenerational improvements in living standards. The costs of this monumental enterprise are discussed, as well as the chances for the continuation of capitalist civilization in the face of the formidable threats it faces.

This book is supplemented by its webpage, saifedean.com/poe, where you can find a full bibliography with live links to the readings listed in this book. Since the internet has become so pervasive, I decided it would make sense to optimize the paper copy of this book for the reader experience by eliminating urls from references, and keeping a live full bibliography on saifedean.com/poe. After concluding this book, I will be offering another online course on saifedean.com to study this material in more depth.

This book benefitted and improved immensely as a result of the feedback of Ross Stevens, Jeff Deist, Per Bylund, Conza, Allen Farrington, Jonathan Newman, Peter Young, and Thomas Semaan. The last two also provided extremely valuable research assistance throughout the writing of this book. I also profusely thank the excellent editors whose thorough and meticulous editing improved this manuscript immensely: Alex McShane, Steve Robinson, Chay Allen, Renata Sielecki, Magda Wojcik, Evan Manning, and Elizabeth Newton. I also thank Tamara Mikler for producing the graphics, and Max DeMarco for editing the audiobook. I am also very grateful for the saifedean.com team of Pavao Pahljina, Marko Pahljina, Dorian Antešić, Flora Fontes, and Valentino Cnappi for all the effort they put into running the website and arranging the publication.

This book would not have been possible without the support, encouragement, and feedback of members of my online learning platform saifedean.com. I am most grateful to them for allowing me to work productively on finalizing my work. In particular my sincere gratitude goes to my readers who supported the publication of this book by buying the pre-ordering signed copies. Thank you A Patel, Aaron Macy, Abdulla Al Abbas, Abdullah Almoaiqel, Adam Higgs, Ágúst ragnar Pétursson, Aidan Campbell, Aleksi Meldo, AJ Garnerin, Alex, Alex Bowe, Alex Vanya, Alex Voss, Alistair Milne, Amit Barkan, Anderson Thees, Andrea Bortolameazzi, Andrew Brasuell, Andrew Rosener, Andrew Stanger, Anthony Clavero, Antonio Caccese, Arnaud Cart,

Ashok Atluri, Avery, Ben Johnson, Bertrand Marlier, BitcoinTina, Björn Tisjö, BK, Blake Canfield, BowserKingKoopa, Brian Daucher, Brian Kim, Brian Lockhart, Bronson Moyen, Browning Hi-Power 9mm, Bryan Matthieu, Bryan Renero, Bryan Wilson, Burcu Kocak, Carlo Barbara, Carlos Chida, Caspar Veltheim, Cedric Youngelman, Charles Smith, Chase Oleson, Chen YH, Chris Cowlbeck, Christian Amadasun, Christof Mathys, Christopher Lamia, Christopher P Valle, Christopher Pogorzelski, Christopher To, Cletus Reynolds, Dale Williams, Dan Skeen, Dane Bunch, Daniel Ostermayer, Daniel Schneider, Dave Hudson, David Heller, David Lawant, Dirk Seeber, Domingo Ochotorena, Donald Johnson, Dylan Parker, Ed Becker, Eduardo Lima, Edward Cosgrove, Elio Fattorini, Ernest Huttel, Fabian von Schilcher, Federico Quintela, Francisco Reyes, Frank Acklin, Gary Lau, Gary Speed, Gen Shin, Glenn Thomas, Greg Doyle, Götz Rößner, Haris M, Harlan Robinson, Hayden Houser, Hugh Starr, Hunter Hastings, Jaap Willems, Jackson Forelli, Jaeger Hamilton, James Seibel, James Weaver, Jason DiLuzio, Jawad Barlas, Jeffery Lee Degner, Jerrold Randall, Jesse Powell, Jim Patterson, Joachim Boudet, John A. Krpan, John Brier, John Dixon, Jon E, Jonas Karlberg, Jonas Konstandin, Jonathan Camphin, Jonathas Carrijo, Jordan Wilby, Jose Areitio Arberas, José Niño, Jules, Julio Neira, Justin Schwartz, Keith G, Kelly Lannan, Kenneth Gestal, Kevin Coffin, Kim Butler, Lachie McWilliam, Larry Salibra, Luis Alonso, Luke and Henley, Maksymilian Korzuchowski, Manuel Tomasi, Marco Daescher, Marco Mouta, Marcus Dent, Marius Kjærstad, Marius Reeder, Martin Brochhaus, Matija Grlj, Matt, Matt Unks, Matthew Robin, Matthew Sellitto, Max Cash, Maximiliano Guimarães, Michael Atwood, Michael Culhane, Michael Felch, Mike Clear, Mitch Soboleski, Mitchell Vanya, Nate Kershner, Nathan Smith, Neal Nagely, Nelson Minier, Nicholas Sheahan, Nick Giambruno, Nicolás Ahumada, Niko Laamanen, Nikolai Maevskii, Noah Amadasun, Noded, Odi Kosmatos, Oleg Mikhalsky, Paola Frapolli, Paweł Sławniak, Per-Olof Vallin, Petar Sutalo, Petr Zalud, Philip Karageorgevitch, Pierre Porthaux, Rasmus Berg, Raycheslav Karagyozov, Rene Bos, Richard Duke, Robert Koonce, Robin Dea, Ron M Dewberry, Ronald Zandstra, Rosie Featherby, Ross Stevens, Rowais Hanna, Ryan Nadeau, Ryan Sandford, Saagar Singh Sachdev, Sam Dib, Sam Shams,

Samuel Douglass, Scott Manhart, Scott Schneider, Scott Shell, Seb Walker, Shakti Chauhan, Shaun McFarlane, Simonna Pencev, Stefano D'Amiano, Stephen Labb, Subhan Tariq, Tami Uitto, Tanner Dowdy, Théo Mogenet, Thierry Thierry, Thomas Jenichen, Timo Oinonen, Tom Karadza, Tomas Hrncir, Travis Tripodi, Trevor Smith, Vik, Viktor Geller, Wendy Hiam, William Azzoli, Wilfred Tannr Allard, Will Phillips, William Green, William Johnston, Winfred Nadeau, Wityanant Thongsawai, Yani Eberding, Yoism, Yorick de Mombynes, Zachary Hollinshead, Zarak Ortega, Zsuzsanna Glasz

PART I

Fundamentals

Chapter 1

Human Action

> Economics is not about things and tangible material objects; it is about men, their meanings, and actions. Goods, commodities, and wealth and all the other notions of conduct are not elements of nature; they are elements of human meaning and conduct. He who wants to deal with them must not look at the external world; he must search for them in the meaning of acting men.[1]
>
> —Ludwig von Mises

Ludwig von Mises' magnum opus, *Human Action*, offered an explicit redefinition of the field of economics as the study of human action and choice under scarcity. Mises believed proper economic reasoning and analysis of economic phenomena must be based on analyzing human action, rather than analyzing material objects and their properties, or analyzing aggregate and abstract units. While Mises' perspective might initially seem pedantic and unproductive, this chapter will explain how it is a very powerful tool for understanding economic reality.

Mises argues that philosophers had long attempted to analyze humanity's evolution and destiny based on an understanding of what history, God, or nature had intended for humans. Such analyses dealt with humanity as a whole or analyzed collectivist concepts like nation, race, or church, and sought to

---

1 Mises, Ludwig von. *Human Action: The Scholar's Edition*. Ludwig von Mises Institute, 1998, p. 92.

find laws to explain the behavior of such entities and their consequences, as if history had ironclad laws to be discovered, akin to the natural sciences.

In writing *Principles of Economics* in 1871, Carl Menger pioneered marginal analysis of economic questions. This "marginal revolution" provided a starkly different alternative to the previous methods of analyzing humans. Rather than analyzing history based on the will of God, nature, or through nation, race, or church, marginal analysis showed that human society is better understood by analyzing its prime driving forces: individual human choice and action. The Austrian school of economics emerged around Menger in Vienna. A few years after him, Léon Walras would develop his own conception of marginalism couched in a concept of general equilibrium. The Walrasian general equilibrium would become the dominant tradition in modern economics, relying on mathematization and relationships between aggregates.

Action, Purpose, and Reason

Mises defines human action as "purposeful behavior,"[2] so as to distinguish it from instinctive, impulsive, or emotional acts. "Action is will put into operation and transformed into an agency, is aiming at ends and goals, is the ego's meaningful response to stimuli and to the conditions of its environment, is a person's conscious adjustment to the state of the universe that determines his life."

Mises' student, Murray Rothbard, defines human action as "purposeful behavior toward the attainment of ends in some future period which will involve the fulfillment of wants otherwise remaining unsatisfied."[3] Mises posits that for action to take place, it requires a human to have a current state, to imagine a more satisfactory state, and the expectation that purposeful behavior can alleviate uneasiness.[4]

Rational action is a quintessentially human quality that distinguishes

2 Ibid. 11.

3 Rothbard, Murray. *Man, Economy, and State, with Power and Market*. Scholar's ed., 2nd ed., Ludwig von Mises Institute, 2009, p. 7.

4 Mises, Ludwig von. *Human Action: The Scholar's Edition*. Ludwig von Mises Institute, 1998, pp. 13-4.

humans from other animals. Humans act purposefully because we are endowed with reason and are able to direct it to the meeting of our ends. Humans are capable of recognizing causal relations in the world around us, and acting upon this understanding to bring about a more favorable state of affairs. We are also able to understand that others have reason and are able to act to their end. As Mises puts it:

> Man is not a being who cannot help yielding to the impulse that most urgently asks for satisfaction. Man is a being capable of subduing his instincts, emotions, and impulses; he can rationalize his behavior. He renounces the satisfaction of a burning impulse in order to satisfy other desires. He is not a puppet of his appetites. A man does not ravish every female that stirs his senses; he does not devour every piece of food that entices him; he does not knock down every fellow he would like to kill. He arranges his wishes and desires into a scale, he chooses; in short, he acts. What distinguishes man from beasts is precisely that he adjusts his behavior deliberatively. Man is the being that has inhibitions, that can master his impulses and desires, that has the power to suppress instinctive desires and impulses.[5]

A useful mental image to explain the primacy of human action is to think of the physical world around us as inert playdough we can mold with our hands into different shapes and objects based on our reasoning and imagination. Inanimate objects are dead matter, and it is human reason shaping human actions that rearranges this matter and gives it value, meaning, and purpose. One understands the material world far better if one studies it as the product of human reason and action. Attempts to explain social phenomena through reference to physical objects, abstract nouns, or collectivist entities are ultimately futile and decidedly inferior to thinking in terms of human choice and action. It is not the stars, nor abstract nouns and entities that act, but individuals. If you want to understand the conditions of the material world, it is most useful to study the actions of the humans who mold it.

---

5 Ibid. 16.

In the Misesean and Austrian tradition, human action is understood and defined as being rational. The word "rational" in this context does not refer to the correctness of the action according to some objective criteria, nor does it refer to the suitability of the action in achieving the ends of the acting man, nor does it pass other moral judgments on the action. Rather, rational here is defined as the product of deliberative reason. Whenever man reasons and acts, he acts rationally. Whether such an action is conducive to achieving his goal or not, and whether such an action meets the approval of another party assessing it are irrelevant to "rationality" as understood and defined by Mises. A person may regret an action and realize it was counterproductive to achieving his ends, but that does not change the rationality of the act, in the sense that it was the product of deliberative reason, correct or faulty. Other individuals may pass judgment on this individual's actions. No matter how wrong they find it, that would also not detract from the rational nature of the act. The Austrian conception of rationality becomes clearer with Mises' explanation that "the opposite of action is not irrational behavior, but a reactive response to stimuli on the part of the bodily organs and instincts which cannot be controlled by the volition of the person concerned." Further, "An action unsuited to the end sought falls short of expectation. It is contrary to purpose, but it is rational, i.e., the outcome of a reasonable—although faulty—deliberation and an attempt—although an ineffectual attempt—to attain a definite goal."[6]

Economic Analysis

Thinking of economics as the study of human action under scarcity allows us to define the most important terms in economics based on their relation to human needs, how human reason treats them, and how humans shape them. When explained, defined, and understood through the lens of human action, economic terminology becomes clearer and economic analysis more fruitful.

Hans-Hermann Hoppe explains:

---

6 Ibid. 20.

> All true economic theorems consist of (a) an understanding of the meaning of action, (b) a situation or situational change—assumed to be given or identified as being given—and described in terms of action-categories, and (c) a logical deduction of the consequences—again in terms of such categories—which are to result for an actor from this situation or situational change.[7]

At the heart of the Austrian approach to economics is the goal of *understanding* the causal processes of economic activity and their consequences. Logical deduction, thought experiments, and common sense familiarity with reality are employed to understand the implications of economic processes. Initially, this approach might appear banal and fruitless compared to the dominant approaches of mainstream economics today, which rely on mathematical analysis. But a closer look shows us why quantitative analysis is unsuited for building an economic theoretical framework. It will also show us why quantitative analysis is meaningless and mute without logical deduction and conclusions to motivate it and understand its results. In keeping with the Austrian critique of quantitative approaches to economic analysis, this book will present and analyze economic acts in plain language, not with mathematical equations. Human action will be understood through logical deduction and thought experiments, not equations and quantitative analysis.

Quantitative Analysis

The Austrian critique of quantitative analysis is summed up in Mises' critique of the application of quantitative methods to economics in *Human Action*:

> The fundamental deficiency implied in every quantitative approach to economic problems consists in the neglect of the fact that there are no constant relations between what are called economic dimensions. There is neither

7 Hoppe, Hans-Hermann. *Economic Science and the Austrian Method.* Ludwig von Mises Institute, 2007, p. 63.

> constancy nor continuity in the valuations and in the formation of exchange ratios between various commodities. Every new datum brings about a reshuffling of the whole price structure. Understanding, by trying to grasp what is going on in the minds of the men concerned, can approach the problem of forecasting future conditions. We may call its methods unsatisfactory and the positivists may arrogantly scorn it. But such arbitrary judgments must not and cannot obscure the fact that understanding is the only appropriate method of dealing with the uncertainty of future conditions.[8]

This is a profound criticism of the methods of modern economics. As discussed in detail in Appendix 1, there is **no standard unit with which economic measurements of value can be made and compared**. As discussed in Chapter 2, value is subjective. The utility that individuals get from goods is also subjective and constantly changing based on the individual, the time at which they are making their valuation, and the relative abundance of the good. There is no possibility for aggregated interpersonal utility comparison, and therefore the mathematization of utility will always be hypothetical and theoretical and never precise and replicable.

Without a common unit with which to measure and compare utility, it is impossible to formulate a quantitative law around, for example, changes in demand and supply based on changes in price, such as a law positing that a 1% increase in price corresponds to a certain percentage decrease in quantity demanded. The impact of a specific change in price on an individual's demand for a good happens through the causal mechanism of changes in individually assessed utility. That factor is not measurable or quantifiable.

Replicable experimentation on economic questions is also impossible. The objects of study of the natural sciences are the structure and behavior of the physical world. It is assumed at the outset that these are regular, that their properties can be isolated and observed by repeatable experimentation, and that they can be appropriately and fully modeled with mathematics. It is fundamental

8 Mises, Ludwig von. *Human Action: The Scholar's Edition*. Ludwig von Mises Institute, 1998, p. 118.

to the intellectual enterprise that the sole and entire purpose of this methodology is to rigorously pin down *causation.* In the physical world, what causes what else? Why do things happen exactly and only the way they do? But the objects of study of the social sciences are the ideas and actions of humans, which are immeasurable and non-quantifiable. Experimentation with ill-defined units of irregular phenomena cannot yield comparable and reproducible results, and so experimentation will fail to produce quantitative laws because there are no units in which these laws can be expressed. Without measurement and repeatable experimentation, it is not possible to find regularities, derive constants, and formulate mathematical relationships and scientific laws. Accurate experiments in economics are also not possible because the subject of economics is the action of humans in the real world, and conditions in testing laboratories cannot replicate the real-world consequences of economic decisions. The real world is the only laboratory that can approximate the real conditions shaping economic decision-making, but it is impossible to experiment on the real world using scientific methods such as those employed in the natural sciences.

Beyond the issues of measurement and experimentation, a deeper logical problem with quantitative approaches to economics is that **they conflate the factors we can measure with the causative factors that shape the world around us**. The quantitative methods which establish relationships between aggregate measures place the aggregates as the driving causal forces for no reason more well founded or coherent than the fact that they can be measured. Whereas in the natural sciences, regularities and constants are discovered through repeated open experimentation, empirical economists simply make the assumption that their data is regular and deduce laws based on it. In the natural sciences, the complexity of the atoms that make up a gas, for example, can be reduced to basic aggregate measures of pressure, temperature, and volume without any loss in analytical accuracy. The atoms have no will of their own, they have no mind, they cannot reason, and they cannot act in response to surrounding conditions, like human beings can. Because they lack reason, the behavior of physical objects can be studied and accurately predicted.

When examining economic questions, however, we are confronted with the reality that human beings and their actions are the causative factors shaping economic reality, motivated by their subjective considerations and personal preferences. Far from being inanimate objects reacting in mathematically predictable ways, humans react in irreducibly complex ways. Attempting to paper over the complexity of the actions of millions of humans by examining only superficial aggregate measures of some economic phenomenon is the core mistake of failed modern pseudosciences like macroeconomics and epidemiology. These fields ignore the actual causative factors of the phenomena they study and instead attempt to hypothesize based on whatever aggregates can be measured. As Hayek explains:

> Unlike the position that exists in the physical sciences, in economics and other disciplines that deal with essentially complex phenomena, the aspects of the events to be accounted for about which we can get quantitative data are necessarily limited and may not include the important ones. While in the physical sciences it is generally assumed, probably with good reason, that any important factor which determines the observed events will itself be directly observable and measurable, in the study of such complex phenomena as the market, which depend on the actions of many individuals, all the circumstances which will determine the outcome of a process, for reasons which I shall explain later, will hardly ever be fully known or measurable. And while in the physical sciences the investigator will be able to measure what, on the basis of a prima facie theory, he thinks important, in the social sciences often that is treated as important which happens to be accessible to measurement. This is sometimes carried to the point where it is demanded that our theories must be formulated in such terms that they refer only to measurable magnitudes.[9]

Just because we are able to construct measures of unemployment, gross domestic production, consumption, investment, and other economic quantities does not mean that these factors are causally related to one another in scientifically

---

9 Hayek, Friedrich von. "The Pretence of Knowledge." *The Swedish Journal of Economics*, vol. 77, no. 4, Dec 1975, pp. 433-42.

preordained relationships based on quantifiable and testable magnitudes. In fact, since the actual drivers of these measures are the actions of individuals, there is no reason to suppose that they are any more than superficial epiphenomena unrelated to the causal mechanisms driving the relationships examined.

Attempting to formulate meaning from the relationships between these aggregates is akin to scientists studying gases and attempting to formulate laws based on the color of different containers, the number of containers used, the brand of the manufacturer, the first letter in the name of the experimenter, and various epiphenomena with no causative effect on the experiment. A scientist can indeed formulate relationships between these (irrelevant) parameters, but it will be impossible for any such relationship to hold after repeated testing by independent parties because they have no connection to the causal process being studied. Repeating the same experiment with an experimenter with a different name or a container of a different color will still yield the same results, making the original experimenter's theorizing pointless. It is the inanimate gas particles whose temperature, pressure, and volume are the control knobs for the system being studied; the container's color and experimenter's name are irrelevant. Similarly, it is the action of humans that shapes economic outcomes, not the aggregate measures constructed in government statistics offices.

This is not to say that all statistical measures are worthless noise, as one can find subjective value when examining these aggregates as close approximations of economic phenomena. The Austrian objection is not to economic statistics per se, but to attempting to build scientific-seeming theories out of statistical aggregates. The most egregious and harmful attempts to ape the methodology of the natural sciences in economics happen in macroeconomics. The physics envy of macroeconomists has, for a century, fueled the search for a system of equations that can explain the dynamics of an economy in the same way equations can explain and predict the movement of objects. Friedrich von Hayek calls this "scientism": the slavish imitation of the method and language of science where it is inapplicable.[10] The hope is that, with an accurate scientific

10 Hayek, Friedrich von. "Scientism and the study of society [Part 1]." *Economica*, vol. 9, no. 35, 1942, pp. 267-91.

system of equations for understanding the working process of an economy, it would become possible to manage economic activity to achieve desirable goals. In the same way that chemists' equations have helped engineers perfect and optimize the working of engines and pumps, scientism searches for economic equations that can help economists improve the state of "an economy."

In macroeconomics, aggregates are constructed from national accounts, and mathematical relationships are sought between them. Such relationships are established theoretically, based on some economist's authority to declare how the causal mechanisms function, not on experimentation. English economist John Maynard Keynes' macroeconomic system is the most prominent example. For decades, economists have formulated equations based on Keynes' theoretical hypothesizing. The state of the economy is primarily a reflection of the amount of spending. If spending is too high compared to output, then inflation and growth are the outcome, but if spending is too low compared to the output, then unemployment and recession are the outcome. Should unemployment be too high, modern macroeconomic equations suggest this can be fixed by increasing aggregate spending through increased government spending or expansionary credit policies. High inflation, on the other hand, can be fixed by reducing aggregate spending through increased taxes or contractionary credit policies.

But accounting identities do not denote real-world causality. There are no mechanisms in macroeconomics to experimentally establish causality as is possible in the natural sciences. Keynes' equations attempting to predict the impact of one aggregate metric on another bear no relation to real-world cause and effect, because there is no way of measuring, testing, and verifying any of it.

No studies can test Keynes' hypothesis, because one cannot experiment on entire economies comprising millions of people who have individual life plans. Nor can one run a suitable control on those same people under different circumstances. But even by observing government statistics collected by adherents of the theory, real-world experience has contradicted the theory for decades. The Keynesian system necessarily implies a trade-off between the unemployment rate and the inflation rate, a relationship termed the Phillips curve, which is supposed to be a downward-sloping curve to illustrate the trade-off. But real-world experience does not show this, as Figure 1, with data from sixty years of U.S. government statistics, shows no such trade-off.

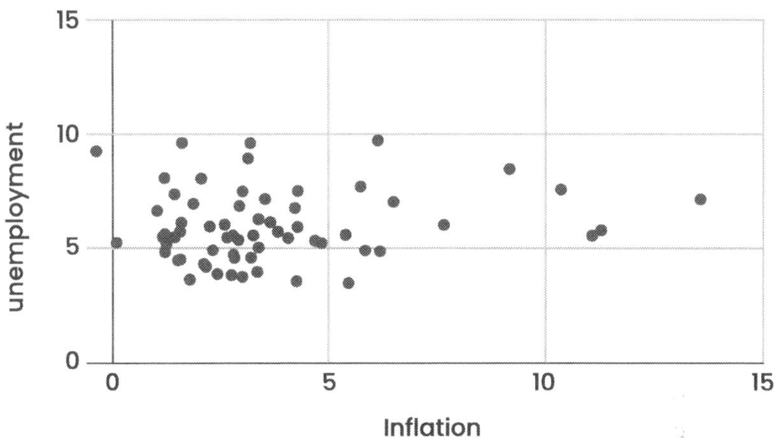

Figure 1. Unemployment and inflation[11]

However, this theory persists to this day, in spite of decades of accumulated evidence that it is not an accurate explanation of how the world works. In the 1970s, as inflation and unemployment both increased at the same time worldwide, the Keynesian trade-off was comprehensively refuted beyond a shadow of a doubt. But the advantage of economics having no systematic and replicable method of experimentation and testing is that theories can always be adjusted after their failure in a way that can justify non-compliant real-world observations. That is the essence of pseudoscience.

Hilariously, Keynesians simply revised their theory to include a new term, "supply shock." Supply shock is an incoherent term, made as an after-the-fact justification to explain how increases in unemployment and inflation can happen simultaneously. Since then, the world's economies have witnessed every imaginable combination of inflation and unemployment rates, and the Keynesians have successfully maintained the delusion that such a trade-off between unemployment and inflation exists. Any diversion away from this

11 Source: FRED, Federal Reserve Bank of St. Louis.

relationship can be explained by invoking a supply shock or various other thought substitutes, and so there can be no observation that falsifies it. It explains everything and therefore explains nothing. The illusion of economics as a precise, quantitative, and empirical science is only maintained through the exemption of its theories from empirical real-world examination.

After a century of aping physics and abandoning classical methodological foundations, economics has failed to produce one quantitative law or formula that can be independently tested and replicated. Macroeconomic equations come and go with the fashions of modern schools of thought, but none of them has been measured objectively and replicated in a way that can allow it to be called a scientific law. That macroeconomics empowers central governments and enriches academics may help explain why it has endured.

A Contrast of Approaches

To illustrate the human action approach to economics, and to compare it with modern quantitative economic methodology, we can use as an example the question of government-mandated minimum wages, which impose a lower limit on what employers can pay their employees. A popular policy intervention in most of the world, the opposing perspectives on it serve as an object lesson in the two different frameworks for thinking about economics: human action and aggregates.

Imagine a politician looking to win an election in a country with no minimum wage laws. As in all times and places in human history, there is a natural variation in the wages earned by workers. The politician decides to center her campaign around improving the living standards of the poorest members of society by mandating a minimum wage, which she imagines guarantees its recipients a decent living. Based on her aggregate-focused macroeconomic framework, the aspiring leader decides to mandate a minimum wage of $10 per hour. The economist concludes that 20% of all workers, supporting 35% of all the population, currently earn less than $10 per hour. The aggregate effect of imposing the minimum wage would lead to a rise in wages equal to $10 billion per year. Based on sophisticated historical and theoretical models, the fiat economist further estimates that the $10 billion increase in payrolls would translate to an $8 billion increase in consumer spending, which models estimate would result in the creation of 40,000 new jobs, a 12% increase in industrial output, a 4% rise in exports, and a $16 billion increase in gross domestic product.

According to this collectivist approach to economic analysis, the aggregates are the causal agents in economic phenomena, and they act according to the theoretical relationships established by fiat economists, in a similar way to how physicists and chemists establish scientific rules. These conclusions were arrived at using scientific-looking equations not very different from those used in the ideal gas law. Using the framework of aggregate economic analysis, the minimum wage law sounds like a great boon to society. The poorest workers will increase their living standards significantly, some unemployed workers will find work as a result of the extra spending, and all of society becomes more productive. What is more, exports rise, helping the economy obtain foreign currency.

If this sounds too good to be true, that is because it is not true. Things look different through the lens of the sound economist's Mises-tinted glasses. Knowing that human action is the real driver of human affairs, the sound economist does not analyze the world through aggregate quantities. Instead, he analyzes the decisions of the real humans affected by this new law. Employment is an agreement between two individuals, the employer and the employee. The sound economist understands that a business owner's choice to hire someone is based on a simple calculus: She will hire him if his contribution to the firm's revenue exceeds his wage. If the minimum legal wage exceeds the marginal revenue he brings, then hiring him costs the business money and is akin to a donation from the business to the worker. Employers know that making such a hire is a costly mistake, and employers who do not know that will soon witness their business fail as it continues to hemorrhage money on wages it cannot afford. Only employers who understand this economic reality will remain employers, and those who do not will lose their businesses. Emotional blackmail by politicians can change nothing about this reality.

Wages, like all prices in a market, are not just arbitrary numbers chosen by greedy employers. They are a reflection of the marginal productivity of the worker. As the law now stipulates that a worker must be paid $10 per hour, the employer now has to reconsider whether it is worth hiring this worker. When the government mandates a minimum wage, it does not magically alter the calculus of the employer, nor does it magically increase the worker's productivity. The employer will still only hire workers whose productivity is higher than their wage. Thus, the minimum wage law makes it illegal for employers to hire anyone whose marginal productivity is less than $10 per hour. Any worker whose productivity is less than that will now become a drain on any business that hires him and pays him that amount. Either he gets fired, or the business that hires him loses money and goes bankrupt. In all cases, these jobs are eliminated, and everyone whose productivity is less than $10 per hour is now legally unemployable; either unemployed or employed illegally.

Viewed through the lens of human action, the effect of a minimum wage law is to make it illegal for workers with low productivity to get jobs, and many of these workers will lose their jobs. Continuing to look through the lens of human action, one would find that the workers who lose their jobs are those with the lowest productivity in society, and these are usually the poorest, youngest, and least experienced workers. Making it illegal for them to work is effectively making it illegal for them to raise their productivity by learning on the job and acquiring valuable on-site work experience. Minimum wage laws are thus particularly pernicious to the people who need to work the most, and they are a causal factor in the emergence of wide-scale unemployment, as well as unemployability. Another possible implication is that some businesses, particularly those that depend on these low-wage laborers for their operation, would pay higher wages but also raise the prices of their goods to finance the higher wages. Consumers would then pay the price through higher prices and lower quantities of goods available. In this scenario, any potential increase in a low-wage worker's income would be counteracted by a corresponding increase in the cost of the goods he must consume.

All these consequences of minimum wage laws are deducible by sound economists who analyze the wage law and evaluate the implications it will have on rationally acting individuals. This turns out to be a far more useful and accurate assessment of the situation than anything that can be conjured from examining mathematical metrics. Prices are a reflection of underlying market reality driven by human action. Attempting to alter the underlying market reality by altering its reflection is unworkable. Every attempt at passing price controls has backfired because this kind of central planning ignores the role of human action. Price controls treat economics as if it were about material objects, rather than human action. Schuettinger and Butler have written a depressingly entertaining history of price controls in *Forty Centuries of Price Controls*, illustrating how this exact dynamic has repeated itself across cultures and nations throughout history.[12] The kings, emperors, politicians, and bureaucrats look at the world of economic transactions as an inhuman process they can alter to suit their needs. They mandate that the observable epiphenomena associated with markets fall within acceptable ranges. They assume humans will just adjust their actions to ensure these laws are upheld. However, in reality, humans adjust their actions to optimize for their own well-being, not to satisfy bureaucrats. The merchant would rather not sell at all than sell at a loss. You will either see the free-market price or you will see no market price at all. In the latter economy, real prices are expressed in underground markets.

Actual economists understand that observable economic phenomena and metrics are but manifestations of the underlying actions of the humans involved. Humans are constantly seeking to improve their own situation in life, and it is futile to mandate that they act against their interests. Mandating laws against humans' self-interested nature does not change human nature; it reduces the incentive to behave legally and so destroys society's respect for laws. This essential realization is why the sound economist is in favor of individual economic freedom and against its restriction by governments. The human spirit is indomitable, and it will not act in a way that is harmful to itself.

The sound economist understands humans are constantly acting to improve their lot in life. Imposing legal punishments on any peaceful economic activity they might choose cannot lead to an improvement in their lives, as it will simply restrict and reduce the choice of actions available to them.

12 Schuettinger, Robert, and Eamonn Butler. *Forty Centuries of Wage and Price Controls: How Not to Fight Inflation*. Heritage Foundation, 1978.

Aggregate analysis blinds the fiat economist to the implications of these laws for the humans whose freedoms it restricts. After formulating mathematical measures of social phenomena, the collectivist economist then assumes that these measures are causal factors in the determination of human affairs.

The world already has far too many economics textbooks written in the pseudoscientific quantitative tradition. This book will definitely not be one of them. It will not try to explain economics in the language of the natural sciences, and it will contain no sophisticated aggregate equations. Such approaches promise much but deliver little in terms of reliable, useful, and actionable insights.

Chapter 2

Value

> Value is thus nothing inherent in goods, no property of them, nor an independent thing existing by itself. It is a judgment economizing men make about the importance of the goods at their disposal for the maintenance of their lives and well-being. Hence value does not exist outside the consciousness of men.[13]
>
> —Carl Menger

The first chapter was a methodological introduction to the topic of economics, illustrating the Austrian approach centered around human action. In this chapter, we turn to the substance of the field of economics, its foundational concepts, and the main questions the field seeks to address.

The foundations of modern economics were laid by Austrian economist Carl Menger in the late nineteenth century. While economics as a field of inquiry had been around since the time of Aristotle, Menger's explanation of the subjective nature of value and economic decisions, and his introduction of marginal analysis, revolutionized the field and gave it a solid theoretical and methodological foundation, allowing for a systematic analysis of how humans economize and act. Menger's groundbreaking work provided a richer understanding of the nature of the consequences for humans of their economic actions. Menger's *Principles of Economics* textbook, written in 1871, is possibly

13 Menger, Carl. *Principles of Economics*. Reprint, Ludwig von Mises Institute, 2007, pp. 120-1.

the oldest economics textbook still relevant and readable. This chapter begins by summarizing some of the main concepts from Menger's book, using his definitions to set the foundation for the analysis of the topics addressed in later chapters. It then discusses the foundational Mengerian concepts on which economic analysis is built: subjective value and marginal analysis.

Utility and Value

Goods

Menger defines a good as something useful that we can direct to the satisfaction of human needs. For something to become a good, it first requires that a human need exists; second, that the properties of the good can cause the satisfaction of that need; third, that humans have knowledge of this causal connection; and, finally, that commanding the good would be sufficient to direct it to the satisfaction of the human need.

Utility

Utility is the capacity of a good to satisfy human needs. Utility depends on our ability to understand the connection between a good and the need it fulfills. Utility is a general prerequisite for an object being a good. Only if something can offer utility can it be viewed as a good by humans.

Scarcity

Goods can be divided into two categories, economic and non-economic. The distinction between the two is **scarcity**: Demand for economic goods is always greater than the quantity supplied, whereas for non-economic goods, their supply exceeds the quantities demanded by humans.

A **non-economic good** is a good available in quantities exceeding the demand for it, which precludes rivalry or competition for securing the good. The best example is air, which is essential for human survival, but is nonetheless plentiful everywhere humans live.[14] Air is, therefore, not an economic good.

---

14 It is scarce in underwater diving and in space, and that is why it becomes an economic good in these settings, requiring sophisticated infrastructure to make it available.

An **economic good**, being scarce, will have a greater demand than its supply, and this creates rivalry around access to it, forcing humans to make choices between it and other goods.

The scarcity of economic goods forces humans to **economize**, making choices between scarce alternatives. To "economize," according to Menger, refers to humans' tendency to want to maintain quantities as large as possible of the goods that can satisfy their needs, to conserve the useful functions of these goods, to prioritize their most pressing needs over less pressing ones, and to obtain the greatest satisfaction from the good's quantity.

Economics

Economics, as a field, is the **study of human choices under scarcity.** It focuses on analyzing how humans attempt to find solutions to the problem of disparity between what they have and what they want and the consequences of their choices.

As scarcity is a permanent condition of existence, humans are constantly making choices between different courses of action, different goods, and different needs to satisfy. The need to make these choices forces us to juxtapose the utility we derive from different goods against each other, so we are able to make informed choices.

Value

Value is our subjective assessment of the satisfaction we derive, or expect to derive, from goods, and what allows us to make economic decisions. Menger defines value as "the importance that individual goods or quantities of goods attain for us because we are conscious of being dependent on command of them for the satisfaction of our needs."[15] Value, according to Menger, is also "the importance that we first attribute to the satisfaction of our needs, that is, to our lives and well-being, and in consequence, carry over to economic goods as the exclusive causes of the satisfaction of our needs."[16]

---

15 Menger, Carl. *Principles of Economics*. Reprint, Ludwig von Mises Institute, 2007, p. 115.
16 Ibid. 116.

Subjective Value

The foundation of economic analysis, and one of the groundbreaking insights from Menger's work, is that **value is subjective.** It exists only in the mind of the person making the valuation. As Menger put it: "Value is thus nothing inherent in goods, no property of them, nor an independent thing existing by itself. It is a judgment economizing men make about the importance of the goods at their disposal for the maintenance of their lives and well-being."[17]

It is not the inherent nature of goods that makes them valuable to us, but only our assessment of their suitability for meeting our needs. As their ability to satisfy our needs changes, so does their value to us. Value, then, is not a physical or chemical property of economic goods; it is a psychic property they attain only when humans assess them. In Menger's famous words, "**Value does not exist outside the consciousness of men.**"[18]

My favorite example to illustrate the subjective nature of value is oil. Up until the nineteenth century, the presence of oil in a plot of land would decrease its value, as it required costly removal before the land could be utilized for agricultural, commercial, or residential use. For as long as human consciousness saw oil as a dirty nuisance, oil had negative economic value. Once humans realized that refined oil could be burned in an internal combustion engine to power machines that satisfy their needs for transportation, electricity, and heat generation, oil went from being a costly nuisance to an enormously valuable and essential commodity, which nobody in the modern world can now live without. Oil in the year 2020 is no different chemically and physically from oil in the year 1620, and yet its value has changed from negative to positive. While our conscious assessment of our needs cannot change the physical and chemical properties of oil, it can change its economic value. Oil went from having a negative to a positive value once human consciousness recognized it as useful. As Menger puts it, "The value of goods arises from their relationship to our needs, and is not inherent in the goods themselves. With changes in this relationship, value arises and disappears."[19]

---

17 Menger, Carl. *Principles of Economics*. Reprint, Ludwig von Mises Institute, 2007, pp. 120-1.
18 Ibid. 120-1.
19 Ibid. 120.

To further illustrate this point, as this book is being written in 2020, a sizable proportion of the world's population is subjected to governments worldwide imposing significant and throttling suspensions of movement and economic production. Oil is produced for immediate consumption, and there is very little spare capacity for its storage, relative to the enormous quantities consumed. As industry and transportation ground to a virtual halt, excess oil production had nowhere to go, and the price of oil plummeted and even became negative for a few days. Given the large surplus of supply over demand, and the lack of storage capacity, owning oil reverted to being a liability, as it was in the preindustrial age, and its owners again had to pay to be relieved of it. The oil price soon recovered to positive territory and continued its rise upward. Nothing changed in the inherent properties of oil as its price went from negative to positive to negative to positive again; the conditions of people making the valuation changed, and so did their subjective valuations.

As the example of oil illustrates, value cannot exist outside human valuation and choice, reflecting their preferences. Value cannot be a constant property of objects; it is a conscious phenomenon in our minds. This does not mean value is not real. Value is real and meaningful, and it shapes our actions and decisions, which direct the production, consumption, and utilization of the real material objects in our world. Menger's recognition of the subjective nature of value was a very important turning point in economic thinking. Previous economists had struggled to explain how goods were valued and why certain goods were more valuable than others. All of these mysteries and paradoxes surrounding valuation were only resolved with the Mengerian insight of subjective valuation and marginal analysis.

Valuation: Ordinal and Cardinal

The first important implication of the subjective nature of value is that it cannot be measured and expressed objectively. Since valuation is subjective to the human making it, and since this valuation is constantly shifting based on the changes in our needs and in our understanding of goods' abilities to satisfy our needs, valuations differ from one person to another, and individual valuations are constantly shifting depending on individuals' conditions. To express any measurement objectively, a scientific unit is needed as the standard measuring rod against which different objects are assessed, as discussed in Appendix 1. Weight, length, temperature, and other scientific measures are expressed in objectively definable units that allow for a precise comparison between different objects. But no such unit can exist for human valuation, since the value of a good is not an inherent objective property of the good, but a subjective psychic property dependent on the person making the valuation, dependent on the ever-changing conditions that determine the usefulness of that good for meeting needs. There is no objective standard by which satisfactions of humans can be compared, as the individuals themselves are the arbiters of value. In other words, there is no way of objectively measuring the satisfaction one person gets from a good in terms of the satisfaction any other person gets from the same good.

Without a standard objective unit, measurement is not possible, and valuation cannot be expressed in objective numerical **cardinal** terms, making it impossible to measure economic value with mathematical precision. Without a constant unit as a reference for value ascertainable for anyone, it is not possible to express the economic value of different goods in relation to one another. It is possible to measure the length of different objects because they can all be measured against the constant reference of an inch, foot, mile, or meter. An individual looking to install a fridge in a kitchen can measure the fridge's allotted space in inches and then look up the fridge's dimensions to see whether it would fit. Such measurement is meaningful and useful because the customer and the manufacturer of the fridge have a very accurate and precise shared definition of what the inch is. Without agreeing on a common constant unit, it would be impossible to know whether the fridge would fit without installing it.

Without a common constant unit, the only way we can express valuation is in **ordinal** terms, in which goods are compared to one another and ordered in terms of the valuing individual's preference, but not valued in explicitly quantitative terms. It is possible for an individual to know their preference for one good over another since there is a constant for this comparison—the individual making the valuation. It is, therefore, possible to *compare* goods in terms of value, as an individual can easily determine if they value good A more than good B, and good B more than good C. But this valuation is purely subjective, expressed in terms of the utility experienced by the person making the valuation. It is impossible for the person to express these preferences in quantitative and cardinal terms, such as valuing good A at a precise numerical value expressed in the same unit with which preference for good B is expressed. In proper economics, there can be no such thing as a statement accounting for the value of goods, such as "the value of A = 14.372x, the value of B = 4.258x, and the value of C = 1.273x," where x is an objective unit of value that can be used for personal and interpersonal comparisons of utility.

As Mises puts it:

> There is a more and a less in the removal of uneasiness felt; but how much one satisfaction surpasses another one can only be felt; it cannot be established and determined in an objective way. A judgment of value does not measure, it arranges in a scale of degrees, it grades. It is expressive of an order of preference and sequence, but not expressive of measure and weight. Only the ordinal numbers can be applied to it, but not the cardinal numbers.[20]

Think of the way you personally value things in relation to one another. Are you able to express them in terms of one unit that measures them all? Can all the things you value, from material goods to friendships, family, and happiness, be measured in terms of the same unit? Is there a set exchange rate between a family member and physical goods? Could you value your child in terms of money? How many cars does a human need to exchange for their child? Human values cannot be measured using one standardized unit. Human valuations can only be compared, but they cannot be added, subtracted, or multiplied. Without a common and constant unit, measurement and mathematical operations are not possible.

---

20 Mises, Ludwig von. *Human Action: The Scholar's Edition*. Ludwig von Mises Institute, 1998, p. 97.

Value and Price

The value of economic goods is distinct from, and not to be confused with, their price. The price of an economic good is not its objective valuation, nor the subjective valuation of either of the transacting parties. The price at which a sale is conducted illustrates only that the seller values the good less than the price, while the buyer values it more. Had this not been the case, the transaction would not have taken place.

A common mistake in economics is to conflate value and price. With that mistake comes the idea that value can indeed be measured objectively, expressed in monetary units. But that cannot be accurate, since market prices only illustrate a bound on goods' valuations, strictly subject to a given time and place. When someone agrees to sell a good for $1,000, she is demonstrating that she values the good at less than $1,000. Had she valued it at more than $1,000, she would not have been interested in exchanging it for $1,000. Only if her valuation is less than $1,000 would an offer of $1,000 tempt her to sell. Equivalently, when the buyer parts with $1,000 to buy that good, all that we can say about his valuation of the good is that it is higher than $1,000, or else he would not have paid that sum for it. It is not possible to determine an individual's precise valuation from their transaction, only its upper or lower bounds. The mere act of exchange tells us a lot about valuation.

Free Exchange

Any time two people freely choose to engage in the exchange of economic goods, it must necessarily be true that they both believe they will benefit from the exchange; otherwise they would not perform it. Mutually beneficial exchange indicates each party received something they value more than what they gave up. The only way this is possible is if we understand that they both have different subjective valuations of the exchanged good. If the value of these goods was objective, it would not differ from one person to another, and the exchange would not be possible, since neither would willingly choose to accept the good with the objective lower value in exchange for the good with the higher objective value. This will be discussed in more detail in Chapter 9 on trade, illustrating the benefits from trade.

Determinants of Value

The fundamental difference between Austrian school economists and other schools is that Austrians view value as subjective, while other schools conceive of value as something objective, or objectively measurable. In order to maintain that pretense, some modern economics textbooks define value as a function of utility, which they measure in terms of an imaginary and undefined unit named *util*. There is no standard for what constitutes a util, and no way of measuring anything in terms of utils. Some modern mathematical economists express value in explicit numerical terms, measured in monetary units, thus conflating value with price and failing to explain why people would engage in transactions to exchange objects if both objects have identical values. Marxists, on the other hand, think that value is determined by the labor that goes into the production of a good, an absurd contention according to which things become valuable if work is expended on producing them, regardless of anyone wanting to own them. If you were to spend equal time baking a normal cake and a cake out of mud, the Marxist would argue that both cakes would be valued the same.

There is an intuitive appeal to the notion that labor determines value. We can see that economic goods always require some element of labor to make them satisfy human needs. Even fruits that grow in the wild require man to expend the labor needed to pick and eat them before they can satisfy his need. It is not possible to conceive of goods that satisfy human needs without any labor being expended on them, and this drives the proponents of the labor theory of value to conclude that it is labor that gives value to goods, and that value can be measured by the amount of labor contributed. However, this is an untenable notion.

Goods are only valued because of their ability to satisfy our needs. A buyer is not interested in how much time and effort went into making a product when he purchases it, but only in the services and utility the product provides him. Labor is expended on producing goods because of the expectation that it can produce a final outcome, which is valuable to the consumer; labor does not magically make things valuable. It is possible to expend labor on a failed production process that does not yield a usable product. The output would not become valuable to others just because of the effort spent producing it; its uselessness renders it worthless to anybody who cares to value it. There is no guaranteed correspondence between the amount of labor expended in production and the value of that production. Workers may overestimate and underestimate the value of their labor, but it is only the choice of consumers in the market that can pass that judgment and determine the value of goods. Producers and workers dedicate labor to production processes they believe will produce these valuable goods. Should the cost of the inputs into the production process turn out to be smaller than the market price of the output, the producer will make a profit. This indicates that her investment in this process was productive to society, as the combined inputs cost less than the price of the outputs produced. Should the market price of the good be less than the inputs that went into producing it, this signals to the producer that she is engaging in a destructive production process, and the longer she engages in it, the more capital resources she squanders.

In Austrian economics, value is subjective and depends on the time and place at which the valuation happens. Value is derived from human choice, which is necessitated by scarcity. Value is assigned by individuals to each unit at the time and place in which they make decisions, but it is not a universal property of the good. Without a subjective conception of value, it is not possible to find coherent explanations for why and how humans make the economic choices they do.

How consumers determine the subjective value of objects is up to them. The same individual will value the same good at different valuations at different times and places, depending on many factors; most notably their existing stockpile of that good.

Marginalism

Menger's other momentous contribution to economics is the concept of marginalism. After establishing that the value of goods is not inherent to them, but is rather subjective and dependent on their ability to satisfy our needs, Menger applied this to the study of the value of different units of the same good and, in the process, laid the foundation for modern economic analysis.

Since the value of goods is derived from their ability to provide us with satisfaction, and since different satisfactions have unequal value to us, the value of different units of the same good will also be unequal, as it depends on the satisfactions they meet. The same good will have a different value to the same person depending on what need of his it meets at a given point in time.

Individuals use the first unit of a good to meet the most important and pressing needs related to it. They will use the second unit to meet the second most pressing need. As the quantity of the good they own increases, the needs that are met are less valuable and less pressing. In other words, identical goods will have different values for individuals, because the utility derived from them is not identical. The first units are the most valuable, and as the number of units consumed increases, each marginal unit is less valuable than the previous one.

Menger thus illustrated that the valuation we place on goods is not dependent on their total or overall utility and that their utility is not something inherent to these goods in the abstract, regardless of their quantities. Rather, the importance that we attach to goods is inextricably dependent on the quantity of those goods, and their quantity in relation to the existing supply of the good we have at our disposal. Humans make decisions based not on the total or abstract utility of an object but on the utility offered by distinct quantities of the good and their ability to satisfy our distinct needs.

Marginal Utility

Although Menger never used the term himself, his student Friedrich von Wieser would later introduce the term "marginal utility" to refer to the importance attached to the least important satisfaction secured by a single unit of the available quantity of a commodity. Mises defines it by saying: "We call that employment of a unit of a homogeneous supply which a man makes if his supply is n units, but would not make if, other things being equal, his supply were only n-1 units, the least urgent employment or the marginal employment, and the utility derived from it marginal utility."[21]

For example, the first unit of food a person eats is extremely valuable, as it is the difference between starvation and survival. The second unit of food will be the difference between mere survival and being well nourished. While still very valuable to the individual, the second unit is not as valuable as the first. Further units of food will be acquired for the enjoyment of taste or for social gatherings, which, while valuable, are not as valuable as the previous units that were used to guarantee survival and health. As an individual's consumption of food continues to increase, they eventually get to the point where they attach no value to an extra unit of food and prefer to go without it even if offered it for free. Increasing the number of units consumed leads to the units being deployed to meet less pressing needs, which means each successive unit has a lower utility than the previous unit and hence, a lower valuation to individuals.

With this important insight, Menger disproved the idea that the value of goods is inherent to them as goods. He illustrated that value is dependent on the needs the goods satisfy, which are, in turn, dependent on the abundance and scarcity of the goods, and only to the person making the valuation. Nobody is ever asked to make a valuation of the total supply of a good, or to value a good in the abstract. Economic decisions pertain only to individual units of goods, and individuals are at any point in time primarily making decisions about the next unit of a good they want to consume, not their lifetime supply of it, nor the good in the abstract.

Law of Diminishing Marginal Utility

An important implication of Menger's approach to valuation is the law of diminishing marginal utility. This law states that an individual's valuation and utility derived from a good will decline as the quantity of the good they hold increases. Since individuals use the first units of a good that they acquire for

21 Mises, Ludwig von. *Human Action: The Scholar's Edition*. Ludwig von Mises Institute, 1998, p. 124.

the fulfillment of the most pressing needs it can address, it must therefore follow that the first unit of any good will be valued highest by that individual. As their holdings of that good increase and each marginal unit goes toward meeting a less pressing need, each marginal unit will have a lower value to the individual. As the value of a good to a person at any point in time depends on the need it satisfies, the more a person has of something, the less the value they attach to it.

The marginal utility of a good declining as its quantity increases is an important insight into individual decision-making. Anyone who has made an expensive purchase may relate. On the first day that you have a new car or toy, the novelty factor is overwhelming, and you are captivated by it. This declines with time as you become more accustomed to its many features and traits. What was novel becomes common and loses the allure it had before you experienced it. You still get joy from driving the car or playing with the toy, but the specific joy declines with each extra use.

The law of diminishing marginal utility is another reminder that there is no such thing as an objective value of good X, as that value changes depending on the abundance of good X and the needs it satisfies. There are only ever subjective values of the next (marginal) unit of good X to the person making the valuation. This is dependent on the subjective preferences of the valuing individual and the abundance of the good.

Valuation by the Least Valuable Use

Another implication from Menger's approach to understanding valuation: As individuals deploy their inventory of a good to meet their most pressing needs, their valuation of the marginal unit will reflect their valuation of the least important satisfaction this good assures. Thus when making purchasing decisions, an individual's valuation of a good will reflect his valuation of the least important satisfaction it provides. A man deciding to pay for a meal will not pay based on how much he values food in the abstract or how much he values all the food he has eaten throughout his life. He will pay up to the value he attaches to the next meal itself. Considerations of the real value of all food to the man are irrelevant. As a man who has had enough food throughout his life to keep him alive and healthy enough to demand a new meal at this point, he does not value the next unit of food the same as he values all the food he has eaten in his life. He is not valuing it as if it was the difference between life and death, because it is not. The decision about the next meal is valued according to the need that the next meal satisfies for the man, which, being one meal, will be significantly lower than the value of food keeping him alive in general or the value of all the previous meals that ensured his survival up to today. We can then see how, when people have to make a choice about any particular good, they are valuing it in light of the least valuable use possible, because that is the only choice that exists at the margin. All the more valuable uses were already met with previous food units.

The person considering purchasing a bottle of water from a restaurant, for example, is not going to pay based on the value they get from water for survival, or for meeting their basic daily needs. They are simply deciding about the marginal (next) unit of water they consume, having already allocated other units of water to their more pressing needs. The price paid for water will be nowhere near the value the individual places on survival, because the decision to buy the bottle of water in a modern city pertains only to the consumption of an extra bottle of water, and not to survival. As water is essential for human survival, all human societies only arise in places with enough water to meet people's essential needs. With these needs secured, the price of marginal units will not reflect the value of the basic needs, but rather, the value of the less pressing needs. This helps us understand why water is relatively cheap even though it is essential. Its essential nature ensures humans are usually in possession of large quantities of it and make their marginal purchasing decisions based on the marginal units going to less pressing needs.

We can see why goods that are vital and important for survival are usually inexpensive. In the modern world, people do not pay for water based on the value they attach to survival, which is dependent on water. They already live in a time and place that secures their most important requirements of water at very low prices. Their individual purchasing decisions pertain to acquiring marginal quantities of water that might alleviate mild thirst but are not necessary for survival or health. But if you were to place an individual in a situation where she is unable to secure water for any of her vital needs for a few days, the least valuable use it would offer her would still be the difference between life and death, and that would make her value it very highly. As Mises explains:

> Acting man is not in a position in which he must choose between all the gold and all the iron. He chooses at a definite time and place under definite conditions between a strictly limited quantity of gold and a strictly limited quantity of iron. His decision in choosing between 100 ounces of gold and 100 tons of iron does not depend at all on the decision he would make if he were in the highly improbable situation of choosing between all the gold and all the iron.
>
> What counts alone for his actual choice is whether under existing conditions he considers the direct or indirect satisfaction which 100 ounces of gold could give him as greater or smaller than the direct or indirect satisfaction he could derive from 100 tons of iron. He does not express an academic or philosophical judgment concerning the "absolute" value of gold and of iron; he does not determine whether gold or iron is more important for mankind; he does not perorate as an author of books on the philosophy of history or on ethical principles. He simply chooses between two satisfactions both of which he cannot have together.[22]
>
> When faced with the problem of the value to be attached to one unit of a homogeneous supply, man decides on the basis of the value of the least important use he makes of the units of the whole supply; he decides on the basis of marginal utility.[23]

---

22 Mises, Ludwig von. *Human Action: The Scholar's Edition*. Ludwig von Mises Institute, 1998, p. 121.

23 Ibid. 121-3.

Water-Diamond Paradox

The immediate significance of Menger's marginal analysis is that it was the first economic resolution to the water-diamond paradox, an explanation of which had evaded economists for centuries. How could economists explain that water, which was essential for human life, was usually very cheap, if not free, whereas diamonds, which are luxury goods that serve no essential purpose for humans, are very expensive? If value really is subjective, then why do people attach so much value to trivial things they do not need, like diamonds, while attaching only little value to essential goods like water? Would this not fit more with a labor theory of value, which would postulate that diamonds are more valuable because they involve more labor in their production?

However, as discussed above, market value does not pertain to some inherent property of the good or to the value that all of its stockpiles afford us; it is based on the least important of the satisfactions the good meets. Since drinking water is usually available in large quantities wherever humans are settled, it, therefore, follows that the most pressing needs of water are already met, and that market choices are being made over units meeting far less pressing needs. Should a person in a modern city forego buying a bottle of water, he will be forgoing only one small need for water at a certain time. He would still have access to the water he needs for his most pressing and important needs of survival and hygiene. Diamonds, on the other hand, being very rare and available in very small quantities, are purchased by people deploying them for some of their highest-valued uses.

It is possible to imagine a scenario in which both water and diamonds are very scarce, and the marginal units available of both would go toward meeting the most pressing needs for these two goods. A man stranded in a desert who has not had a sip of water for days would be willing to pay a far higher price for the first unit of water than the first unit of diamond, as water would be the difference between life and death for him.

It is, therefore, inaccurate to say that diamonds are more valuable than water. The water-diamond paradox illustrates the importance of individual circumstances to the assessment of subjective value. In situations where water is plentiful and diamonds are scarce, water going to its least valuable uses is less valuable than diamonds, whose scarcity ensures that their least valuable uses still remain highly valuable. In situations in which water is scarce enough that the marginal unit will be deployed to satisfy the need for survival, water would undoubtedly be more valuable than diamonds.

Chapter 3

Time

> Man is subject to the passing of time. He comes into existence, grows, becomes old, and passes away. His time is scarce. He must economize it as he economizes other scarce factors. The economization of time has a peculiar character because of the uniqueness and irreversibility of the temporal order.[24]
>
> —Ludwig von Mises

The Ultimate Resource

Human action happens across time. All economic decisions take place across time, and production requires time. Being mortal, man's time on Earth is scarce, and that scarcity makes it an economic good and gives it value. Time's irreversible nature makes it a unique economic good. You cannot buy back the time you spent on something, or continue to increase your time indefinitely, as you could with other goods. Mises and the Austrian economists wrote eloquently about the importance of understanding the temporal dimension of human action and the unique nature of time as an economic good. This chapter will also build on the work of economist Julian Simon to argue that human time is the ultimate resource and that economic scarcity is a consequence of the scarcity of human time. The economizing of time is the ultimate

24 Mises, Ludwig von. *Human Action: The Scholar's Edition*. Ludwig von Mises Institute, 1998, p. 101.

economizing act, from which all economic decisions flow. Given more time, humans can make more of any economic good.[25] There are no binding physical constraints on the production of economic goods, and with the dedication of more human time and effort, the output of any good can be increased indefinitely. Only the scarcity of time is what forces us to make choices between economic goods, creating their scarcity.

When a child is born into this world, his time in it begins. That time is uncertain. It may be as brief as an hour, or it could last a whole century. Nobody knows how long he will live, but everyone soon realizes it is impossible to live forever, and one's time will only decline until it runs out completely. With that realization, and with maturity, humans economize time.

In contrast to the relative and constantly decreasing scarcity of material objects, human time's absolute scarcity increases with time. This is intuitively true individually, as growing and aging make man realize that his time on Earth only gets scarcer, giving it more value. It can also be seen in the market price paid for human labor across time. As humans spend more time working and producing, they increase the abundance of material objects, making them drop in value across time, when measured in terms of human labor.

In his book *The Ultimate Resource*, Simon argues that human time, or human labor, is the ultimate resource because it can be used to make all economic goods and resources.[26] The dedication of time to any production process would lead to an increase in the supply of its output, which leads Simon to argue that using the term "resource" to describe material goods is a misnomer, as material resources are the products of deploying the one ultimate resource, human time, to transform materials that are practically infinitely abundant into useful economic goods. The term "resource" suggests a fixed pool that humans draw down as they consume, but in reality, resources need to be produced before they are consumed, and their production is limited not by their physical abundance on our enormous planet, but by the amount of time humans dedicate to producing them, and their opportunity costs in terms of other goods. Raw

---

25 Bitcoin, as will be discussed later, is the only exception.

26 Simon, Julian. *The Ultimate Resource 2*. Princeton University Press, 1996.

materials, metals, and fuels are not given to us as manna from heaven; they are the complex output of sophisticated production processes to extract and deploy them to meet human needs.

Simon's conception of human time as the ultimate resource clarifies the nature of economic scarcity. Whereas economists had generally posited the scarcity of material goods as the starting point of economic analysis, it would be more accurate to understand scarcity as a function of the finite nature of human time. While material goods are technically scarce on Earth, their absolute quantities within the planet are far beyond our ability to exploit. The amount of raw materials is, therefore, not what makes them scarce. What makes them scarce for us is the time that is required to produce them, since that is limited and constrained in a very vivid sense to us.

Opportunity Cost

The scarcity of time is why humans have to think not just about direct monetary costs associated with any activity, but about its **opportunity cost**: the cost of an activity in terms of the forgone value of a different activity in which a person could have engaged. The fact that our time is scarce means we cannot engage in all activities at all times. We must choose. Even if physical resources were not a constraint, the time needed to carry out activities is always a constraint, and humans must factor in the alternatives they forego every time they partake in an activity.

The inevitability of death, and the finitude of time, and hence its scarcity, necessitate a constant accounting for opportunity cost, and from that comes all of man's economic thinking and action. All human actions consume time and therefore come at the cost of forgone actions. Understanding scarcity in general as resulting from the scarcity of time helps us understand opportunity cost, and why the economic way of thinking must always include the cost of the forgone alternative. Since human time is scarce, it is valuable to humans. There is thus always an alternative valuable use of time available for an individual, which must be taken into account.

Material Abundance

The most common measure to discuss the abundance of resources is "known or proven reserves," which refers to quantities of a resource that are definitively known to exist in particular locations and that can be extracted with current technology and prices.[27] This measure has increased in the long run for every resource known to man. As we consume more of a resource, it gets deployed in more uses, and that creates more demand for it, incentivizing more searching for it, thus increasing its reserves. Simon illustrates how these proven reserves increased between 1950 and 1990 for some important industrial metals. The world's population in 1950 was around 2.5 billion people, and, by 1990, had grown to around 5.32 billion people.[28] Measured in 2011 dollars, world GDP in 1950 is estimated to have been $9.25 trillion, and $47.04 trillion in 1990.[29] So in a forty-year period in which the human population grew by a multiple of 2.13, and in which human production grew fivefold, the proven reserves of most metals grew, instead of being depleted, and at rates higher than the population growth. Lead proven reserves grew by a multiple of 3, zinc by 4.21, copper by 5.66, iron ore by 8.27, oil by 13.1, phosphate by 14, and bauxite by 16.6.[30]

Clearly, the measure of proven reserves does not serve as a reasonable measure of the Earth's total resources, but as a measure of the amount of effort we put into the search and exploration of resources. Proven reserves are a measure of how much we are looking for resources using current technologies at current prices. As our exploitation of these resources and our standards of living grow, we develop better tools for digging, and we excavate in more areas, resulting in the growth of these proven reserves. Proven reserves are but the tip of the giant submerged iceberg of the Earth's total resources, which we cannot ever hope to estimate with any accuracy. Earth is enormous, and its exact composition is very difficult to ascertain from the surface. Digging up the entire

27 Simon, Julian. *The Ultimate Resource 2.* Princeton University Press, 1996, p. 44-8.

28 Roser, Max, Hannah Ritchie, Esteban Ortiz-Ospina, and Lucas Rodés-Guirao. "World Population Growth." *Our World In Data,* 2013.

29 Roser, Max. "Economic Growth." *Our World In Data,* 2013.

30 Simon, Julian. *The Ultimate Resource 2.* Princeton University Press, 1996, p. 45.

Earth to conduct a conclusive inventory is a futile and impossibly expensive job nobody could ever seriously contemplate.

Getting a sense of the magnitude of Earth supports Simon's contention. Earth's surface area is 510.1 million km^2, and the total area used for mining between the years 2000 and 2017 was estimated at 57,277 km^2, or 0.011% of the planet's surface area.[31] For perspective, if Earth was the size of a soccer field (105m × 68m, or 7140 m^2), the surface area of all of the world's mines would be 0.785 m^2, roughly the size of a small desk (a 122 cm × 61 cm desk has a surface area of 0.744 m^2).

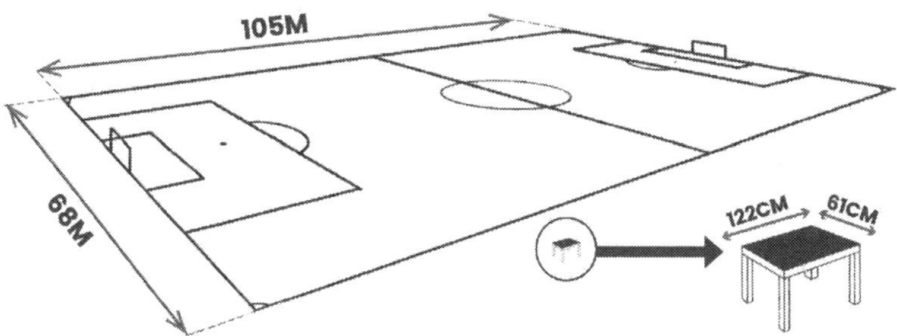

Figure 2. If Earth was a football field, all mines would be a small desk

The diameter of Earth is 12,742 kilometers. By contrast, the deepest mine in the world, Mponeng gold mine near Johannesburg, is "only" 3.16 km to 3.84 km deep, or from 0.024% to 0.03% of Earth's diameter. For perspective, if Earth was a ball with a diameter of 1 meter (or 3.28 feet), the deepest hole ever dug in its crust would be 0.027 cm (or 0.011 in) deep, less than the thickness of three pages of this book. The vast majority of Earth's surface has not been dug in search of resources, and in the few places where we have dug, we have, quite literally, barely scratched the Earth's surface. All of the resources humanity has used in millennia of consumption and exploitation are but a tiny fraction of the bounty available in the superficial 0.027% of Earth's diameter.

31 Maus, Victor et al. "A Global-scale Data Set of Mining Areas." *Scientific Data*, vol. 7, no. 289, 2020.

Most mines are closer to 300 meters in depth. For the sake of argument, let us assume a very generous average mine depth of 1 km. This would imply that the total volume of mines in the period between 2000 and 2017 was 57,277 km^3. The Earth's volume is 1,083,206,916,845.80 km^3 (around a trillion cubic kilometers). The volume of all the world's mines is, therefore, 0.00000529% of the Earth's volume. In other words, the Earth is 18,911,725.8 times larger than all the mines that exist on it, from which we have extracted all our resources. For perspective, if the Earth's volume was that of an Olympic swimming pool, all the world's mines would be roughly the size of half a cup.[32]

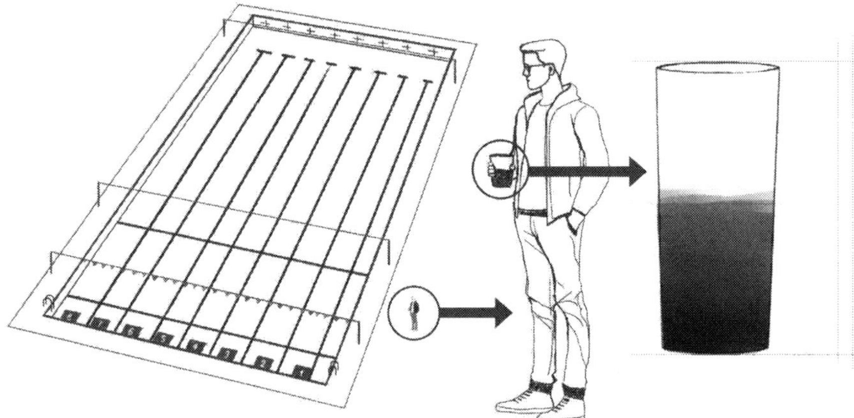

Figure 3. If Earth was an Olympic swimming pool, all our mines would be half a cup

If all the resources humans consume come from the equivalent of half a cup of the Olympic swimming pool that is Earth, it becomes apparent why worrying about the total amount of resources is so misguided. If eight billion people can subsist on the equivalent of a half cup out of an Olympic pool, it is clear that the total magnitude of water in the pool is irrelevant to human life and all economic considerations. The world's population would need to double for us to be digging into one cup's worth of an Olympic swimming pool. Even with enormous

32 An Olympic swimming pool has a volume of 2,500,000 liters. 0.00000528% of that is 0.132 liters. A cup is 0.25 liters.

growth in the world's population, we will barely scratch the surface of our vast, bountiful planet. Even the most conservative estimates find that the total crustal abundance of any particular naturally occurring substance is many uncountable multiples of the total amount humans consume of it and that quantity constitutes no meaningful limit or binding constraint on our level of consumption. It is quite likely that the total crustal abundance of any particular metal is equal to millions of years of human consumption. Even if the current, supposedly unsustainable, consumption trends were to continue for thousands of years, we would not be able to dig through the entirety of the Earth's contents of any particular metal. The limit and constraint on how much we can produce from each metal in any given year will continue to be the amount of time and resources we direct to its production and the amount of other goods and services we are willing to forego for its production.

Beyond being used as an illustration in this economics textbook, these aggregate measures of Earth's resources are completely pointless and irrelevant metrics that do not factor into the economic decisions carried out by anyone anywhere. There are no economic decisions that pertain to the total stock of metal on Earth, and all individual economic decisions pertaining to a resource are made at the margin, based on the next marginal unit of land to be exploited, the marginal cost of extracting the next unit, and the marginal revenue expected from selling it. At no point can any individual or entity make any economic decision pertaining to the total aggregate stock of a material on Earth. Economic calculations are constantly being done at the margin, and they pertain only to scarce resources that involve an opportunity cost. Minerals in the Earth's crust are not scarce, and they offer no utility to humans. Producing usable materials from them, on the other hand, requires real decisions to be made about allocating marginal units of scarce resources into the exploration, excavation, extraction, refining, and production processes.

A useful analogy here is to think of Earth's resources as rocks, and our consumption of resources as the use of rocks to build houses. No economic decision needs to factor in the total quantity of rocks on Earth; economic decisions pertain only to the application of scarce resources, labor, capital, and land, to the process of excavating and applying rocks. It would be insane for a homebuilder to concern himself with the availability of rocks in nature, when all our houses require an infinitesimally tiny fraction of Earth's rocks for their construction. The only economically pressing concern for the homebuilder is whether he can secure the human labor and human-produced capital that is necessary to convert those rocks into homes.

What we really value are not resources, but economic goods made from resources. That is what requires time, and that is what is scarce. That is the scarcity from which all other scarcities originate. The raw material is everywhere around us, but the time to produce economic goods from it is scarce. Humans are not passive recipients of manna that can run out. Humans are the producers of all these resources, and when demand for these metals increases, the most important determinant of their scarcity is the action of the humans who produce them, and the incentives they face. As they face greater demand for a resource, they have the incentive to produce more of it and invest more in its production. As productivity increases, we are able to obtain larger quantities of the supply of the good per amount of time invested in producing it, meaning that the real price of the good, as measured in terms of human labor, will continue to decline. This fact is borne out by decades of commodity market data.

While commodity prices can and usually do rise in terms of national currencies, that is a result of the debasement of national currencies. When measured against wage rates, or the price of human time, all commodities are in long-term price decline, even as consumption steadily increases. In a world of hard money, as under the gold standard, it would be perfectly normal to expect the prices of all commodities to consistently decline over time, with only occasional and temporary increases precipitated through sharp, sudden rises in supply and production disruptions. Gold, or whatever is used as money, would always be the good whose supply increases at the slowest rate, allowing its holders to command more of all other goods, whose supply becomes more abundant.

Economists Gale Pooley and Marian Tupy constructed an economic index in honor of Julian Simon that measures the prices of 50 basic commodities in terms of wages. They find that the time needed to earn a basket of 50 commodities has fallen by 75.2% over the period between 1980 and 2020, which means that an hour of work in 2020 could buy 4.03 times as much of the 50 basic commodities as it could buy in 1980, implying an annual growth rate of 3.55% and a doubling of commodity abundance every 20 years.[33] Even though the human population increased by 75.8% over these 40 years, decades that witnessed the largest human population growth, and the highest consumption and standards of living in history, the prices of 50 basic commodities have declined by 3 quarters in terms of the human time needed to purchase them. This data is only possible to understand in the context of an infinitely large Earth whose physical limits are nowhere near our grasp, a grasp limited by the scarcity of our time and the opportunity cost involved in increasing the production of any particular resource.

Basic 50 Commodities 1980–2020	Percentage Change in Time Price	Abundance Multiplier	Basic 50 Commodities 1980–2020	Percentage Change in Time Price	Abundance Multiplier
Sugar	-86.2%	7.25	Sorghum	-74.0%	3.85
Hides	-86.2%	7.23	Soybeans	-72.4%	3.62
Pork	-86.1%	7.20	LNG, Japan	-71.6%	3.52
Coffee	-85.9%	7.11	Fertilizer	-71.6%	3.52
Salmon	-85.1%	6.72	Coconut Oil	-70.8%	3.42
Natural Gas, EU	-85.0%	6.68	Orange	-70.8%	3.42
Cotton	-85.0%	6.66	Coal	-70.5%	3.39
Groundnuts etc.	-83.0%	5.89	Logs	-70.4%	3.38
Cocoa	-82.2%	5.63	Rapeseed	-69.9%	3.32
Uranium	-82.0%	5.54	Wool	-69.7%	3.30
Aluminum	-81.3%	5.34	Tea	-68.3%	3.15
Lamb	-81.1%	5.30	Sawnwood	-67.6%	3.09
Silver	-80.7%	5.19	Beef	-67.0%	3.03
Tin	-80.1%	5.03	Plywood	-63.6%	2.75
Crude Oil	-78.2%	4.58	Sunflower Oil	-63.0%	2.70
Rice	-76.4%	4.24	Tobacco	-62.5%	2.67
Rubber	-76.3%	4.21	Lead	-60.7%	2.55
Wheat	-76.1%	4.18	Nickel	-58.8%	2.43
Barley	-75.7%	4.11	Chicken	-58.3%	2.39
Shrimp	-75.6%	4.11	Copper	-44.8%	1.81
Natural Gas, U.S.	-75.2%	4.04	Fish Meal	-44.6%	1.81
AVERAGE	-75.2%	4.03	Gold	-43.2%	1.81
Palm Oil	-74.8%	4.04	Zinc	-42.0%	1.72
Platinum	-74.6%	4.05	Banana	-37.5%	1.60
Pulpwood	-74.5%	4.06	Iron Ore	-24.4%	1.32
Corn	-74.2%	3.88			

Figure 4. Changes in time prices and abundance of basic 50 commodities (1980 to 2020)

33 Pooley, Gale, and Marian Tupy. "The Simon Abundance Index 2021." *Human Progress*. • See also *The Bitcoin Standard Podcast* with guest Gale Pooley.

The only scarcity, as Julian Simon brilliantly demonstrated, is the time humans have to produce these commodities, and that is why global wages continue to rise worldwide, making products and materials continuously cheaper in terms of human labor. The one resource whose price has risen almost continuously throughout history is human time, as measured by wages. As we continue to find more ingenious ways of increasing the output of physical resources, their real price, in terms of human time, continues to decline, while the value of human time continues to rise.

Only with this framework can one understand why humanity has never run out of any resource, even after many millennia of exploiting the Earth, and the relentless predictions of imminent doom caused by resource exhaustion. Not only have we not run out of any of these resources, but, in fact, real prices continue to decline, the annual production of virtually all resources continues to rise every year, and the proven reserves of each resource have only increased with time as our consumption has gone up, as mentioned above in Simon's data. If resources are to be understood as finite, then the existing stockpiles would decline with time as we consume more. But even as we are always consuming more, prices continue to drop, and the technological improvements for finding and excavating resources allow us to find more untapped stockpiles.

Oil, the vital bloodline of modern economies, is the best example as it has fairly reliable statistics. As Figure 5 shows, even as oil consumption and production continue to increase year-on-year, the proven reserves increase at an even faster rate. According to data from BP's Statistical Review of World Energy, annual oil production was 46% higher in 2015 than in 1980, while consumption was 55% higher. Oil reserves, on the other hand, have increased by 148%, around triple the increase in production and consumption.

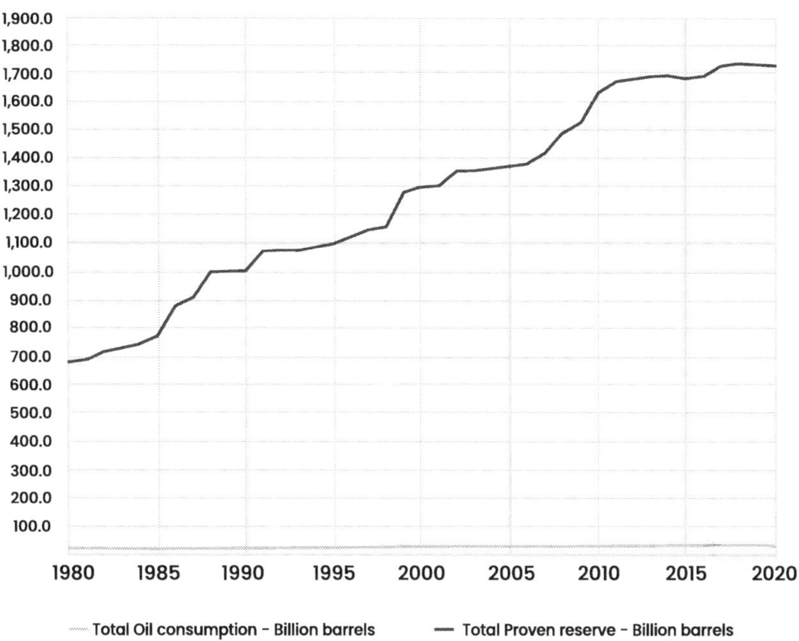

Figure 5. Oil consumption and proven reserves[34]

Similar statistics can be produced for resources with varying degrees of prevalence in the Earth's crust. The rarity of a resource determines the relative cost of extracting it from the Earth. More prevalent metals, like iron and copper, are easy to find and relatively cheap as a result. Rarer metals, such as silver and gold, are more expensive. The limit on how much we can produce of each of those metals, however, and not their absolute quantity, remains the opportunity cost of their production relative to one another, in subjective human valuation. There is no better evidence for this than the fact that one of the (if not the) rarest metals in the Earth's crust, gold, has been mined for thousands of years and continues to be mined in increasing quantities as technology advances over time.

34 BP Statistical Review of World Energy.

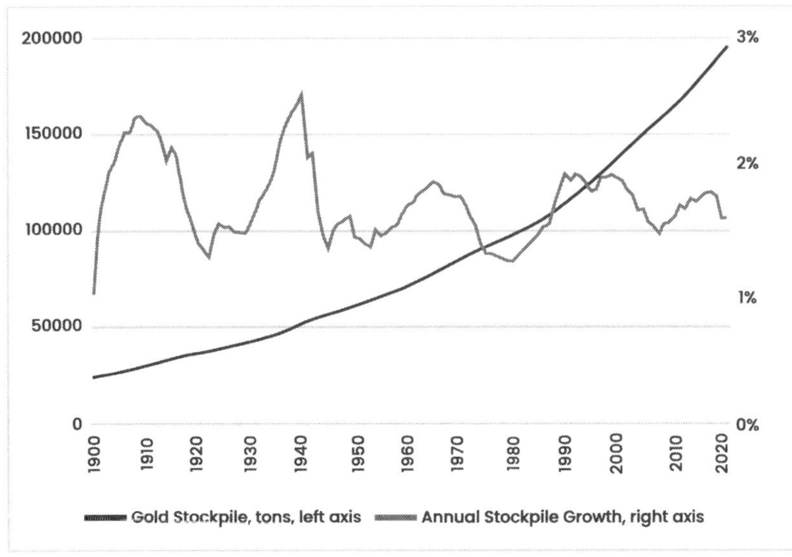

Figure 6. Global gold annual production[35]

If there are other metals that are rarer than gold, they have all been discovered recently, and we have not dedicated as much time to finding their reserves and accumulating their stockpiles as with gold. But gold has been sought and mined for thousands of years, and its annual production goes up every year, so it makes no sense to talk of any natural element as being limited in its quantity in any practical sense. Scarcity is only relative to material resources, with the differences in the cost of extraction determining the scarcity.

Simon's Bet

After U.S. President Richard Nixon suspended the convertibility of the U.S. dollar into gold in 1971, all prices began an inexorable rise, a trend that continues to this day. For people in the 1970s accustomed to relatively stable prices under the gold standard, these price rises seemed like a sign of an economic apocalypse, as it gave the impression that all our precious resources were

35 Source: U.S. Geological Survey.

running out. As the world was swept up in the hysteria about the depletion of resources and overpopulation, Simon was not content with merely writing to counter the hysteria. He sought to expose the vacuity of the hysterics by challenging one of the twentieth century's foremost hysterics, Paul Ehrlich, to a public bet on the question.

Ehrlich had published a large number of hysterical diatribes unworthy of inclusion in this book's bibliography in which he had predicted the exhaustion of several essential resources to humanity due to overpopulation and added trademark misanthropic rants about eugenics and coercive sterilization and other measures to reduce the human population. Simon challenged Ehrlich to specify any resources he was confident would run out or become much scarcer over any period longer than a year, and Simon would bet him $1,000 that each of them would actually be cheaper, in real terms, by the end of the period.

The bet must have seemed like a donation to Ehrlich, such was the conviction of his warnings about the imminent depletion of critical resources. Ehrlich specified 5 metals and a period of 10 years to assess their price, from 1980 to 1990. By the end of the period, each of these metals was cheaper than at the start in real terms. Thirty years later, these metals have only gotten cheaper in real terms, while their annual production continues to increase every year.

The reason that the price of all these metals dropped is that their scarcity is relative, not absolute. They are scarce to us because the time and resources required to produce them must be diverted away from the production of other resources. Simon understood that as the human population increased and demand for these metals increased, these metals would have more resources directed toward their production, their quantities would increase, and their prices would decrease. The rise in demand causes a rise in prices, which affords larger profits to producers of these metals, which provides them with more money to spend on investment, and allows them to attract more investment. This investment goes into prospecting, extracting, refining, and distributing the metals, all of which leads to an increase in productivity, the output per unit of input. As will be discussed in more detail in Chapter 4, larger capital investments allow the employment of more complex and longer methods of production that yield a higher productivity per worker.

As a geologist, Ehrlich's conception of scarcity was based on estimates of consumption compared to reserves, without regard for the role of human action in bringing about changes in these numbers. Ehrlich essentially compared the proven reserves of metals to their annual consumption numbers and estimated the number of years it would take humanity to run through its reserves.

Simon, as an economist, understood the dynamics driving the production of these metals, even though he had little familiarity with the geological realities. By understanding economics as the study of human action, as discussed in Chapter 1, Simon knew that the scarcity of these metals depended ultimately on the amount of time humans dedicated to them, and that was, in turn, dependent on the incentive humans had to produce these resources, not on geological limitations. Should the demand for a metal increase, there is no limited pool to be depleted. There are always other lands to prospect and deeper mines to dig.

Time Preference

Human time being finite and uncertain means that no person knows with certainty how long they will live, or when they might die. This creates in man a **time preference**, a universal preference for earlier over later satisfaction. Individuals always prefer consuming or having a good today over any future period, because survival is never certain. Time preference is always a positive value, meaning that utility today is always preferred to the same utility tomorrow. Humans also prefer to have resources sooner rather than later, since, in the case of durable goods, they would be likely to enjoy their services for longer the earlier they receive them.

While time preference is always positive, its value varies depending on the degree to which humans discount future utility compared to present utility. A relatively low time preference indicates a low degree of discounting of future utility, indicating a relatively greater concern with the future. A higher time preference implies a higher degree of discounting of future utility, a relatively lower concern with the future, and a strong present orientation.

Economizing Time

As discussed above, economic scarcity is ultimately the scarcity of human time. We can then also understand the entirety of human economizing as centering around economizing time. That is, we seek to increase the amount and subjective value of our time on Earth. That time is scarce means humans are constantly looking to economize it into being spent in the ways that offer them the most satisfaction, or that are the most valuable. The future being uncertain and time preference being universally positive mean that humans constantly seek to maximize the value of their present time.

Leisure is the term used to denote the time people spend doing things they enjoy for their own sake, things that bring them immediate pleasure, as opposed to things they do in exchange for a future reward or satisfaction. Leisure is how economists refer to good times. Everyone likes to have a good time. Life is finite, and humans naturally want to spend it doing the things they enjoy rather than the things they do not enjoy. Time preference, in other words, is always going to be positive.

Everyone would like to spend all their life in leisure. But since we are not eternal creatures living in the Garden of Eden, too much leisure will inevitably mean an early death through starvation or the forces of nature. We also cannot just enjoy leisure indefinitely, because we are always capable of conceiving of ways in which we can improve the quality and quantity of time we have on Earth. It is not just the value of our present time that humans seek to economize. We would also like to maximize the quantity of time we have on Earth; in other words, try to live long lives and not die early. We would also like to maximize the value of our future time. Human reason allows us to conceive of ways to act to increase our chances of survival and to provide for our future selves. Reason allows us to conceive of a better future, to work for it, and to sacrifice present enjoyment for its sake. Reason also allows us to conceive of the consequences of failing to provide for the future, and to compare them to other courses of action. Humans can spend every minute of their lives caring only about their present, but they would eventually arrive at a very precarious present moment because of their failure to have provided for it in the past. The more an individual values the future and works and provides for it, the more likely they are to survive into the future.

Ultimately, the economic question is how we trade off present utility against longer survival and future utility. The most important trade an individual conducts is their trade with their future self. The simplest trade is the one involving forgoing immediate pleasure in favor of labor to provide for the future. As a person is enjoying their present, they will experience a need for sustenance and shelter, at the very basic level. But food needs to be hunted, grown, or acquired, and shelter needs to be built or acquired. That requires the sacrifice of present enjoyment in favor of labor.

Man's reason leads him to realize he can provide for his future self and improve his chances of survival. He understands that labor, while unpleasant in the moment and involving the cost of forgoing pleasure, will allow him to reap the rewards in the future. Reason, and the desire to live long and well, conspire to lower man's time preference. They call on him not only to abandon leisure in search of the hardships of work, but also to provide for his future self through deferring current consumption, saving for the future, and accumulating durable goods and productive capital.

It is this process of lowering time preference, future orientation, and provision for the future that sets in motion the process of civilization. Or, as Hans-Hermann Hoppe put it, "once it is low enough to allow for any savings and capital or durable consumer-goods formation at all, a tendency toward a fall in the rate of time preference is set in motion, accompanied by a 'process of civilization.'"[36]

As humans reap the benefits of future provision and low time preference, they become more likely to engage in it. Work, and the accumulation of capital, lead to increases in productivity, increasing the value of an individual's time. The more people are able to provide for their future, the less uncertain it becomes, which in turn encourages further concern for the future, saving, capital accumulation, and a likely increase in the quantity and the value of an individual's time on Earth.

---

36 Hoppe, Hans-Hermann. *Democracy: The God That Failed.* Transaction Publishers, 2001, p. 6.

Economizing Action

There is no opting out of economics and economic choice except through death. You may not like specific institutions such as private property or labor, but choosing to not engage in them simply excludes you from larger, more productive circles of economic activity. If you are alive and you strive to remain alive, you are bound to seek to survive through the tools of economizing action. Everyone engages in economizing acts every day of their lives without having to learn economics. But learning economics can help the mind consciously understand the importance of acts in which it engages, and how complex structures and institutions emerge from them. While learning economics is not necessary for economizing, which is a natural function of our reason, it is necessary for the fostering and survival of an extended market order in which humans are able to economize freely, cooperate with one another, and prosper. Individuals are capable of engaging in market transactions but can lose sight of their importance, resulting in political structures that suppress this type of economic action, with devastating consequences.

The following nine chapters of the book will each focus on important tools we humans have developed, consciously and spontaneously, to increase the quantity and value of our time. This list is not meant to be exhaustive or conclusive, and these categories contain significant practical overlaps, but this book will still focus on explicating each of these concepts individually. They are listed below alongside their chapter numbers:

4. **Labor**
5. **Property**
6. **Capital**
7. **Technology**
8. **Power**
9. **Trade**
10. **Money**
11. **The Market Order**
12. **Capitalism**

These tools are, in essence, how we humans economize our time. The ultimate trade-off we all face is that our time can be spent on leisure, enjoying things we like, or it can be spent on economic activity, with the aim of increasing the length and value of our time. All of these economic tools share one thing in common: they are peaceful, and everyone involved does so of their own volition. Chapter 16 discusses non-peaceful means of human interaction, and Chapter 17 discusses how humans defend these forms.

PART II

Economy

Chapter 4

Labor

> The employment of the physiological functions and manifestations of human life as a means is called labor... Man works in using his forces and abilities as a means for the removal of uneasiness and in substituting purposeful exploitation of his vital energy for the spontaneous and carefree discharge of his faculties and nerve tensions. Labor is a means, not an end in itself.
>
> Every individual has only a limited quantity of energy to expend, and every unit of labor can only bring about a limited effect. Otherwise human labor would be available in abundance; it would not be scarce and it would not be considered as a means for the removal of uneasiness and economized as such.[37]

—Ludwig von Mises

Labor and Leisure

Human time is the ultimate and scarcest resource. Spending it is irreversible, and its quantity cannot be increased indefinitely. Time's scarcity and unpredictability create in humans a positive time preference: a preference for a present good over an identical future good. This preference applies to time itself. Humans value their present time period more than they value identical

37 Mises, Ludwig von. *Human Action: The Scholar's Edition.* Ludwig von Mises Institute, 1998, p. 131.

future time periods. This preference varies over time and from person to person, but it is nonetheless always present and always positive.

Humans can spend their time in two ways. The first involves doing the things we desire, like, and want to do for their own sake. These activities are subjectively valuable to the individuals who engage in them; they provide utility in their own right. They are, in a sense, their own reward. Economists refer to this use of time as **leisure**, which includes rest, time spent with loved ones, entertainment, recreation, and anything else an individual enjoys. Leisure is what you would do if you did not have to work. The second way to spend time is doing things for the sake of their results and outputs. This is the time man spends doing an activity that he does not find valuable in and of itself, but whose output he values. Economists refer to this use of time as **labor**, which Mises defines as "the employment of the physiological functions and manifestations of human life as a means."[38]

The distinction between leisure and labor is the distinction between what you want to do and what you have to do. Or, put differently, it is the distinction between what you do for its own sake and what you do for the sake of its future outcomes. If a person were engaged in an activity because they enjoyed it, regardless of its outcome, it would not be labor; it would be leisure. Labor itself has negative utility, or disutility, by definition; it reduces human satisfaction to engage in work, but man engages in it nonetheless because he expects it to produce outputs that offer him greater future utility. The present utility of leisure is sacrificed in favor of the expected future utility from the outcomes of the labor. **The opportunity cost of labor is leisure forgone.**

Humans have an infinitely high time preference when they are very young, as they are unable to conceptualize labor or anything but their immediate basic desires. As humans grow and mature cognitively, they realize they care about more than just increasing the value of their present time. As soon as children become capable of conceiving of the future and valuing it, they begin deferring instant gratification in exchange for future rewards. Our valuing of the future is what begins the process of lowering our time preference with age. With the

---

38 Ibid.

ability to conceive of the future comes the ability to reason about it, plan for it, and work for it. Toilet training, or any activity carried out in anticipation of parental reward, might be the first activity that teaches a child to trade current present labor for future reward.

With maturity, a man transcends the narrow concerns of immediate gratification and begins economizing for the future. This takes two forms: economizing to lengthen the time period in which he is alive and economizing to provide for future time periods in his life. The human struggle to survive and thrive is the struggle to increase the amount and value of time we have on Earth, and it is inextricable from the need to work in the present. Surviving and prospering, in the long run, require work and sacrificing pleasure today, and this incentivizes the lowering of our time preference. When man values the return of labor more than the disutility of sacrificing leisure, man will work.

Man's reason drives him to realize he can expend labor in the present to provide himself future utility, improve his future subjective well-being, and extend his life. No matter how favorable or unfortunate his circumstances, man will always think of ways to improve his situation. In a tropical paradise, in a desert, on a farm, or in a modern industrial society, reason will always find a way to direct man's physiological functions and time toward improving his condition. There will always be present utility to sacrifice on the altar of future utility, and reason will always drive man to it.

The castaway stranded in an idyllic tropical island paradise might appear to modern people to be living the ideal life, but such a life will nonetheless inevitably involve labor. Man can be happy on the beach for a while, but as time passes, his contentment declines, and other needs arise. Time on the beach, like leisure in general, and like all goods with positive utility, exhibits diminishing marginal returns. The joy of the beach declines the more time the individual spends there. Other desires only intensify, as they go unsatisfied for longer periods. The castaway will soon get hungry, and his reason will lead him to conclude he can satisfy his hunger by working to secure food. His reason leads him to devise ways to transform wild animals into nutrition. He tries to catch a fish with his bare hands, or he hunts down rabbits and deer. There is no guarantee his toil will produce a worthwhile return, but hunger becomes more pressing as time goes by, increasing the urgency of the hunt, and decreasing the value of the leisure that would be attained without labor, thus incentivizing more, better, and smarter toil.

The motivation for work, ultimately, is that failure to do it, or failure to carry it out successfully, will result in death, sooner or later. Outside the Garden of Eden, man has always had to work to survive and thrive. At any point in time, each individual faces the choice between labor and leisure, as well as the choice of what kind of labor to perform to increase productivity. Labor is our first conceptual tool for increasing the amount and value of our time. Yet labor is not uniquely human. Instinctively, animals have the ability to engage in activities for which the rewards are not immediate, trading off present utility for future utility. Birds build nests, beavers build dams, and predators spend significant time chasing their prey. Unlike animals' instincts, though, human reason can devise many other methods for economizing and increasing the productivity of our labor, discussed in the next chapters.

The primary way humans influence their surrounding environment is through the process of production. The following section defines the main terminology of production, which will be foundational to the rest of the book's discussion.

Production

Production is defined by Mises as the "alteration of the given according to the designs of reason." According to Mises, "These designs—the recipes, the formulas, the ideologies—are the primary thing; they transform the original factors—both human and nonhuman—into means. Man produces by dint of his reason; he chooses ends and employs means for their attainment. The popular saying according to which economics deals with the material conditions of human life is entirely mistaken. Human action is a manifestation of the mind."[39]

Labor is "the employment of the physiological functions and manifestations of human life as a means."[40] People work only when they value the

39 Mises, Ludwig von. *Human Action: The Scholar's Edition*. Ludwig von Mises Institute, 1998, p. 142.

40 Ibid. 131.

expected return of labor more than the lost satisfaction brought about by the curtailment of leisure. To work involves disutility.

Consumer goods, final goods, or first-order goods satisfy human wants directly, independent of other goods. This is the end goal sought from the production process and the reason the process is undertaken.

Producer goods, intermediate goods, factors of production, or higher-order goods are goods that satisfy human wants indirectly when used to produce consumer goods. Human labor can be viewed as a producer good, but this term is usually used to refer to **capital**. A capital good is any good that is acquired not to be consumed, but to produce other goods. The existence of a capital good requires the sacrifice of consumer goods.

Productivity is understood as the quantity of output produced by one unit of input in a specific period of time.

Exchange or trade: Willfully induced substitution of a more satisfactory state of affairs for a less satisfactory one. Production itself can be understood as an exchange of leisure time and capital inputs for the outputs of labor production.

Price: The thing that is given up in an exchange.

Cost: The value of the price; the value of the satisfaction one must forego in order to attain the desired end.

Profit, gain, or net yield: The difference between the value of the price paid (the cost incurred) and that of the goal attained. Profit in this primary sense is purely subjective; it is an increase in the acting man's happiness, a psychic phenomenon that can be neither measured nor weighed.

Productivity of Labor

Man can work to produce products for himself, or he can work to produce products for others, receiving compensation in exchange for his time. Wage labor is distinct from performing a service for someone as a favor or gift, because the former involves compensation. Wage labor is distinct from slave labor in that it is voluntary; the laborer can stop working, and the employer can only seek to keep him by trying to convince him to return willingly through incentives such as better payment, better work conditions, or similar noncoercive means. Labor is, by definition, a consensual agreement between the employee and employer.

The decision of an employer to hire an employee is a market transaction, like all others. The difference between it and the exchange of a consumer good lies in the fact that employers do not value labor based on their own subjective preferences because labor is not a consumer good for the employer. Instead, since labor is a producer good, the employer values labor based on how much output it can produce, multiplied by the subjective valuation the market assigns to the product produced.

For the employer and employee to willingly agree on an arrangement to exchange labor for compensation, the conditions of the exchange must be satisfactory for both. For the laborer, this means his compensation is higher than the valuation he places on the alternative use of his time, which is leisure, or the next best available job. The value of the employee's labor to the employer must also be greater than the wage paid, or else the employer would not pay it. At the margin, when an employer is deciding whether to hire an extra worker, she will only do so if the extra worker provides her with a marginal increase in revenue that is higher than the wage. Each extra worker must contribute to an increase in output production at the margin. The marginal increase in quantity produced is referred to as the marginal product of the worker. When that number is multiplied by the price of the product, we obtain the **marginal revenue product**, a measure of the revenue provided to the employer by the marginal worker. If the wage is higher than the laborer's valuation of leisure or the next best use of his time and lower than the employer's marginal revenue product, then the two can agree to work together for their mutual benefit. Otherwise, there will be no exchange of labor for compensation between the two parties.

Labor occupies a unique position in our world due to what Mises calls its "nonspecific character."[41] Unlike specialized capital equipment, human time can be directed toward all kinds of production processes. Capital that can no longer be productive in a specific line of business will likely be rendered

41 Ibid. 133.

obsolete, but human time can always be repurposed for more productive uses. There is always more demand for more human minds and hands to work in the world due to the ultimate scarcity of human time, and employers will always be willing to take the next worker at a wage lower than their marginal productivity.

Productivity is understood as the quantity of output produced by one unit of input in a specific time period. As discussed in the previous chapter, the value of human time has appreciated significantly throughout human history. Over time, labor wages continue to rise in real terms, because worker productivity continues to rise, driving employers to pay higher wages to obtain the labor they need and prevent it from going to competitors.

In the past 200 years, following the Industrial Revolution, the value of human time has continuously risen as humans have accumulated more capital, invented higher productivity technologies, utilized more powerful energy sources, and extended the division of labor to larger markets and more participants. All the inventions, tools, and technologies that increase human productivity have led to the extension of human lives and an increase in the value of human time, because now we need to be paid significantly more to part with our leisure. The end goal of economizing, after all, is to allow humans more, and better, time on Earth.

Unemployment

In the twentieth century, the concept of unemployment became closely intertwined with the concept of labor. Many schools of thought have posited that unemployment is an unavoidable and inevitable part of the workings of the market economy. Various reasons have been presented to explain why a free labor market will inevitably malfunction in a way that leaves significant numbers of people who are willing to work at prevailing wages unemployed.

But unemployment is as much a normal part of the labor market as burning crops is a part of the food market. As will be discussed in Section IV of this book, inflationary credit expansion and minimum wage laws are the root cause of unemployment. Inflation causes prices to rise, requiring workers to ask for higher wages to cover their increasing living costs. But since an increase in monetary media does not result in an increase in economic resources, employers often have no ability to pay higher wages to workers and remain operational. They will either lay off workers, or go out of business. Inflation reduces the wealth and holdings of both worker and employer and increases the price of the market goods they seek to purchase. Further, credit inflationism also causes the business cycle. The inflationary boom results in the financing of unsustainable investments, and their inevitable collapse causes entire economic sectors to witness bankruptcies, with large numbers of workers laid off and left with skills for which there is little demand.

As inflation causes unemployment through rising prices and recessions, governments and government-employed economists prefer to shift the blame onto the market economy itself or greedy capitalists, or they provide other flimsy explanations. Instead of tackling the inflation at the root of the problem, modern economists invariably propose counterproductive measures like minimum wage laws. Rather than a command for employers to pay workers more, minimum wage laws should be thought of as a prohibition against workers choosing the price of their own labor. Minimum wage laws prevent the market from adjusting to inflation, resulting in constant waves of unemployment that coincide with the business cycle.

It is telling that the concept of unemployment did not really exist as an economic term before the twentieth century. In a free market, people choose whether or not to work for the wage offered to them, so nobody can be involuntarily unemployed. With the introduction of monetary inflationism and minimum wage laws, a permanently unemployed part of the population became a fixture of modern economies, and blaming this unemployment on the market process became a fixture of the pseudoscientific economics dominant in modern academia, financed by those with vested interests in maintaining inflation in order to provide rationales for it.

Switzerland, the last country in the world to go off the gold standard, provides a good example of this dynamic. As the fiat world struggled through severe unemployment crises throughout the twentieth century, Switzerland had practically no unemployment until it went off the gold standard in the mid-1970s.[42] After adopting the dollar standard and engaging in inflationism, Switzerland has witnessed a rise in unemployment that follows the same cyclical pattern observed in every country that runs on fiat money.

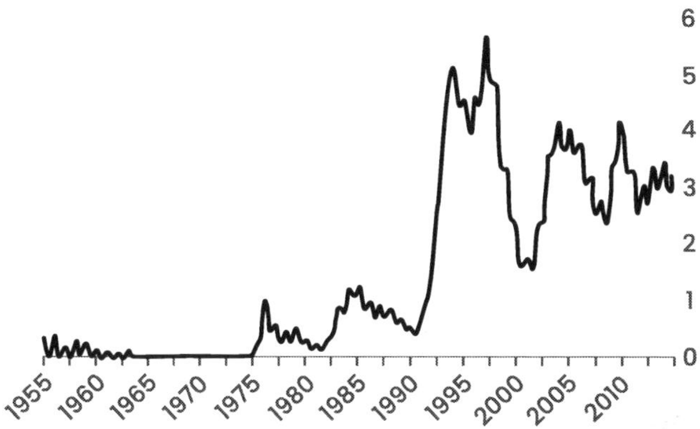

Figure 7. Unemployment rate in Switzerland

Under a free market with sound money, savings appreciate in market value over time, and individuals have the freedom to work or not, and to ask for any wage they want. Employers also have the freedom to pay any salary they want. In such a world, with savings appreciating, it is perfectly rational for many to forego employment. A worker who cannot find employment at a prevailing wage is simply unable to find someone who values the marginal revenue product of his labor at a price higher than the worker's valuation of leisure. The modern phenomenon of mass involuntary unemployment can only occur when there are laws, rules, or restrictions that make it illegal, and subject to punishment, to engage in labor at specific wage rates.

In the context of free exchange, there can be no such thing as unemployment among people who are willing to work, because this implies they are entitled to earn a wage that nobody is willing to pay them. The worker could always find work by increasing his productivity or decreasing his asking wage. Involuntary unemployment is impossible in a free-market economic system; it

42 "Unemployment Rate in Switzerland." *Federal Reserve Economic Data.*

is the worker's choice to ask for a wage that nobody is willing to pay, and thus it is their choice to remain unemployed.

Will Work Ever End?

Labor, as a resource, is very precious precisely because it competes with leisure for the scarcest of resources—human time. Further, as income and utility produced from labor increase, they lead to an increase in workers' wealth; this results in workers who can afford to spend more time enjoying leisure, further increasing the disutility of their labor and discouraging them from working. Labor may be the only economic good or activity whose supplied quantity can decline as its price rises, because the increase in the price of labor causes an increase in the worker's wealth, which might allow the worker to purchase more leisure and sell less labor. The scarcity of time means that the supply of labor has an opportunity cost that becomes more valuable the more a person earns from working. This dynamic has led many to speculate that economic progress might one day mean humans will no longer need to work.

Will we ever get to a point where we don't need to work? This is a common fantasy among many politicians and economists who have no conception of the economic way of thinking, such as John Maynard Keynes and his many followers. Writing in the 1930s, Keynes speculated that productivity will continue to increase so much that by 2030, humans would only need to work a fifteen-hour work week to produce what they need. Keynes imagined technological progress would bring about technological unemployment, which he defined as "unemployment due to our discovery of means of economising the use of labour outrunning the pace at which we can find new uses for labor."[43]

"All this means in the long run *that mankind is solving its economic problem,*"[44] Keynes concluded, because he naively imagines the economic problem is like a math problem that needs to be solved once to stay solved, as if it pertains to securing some specific set of goods and services needed for a happy

43 Keynes, John Maynard. "Economic Possibilities for our Grandchildren (1930)." *Essays in Persuasion*, Macmillan, 1931, pp. 358-73.

44 Ibid.

life, and once these are secured, the economic problem is solved once and for all, and there is no longer a need for anyone to economize. But in reality, the economic problem is a permanent part of the human condition, as we are constantly facing choices between scarce objects, because that scarcity comes from our scarce and extremely valuable time. So long as humans are alive and need to decide what to do with their time, the economic problem exists, and humans attempt to solve it by working. There can be no final solution to the economic problem, only the replacement of bad choices with better choices.

"I draw the conclusion that, assuming no important wars and no important increase in population, the economic problem may be solved, or be at least within sight of solution, within a hundred years... Thus for the first time since his creation man will be faced with his real, his permanent problem—how to use his freedom from pressing economic cares, how to occupy the leisure, which science and compound interest will have won for him, to live wisely and agreeably and well."[45] Keynes seems unaware that what he posits as a replacement to the economic problem is just the economic problem itself, but applied to choices slightly different from the ones he was used to seeing in the very few economic books he had read. Deciding how to occupy his time is man's eternal and universal economic problem because time is scarce, and Keynes' simplistic conception of economics prevents him from recognizing that use of time is an economic choice.

No matter how many material objects we have, we will always have a choice to make at the margin between immediate and future satisfaction. We can always forsake present satisfaction for more future satisfaction. There will never be complete satisfaction because human reason will always foresee a better possibility and work toward it. It would be very inexpensive for someone to live today by the living standards of Keynes' day. Yet, even the poorest people today can use and own many things Keynes was never able to own. And they continue to yearn for a better living, as do the richest people. As long as humans economize, they use reason to produce new goods, services, and objects that others desire.

---

45 Ibid.

Keynes bases his fantastic vision of the future on the completely unjustified assertion that there are two types of needs, absolute and relative needs. Absolute needs, Keynes asserted, are needs felt "whatever situation of our fellow human beings may be," while relative needs are felt "only if their satisfaction lifts us above, makes us feel superior to, our fellows."[46] Keynes posits that demand for the latter may be insatiable, but demand for the first class of needs could be completely satisfied. Keynes thought the economic problem has always been the primary and most pressing problem of the human race and the entire biological kingdom, and solving it would be a momentously important transformation of the nature of human life. He did not understand that the economic problem always exists for as long as human time is scarce and humans have choices to make. Even if humans were in an imaginary world where everything a person wishes for materializes in front of them immediately, the economic problem would not be solved, as humans' mortality still forces them to economize their scarce time. The economic problem is solved every instant in which a human reasons about their time and makes a choice, only for a new economic problem to emerge in the next instant and force the same human to make another choice. The only final solution to the economic problem is death, the point at which there are no further choices to be made regarding time allocation.

As such, it is nonsensical to imagine, as Keynes does, that work could ever end, or the need for work could ever go away, or that abundance will reach a point where labor will not be needed. We are always economizing, and we always have to make choices between alternatives. As our living standards improve, our choices improve, but the act of choosing must remain, at least for as long as humans are mortal.

Is Labor Exploitation?

Are laborers exploited by capitalism? Millions of pages have been written on the topic of worker exploitation, based largely on the incoherent ramblings of Karl Marx, a semiliterate German bum who never had a job that could support

46 Ibid.

him. Marx lived off the support of rich benefactors in England as he pontificated about reengineering the world into a dystopia run by people incapable of supporting themselves through their own labor.

Marxist economic analysis is based on the labor theory of value, discussed in Chapter 2. Since all economic goods require some labor input to transform them into economic goods that can serve our needs, the Marxist falsely concludes that labor is what gives economic goods value, and the quantity of labor that goes into the production of a good is what determines its value. This means the value of goods is based on the amount of labor that goes into producing them. Using the baseless assumption that economic value is imparted onto objects purely as a function of the amount of labor that goes into them, the Marxist automatically eliminates the value of the capitalist's contribution. Workers need to turn up and work, whereas capitalists, as socialists maintain, do nothing. According to this view, because the worker does not receive the entire profit from the process of production, the capitalist is exploiting the worker.

This is obviously nonsensical because workers willingly choose to work for capitalists. Marxists do not attach any significance to the fact that workers willingly choose to sign up for this supposedly evil exploitation. As long as capitalists do not use violence or the threat of violence to force workers to work for them, then workers are willingly choosing to work, which indicates the work opportunity is the best option for spending their time. An observer or economist might resent this reality, but they cannot blame capitalists for providing workers with the best option available in exchange for their time. It is telling that Marxists who complain about this arrangement cannot offer workers better jobs than the capitalist "exploiters" offer.

But the understanding of work as exploitation betrays a deep ignorance of what capital and its value to economic production are. Capitalists defer consumption to provide capital for workers, which increases the workers' productivity. At any point in time, the capitalist is choosing to forego consumption in order to provide workers with capital to increase their productivity. At any point in time, the capitalists can liquidate their capital goods and use the proceeds to finance consumption. By choosing to forego consumption and make the capital available to a worker, the capitalist is allowing the worker to have a higher productivity level. This higher productivity makes the worker happy to receive only part of the proceeds. The alternative to capitalist exploitation is not just that the worker receives all of the revenues from the sale of the goods they produce; it is that the revenue is much lower without capital. A Marxist might consider a cab driver as being exploited by the owner of the car he drives, but that is only because the Marxist cannot conceive of what would happen if the driver denied the capitalist compensation for allowing them the use of their car. Without earning a return, the capitalist would prefer to use the car as a consumer good or sell it and consume its proceeds. Without the car, the driver would have to carry people on his back, which would be a highly uneconomical and physically destructive job. Only by allowing a capitalist to "exploit" him by providing him with capital (the car) is the job of a driver productive and safe enough to provide the worker with a good life.

The production process requires the worker to dedicate his time, but it requires the capitalist to contribute capital, which can only be acquired through previous work and can only be retained through continuous deferral of consumption throughout the entire production process. Without compensating the capitalist for her decision to delay gratification and invest, there would be no capital, and the worker's productivity would decline significantly. The capitalist does not exploit the worker by taking part of his output forcibly; the worker willingly pays part of his output to the capitalist in exchange for securing a much higher productivity level.

The laborer-capitalist relationship is a feature of human relations that has existed in all human cultures, and it reflects a natural trade between an individual who has the ability to work but lacks the means to secure the necessary capital, and another individual who has more capital than she can, or wants to, utilize herself. The continued existence of this relationship is what incentivizes humans to accumulate capital, while pathologizing it and punishing it has led to societies experiencing calamitous economic destruction.

Chapter 5

Property

> [O]nly because scarcity exists is there even a problem of formulating moral laws; insofar as goods are superabundant ("free" goods), no conflict over the use of goods is possible and no action-coordination is needed. Hence, it follows that any ethic, correctly conceived, must be formulated as a theory of property, i.e., a theory of the assignment of rights of exclusive control over scarce means. Because only then does it become possible to avoid otherwise inescapable and unresolvable conflict.[47]
>
> —Hans-Hermann Hoppe

Scarcity and Property

Chapter 3 covered the process of economizing as a consequence of the scarcity of human time. Chapter 4 examined how humans economize their time by making a choice between leisure and labor and explained the basics of the process of production. Chapter 5 examines the process of economizing with goods and the economic rationale for the emergence of property. After explaining the economic meaning of property, this chapter will discuss different types of property, the application of property to self-ownership, and how property as an institution helps in the eternal quest to increase the value and quantity of human time.

---

47 Hoppe, Hans-Hermann. *A Theory of Socialism and Capitalism*. Ludwig von Mises Institute, 2010, p. 158.

Scarcity, as discussed in the first chapter of this book, is the starting point of economics and the origin of all economizing. It is the mismatch between the desired and available quantities of a good that forces humans to treat the good carefully, try to maintain it in an optimal condition to serve its functions, and protect it from being taken by others. Scarcity is what compels us to value objects, and in valuing them, we develop command over them over time. Scarcity, then, is also the origin of property. As Menger explains:

> Property, therefore, like human economy, is not an arbitrary invention but rather the only practically possible solution of the problem that is, in the nature of things, imposed upon us by the disparity between requirements for, and available quantities of, all economic goods.[48]

To take ownership of a good is to exercise full control of the services that can be derived from it. Menger defines property as "the entire sum of goods at an economizing individual's command for the satisfaction of his needs."[49] Legal scholar A. N. Yiannopolous writes:

> Property may be defined as an exclusive right to control an economic good... ; it is the name of a concept that refers to the rights and obligations, privileges and restrictions that govern the relations of man with respect to things of value. People everywhere and at all times desire the possession of things that are necessary for survival or valuable by cultural definition and which, as a result of the demand placed upon them, become scarce. Laws enforced by organized society control the competition for, and guarantee the enjoyment of, these desired things. What is guaranteed to be one's own is property... [Property rights] confer a direct and immediate authority over a thing.[50]

---

48 Menger, Carl. *Principles of Economics*. Reprint, Ludwig von Mises Institute, 2007, p. 97.

49 Ibid. 76.

50 Yiannopoulos, A. N. "Property." *Louisiana Civil Law Treatise*, 4th ed., vol. 2, 2001.

Property is distinct from wealth, which Menger defines as the "the entire sum of *economic* goods at an economizing individual's command."[51] One's property includes all non-economic goods, but wealth refers only to economic goods.

The economic rationale for owning property is obvious and straightforward. If the use of an economic good does not consume it and render it obsolete, it can be reused for the same purpose, and the user would naturally seek to maintain its ownership until she needs it again. The hunter who builds a spear to successfully hunt a rabbit will instinctively understand that the spear can be reused for hunting another rabbit and will choose to maintain possession of it. Very few animals have the instinct to take property of objects, and perhaps nonhuman species assume ownership only of their homes, nests, or dens. Humans' superior intellect allows us to develop ownership behavior in a much more sophisticated and complex manner, and we own things for years, decades, and even centuries through generations of the same family.

By taking property of valuable objects, humans can reduce the cost and time required to perform future tasks. The owner of durable property goods is capable of arriving at her desired end with a smaller exertion of effort and cost than someone who does not own the same property. Investing labor in the construction of a durable house for the long term is a more effective way of obtaining shelter than finding a new makeshift arrangement every day. Domesticating and husbanding animals can be a more reliable way of obtaining food than trying to hunt every day. Growing your own trees and crops can be more reliable and productive than needing to forage for plants every day. These are all methods by which humans economize to improve their chances of survival and to increase the value of their time, in other words, to increase the amount and value of time they have on Earth.

We can also think of property as a way to convert time spent in labor into future utility. By employing his labor to produce a durable good, man is forgoing present satisfaction in order to produce a good that provides continuous utility over a future period. Man's most basic needs can be met more effectively by investing in durable property. Expending labor to cultivate a piece of land

---

51 Menger, Carl. *Principles of Economics*. Reprint, Ludwig von Mises Institute, 2007, p. 109.

creates an incentive to stay on the piece of land and continue to benefit from it. Owning land allows for long-term investment and the improvement of its utility, more than if it had been left without owners, as a lack of ownership would discourage investment.

The importance of property within the social context is that it prevents conflict over scarce resources. As Stephan Kinsella puts it:

> There is always the possibility of conflict over contestable (scarce) resources. This is in the very nature of scarce, or rivalrous, resources. By assigning an owner to each resource, the legal or property rights system establishes objective, publicly visible or discernible boundaries or borders that nonowners can avoid.[52]

Types of Property

Property in physical goods can be classified into four types: consumer goods, durable goods, capital goods, and monetary goods. Consumption goods are the ultimate ends of economic action, the goods that humans acquire for their own sake. A particular kind of consumer good is durable consumption goods, which are distinct from consumption goods in that they are held for long periods because their consumption can span long durations. Examples of durable consumption goods are houses, cars, televisions, or washing machines. Capital goods are the goods acquired for their ability to produce other consumer goods, and monetary goods are goods that are not held to be consumed or produce consumer goods, but to be exchanged for other goods later on.

In a social system conducive to individuals economizing and seeking to eliminate conflict as much as possible, property claims can be established based on "the existence of an objective, intersubjectively ascertainable link between the owner and the resource claimed," as Hoppe puts it.[53] In a free

52 Kinsella, Stephan. "What Libertarianism Is." *Property, Freedom, and Society: Essays in Honor of Hans-Hermann Hoppe*, Ludwig von Mises Institute, 2009, p. 184-5.

53 Ibid. 12.

market, or in a social order free from coercion, there are three ways for individuals to obtain legitimate property, as explained by Rothbard:

1- Homestead objects that were previously unowned
2- Products derived from these objects
3- Objects obtained from rightful owners willingly, either as part of a trade or a gift.

Self-Ownership

Since humans are scarce, and so is their time, it is only natural that the same implications of scarcity for economic goods would also apply to humans, and that property is the "only practical solution," as Menger put it. While the idea of ownership of humans sounds jarring and morally wrong, in economic terms, it is inevitable. As humans and their time are scarce, the decisions about how a human behaves and what he does with his time must be made by someone, and that is the essence of property. The person who decides what to do with a person's body and time *de facto* owns them, in economic terms. The abhorrent nature of the question is only applicable and appropriate when the question of ownership is resolved in favor of anyone other than the person himself.

There are only three potential ways of organizing the ownership of human beings:

1- Self-ownership, wherein a person owns himself completely, and others have no ownership claims over his body and time.

2- Communal ownership, wherein all members of society jointly own all their bodies and decide jointly what each body does.

3- Slavery, wherein a person is owned by someone else, and his owners get to dictate what they can do with the body and time of the slave, from assigning his time to tasks to inflicting bodily harm. The rights of slave owners extend even to the right to murder the slave. In a social order of slavery, some people have ownership over both themselves and others, while others have no right to ownership over themselves or others.

The second option is not practically workable beyond the scope of a handful of people who know each other intimately, and even then, it would not be easy. Humans would find it very difficult to have all the knowledge to decide what others should do with their lives and time. The complexities of devising a mechanism for information communication, decision-making, and execution in such a system are practically insurmountable at any large social scale.

The third option fails on the grounds of consistency, ethics, and consequence. What ethical basis can there be to justify why some people should own themselves while others are owned by others? There can be no logically and ethically coherent way to justify this drastic difference in property rights assignment. Further, this difference is likely to be a recipe for conflict. The individual who does not have property rights over himself will seek to gain it and may feel justified in the use of violence against those who own him. Everywhere slavery has existed as a system, it has resulted in conflict.

Self-ownership is the only logically and ethically consistent solution to the problem of human ownership, and it is the only one likely to result in peaceful cooperation rather than violent conflict. Self-ownership means an individual has full claim over his own body and time. Once one accepts the premise of self-ownership, a coherent framework for understanding rights, justice, and non-aggression emerges. This principle extends to what a man may produce as a consequence of these choices, i.e., property. Aggression can be understood as the use or threat of violence to control another person's body or time, and any physical aggression against an individual would be a violation of his right to property of himself.

It is difficult to argue against self-ownership and the system of property rights if one understands property rights as the only workable solution to economic scarcity and subjectively values peace and civilization. Any such argument can be seen as transparently self-serving hypocrisy. Rather than an intelligent argument arising from human reason, this argument is nothing more than an appeal that we return to the mores of subhuman animals controlled entirely by their instincts, unable to employ reason. Arguing against self-ownership is effectively arguing against your own personhood, because it makes it clear you cannot respect property rights and cannot be part of a civilized social order. It is a plea to be considered an animal. Although economic theory does not dictate political ideology, understanding economic scarcity and subjectively valuing peace and civilization will incline a person to adopt a libertarian outlook. There are no alternatives to self-ownership that do not result in propagating conflict and engendering enmity and resentment between individuals and groups.

While most ideologies will not argue for slavery explicitly, only libertarians consistently apply this standard to its logical conclusion. All other ideologies believe in at least some form of slavery, in the form of a legitimate claim by others against a person's body or time. Supporters of taxation, conscription, drug prohibitions, or medical mandates may not like to think of themselves as supporters of slavery, but they are placing a partial ownership right over a person's body in the hands of the state because they support the state treating its citizens like property when it forcibly takes their income, locks them in jail for consuming drugs, or bans them from employment for not taking state-mandated pharmaceutical products.[54]

Importance of Property Rights

Understanding the concept of property makes an individual able to economize more effectively and increase the productivity and value of his time. By investing his labor in the production of durable goods, man is able to draw on their services for longer, lowering his time preference in the process and learning to prioritize the future more.

When the acceptance of property rights becomes the prevailing norm in a society, individuals are able to invest in capital goods to trade with others, their productivity increases further, and the market economic order emerges, as will be discussed in subsequent chapters. Property rights can be understood

54 Ibid. 179-96.

as the social scaling mechanism that allows people to hold property in close proximity to others who might want to hold it. As Mises put it, "Private ownership of the means of production is the fundamental institution of the market economy. It is the institution the presence of which characterizes the market economy as such. Where it is absent, there is no question of a market economy."[55]

The market economy, and civilization itself, are predicated on the respect of property rights, as it is only when property rights are secure that individuals can accumulate any amount of capital significantly larger than what they can keep on their person for basic primitive needs. A society in which property rights are not respected is one where conflict is rife, and one where individuals cannot afford to think of investing their precious labor in the future, as all the property that can store this value is risky to own. Civilized society is only possible when the right to property in self and objects is widely respected, and individuals can expect to maintain their property into the future.

In the context of a market economy, Mises beautifully explains how the institution of private property ensures the responsible stewardship of resources:

> The meaning of private property in the market society is radically different from what it is under a system of each household's autarky. Where each household is economically self-sufficient, the privately owned means of production exclusively serve the proprietor. He alone reaps all the benefits derived from their employment. In the market society the proprietors of capital and land can enjoy their property only by employing it for the satisfaction of other people's wants. They must serve the consumers in order to have any advantage from what is their own. The very fact that they own means of production forces them to submit to the wishes of the public. Ownership is an asset only for those who know how to employ it in the best possible way for the benefit of the consumers. It is a social function.[56]

---

55 Mises, Ludwig von. *Human Action: The Scholar's Edition*. Ludwig von Mises Institute, 1998, p. 678.

56 Ibid. 680.

The absence of private property rights results in conflict between people, as well as the degradation of economic goods and natural resources. When economic goods do not have clear ownership rights, the individuals who happen to use and command them will do so without the expectation of utilizing them in the future, which will naturally lead to them deprioritizing the future state of these resources. This heavy discounting of the future is the inherent characteristic of utilizing resources without a clear owner. Private property incentivizes owners to care about the long-term state of their property, and thus to preserve it for the long term. As Mises explains:

> If land is not owned by anybody, although legal formalism may call it public property, it is utilized without any regard to the disadvantages resulting. Those who are in a position to appropriate to themselves the returns—lumber and game of the forests, fish of the water areas, and mineral deposits of the subsoil—do not bother about the later effects of their mode of exploitation. For them the erosion of the soil, the depletion of the exhaustible resources and other impairments of the future utilization are external costs not entering into their calculation of input and output. They cut down the trees without any regard for fresh shoots or reforestation. In hunting and fishing, they do not shrink from methods preventing the repopulation of the hunting and fishing grounds. In the early days of human civilization, when soil of a quality not inferior to that of the utilized pieces was still abundant, people did not find any fault with such predatory methods. When their effects appeared in a decrease in the net returns, the ploughman abandoned his farm and moved to another place. It was only when a country was more densely settled and unoccupied first-class land was no longer available for appropriation, that people began to consider such predatory methods wasteful. At that time they consolidated the institution of private property in land. They started with arable land and then, step by step, included pastures, forests, and fisheries.[57]

---

57 Ibid. 652.

Chapter 6

Capital

> Wherever we turn among civilized peoples we find a system of large-scale advance provision for the satisfaction of human needs. When we are still wearing our heavy clothes for protection against the cold of winter, not only are ready-made spring clothes already on the way to retail stores, but in factories light cloths are being woven which we will wear next summer, while yarns are being spun for the heavy clothing we will use the following winter. When we fall ill we need the services of a physician. In legal disputes we require the advice of a lawyer. But it would be much too late, for a person in either contingency to meet his need, if he should only then attempt to acquire the medical or legal knowledge and skills himself, or attempt to arrange the special training of other persons for his service, even though he might possess the necessary means. In civilized countries, the needs of society for these and similar services are provided for in good time, since experienced and proven men, having prepared themselves for their professions many years ago, and having since collected rich experiences from their practices, place their services at the disposal of society. And while we enjoy the fruits of the foresight of past times in this way, many men are being trained in our universities to meet the needs of society for similar services in the future.[58]
>
> —Carl Menger

58 Menger, Carl. *Principles of Economics*. Ludwig von Mises Institute, 2007, p. 79.

The previous chapter presented the concept of property in economic terms and discussed the development of this human tool over time. Of the forms of property humans can own, economics makes a distinction between consumption goods, which are owned for the utility they offer their owners, and capital goods, owned not for their utility but because they can be used to produce consumption goods that offer utility. Capital goods, or higher-order goods, are any goods that are not consumed but used for the production of consumption goods or lower-order goods. What makes a good a consumption good or capital good is not inherent to the good itself but is a function of how the good is utilized by the person who owns it. The same good can be used as a capital or consumption good, depending on the context. A computer used for watching movies and browsing the web is a consumption good, but the same computer used to write a book is a capital good. A car can be a capital good if operated as a taxi, but a consumption good if used purely for recreational travel. Grains of corn can be a consumption good if eaten but a capital good if planted to grow more corn.

This chapter discusses capital conceptually in an abstract sense. After introducing money and the extended market order in the forthcoming chapters, Chapter 12 will discuss capital in the context of a modern monetary economic order, and Part IV of the book will discuss the problems of central planning in capital markets.

Lengthening Structure of Production

The introduction of capital into economic production necessitates the lengthening of the period of production. Without capital goods, man engages in the production of the final consumption good directly, but when a capital good is involved, man needs to first produce the capital good and then use it to produce the consumer good. By adding an intermediate stage of capital production, the process of production from start to finish becomes longer.

This might initially sound counterintuitive. Why would humans engage in longer processes of production? Time preference is positive, as discussed in Chapter 3; humans prefer the same good sooner rather than later. Why spend hours building a fishing rod to catch a fish when you can just catch fish directly with your hands in less time? The answer lies in the productivity of the fishing rod. While producing the fishing rod takes time, once it is completed, its use should hopefully allow the fisherman to catch a larger amount of fish per unit of effort. Even though the immediate investment in manufacturing a fishing rod delays the arrival of the fish, the increase in productivity makes its long-term output more valuable than the smaller output from fishing with your hands, which arrives sooner. The success of this investment is not guaranteed, but the potential extra reward is the only motivation for engaging in capital accumulation, lengthening the process of production, and forgoing closer need satisfaction.[59]

Should a man choose to catch fish with his hands, the period of production would last from the moment he began heading to the sea to catch the fish until the moment he caught it. Assume this process takes two hours. There is no faster and more direct way of catching fish, but there are more productive ways, albeit ones with longer production processes. Should the man engage in producing a fishing spear, the time required to find a suitable branch, sharpen it, and learn to use it would now lengthen the entire production process. We can reasonably assume that the time from initiating the search for the stick until the fish was caught would now be 4 hours instead of 2. However, once the fish was caught, the fisherman's spear would still function, and catching the next fish would take much less time than the 2 hours, on average, that it used to take the man without the spear. The entire production process would become longer, but once the capital was produced, the marginal time needed to produce an extra unit would become shorter. As the process of capital accumulation intensifies in fishing, the production process just becomes longer: The fisherman builds a small boat, which requires an entire week of production before he can use it to catch a single fish, but once he can start catching fish with it, it appreciably increases the fisherman's marginal productivity. As capital accumulation continues to proceed, the fisherman could build a large boat that requires an entire year of production before it yields a single fish.

---

59 Böhm-Bawerk, Eugen von et al. *Capital and Interest.* Libertarian Press 1959. • Böhm-Bawerk, Eugen von. *The Positive Theory of Capital.* Bubok Publishing, 2018.

Saving

> The sine qua non of any lengthening of the process of production adopted is saving, i.e., an excess of current production over current consumption. Saving is the first step on the way toward improvement of material well-being and toward every further progress on this way.[60]
>
> —Ludwig von Mises

Lengthening the period of production cannot take place without initially providing the consumer goods needed to sustain the producers during the production process. Providing for the future makes it possible to engage in production processes that are longer and more productive. But man can save resources to provide for the future only if he is able to meet his current needs. The farmer must produce enough grain to feed himself before he can plant any grain, and every grain he plants is a grain he cannot consume this year. If the fisherman is going to spend a day building a fishing rod, he must already have provided for this day from his previous day's production by delaying consumption that was possible the previous day. It is impossible to engage in building a fishing rod without forsaking time away from leisure, which has positive utility, or from labor, which produces consumer goods with positive utility. Saving is the mother of capital; only by deferring consumption can capital goods exist.

The same is true even in the longest and most sophisticated production processes, such as that of creating an airplane. Today there are engineers designing the next line of airplanes for Boeing that will likely need more than a decade of design, production, and testing before they can be sold to generate revenue for the company. The airplane maker requires capital investment to provide these workers with the resources necessary to sustain them before the production process can be completed and the company can generate revenue from the sale of the planes, in addition to compensating the owners of the capital stock that will be used in the production process. Time preference is

60 Mises, Ludwig von. *Human Action: The Scholar's Edition*. Ludwig von Mises Institute, 1998, p. 487.

positive, and capital owners and laborers need to consume during the production process to survive and part with their capital or labor. Even if Boeing were somehow able to procure all the capital equipment and labor it needed by promising to pay the workers and equipment sellers when the airplanes were completed, the production would have been financed by the workers and equipment sellers, who would have had to delay gratification to produce.

To lengthen the production process, someone somewhere must forego the consumption of resources in order to provide them to the producers. In the simple fisherman's economy, that sacrifice was made by the fisherman himself when he saved some of the previous day's food for the subsequent day, so he could spend time building a fishing rod. In a modern capitalist economy, the sacrifice is made by investors who forego consumption to provide financing to entrepreneurs. The entrepreneurs compensate the workers and the owners of capital, in the present, for providing their labor and capital for his production process, whose output will materialize in the future. Not only does a longer production process require more delayed gratification, but it also requires more cognitive skills and can incur more risks. Without an entrepreneur imagining a longer structure and an investor sacrificing present satisfaction for the chance of a larger future return, the capital and labor resources needed for the production process cannot be procured. Every process that lengthens production is only possible because of the sacrifice and delayed gratification made by capitalists. This seemingly obvious point is worth reemphasizing because a sizable portion of the world's economic problems have come from cranks laboring under the delusion that they have found an exception to this necessity.

Higher Productivity

Ludwig von Mises described capital goods as "labor, nature, and time stored up.[61]" He made a distinction between capital and independent factors of production, nature-given material resources, and labor. This mental framework is very useful for understanding the economic function and significance of capital.

61 Ibid. 490.

Humans are able to take nature's given resources, combine them with their labor, and over time produce capital goods as an output. The time, labor, and resources that went into making the capital good will then result in higher productivity.

Producing using capital goods can be thought of as producing with the aid of the labor, nature, and time that went into making the capital good. This results in an increase in productivity, allowing the production of one unit of the final output to take less time than it would have taken without capital. Time is spent on longer processes of production to achieve higher outputs per unit of time, which is why capital is another way of economizing on human time, as Mises explains: "The difference between production without the aid of capital goods and that assisted by the employment of capital goods consists in time... He who produces with the aid of capital goods enjoys one great advantage over the man who starts without capital goods; he is nearer in time to the ultimate goal of his endeavors."[62]

It is important not to confuse the longer period of the entire production process with the shorter production time of the final good. Accumulating capital leads to an increase in the total time taken to produce goods when including the higher-order goods that go into the process. However, it also results in a decrease in the production time of each marginal unit. Beyond just increasing productivity, capital goods allow for the production of goods that were entirely impossible without capital. As the fisherman goes from catching fish with his hand to using a fishing rod or fishing boat, not only will he have a higher output, but he will also be able to catch species of fish that were not within his reach before he had the capital. Without capital accumulation, most of the products we take for granted in the modern world would not be possible, as there is no way to produce them with our bare hands.

Capital goods are built and acquired to increase the productivity of labor, and in the process, they inevitably make the entire production process longer. Capital is the difference between fishing with your bare hands and fishing with a fishing rod, a small fishing boat, or the *Annelies Ilena*, the world's largest open-sea trawler. A day spent fishing with your hands will produce a few fish, if you are lucky. With a fishing rod, you could catch around a dozen fish a day;

62 Ibid.

and with a fishing boat and net, a few hundred. On the other hand, if you were one of the approximately 70 crew members of the *Annelies Ilena*, you would collectively produce approximately 350 tons of fish every day, or around 5 tons of fish per worker per day. The same human being, spending the same number of hours during the same day, could catch one fish or 5 tons of fish, depending entirely on the capital he is able to deploy to the task.

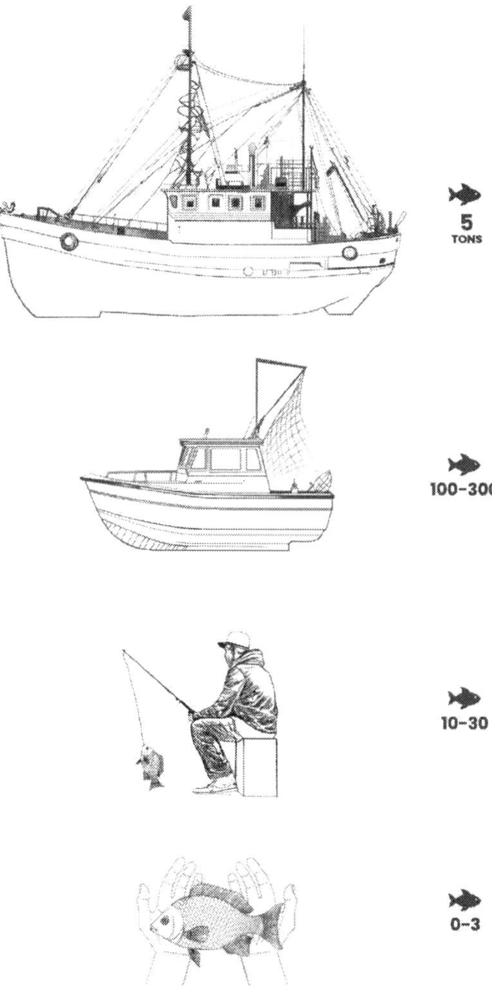

Figure 8. Productivity and capital

This increase in productivity is what ultimately drives the disparity in living standards between people who can work with large amounts of capital and people who cannot, between people who fish with their bare hands and those who fish with the *Annelies Ilena*, between countries with a large amount of industrial capital and those without.

This increased productivity is what makes our modern life possible. As a thought exercise, try to imagine securing your survival without using any capital goods. If all production processes were to be carried out with your bare hands, survival would be a very difficult ordeal. It would be uncertain whether you could secure enough food for your daily survival from foraging or hunting. A shelter built only by hand would be flimsy and vulnerable to destruction by nature. Under such conditions, survival would be uncertain. However, were you to survive, it is almost inconceivable that you would not recognize the enormous value of investing in the production of goods that increase the output of your time spent in production processes. The inevitable need to resort to using rocks and tree branches to fight off animals, or trying to hunt them, is itself a form of capital use. Individuals and ideologies that decry the evils of capital are impotently and ignorantly railing against the inevitability of the human mind resorting to using tools to achieve its ends.

Should these investments succeed in raising your productivity, securing a day's food becomes less demanding and uncertain. Less time needs to be dedicated to securing basic survival, and more time can be directed toward investing in more capital production to increase productivity further.

The surest and most important way of increasing human quality of life is through the accumulation of capital goods, because they serve to increase work productivity. There is no guarantee that investing in capital will result in increased productivity, and that is the risk inherent in the process of capital accumulation. But if investment yields capital that does not result in increased productivity, then the investment fails and its outcome will not be deployed as capital. It will be consumed if it can be, or otherwise discarded. There have, undoubtedly, been many attempts at producing capital goods that increase the productivity of fishing, but only the ones that succeeded remained. All the others have long been forgotten, and the investment that went into them wasted. Capital is not just the product of any investment in lengthening the production process; capital consists of only the investments in the lengthening of the production process that yield higher productivity. The risk of waste is but one facet of the high cost of capital.

The longer the production process, the more capital is deployed successfully, the higher the productivity of labor, the less of a day's labor needs to be dedicated to securing basic survival, and the larger the margin of safety separating man from starvation. It is primarily thanks to capital accumulation and longer production processes that most of the world's population can buy nutritious food for a fraction of a day's wages. Without modern capital, the output of a day's work would be in the rough range of what an individual needs to survive for a day, making existence precarious and uncertain. Extreme poverty today exists only where capital is scarce, and people need to work daily to survive. With modern capital, on the other hand, most workers can produce several multiples of their food needs every day, providing them a considerable margin of safety to protect them from destitution and starvation and allowing them to consume many other goods.

To understand the importance of capital, try to perform your job without any capital, and measure the change in your productivity. If you are a farmer, try farming with only your bare hands and no tractor or shovel to help. Try hunting without a rifle, spear, or bow and arrow. Try to be a taxi driver without a car. Try to survive a winter without the capital equipment we use to build our modern homes, warm them, and protect them from storms. It is accurate to think of poverty as the lack of capital.

A good literary illustration of the value of capital comes from George Orwell's *Down and Out in Paris and London*.[63] Orwell spent a lot of time with low-income workers in both major European cities in the 1920s and '30s. One of his most astute and profound observations about the state of poverty in which he lived was how expensive everything was for poor people. A rich man who has a home with all the essentials of survival can take survival for granted on any given day, at least when compared to what a poor tramp has to persevere in order

63 Orwell, George. *Down and Out in Paris and London*. Victor Gollancz, 1933.

to secure his basic needs. Without a kitchen, every meal is expensive. Without a car, walking is very time consuming. Without a wardrobe, it is expensive to find decent clothes to look good for a decent job. Many things are made cheap by owning the capital, and capitallessness is a prime reason why poverty can appear insurmountable. Low stocks of capital induce low productivity, and that, in turn, leaves very little income for saving and investing in capital to raise productivity. Breaking out of this cycle requires the deferral of consumption when consumption is already very small, and survival is precarious. Many of the world's poor have struggled to break out of this poverty trap.

The High Cost of Capital

It is common to hear capital and its owners mentioned disparagingly in mainstream media, academia, and other fountains of economic illiteracy. Capital is presented as if it is a means of exploiting labor, and its owners the beneficiaries of an unfair advantage over the rest of society. Rarely does one hear the true costs required for capital ownership and the responsibility it implies. To be a capital owner, you first have to earn it. Then you have to abstain from consuming it by saving it. Then you have to deploy it in the market well enough to earn a return sufficient to maintain it. The economic cost of capital manifests in several ways:

Delayed gratification

The drawback of capital accumulation is that it is expensive and uncertain. It requires sacrificing present consumption in order to invest resources that will only bear fruit in the future and may not bear fruit at all. Capital requires the constant delay of gratification and deferral of consumption. The opportunity cost of capital is always forgone consumption. Any person who owns any capital is at any point in time capable of selling the capital in exchange for present consumption goods. The moment his fishing rod is completed, the fisherman could find someone to pay him a significant sum of fish in exchange for the rod. In order to continue to produce at the more productive level allowed by the fishing rod, its owner must every day reject the chance to accept a sum of fish in exchange for it. Every productive machine on the planet could be sold by its owner in exchange for consumer goods that give him more immediate pleasure. The owners of the *Annelies Ilena* could live outrageously well over the next year if they sell it and spend the proceeds, but they continue to sacrifice that splendid year in favor of maintaining capital that will produce a stream of income for decades into the future.

For any capital accumulation to occur, individuals must lower their time preference; they must reduce their discounting of the future enough to provide for it at the expense of the present. This point is worth bearing in mind when economic illiterates rail against capital owners for being parasites on the workers. The sacrifice of present consumption by capital owners in exchange for future reward is economically no different from the sacrifice of leisure by workers in exchange for future reward. Had capital owners actually contributed nothing to the production process, then their consumption of the capital good instead of offering it to the workers would make no difference to the workers' productivity. But ask any worker what would happen to their productivity without capital, and the absurdity of hating capital becomes apparent.

It is worth noting that neither the Marxist nor Keynesian economic schools of ill-thought have ever developed the intellectual capacity to deal with a concept like time preference, and what it implies for capital accumulation. Nor have they ever demonstrated a grasp of the concept of opportunity cost, as is apparent from their policy proposals, which are made for a Garden of Eden that has no scarcity, and forces no choices on governments or individuals. No appreciation of the difficulty and importance of capital accumulation can be obtained without understanding scarcity and opportunity cost, and that helps explain why socialist governments culminate in the wholesale destruction of society's capital.

Destruction

Producing capital is expensive and uncertain, and destroying capital is very easy. Capital is similar to a living organism that needs to be continuously receiving inputs from, and producing outputs into its environment to survive. It needs to operate in a market where prices dictate its most productive uses and modes of production. Prices inform capitalists as to where to allocate their capital, and they inform entrepreneurs as to how to manage production processes. Without free markets, prices give no signals to capitalists or entrepreneurs on where and how to allocate their resources, leading to misallocation, waste, and a decline in capital stocks. Without being employed and properly maintained, machines malfunction and deteriorate. Disruptions to production processes can cause very expensive, and often irreparable damage, to capital goods. It takes a lot of time for our fisherman to build his fishing boat, but it only takes a few seconds of losing control of the boat for it to crash onto a rocky shore and disintegrate into irreparable pieces. This is equally true for the small fishing boat and the giant open-sea trawlers.

Depreciation

It is also the nature of capital to depreciate over time as it gets used. Capital is not eternal, and its employment and daily wear and tear will take their toll on it. Producers who invest in capital cannot expect it to keep producing consumer goods indefinitely at the same level of productivity. The productivity of capital constantly declines with use, and more capital expenditure is needed to maintain capital and its productivity. The fishing spear going into the sea's salty water degrades and becomes less effective with time. The small fishing boat deteriorates with use and over time, and it requires the investment of more time in repairing it. The most advanced modern trawler requires constant maintenance to remain operational, and it will have a large team of engineers and workers specialized in maintaining its operation, constantly inspecting critical parts, replacing worn ones, oiling the gears, and refilling it with the fuel it needs.

Risk

Capital accumulation is also inherently risky and uncertain. On top of the risk of destruction discussed above, there are countless reasons why capital could fail to produce the desired quality and quantity of final goods. Capital is at risk of being rendered obsolete by the invention of newer products and newer methods of production. Through no fault of her own, an entrepreneur may find her entire investment rendered obsolete when a competitor develops a superior product to hers, or a much cheaper way of making a product. **Capital accumulation not only requires the sacrifice of the present for the future, but it also requires the sacrifice of the certain for the uncertain.** The capitalist is constantly speculating that her investment will yield a positive return in the future, but she could always be wrong.

In order to become a capitalist, one needs to first produce something of value for which others can pay him. He then needs to abstain from using that payment to satisfy his own needs, and instead deploy it into a business whose goal is to serve others, by producing outputs, which they subjectively value higher than the market price of the inputs into the production process. At any point in time, failure to provide customers with this value will result in a collapse in revenue and profitability, inevitably leading to bankruptcy and the loss of capital. The causes of such failure are endless: laziness, disinterest, bad luck, better competitors, but the outcome is always the same: the loss of capital.

These are the reasons why capital ownership is so valuable and productive and why workers continue to choose to work for capital owners. As Murray Rothbard put it:

> [I]f they wanted to, all workers could refuse to work for wages and instead form their own producers' cooperatives and wait for years for their pay until the products are sold to the consumers; the fact that they do not do so, shows the enormous advantage of the capital investment, wage-paying system as a means of allowing workers to earn money far in advance of the sale of their products. Far from being exploitation of the workers, capital investment and the interest-profit system is an enormous boon to them and to all of society.[64]

The extent that an individual owns capital in a free-market economic system is the extent to which he is able to serve people enough to maintain his capital. No privilege or inheritance is above this, and no wealth too large.

---

64 Rothbard, Murray. *Egalitarianism As a Revolt against Nature and Other Essays*. 2nd ed. Ludwig von Mises Institute, 2000.

Fail to serve customers, and your capital will depreciate until it becomes dysfunctional junk requiring disposal. Owning capital, as Mises explained, is a responsibility, and a liability, not a privilege:

> Capitalists and landowners are compelled to employ their property for the best possible satisfaction of the consumers. If they are slow and inept in the performance of their duties, they are penalized by losses. If they do not learn the lesson and do not reform their conduct of affairs, they lose their wealth. No investment is safe forever.[65]

Modern schools of economics do not teach the reality of economics as the study of human action, which results in their adherents being incapable of understanding the hard work, sacrifice, and risk needed for anyone to become a capital owner. This inability to understand cause and effect leads to imagining capital as some sort of heavenly privilege bestowed upon a particular race of people. You either belong to that race or you do not. There is little appreciation or understanding of the actions necessary to accumulate capital and hold on to it successfully, and as a result, many people waste their time, and the fruit of their labor, complaining bitterly about capital, rather than working to acquire it and raise their productivity and living standards. This economic ignorance is the wind in the sails of demagogue politicians who exploit it to achieve power and use it to expropriate capital owners.

The denigration and vilification of capital ownership by Keynesians and Marxists and their inability to understand the costs needed for capital accumulation has meant that governments under the influence of these ideologies have too often attempted to finance investment without preexisting savings. Whether it is through printing physical money or credit expansion, the underlying delusion is the same: Creating claims on capital can replace the need for saving to produce capital. This dynamic, and its disastrous consequences, will be studied more closely in Part IV of this book.

---

65 Mises, Ludwig von. *Human Action: The Scholar's Edition*. Ludwig von Mises Institute, 1998, p. 308.

Capital and Time Preference

> Once it is low enough to allow for any savings and capital or durable consumer-goods formation at all, a tendency toward a fall in the rate of time preference is set in motion, accompanied by a "process of civilization."[66]
>
> —Hans-Hermann Hoppe

The cost of capital accumulation lies in the sacrifices of present goods that must be undertaken in order to invest resources in the production of future goods. The more that people value the present compared to the future, i.e., the higher their time preference, the less they will be inclined to defer consumption and invest in future production. As their time preference declines and their valuation of the future increases, they become more likely to forego present consumption in search of future returns. As far as anyone knows, capital goods cannot be conjured out of thin air by visualizing or wishful thinking. The only way of making capital goods lies in the deferral of the consumption of present goods. Like all economic phenomena, capital can only be understood in terms of human action, and the action needed to make it happen. The constraint on capital accumulation is not natural or physical; it is human and lies precisely in how much of their output humans want to invest in future production versus present consumption; in other words, **the constraint on capital production is time preference**. As Hoppe explained, "the lower the time-preference rate, the earlier the onset of the process of capital formation, and the faster the roundabout structure of production will be lengthened."[67]

Seeing as time preference is the limit on the production of capital, it, therefore, follows that the price of capital is a reflection of time preference. The lower a person's time preference, the less they discount the future compared to the present, and therefore the cheaper it is for them to sacrifice the present consumption for future reward. When a person's time preference is high, on

---

66 Hoppe, Hans-Hermann. *Democracy: The God That Failed.* Transaction Publishers, 2001, p. 6.

67 Ibid. 3.

the other hand, the sacrifice of present consumption is going to appear very costly compared to future reward. The price of capital is thus a negative function of time preference. This is the intuitive basis for the pure time preference theory of interest rates, which will be discussed in detail in the last section of this book, after introducing money, entrepreneurship, and the monetary market economic order in the forthcoming chapters.

Since time preference is positive, only the expectation of a positive real return encourages saving. The value of capital goods is derived entirely from the goods they produce; capital has no value independent of its product because it offers no direct utility to humans as a consumer good; it has utility only to the extent that it can produce goods with utility. Only investment in activities which offer a positive return in terms of utility and final goods is undertaken. As Rothbard put it:

> We may explain the entire act of deciding whether or not to perform an act of capital formation as the balancing of relative utilities, "discounted" by the actor's rate of time preference and also by the uncertainty factor.[68]

When a man values the future output of the production process, discounted for their time preference and uncertainty, at a higher value than the initial investment required, he is likely to invest and build or acquire capital goods. Should the investment succeed, he can use more of the resources to acquire more capital goods, increasing his profits and productivity further. In turn, as the stock of capital and productivity increase over time, he becomes less uncertain about his financial future, and that lowers his time preference further, encouraging more capital accumulation. As more capital is accumulated across society and time preference declines, the price of capital (determined by interest rates) also declines. This process of lowering time preference and increasing investment can be understood as the process of civilization.

---

68 Rothbard, Murray. *Man, Economy, and State, with Power and Market*. Ludwig von Mises Institute, 1962, p. 61.

Saving Fallacies

Any modern economics textbook will have little focus on the process of capital accumulation. When people think of a capitalist system, they are more likely to think of free trade as its hallmark, rather than capital accumulation. International development organizations promoting economic growth in developing countries also emphasize the role of trade and countless trade policy reforms, but place little value on capital accumulation. To the extent that capital accumulation is mentioned, it is used as a pretext for justifying public and private borrowing, as though that would be the equivalent of accumulating capital, when it is, in fact, the exact opposite. International financial institutions have a vested interest in generating more loans for developing countries, but not much of an interest in watching domestic savings grow.[69]

There is very little discussion of savings in modern economic textbooks, particularly with regard to the essential role of savings in generating economic production. Saving financial instruments, instead of spending them, is no different from saving economic resources from present consumption in order to deploy them in economic production, or from delaying the enjoyment of leisure and engaging in labor. There is also no discussion of the inescapable need for saving to precede investment. Rather than emphasize the commonality of delaying gratification in all of these acts, and their indispensable role in economic growth and progress, the typical Keynesian textbook portrays savings as an antisocial and borderline sociopathic personality trait.

The starting point of Keynesian analysis is to assume that society's income will be divided into spending and saving according to a predetermined mathematical formulation. There is little discussion of the factors that determine the level of saving in a society. There is no recognition of the importance of human agency in making this choice, and no discussion of its consequences. The Keynesian model uses a highly contrived definition of savings, whose explication and debunking are not worth including in this book in more than a

69 See Chapter 12 of *The Fiat Standard.*

footnote.[70] Suffice it to say that after extensive definitional and mathematical shenanigans, the Keynesian analysis concludes that equilibrium is reached only when the quantity of savings equals the quantity of investment, even though these are two completely distinct concepts and accounting entries, and there is no reason for them to be equal, other than by coincidence. But, according to this model, when aggregate savings exceed aggregate investment, that must mean society is not consuming enough, or, in other words, is saving too much. Under the Keynesian model, when people decide to stop spending a lot and instead save and hold on to cash, the economy slows, causing widespread unemployment and bankruptcies.

The Keynesian textbook implicates savings for damaging the economic order and causing unemployment. It does so based on a deference to Keynes' authority and through the application of more recent completely invalid mathematical equations and models. It also concludes savings would prevent the market from recovering as the economy falls into a deflationary spiral, with

---

70 This is how Mankiw's *Principles of Economics* explains savings and investments. Identifying the many category errors necessary to make the Keynesian system of equations workable in this excerpt is left as an exercise for the reader:

"The terms saving and investment can sometimes be confusing. Most people use these terms casually and sometimes interchangeably. By contrast, the macroeconomists who put together the national income accounts use these terms carefully and distinctly.

"Consider an example. Suppose that Larry earns more than he spends and deposits his unspent income in a bank or uses it to buy some stock or a bond from a corporation. Because Larry's income exceeds his consumption, he adds to the nation's saving. Larry might think of himself as "investing" his money, but a macroeconomist would call Larry's act saving rather than investment. In the language of macroeconomics, investment refers to the purchase of new capital, such as equipment or buildings. When Moe borrows from the bank to build himself a new house, he adds to the nation's investment. (Remember, the purchase of a new house is the one form of household spending that is investment rather than consumption.) Similarly, when the Curly Corporation sells some stock and uses the proceeds to build a new factory, it also adds to the nation's investment.

"Although the accounting identity S = I shows that saving and investment are equal for the economy as a whole, this does not have to be true for every individual household or firm. Larry's saving can be greater than his investment, and he can deposit the excess in a bank. Moe's saving can be less than his investment, and he can borrow the shortfall from a bank. Banks and other financial institutions make these individual differences between saving and investment possible by allowing one person's saving to finance another person's investment."

less spending causing less employment, which in turn causes less spending in a never-ending downward spiral. Such an absurd scenario is understandable since Keynes had no comprehension of how prices function and adjust in a market economy, where final products are discounted and sold off, and unprofitable factors of production are deployed in new, more productive lines of production. But according to Keynes, markets would fail to adjust if people continued to selfishly look out for their own self-interests by saving, rather than doing the responsible thing and spending.

According to Keynesians, only the omnipotent and omniscient hand of coercive government intervention could rescue the market from the catastrophe that low-time-preference savers had inflicted upon it by providing for their future at the expense of the present. By devaluing the misers' savings to finance credit expansion and fiscal spending, the government would, at once, be able to increase the aggregate level of spending in society, increase the amount of investment, reduce the level of savings, and, for good measure, teach savers a lesson and set a precedent that discourages them from saving in the future. The assumption is that, through central planning, all things are possible. This was, after all, the doctrine of a man whose time preference was so high, who cared so little for the future that he made his motto "In the long run, we are all dead." Given that saving is a means of providing for the future, Keynes never failed to denigrate it, discourage it, and seek to undermine it, and in this, his economics conformed with his personal morality, as discussed in Chapter 18.

The triumph of Keynesian economics in modern universities is reflected in the destruction of savings and the culture around it. The western societies that experienced the Industrial Revolution and the benefits of modern capitalism, thanks to many decades of saving and capital accumulation, currently have savings rates in the low single digits, and they have been at these levels for decades. The inflationary monetary policy, which Keynesians tout as the driver of economic growth discourages people from saving, and when this inflation results in the inevitable crises discussed in the latter chapters of the book, the Keynesians blame the crises on saving, and suggest more inflation to remedy the effects of inflation.

Limits to Capital

As quantities of capital are accumulated beyond a certain point while other factors remain constant, capital marginal productivity diminishes. A textile factory that gets machines for its workers will witness very fast productivity growth with the first machine it procures. Productivity increases with each worker that moves from using his hands to using a sewing machine. However, each additional machine will have a smaller marginal benefit than the previous machines. The extra machine will be used as a backup in case any of the others break down, so its marginal contribution will be lower than the previous machine that was employed full-time. As more machines are accumulated without corresponding increases in workers and other factors of production, and without technological improvement, the marginal productivity of each unit decreases. Going from fishing by hand to using a fishing rod increases the productivity of the fisherman by more than going from one fishing rod to two.

This relationship has driven some economists to hypothesize that there are limits to capital accumulation, or that capital accumulation cannot drive economic growth in the long run. While strictly true in a world in which capital grows while other factors of production remain stationary, a cursory look at the real world around us illustrates how far this is from reality. In the real world, the accumulation of capital does not run into diminishing returns because technological knowledge is constantly advancing, thus allowing us to accumulate better capital, not just more capital. The technological advance is itself a function of increasing capital accumulation. In other words, the more capital available, the more technologies can be attempted, and the more technologies will be found. The availability of capital is the prerequisite for elongating the structure of production and introducing new technologies. Ideas for technologies are quite cheap to come by, but execution is expensive because it requires capital, which is expensive.

In the real world, a fisherman does not continue to invest in accumulating an ever-growing number of fishing rods with declining marginal productivity. Instead, he will invest in other, more productive technologies, such as a fishing net, a fishing boat, and eventually, the *Annelies Ilena*. While it may seem like we can have too much capital, in practice, as long as any fisherman is less productive than the *Annelies Ilena*, there is still a lot of room for capital to be accumulated in the fishing industry without even any innovation taking place. Even the *Annelies Ilena* itself cannot be viewed as the pinnacle of capital productivity in the fishing industry. There is nothing about this boat that makes it the highest level of productivity possible for fishing. A capitalist with more resources could commission the building of an even more productive boat, with an even longer production process for designing, building, and operating it. More engines could increase its speed, larger freezers could increase its holding capacity, more nets could increase its catching capacity. Should the capital and time be made available to the world's best and most experienced boat engineers, it is extremely doubtful they would not be able to come up with a more productive boat than the *Annelies Ilena*. The reason we have no boat more productive than the *Annelies Ilena* is simply that we have not deployed more capital into the construction of fishing boats, the accumulation of which is limited by our ability to save and our time preference. It is not that we have reached the end of capital accumulation, nor that we have run out of ideas to improve the fishing boats we currently have.

The limit on capital investment is the present opportunity cost in terms of present goods. We can never run out of the high opportunity cost of capital for us to have too much capital. The reason a more productive boat than the *Annelies Ilena* has not been built is that potential investors value other investment opportunities or consumption more than they value taking a risk on producing these larger boats. The more capital we accumulate, the higher the productivity of our time, the more we value our time, the higher the value of leisure, and thus, the more expensive it is to sacrifice leisure for labor and capital. With time and capital accumulation, newer and better boats will be made. More advanced trawlers do not simply take away from the fish that would be caught by the fishermen with less advanced machinery. Instead, they allow fishermen to reach deeper into the sea, find the fish that would not have been caught by the other fishermen at all, bringing more fish to market, satisfying the needs of more customers.

Chapter 7

Technology

> What is wrong with our age is precisely the widespread ignorance of the role which these policies of economic freedom played in the technological evolution of the last two hundred years. People fell prey to the fallacy that the improvement of the methods of production was contemporaneous with the policy of laissez faire only by accident.[71]
>
> —Ludwig von Mises

Before the process of economic production takes place in the real world, it is planned in the mind of the individual undertaking it. Human reason allows us to develop concepts and ideas to achieve economic outcomes. Technology can be thought of as the plan for economic action, and the mechanism by which man achieves his ends. Technology is akin to a recipe for cooking a meal; it is not a physical part of the meal, but the cognitive knowledge that brings it all together. Ideas, recipes, and technology are forms of capital, in that they increase the productivity of the production process. However, they are non-material forms of capital, which makes them abundant. A person using a technology or an idea does not reduce the ability of others to use it, nor does he reduce its productivity. The implications of the non-physicality of this form of capital are significant.

---

71 Mises, Ludwig von. *Human Action: The Scholar's Edition*. Ludwig von Mises Institute, 1998, p. 9.

The process of technological advancement is the continuous development and application of new and better ideas and methods to the process of production, leading to a progressive increase in output per unit of time. Capital accumulation will quickly run into diminishing returns without technological advancement. As the fisherman begins using a fishing rod, his output increases. Without technological advancement, he would continue to invest in more fishing rods, to the point he had no use for more fishing rods, and the extra investment was just providing him with rods he never needed to use. He would, of course, stop investing at that point.

But if the fisherman is able to think and come up with new ideas for technologies to deploy capital to create, he can produce new capital goods that are more productive than the fishing rod. The process of capital accumulation will then continue to increase productivity without running into diminishing returns. The fisherman's reason makes him suspect that fishing will be more productive if he is able to do it from a boat rather than from the shoreline. He invests some of his time and output into building the boat, and then tries it. As discussed in the previous chapter, this investment is expensive and uncertain. It necessitates deferring consumption, it suffers depreciation, and it entails the risk of failure. But if it does succeed, his productivity will increase. Continuing to invest in more identical boats will now also run into diminishing returns, but human reason will continue to look for new technologies to employ. With each new technology and invention, new limitations to production emerge, and capital can be deployed to improve them. A better, bigger, faster, safer boat, and new specialized equipment can continue to be invented as long as capital is being accumulated to finance it. Not only will the new technologies allow you to pull in more fish, but they will also enable you to catch types of fish that were unattainable before.

Technology and Labor

> The substitution of more efficient methods of production for less efficient ones does not render labor abundant, provided there are still material factors available whose utilization can increase human well-being. On the contrary, it increases output and thereby the quantity of consumers' goods. "Labor-saving" devices increase supply. They do not bring about "technological unemployment."[72]
>
> —Ludwig von Mises

The rise of industrialization and the utilization of large amounts of power in economic production has been accompanied by incessant complaints about technology replacing labor. On an intuitive and superficial level, this appears to make sense. The more machines are used to increase output and productivity, the less reliant producers are on workers to generate the same level of output. As individual factories procure machines, they lay off unnecessary workers. Perhaps the most famous and original example of rage against the machine in response to the fear of job loss came from the Luddites, who organized campaigns to break automated looms, which they argued would destroy the livelihood of the British textile worker. Mechanized farming was said to put farmers out of work. The steam engine was going to make large chunks of the labor force redundant. Telephone operators were needed to connect phone calls when telephones were first invented and deployed, but as automated switchboards were invented, the demand for operators collapsed. More recently, many fast food restaurants are deploying increasingly sophisticated automated tellers that reduce their need for workers. This line of thinking is also central to the Marxist creed, as Marx argued that the gains of mechanization would accrue to the capitalists at the expense of the workers, whose pay would not increase, and whose ranks would dwindle as the rapacious capitalists abandoned them to unemployment.

Were the Luddites right? Would continued automation result in the unemployment of large chunks of the population, leading to horrible societal

---

72 Mises, Ludwig von. *Human Action: The Scholar's Edition*. Ludwig von Mises Institute, 1998, p. 136.

consequences? The commonalities between their complaints and Marxist theories are an obvious red flag to the contrary. Moreover, empirical observation does not support the Luddites' contentions. But the definitive answer can only be attained through the economic way of thinking.

After more than two centuries of automation and industrialization, we somehow find that the vast majority of British adults who want employment can find it, and at wages that far exceed those the Luddites fought for. While it is true that very few, if any, Brits are doing the menial jobs their ancestors performed in the eighteenth century, they have jobs nonetheless. Even as the population of Britain continued to increase, more jobs continued to be found, and Brits today earn more and work in much better conditions than their ancestors did in the eighteenth century. Had the Luddites and Marxists been right, one would imagine that two centuries of technological progress would have left absolutely nobody with a job today, let alone leaving them with better jobs.

The root of the Luddites' confusion was their treatment of labor as if it were a consumer good, acquired for the utility it provides, rather than a producer good, acquired for the production of consumer goods. A consumer good for which a superior alternative can be found is no longer demanded and can lose its economic value, which is what happened to typewriters after the invention of computers. But demand for a producer good is not necessarily contingent on its utility to the purchaser; it is dependent on the good's usability for production. Even if a factor of production was to be replaced in one production process, it would still be valuable if it could be utilized in another production process.

Labor, in particular, is the least specific factor of production, and it can be redirected to other jobs or industries. And labor, being made up of human time, is also the ultimate resource, whose scarcity underpins the scarcity of all other resources. Everything is made with the input of human labor, and we live in a world of scarcity where there is always a large demand, at the margin, for more goods and services. As technological advancement increases the productivity of labor, and therefore makes labor more valuable, it allows for the production of more economic goods, alleviating scarcity. However, it does not, and cannot, eliminate scarcity, which is, after all, the scarcity of human time itself. As long as humans have unmet needs, there will be avenues for directing human labor to meet those needs. No matter how much human productivity increases, human wants can increase further, and human reason can continue to devise better solutions to the problems of scarcity. It can always invent better products, better technologies, and safer production methods and generate new demand. We will never "run out of jobs," because we can always use more humans making more scarce products to meet other humans' ever-increasing wants. Scarcity can never be eliminated, because time is always scarce. Work can never end, and man can only choose which tasks to prioritize. The more tasks he can delegate to machines, the more time he has to perform many of the infinite number of tasks he would like to carry out but cannot because of the scarcity of his time.

There was a time when moving humans or luggage around could only be accomplished by hiring other humans to carry them. A strong, healthy man would be able to carry another man, or several dozen kilograms of weight, and move them a few kilometers in a day. The job of carrying heavy things without the support of capital had very low productivity, and it was so unpleasant to perform that it seems to have mainly been the purview of slaves. Only those who could own slaves could afford this kind of labor with any sort of regularity. The vast majority of the population, however, could only move their own bodies and things as far and fast as their own feet could carry them.

As humans developed the wheel, the possibilities for moving weighty matter around were expanded. By pulling a carriage with wheels, the worker could now move heavier weights over longer distances; in other words, his productivity increased. Combining the carriage with a horse would increase the productivity of the worker even further. With the dawn of the Industrial Revolution, and the invention of the train, car, truck, shipping container, and airplane, the productivity of modern transportation increased far beyond pre-industrialization levels. One truck driver can now move up to 50,000 kg of weight at a speed of 100 km/h for 16 hours a day. A handful of crew members can fly an Airbus A380 weighing 575 tons, 300 of which are cargo, at a speed of 903 km/h. With a crew of 20–40 people, the world's largest container ship, the HMM Algeciras, can move 24,000 twenty-foot shipping containers, each weighing up to 25,400 kg, with a total shipping weight of around 672,000 tons at a speed of 15.2 knots, or 28 km/h.

From the domestication of the horse to the building of the HMM Algeciras, there has been a succession of inventions—the wheel, carriage, horseless carriages, trucks, trains, and airplanes—and somehow jobs in the transportation industry have yet to be eliminated. Not only that, but there is certainly a larger percentage of full-time jobs in the transportation sector today than existed before the invention of the wheel. In primitive societies that predate the wheel, there cannot be the level of specialization that would have allowed for many careers dedicated to transportation, as all individuals had to spend the majority of their working hours providing their own basic needs. With low levels of capital, low utilization of nonhuman energy sources, and primitive technological development, labor output was close to the level needed for basic survival. In such a world, most people need to work on producing their own food, and very few people can specialize in other jobs. Given the very low productivity of pre-wheel transportation technologies, it is unlikely many people had enough surplus economic production to hire someone to work in transportation full time, as that person's opportunity cost would represent a significant part of the food they would otherwise produce for himself. Only someone who was enslaved and had no free will would be forced into this kind of job.

As technology advances and productivity increases, each person's production rises above their daily survival needs. Scope for specialization then emerges, as more workers can be fed by the efforts of others, thus freeing them from having to engage in subsistence labor and allowing them to produce more sophisticated goods. As productivity increased in the transportation industry, it became feasible for free people to willingly want to work in transportation. As technology and productivity continued to improve, the conditions and pay for jobs in transportation continued to improve.

Many people continue to find more work in transportation as the productivity of transport increases. Instead of one worker carrying one man, we now have one worker sailing a ship that carries thousands or an airplane that carries hundreds. The amount of work done increases proportionately to the increase in productivity. More people travel, more work gets done, more trade takes place, and more needs are met. The more capital is employed in transportation, the more productive a transportation worker becomes, and the more they are paid.

To Luddites and Marxists, the invention of the wheel would have appeared as an unmitigated disaster—just think of all the lost jobs in the carrying-painfully-heavy-stuff industry! But in reality, it was a great boon for humanity, as it freed humans from carrying heavy loads and allowed them to focus on more productive jobs instead.

The value of goods, as discussed in Chapter 1, comes from their suitability to fulfilling human needs. The human need for movement and transportation cannot be eliminated by being met more efficiently. Humans are mobile, and they do not like to stay in the same place for long. Diminishing returns set in as a result of being in the same place, and individuals seek to move. Trade requires the movement of goods, and the larger the scope for trade, the more productivity gains can be had. These economic realities make transportation a need that has existed in all times and places, and one has no reason to expect it will be eliminated any time soon. Individual jobs in transportation at any time represent the most productive and technologically advanced solutions available to the problem of transportation up to that point. When a new technology is invented, it does not eliminate the need for transportation; it allows labor to be directed to a more productive solution for transportation.

Therefore, it is no coincidence that humanity's economic conditions continue to improve with technological advancement. The more productive our technology, the better off we are. If humanity were to listen to the Luddites and fight technological advancement, none of us would have any time to do any of the immensely productive things we do in today's modern society. We would be too busy engaging in very primitive tasks, like carrying heavy loads, to be able to do anything else.

The bad news for Luddites is that their opponent is far more powerful than even they imagine. They are not up against greedy capitalists looking to cheat workers; they are up against the full force of economic reality and human action responding to economic incentives. The value that accrues to humanity from new inventions that enhance our productivity is far too significant and tempting for legislation and machine breakers to overcome. The Luddites are always destined to lose to whoever appreciates technology, because its adopters can use it to gain much higher productivity.

While the Luddites of the early nineteenth century did succeed in destroying many machines and some factories, these victories against human advancement were few and far between. Their movement died and their ideas became the butt of jokes, while technological advancement continued to make life better for everyone. They were utterly powerless to stop the ingenuity of billions of human beings from making life better for all of us. Once a wheel, loom, car, airplane, or software code is invented, people recognize the value it provides in terms of increased productivity. Violent restrictions may succeed in delaying these technologies, but they also serve to increase the returns for those who manage to get around them. The individuals, businesses, or regions that utilize a productive technology not utilized elsewhere can produce at lower prices.

Technological advancement does not eliminate demand for labor, but there is compelling evidence that it does eliminate slavery.[73] As specialization and productivity increase along with capital accumulation, a worker's output becomes increasingly valuable, allowing him to command a more valuable reward for his labor. Rather than "exploiting" workers, the market allows them to produce with the highest productivity, which makes them more valuable to those who employ them, and reduces the returns on enslaving them. The benefits of mutual cooperation grow as the productivity of workers increases.

Slavery and highly productive capital goods do not coexist. The deployment of highly productive capital goods makes the willing cooperation of the worker increasingly valuable, as they can willingly or negligently sabotage very expensive equipment worth orders of magnitude more than the wage they are paid. Unless he is paid enough to willingly want to work, forcing a slave to manage expensive capital goods carries a large risk. In this way, capitalism encourages the rise of more mutually beneficial exchange at the expense of coercive arrangements like slavery.[74]

---

73 Ridley, Matt. *The Rational Optimist: How Prosperity Evolves*. Harper, 2010.

74 Boudreaux, Don. "Capitalism & Slavery." Learn Liberty, 15 Dec 2016.

Capital accumulation and the division of labor have also resulted in the development of advanced power sources, which allow us to deploy ever-increasing amounts of energy to meet our needs. As will be discussed in the next chapter, before the deployment of modern capital-intensive energy sources from hydrocarbons, human energy consumption was very close to human energy production. In a pre-capitalist world, a person's own hands and legs produced most of the energy he could command. In such a world, acquiring the service of another man is highly valuable. With very little energy available to meet a person's needs, a second person's energy output has a huge marginal value, making slavery economically attractive and slaves valuable. But as energy consumption increases with new technologies, to the point where the average citizen of a rich country now consumes as much energy as the output of 200 slaves, most of the work slaves did can now be outsourced to machines that are much more productive, reliable, and accurate. With hundreds of machine slaves providing energy, the marginal value of one extra human slave becomes increasingly low. As the number of machines we have grows, the economic logic of slavery becomes less and less compelling. It is no exaggeration to say that technological innovation and capital accumulation made slavery obsolete and set slaves free.

When there was little or no capital, transportation was a job that was only acceptable for slaves. When there were carriages, you had free men willingly take on a job in transportation, because the productivity was high enough to compensate them sufficiently for their time. This allowed them to buy sufficient sustenance from others specialized in the production of food. With the introduction of the car, the job of a taxi or truck driver became even better rewarded, and working as a driver was an attractive occupation for millions of people all over the world. The more technology advances, the more capital is invested in a job, the more productive the job becomes, and the more rewarding the work is. Today, many highly skilled engineers, technicians, and various other professionals work in the shipping and transportation industry, and their productivity is high, allowing them a high standard of living.

Technology and Productivity

> We have inherited from our forefathers not only a stock of products of various orders of goods which is the source of our material wealth; we have no less inherited ideas and thoughts, theories and technologies to which our thinking owes its productivity.[75]
>
> —Ludwig von Mises

As better technologies are deployed, productivity rises and living standards increase. But the non-scarce nature of technology makes it unique as a method for increasing the value of human time. Whereas labor, property, capital, energy, and money are scarce, ideas are not. When the wheel's inventor used it, his productivity increased. When his neighbors copied him, they, too, were able to increase their productivity without decreasing the productivity of the inventor. As people emulate an invention, they benefit from it, and everyone's productivity increases. As more people benefit from the invention of the wheel, they are likely to add innovations to it, thereby allowing everyone to benefit from the higher productivity such innovation brings.

The non-scarce nature of technology makes it arguably the fundamental driver of long-term economic growth. Labor is expensive, as it comes at the cost of our leisure, and the more our income grows, the more we are able to afford leisure. Capital is also expensive, as it comes at the expense of increasingly valuable consumption, and it inevitably runs into diminishing returns without technological advancement. There are only so many fishing rods you can employ. Trade and specialization will have limits if they are not combined with technological progress, which itself faces no such limits and allows for indefinite increases in economic productivity. After the wheel was invented, it allowed for a large array of technologies to be built on top of it. These then opened additional possibilities for innovation. Carriages, trolleys, pushcarts, cars, buses, trucks, trains, and airplanes were developed with wheels. These

---

75 Mises, Ludwig von. *Human Action: The Scholar's Edition.* Ludwig von Mises Institute, 1998, p. 178.

devices, and the wheel itself, will continue to be improved upon by users and engineers. Only the improvements that increase productivity are adopted, while the ones that do not improve it are discarded. Technological improvement creates new, more intensive divisions of labor, increasing specialization and allowing for increased productivity.[76] As long as humans economize, they will continue to dedicate their reason to finding better solutions to their problems.

One can see support for the argument that technological innovation is the driver of long-run growth in the empirical observation that larger populations witness faster economic growth than smaller populations. Had economic growth been a product of resource availability, then you would expect a smaller population to have a greater abundance of resources per capita, allowing it to increase its productivity and living standards faster than a more densely populated area. If resources alone drove economic well-being, one would expect that sparsely populated areas would have higher incomes than more crowded areas. But if technological innovation is the driver of long-run growth, then one would expect the opposite to be true: Larger populations would lead to more individuals coming up with productive ideas, and since these ideas are non-rival, they would spread to the whole population, leading to higher productivity growth. A society of 100 million people will have many more people able to devise new ideas like the wheel than a society of 100 people. Imagine if one out of 100 people comes up with an innovation every year. The smaller society would have one innovation every year to improve their productivity, while the larger society would have 1,000,000 innovations every year. Since these are non-rival, everyone in the society could copy them and benefit from the increased productivity they entail.

The preceding discussion is the essence of a paper by economist Michael Kremer, who finds that population growth rates across time correlate positively with population size.[77] If the driver of economic growth were the availability of physical resources, then you would expect that lower-population societies

---

76 Bylund, Per. *The Problem of Production: A New Theory of the Firm*. Routledge, 2016.

77 Kremer, Michael. "Population Growth and Technological Change: One Million B.C. to 1990." *The Quarterly Journal of Economics*, vol. 108, no. 3, 1993, pp. 681-716.

would be able to grow faster since more resources are available per capita. But if the driver of economic growth were technological advancement, then you would expect to witness the opposite: Societies with high populations produce more technological discoveries and thus achieve faster economic and population growth. In another test of the same hypothesis, Kremer compares the population density and economic growth rates across different geographic regions that were historically isolated. The data show that the more highly populated geographic areas had faster economic growth than sparsely populated, again, supporting the notion that technological innovation, not economic resources, drives economic growth. More population density means more non-rival innovations and technologies will spread to the entire population, allowing higher productivity and increasing living standards.

Another unique aspect of ideas and technological innovations is that they are very difficult to destroy, unlike physical property and capital. Once the wheel was invented, destroying any particular wheel would not have destroyed the idea of the wheel. The idea would have lived on in the minds of everyone who saw it, and it could be reproduced indefinitely. Natural calamities, and man-made ones like vandalism, theft, and government, can and have destroyed unfathomably large quantities of capital over the millennia. But technologies and ideas have always been much harder to destroy. They live on in the minds of people who observed them, or in their writings. And while writing can be destroyed, what is in the minds of humans cannot be controlled. It is more difficult to kill ideas than to kill a person or destroy an object. You may violently assault or kill a person holding an idea or use physical torture to get him to denounce it, but you cannot stop him from thinking it. The last bastion of human freedom will always be the thoughts humans hold in their minds, which no force on Earth can overrule.

Physical capital, as discussed in the previous chapter, also suffers from the problem of depreciation, an inevitable consequence of its physical nature. Physical capital is constantly decaying, on top of the risks of destruction it also faces. Not only do material objects originate in ideas, they only survive in the long term as ideas as their individual physical manifestations decay and are destroyed. The ideas, technologies, and knowledge that go into making bridges, buildings, engines, computers, wheels, or medicines are all more economically significant than any individual manifestation of these technologies.

The introduction of the printing press was a monumentally important technology for humanity because it allowed for the mass printing of ideas, making it far harder to destroy them as they spread via a growing number of copies. The invention of digital media and the internet was another aid to humanity's capacity to preserve its ideas and technologies, as it made copies of information far cheaper to produce. A simple digital data storage device worth a few dollars, or the wage of a few hours' labor for the majority of people worldwide, can store the books of the world's largest library.

Technological Innovation and Entrepreneurship

This evolutionary process of selection and variation continues indefinitely with technologies, and there are no good reasons to expect it to stop, because it is ultimately driven by humans' need to economize—an eternal problem that cannot be evaded. Humans are always economizing, and that requires the application of reason to improve the process of production. Technological innovations increase productivity, but they do not end economizing action; humans still need to economize and seek ways of improving their productivity, and the new innovation simply opens up more horizons for finding newer innovations.

The predominant model for understanding technological innovation is that it is a product of scientific advances discovered by scientists. While understandably popular among the universities that teach it, a closer look at the realities of technological innovation shows a far more dynamic and market-driven process. Technological innovations are only innovations if they pass the market test and increase productivity, commanding enough of a market price to compensate the producer for deploying them. Failing to achieve success on the market implies that the productivity increase of the technology does not justify the initial cost. The difference between a curiosity or a toy and a technological innovation lies purely in the latter's ability to raise productivity.

In *The Economic Laws of Scientific Research*, Terence Kealey provides a very compelling illustration of the inextricable link between markets and technological innovation.[78] Kealey rejects the linear model for technological advance, in which academic science findings are applied to produce technological innovations, and offers a wealth of compelling evidence to the contrary. The increase in the productivity of the textile industry in the eighteenth century came through the inventions of craftsmen who owed nothing to academics. British agricultural productivity growth in the nineteenth century came without government support for agricultural research and development, but from farmers and inventors. Most significantly, the Industrial Revolution was not birthed from the laboratories of scientists, but from the workshops of workers, sometimes illiterate. Thomas Newcomen, who invented the first commercial steam engine, was a barely literate provincial blacksmith who had no knowledge of whatever scientific advances were supposed to have inspired the industrial engine. His work with pumps led him, after a decade of experimentation, to reverse the process of a pump in order to produce an engine. Whereas the pump uses mechanical power to move fluids, an engine uses moving fluids to produce mechanical power. It was a simple idea, inspired by the enormous economic reward for producing an engine, not by theoretical scientific discoveries. Kealey illustrates this to also be the case for James Watt, Richard Trevithick, and George Stephenson, and other pioneers of engines:

> It will be seen, therefore, that the development of the steam engine, the one artefact that more than any other embodies the Industrial Revolution, owed nothing to science; it emerged from pre-existing technology, and it was created by uneducated, often isolated, men who applied practical common sense and intuition to address the mechanical problems that beset them, and whose solutions would yield obvious economic reward.
>
> Looking back at the Industrial Revolution generally, it is hard to see how science might have offered very much at all to technology, because science itself was so rudimentary. Chemists who subscribed to the phlogiston

78 Kealey, Terence. *The Economic Laws of Scientific Research*. Macmillan Press, 1996. See also *The Bitcoin Standard Podcast* episode 80 with guest Terence Kealey.

> theory, or to the view that heat was a substance, or who tried to build perpetual motion machines, were not likely to be of much use to engineers. Indeed, during much of the nineteenth century, the reverse was true; scientists scrambled to catch up with engineers. Carnot' s descriptions of the laws of thermodynamics, for example, emerged from his frustration with Watt's improved steam engine, because that steam engine broke all the rules of contemporary physics. Watt's engine was more efficient than theory stated it could be, so Carnot had to change the theory.[79]

It is more accurate to say that the invention of the steam engine created thermodynamics, rather than the other way round. A similar story can be seen with the invention of the airplane. The majority of scientists at the beginning of the twentieth century were adamant that flight was not possible,[80] even after it happened. Yet it was two bike-shop-owning brothers who had no scientific training who managed to achieve it. Physics was then revolutionized to explain and rationalize flight. Technological innovation is born from the desire to achieve ends and secure profits by serving others.

Further, Kealey illustrates that technological advances of the Industrial Revolution happened in Britain, which had virtually no government support for science, and not in countries like France, which spent profligately on financing official science.

Software

As human knowledge has advanced, our ideas have resulted in the creation of ever-more complex machines to produce the outputs we value. As operating machines became increasingly repetitive and predictable, humans began to devise ways to automate the instructions machines needed. Cloth-making looms were equipped with guiding patterns and punch cards that would produce reliable patterns in fabric without requiring conscious and continuous human

79 Kealey, Terence. *The Economic Laws of Scientific Research*. Macmillan Press, 1996

80 Ammous, Saifedean. "Slowdown: Aviation and Modernity's Lost Dynamism." *SSRN Electronic Journal*, 25 May 2017.

supervision. Some mechanical devices were utilized to perform mathematical calculations at a faster and more reliable rate than humans could achieve.

In 1822, English polymath and inventor Charles Babbage worked on developing a "difference engine," which was used to compute polynomial functions.[81] He was unable to complete its construction, although his design survived, and in 1991 the London Science Museum constructed an operational machine based on his design. In 1833, Babbage started work on a more general design, the Analytical Engine, which would incorporate many of the essential features of modern-day computing, a century before any modern computer manufacturer achieved commercial success.

Perhaps the most fascinating aspect of Babbage's design was that it was programmable using punch cards. Ada Lovelace, the daughter of Lord Byron, developed an algorithm in 1842 to calculate a sequence of Bernoulli numbers on Babbage's machine, giving her a strong claim to the title of world's first programmer.[82] While Babbage and Lovelace were unsuccessful in developing commercial computers, they were instrumental in advancing the science and art of computer development until it bore fruit in the twentieth century. The Babbage Analytical Engine was too difficult and expensive to successfully construct and operate commercially, given the industrial and technological reality of the nineteenth century; but by the twentieth century, it had become possible.

Electricity would enter into the operation of these machines, increasing their productivity and complexity. Highly sophisticated wiring boards and circuits would be needed to control them. As the sophisticated new breed of electric machines could compute difficult mathematical problems, they were termed "computers." In 1941, Konrad Zuse, a German engineer, constructed what is regarded as the first programmable computer, the Z3.[83]

The instructions that operated the early computer machines were coded into them through electric circuits or punch cards. Getting an early computer

---

81 "The Engines." *Computer History Museum*, 2021.

82 Woolley, Benjamin. *The Bride of Science: Romance, Reason, and Byron's Daughter*. McGraw-Hill, 1999.

83 Trautman, Peggy Salz. "A Computer Pioneer Rediscovered, 50 Years On." *The New York Times*, 20 Apr 1994.

machine to perform a slightly different function usually required adjustments to its hardware and processes, as well as sophisticated rewiring. By the late 1940s, it became possible to store these instructions in computers electronically with the ENIAC (Electronic Numerical Integrator and Computer). In the 1950s and 1960s, computer programming languages were developed that would allow for programs to be specified in a more abstract way, independent of the computer's architecture. The development of these standardized programming languages, and the growing number of people worldwide who could read, understand, and write them, brought about an entirely new type of economic good with enormously transformative implications.

Software can be thought of as the purest form of technological good. It consists entirely of data and has no physical form, but it increases productivity enormously. It can be communicated around the world very quickly with modern communication tools, and it is non-rival and non-scarce. Applying software to an industrial process allows for the increased automation of the machines' functions, requiring less human supervision and labor. Software allows for far better organization of resources and supply chains, reducing costs and increasing efficiency.

This economic development has had an outstanding impact on the world over the past seven decades. Ideas and technologies can now be coded, through abstract letters and numbers, into hardware that controls a program's operation and allows it to perform evermore complex tasks. For most of the population of nineteenth-century Britain, the punch cards inserted into obscure and highly complex machines must have seemed unintelligibly insignificant. Today, software, the instructions codified into standard languages that tell machines to perform functions, has invaded every industry in the world. It is impossible to imagine a single avenue of economic production that has not increased its productivity through the utilization of machines that run on software.

Property in Ideas

Can ideas and technology be considered property? To answer this question, we return to the discussion in Chapter 2, in which a distinction was made between economic and non-economic goods. Both types of goods offer utility to individuals, but economic goods have value because they are scarce. Scarce goods are those available in supplies so limited it is impossible to satisfy the demand for them; this forces humans to make choices about how to consume and allocate them. In other words, scarcity forces humans to assign value to goods. Ideas, being immaterial, have no limit on their supply, so the available supply can always meet whatever demand exists. This precludes the development of a market value for ideas, unless the individual who possesses an idea creates a market for it by restricting access.

There are two ways of creating scarcity in the access to ideas in order to generate a market value for them. The first is for the person with the knowledge to choose not to disclose it publicly, and to only disclose it to individuals who pay for it. Trade secrets, secret recipes, and proprietary technological processes are examples of this voluntary and peaceful method of establishing property in technology and ideas. The second is to make the knowledge public but use the coercive power of the state to prevent others from using the knowledge for profit. Examples of this include intellectual property laws, like copyrights and patents. Kinsella explains these:

> A patent is a grant by the state that permits the patentee to use the state's court system to prohibit others from using their own property in certain ways—from reconfiguring their property according to a certain pattern or design described in the patent, or from using their property (including their own bodies) in a certain sequence of steps described in the patent.
>
> Copyrights pertain to "original works," such as books, articles, movies, and computer programs. A copyright is a grant by the state that permits the copyright holder to prevent others from using their own property—e.g., ink and paper—in certain ways.

> In both cases, the state is assigning to A a right to control B's property—A can tell B not to do certain things with B's property. Since ownership is the right to control, IP grants to A co-ownership of B's property.[84]

An excellent treatment of this topic from a legal and economic perspective can be found in Stephan Kinsella's *Against Intellectual Property*.[85] A key insight is that when information and knowledge of certain production processes become publicly known, the only way to prevent others from using it is to impose restrictions on the ways in which they can use their own property. The only way to copyright published information is to make it illegal for owners of the published good to use their own property of ink and paper to recreate the copyrighted, published work. Similarly, patents can only work by imposing restrictions, with the threat of government violence, on producers' ability to use their own equipment in a similar way to that described in the patent.

Both patents and copyrights require the use of violent threats against individuals engaging in peaceful economic production. In both cases, the government assigns to the copyright or patent holder the right to control the property of others. From a legal perspective, intellectual property laws must involve the assignment of a claim of ownership and control on the physical property of others: The copyright or patent holder asserts control over the property of everyone on the planet who could use their own property.

As Wendy McElroy explained in *Contra Copyright, Again*:

> My ideas are like stacks of money locked inside a vault which you cannot acquire without breaking in and stealing. But, if I throw the vault open and scatter my money on the wind, the people who pick it up off the street are no more thieves than the people who pick up and use the words I throw into the public realm.[86]

---

84 Kinsella, Stephan. "The Case Against IP: A Concise Guide." *Mises Daily Articles*, Ludwig von Mises Institute, 4 Sep 2009.

85 Kinsella, Stephan. *Against Intellectual Property*. CreateSpace, 2001.

86 McElroy, Wendy. "Contra Copyright, Again." *Libertarian Papers*, vol. 3, no. 12, 2011.

Chapter 4 elaborated on how property is, according to Menger, "not an arbitrary invention, but rather the only practically possible solution of the problem that is, in the nature of things, imposed upon us by the disparity between requirements for, and available quantities of, all economic goods.[87]" Understanding the praxeological rationale for the development of the institution of property explains the arbitrary, unworkable, and contradictory nature of the concept of intellectual property. Ideas are not scarce, so their demand can never exceed their supply—there is no limit on how many wheels can be produced from the idea of the wheel. The absence of scarcity makes the application of the framework of property inapplicable to ideas, as there is no conflict over scarcity to be avoided. This makes intellectual property incompatible with property rights.

With the economic approach to these questions, the notion of intellectual property laws is intellectually untenable, and it reduces to nothing more than aggression on the part of the bodies that impose these laws on the property of anyone who may fall foul of them. Abolishing intellectual property laws does not prevent producers from keeping trade secrets; it just places the cost of maintaining the secret on the producer and requires him to only resort to peaceful methods of enforcing it. There is nothing about ideas that makes enforcing their scarcity an acceptable exception to the non-aggression principle, which will be discussed in more detail in Chapter 16. Even if there were an increased benefit to some segment of society, or to society overall, it does not justify the initiation of aggression against peaceful people.

Yet a closer look at the alleged benefits of intellectual property shows that they have been massively exaggerated. Intellectual property laws, at the margin, increasingly incentivize innovators to obtain monopoly licenses at the expense of innovating to meet consumer demand. At the margin, these laws magnify the reward for obtaining state monopoly licenses for ideas and lead innovators to dedicate growing quantities of resources toward meeting that end, rather than seeking to satisfy consumers.

This is most apparent in the pharmaceutical and software industries, where large bureaucratic corporations can be increasingly seen as enormous patent

---

87 Menger, Carl. *Principles of Economics*. Ludwig von Mises Institute, 2007, p. 97.

trolls, whose primary focus is on hiring lawyers, patenting, litigating, and defending against litigation; while developing consumer software and drugs are an increasingly secondary focus.

While we are taught to value innovations for their own sake, valuable innovations are those that consumers value enough to make them profitable. Without intellectual property laws, the only way to monetize ideas and innovations is for idea holders to ensure their ideas provide greater value to consumers than the available alternatives.[88] With intellectual property laws, entrepreneurs can legally ban their competitors from competing, and succeed by dint of their monopoly power over their ideas. The satisfaction of consumer wants becomes a secondary concern. By limiting the number of providers on the market, government enforcement of intellectual property laws effectively comes at the cost of consumer satisfaction.

A common argument from supporters of intellectual property rights is that rewarding innovators with monopoly profits for a period of time will incentivize them to produce more than they otherwise would. Society overall would be better off allowing this form of aggression against peaceful property owners in order to protect innovators and incentivize them to come up with new ideas. Yet the theoretical and empirical arguments for the increased benefits to society from intellectual property laws are very weak. In an excellent study of the patent and intellectual property system, Levine and Boldrin present compelling evidence suggesting that intellectual monopoly laws are counterproductive to innovation. The focus on patents directs companies' energies away from innovation toward lawsuits and a patent arms race, where competitors seek to acquire as many patents as possible to use as bargaining chips to avoid getting sued and to derail each other with lawsuits. The high cost of drug development, usually cited as the justification for monopoly profits, comes predominantly from the cost of litigation and regulatory approval required to secure drug approval and patents.

Boldrin and Levine examine these laws and find little empirical support for the idea that intellectual property leads to greater innovation or growth:

88 Bylund, Per. "Intellectual Property: Innovation Should Serve Consumers, Not Producers." *Mises Wire*, Ludwig vonMises Institute, 6 Feb 2020.

> [T]here is no empirical evidence that they serve to increase innovation and productivity, unless productivity is identified with the number of patents awarded—which, as evidence shows, has no correlation with measured productivity. This disconnect is at the root of what is called the "patent puzzle": in spite of the enormous increase in the number of patents and in the strength of their legal protection, the US economy has seen neither a dramatic acceleration in the rate of technological progress nor a major increase in the levels of research and development expenditure.
>
> In 1983 in the United States, 59,715 patents were issued; by 2003, 189,597 patents were issued; and in 2010, 244,341 new patents were approved. In less than 30 years, the flow of patents more than quadrupled. By contrast, neither innovation nor research and development expenditure nor factor productivity has exhibited any particular upward trend. According to the Bureau of Labor Statistics, annual growth in total factor productivity in the decade 1970 – 1979 was about 1.2 percent, while in the decades 1990–1999 and 2000–2009 it has been a bit below 1 percent.[89]

The simplistic view of intellectual monopoly rights is that they incentivize innovators. But on closer inspection, it is clear they have the opposite effect. Innovation itself always has strong motivation driving it, and it is facilitated by building on others' innovations. Intellectual monopoly laws do not provide an added incentive for innovators as much as they hinder innovators by preventing them from building on the work of others. Most inventors come across their inventions when trying to scratch their own itch, and the invention will provide them value in itself regardless of what others do with it. Further, being the first to come across an innovation provides the inventor an enormous advantage in being able to market and sell it without having to resort to coercive intellectual property laws. Over the centuries, the greatest inventions, along with the most innovative works of literature, music, and art, have been

---

89 Boldrin, Michele, and David Levine. "The Case Against Patents." *Federal Reserve Bank of St. Louis*, Working Paper 2012-035A, 2012.

produced without the need for copyright or patents. In fact, one could argue they were developed precisely due to the absence of copyright laws, allowing their producers to cheaply access the work of those who inspired and provided them with the foundations for their own creations. It is common for intellectual property law advocates to focus on the benefits to the inventor of greater earnings, but they are very quiet on the topic of the enormous cost this entails to the many more potential inventors who cannot access ideas or build on them without paying exorbitant fees.

Ideas are the only non-scarce productive assets. As technology and telecommunication become cheaper, copying productive ideas just becomes easier and cheaper. The cheaper it is to spread and copy good ideas, the more productive the world becomes. Intellectual property laws impose a higher cost on the transfer of ideas. In today's world, this primarily benefits the people who work in the field of intellectual property, but not the creators or the producers, and not the copiers or society at large. "If I have seen further, it is by standing on the shoulders of giants" was how Isaac Newton paid tribute to the many people from whom he learned. In his time, obtaining the knowledge of others required paying large sums of money to obtain expensive manuscripts. The printing press, industrialization, and the internet have decimated the cost of acquiring knowledge and made virtually all of humanity's knowledge accessible to anyone with a $20 phone and an internet connection. Intellectual property laws raise this cost again, reversing centuries of technological progress in reducing the cost of communicating knowledge, leaving countless millions of geniuses and producers deprived of knowledge they could use to become more productive. If the past hundreds of years of progress have given the vast majority of humans on Earth access to a very large number of giants' shoulders, intellectual property laws are a tax for standing on these shoulders. One can only imagine how much more creative and productive humanity would be if all of the world's books were available freely online.

Chapter 8

Energy and Power

Using energy is an economic act that deserves close inspection by economists, as it is similar to trade, capital accumulation, and money as a method for increasing the quality and quantity of our time on Earth. While economics textbooks, both the mainstream and Austrian variety, generally avoid discussing the economics of energy as a main topic, I believe the economic reality of the modern world demands a discussion of energy production and use in any book on economics. Understanding the role of energy production and utilization is essential to all economic decision-making in the modern world. One cannot understand the economics of the division of labor and capital accumulation without reference to the increased consumption of energy that inevitably accompanies each and without which they would not be possible.

Remarkably, modern science is not very clear on what exactly energy is. The word defies clear definition, so much so that the famous physicist Richard Feynman said, "it is important to realize that in physics today, we have no knowledge of what energy is. We do not have a picture that energy comes in little blobs of a definite amount."[90] The world's most popular thermodynamics textbook, written by Yunus Çengel and Michael Boles, has this to say on the subject: "Thermodynamics can be defined as the science of energy. Although everybody has a feeling of what energy is, it is difficult to give a precise definition for it. Energy can be viewed as the ability to cause changes."[91]

A common definition is that energy is "the ability to do work," or "the ability to do work and transfer heat." Wikipedia has a more precise definition: "In physics, energy is the quantitative property that must be transferred to an object in order to perform work on, or to heat, the object." Energy is in the food you eat that makes you do what you want, in the battery that powers your electric device, in the electric socket that powers your TV. I like to think of energy as an animating force that can move or heat objects and access to energy as the ability to command this force to perform tasks valuable to humans. Energy can be defined in terms of work or heat, based on the standard international units discussed in Chapter 1.

Work can be measured in terms of the work produced by a force or through heat. A force acting on one kilogram of mass to produce an acceleration of 1 m/s^2 is defined as one *newton*, named after physicist and polymath Isaac Newton (who, incidentally, was responsible for placing England on the gold standard). A force of one newton acting over a distance of one meter produces one joule of work, a unit of measuring energy named after physicist James Joule. Lifting a 1-kg object over a distance of 1 meter against gravity (whose acceleration is measured at 9.81 m/s^2) will require 9.81 joules of work. The measurement of energy through heat is done by defining a calorie as the amount of heat needed to raise the temperature of 1 cm^3 of water by 1 degree Celsius. As these are all precisely defined scientific constants, a calorie is the equivalent of precisely 4,184 joules. The joule remains the more common scientific measure of energy. **Power** is defined as the amount of energy brought

90 Feynman, Richard. *The Feynman Lectures on Physics*. Vol. 1, lecture 4, "Conservation of Energy," section 4-1, "What is energy?" California Institute of Technology, 1963.

91 Çengel, Yunus, and Michael Boles. *Thermodynamics: An Engineering Approach*. 5th ed., vol. 1, McGraw-Hill, 2006, p. 2.

to bear on a process in a specific period of time. The common unit for power is the watt, which is defined as joules per second.

Human bodies obtain energy primarily from eating, but also from sunlight. This energy allows humans to function cognitively and physically—it is what allows human action. And beyond the energy of our own bodies, we can act by directing outside energy sources to satisfy our needs and achieve our ends. In his book, *The Moral Case for Fossil Fuels*, Alex Epstein presents an intuitive way of understanding energy as "machine calories."[92] Energy is what machines need to consume in order to produce the output we value from them. In the same way humans need to consume energy to act, machines need their own joules to function. From ancient times, humans have used their reason to devise ways of deploying power sources to perform work for them, allowing them to achieve higher productivity with their actions. This has helped us economize time in achieving our ends, increasing our chances of survival.

Take transportation as an example, a perennial feature of human action. Assume a hypothetical man wants to transport 500 kg of butter from his farm to town to sell it. This man needs to consume food to gain the energy necessary to move his body and the butter to town. Given the amount of power the man can produce, he would have to carry the butter over 10 trips, each trip taking 2 hours to complete, which is 2 entire working days for the man. If this man had a horse and carriage, he would have a larger amount of power at his disposal to achieve his end. Provided he feeds the horse and maintains its health, the horse will be able to pull the man and all the butter to town in only one trip, taking 2 hours in total, around one-tenth of the time the man would have needed to complete the trip on his own. Should he have a car at his disposal, he would be able to complete the trip in a matter of minutes. The car is a machine that produces around 100–500 times the power of a horse, or 1,000–5,000 times the power of a human, and thus minimizes the human time required to complete tasks.

The role of power in economics is similar to the roles capital and technology play. In fact, the three are often intertwined and even overlap in what they signify. Capital accumulation is a process that is usually accompanied by

92 Epstein, Alex. *The Moral Case for Fossil Fuels*. Portfolio Penguin, 2014.

increases in the amount of energy brought to an act and to any technological improvement used in its performance. The move from transporting the butter by foot to horse and then to car involves an increase in energy consumed in the task, a technological improvement, and the deployment of increasing quantities of capital.

Energy in Human History

In nomadic, pre-agricultural societies, humans used the raw energy of nature to survive. The sun helped them stay warm and grow their food, and running rivers washed their bodies. As humans became more sedentary and settled, they developed the capacity to invest in more powerful, sophisticated, and reliable power sources. The domestication of animals offered us the ability to direct the power of these animals to meet our needs, such as transport and soil tilling. The fat of these animals was used for lighting. Humans were likely to settle near rivers to utilize the energy of the running water through watermills, as well as to construct windmills that turned the energy of wind into usable power. Logging wood provided warmth and allowed for cooking. The productivity of human labor was enhanced by these sources of energy, and the likelihood of survival increased through the protections these energy sources afforded us.

Around the middle of the second millennium A.D., humans began to extract and burn coal, which had a higher energy content than wood, allowing us to pack more energy into smaller weights of fuels, thus increasing our productivity. By the nineteenth century, humans had also learned to utilize crude oil and natural gas from the Earth for their energy content. The most obvious testament to the incredibly transformative and valuable power these fuels provide is the speed with which the utilization of these energy sources has spread around the world in the past two centuries. The levels of productivity afforded to workers who have access to these fuels made the fuels highly desirable worldwide, resulting in increased standards of living wherever they are available. The twentieth century witnessed the invention of nuclear power, a technology that allows humans access to fuels with a much higher energy content per unit of weight than hydrocarbon fuels. The utilization of nuclear power has, however, been limited in this century due to popular opposition and fears about its safety.

At all points, technological progress would provide power sources that would contain a higher energy per unit of mass. Wood contained 16 MJ/kg, and in comparison, coal, a solid hydrocarbon fuel, was a significant leap forward, with 24 MJ/kg. Liquid hydrocarbon, oil, has a higher energy density with 44 MJ/kg, and natural gas is the densest of the hydrocarbons, at 55 MJ/kg. Nuclear power, on the other hand, is in a completely different league, with 3,900,000 MJ/kg.[93]

Energy Abundance[94]

One of the most common misconceptions about energy is that it is limited and scarce. In the popular imagination, the Earth has a limited supply of energy that humans consume whenever they heat or move anything. This scarcity perspective views energy consumption as a bad thing because anything that consumes energy depletes our planet's finite supplies of it. The reality is very different.

The total amount of energy resources available for humans to exploit is practically infinite and beyond our ability to even quantify, let alone consume. The solar energy that hits the Earth every day is hundreds of times larger than the total daily global energy consumption. The rivers of the world that run every hour of every day also contain more energy than the global energy consumption. The same is true of the winds that blow and the hydrocarbon fuels that lie under the Earth, not to mention the many nuclear fuels we have barely begun to utilize.

To begin with the most obvious of energy sources, the sun alone showers the Earth with 3,850,000 exajoules of energy every year. That is more than 7,000 times the amount of energy humans consume every year. In fact, the amount of solar energy that falls on Earth in one *hour* is more energy than the entire human race consumes in one year. The amount of wind energy blowing

93 Hore-Lacy, Ian. "Future Energy Demand and Supply." *Nuclear Energy in the 21st Century*, 2nd ed., World Nuclear University Primer, 2011, ch. 1, sec. 6, p. 9.

94 This section draws heavily on the text of *The Fiat Standard*.

around the world alone is around four times the total energy consumed worldwide. Some estimates put the potential hydroelectric yearly power capacity at around 52 petawatt hours (PWh), or one-third of all energy consumed worldwide. There are no accurate estimates of the amounts of hydrocarbon fuels that exist on Earth, but the closest estimate we have (proven oil reserves) is constantly increasing as a result of new discoveries, which occur at a pace greater than the increase in oil consumption, as discussed in Chapter 3.

The belief that resources are scarce and limited is a misunderstanding of the nature of scarcity, which is the key concept behind economics. The absolute quantity of every raw material present on Earth is too large for us as human beings to even measure or comprehend, and in no way does it constitute a real limit to the amount humans can produce. We have barely scratched the surface of the Earth in search of the minerals we need; the more we search and the deeper we dig, the more resources we find. What constitutes the practical and realistic limit to the quantity of any resource is always the amount of human time that is directed toward producing it, as this is the only real scarce resource. As a society, our only scarcity is in the total amount of time available to members of a society to produce goods and services. More of any good can always be produced if human time is directed toward its production. The real cost of a good, then, is always its opportunity cost in terms of goods forgone to produce it.

In all human history, we have never run out of any single raw material or resource, and the price of virtually all resources is lower today than it was at past points in history because our technological advancement allows us to produce them at a lower cost in terms of our time. Not only have we not run out of raw materials, the proven reserves of each resource that exist have only increased with time as our consumption has gone up. If resources are to be understood as finite, then the existing stockpiles would decline with time as we consume more. But even as we are always consuming more, prices continue to drop, and the improvements in technology for finding and excavating resources allow us to find more and more. Oil, the vital bloodline of modern economies, is the best example, as it has fairly reliable statistics. As shown in Figure 5, according to data from BP's Statistical Review, annual oil production was 46% higher in 2015 than in 1980, while consumption was 55% higher. Oil reserves, on the other hand, have increased by 148%, around triple the increase in production and consumption. In *Energy: The Master Resource*, Robert Bradley argues that proven reserves will usually be in the range of 20 times annual consumption because there seems to be little incentive to speculate for more reserves beyond this point.[95] As consumption increases with time, more reserves are invariably found.

There is no energy scarcity problem, because energy cannot run out as long as the sun rises, the rivers run, and the wind blows. Energy is constantly available for us as humans to utilize as we like. The only limit on how much energy is available to us is how much time humans dedicate toward channeling these energy sources from places where they are abundant to places where they are needed, in the time frame in which they are needed. All energy is ultimately free, but the costs lie in paying the supply chain of individuals and firms involved in transporting this energy to where it is needed, in a usable form. It thus makes no sense to discuss energy itself as a scarce resource, which implies there is a fixed, God-given quantity for humans to consume passively. In its usable form, energy is a product that humans create by channeling the forces of nature to where they are needed. As with every economic good other than bitcoin, there is no natural limit to its production; the only limit lies in how much time humans dedicate to producing it, which in turn is determined through the price mechanism sending signals to producers. When people want more energy, they are willing to pay more for it, which incentivizes more of its production at the expense of producing other things. The more people desire it, the more of it can be produced. The scarcity of energy, like all types of pre-bitcoin scarcity, is relative scarcity, whose cause lies in its opportunity cost in terms of other resources.

The non-scarce nature of energy implies that it cannot be an economic good, as discussed in Chapter 2. Further, based on Menger's work, a good is something useful that can be directed to the satisfaction of human needs. Energy sources in the abstract cannot be viewed as goods in that regard. The total quantity of energy available on Earth is not a metric with any relevance to any individual. It is neither scarce, nor can it be directed to the satisfaction of our

95 Bradley, Robert. *Energy: The Master Resource: An Introduction to the History, Technology, Economics, and Public Policy of Energy*. Kendall Hunt Publishing, 2004.

needs. Solar, wind, hydrocarbon, nuclear, or hydroelectric energy that is not directed to satisfying human needs is not a good any more than the energy of a distant star is. Only when directed to the satisfaction of our needs can energy sources be considered goods, and only when directed to the satisfaction of our needs does energy indeed become scarce, and thus, an economic good. Energy, then, is not an economic good, but power is.

Humans cannot value energy sources in the aggregate, but only at the margin; they value the next unit of energy directed to the satisfaction of their needs over a forthcoming period. Applying the framework of subjective valuation at the margin to understand energy is a powerful explanatory tool that illuminates the nature of energy markets.

Power Scarcity

Whereas energy is understood as the capacity to do work, power is a measure of that capacity divided by the period of time in which the work is performed. Power measures the intensity of energy over time, which is what is necessary to make energy sources useful for satisfying human needs. The latter are time sensitive, since time is finite and scarce, and time preference is positive. The total amount of solar and wind energy that hits your home in a day is irrelevant to your economic needs, as is the amount of energy contained in the hydrocarbon fuels under your house. Consumers do not pay for these energy sources, nor should they, as they are not performing any tasks valuable to human beings.

Mises and Menger's explanation of marginal valuation can be applied to thinking about the energy market. Mises explained that nobody ever has to choose between all the iron and all the gold in the world; they only have to make choices concerning the next marginal unit of these substances they want to consume. Whereas iron might be more useful for humans than gold, this will not be reflected in a higher price on the market, because nobody ever has to choose whether to bid on gold or iron for his entire life. People only make choices about the next marginal unit, and due to the relative scarcity of gold next to iron under normal market conditions, people usually value the marginal unit of gold more than iron.

Energy is analogous to the total supply of gold and iron in that they are more akin to nebulous concepts than economic goods that can be directly brought into satisfying human needs. People do not buy the total supply of iron, but only the marginal quantity they need to satisfy their marginal need at the particular time and place in which they buy it. Similarly, **people do not buy energy in total. They buy definite quantities of energy delivered with a desired intensity over periods of time in which they want work done. They buy energy over the marginal time unit. They buy *power*.**

It makes little sense to speak of "energy markets," or "buying energy." Energy as a good cannot be divorced from the time in which it performs the work required for it to satisfy human needs. A breeze blowing at your house for a week may be enough to operate the lights in your home for an evening, but managing to concentrate that energy into operating the lamps over a week is what matters. The breeze blows for free, but channeling it to light the lamps is not.

Energy's scarcity lies not in its absolute availability, but in its availability in sufficient quantities when and where it is needed, in the form in which it is needed. Energy in its raw form is not an economic good because it is highly abundant, and because it has very little utility in its naturally occurring levels without being channeled into productive uses, at the margin, as power. In order to operate a car, airplane, computer, phone, loudspeaker, ventilator, or any of the many critical and ubiquitous technological devices of the modern world, a specific amount of energy needs to be directed at the device per second of operation. The economic value that accrues from operating these devices is dependent on this continuous stream of energy entering the machine at the required rate—i.e., the power supply. **To the extent that energy provides utility to humans, it does so at the margin, in the form of power.**

As humans value goods at the margin, humans value energy in the form of power, the quantity of energy provided per second. With valuation being performed at the margin, we can understand the enormous value humans find in energy sources that can deliver high amounts of power over short periods of time, in particular, hydrocarbons. Hydrocarbons are also a highly mobile form of stored energy that can provide high amounts of power virtually anywhere an engine can be taken.

Hydrocarbons have enormous value to humans because they are chemically stable, light, and easy to transport and lend themselves to being used for purposes that demand high power on demand and on location. Individuals, small groups, or large populations anywhere in the world can access large amounts of power on demand by acquiring hydrocarbon fuels and putting them into increasingly cheap and ubiquitous engines. There are several billion engines deployed in various capacities worldwide to meet the human need for light, warmth, transportation, production, and construction, among many others.

The introduction of hydrocarbon fuels has vastly increased humanity's potential for generating power, as is explained thoroughly in Vaclav Smil's *Energy and Civilization: A History*.[96] It is instructive to use Smil's analysis of the evolution of energy and power consumption over history to examine the technical possibilities for the division of labor and productivity, and how much they were enhanced by the development of hydrocarbons.

The amount of power that a strong man can produce by treading a wheel is around 200 watts. A Roman waterwheel turning a millstone produces 1,800 watts. Around the sixteenth century, German windmills could deliver 6.5kW to crushing seeds. By 1750, a large Dutch windmill could drain a polder by producing 12kW. In 1832, the first water turbine could produce 38kW. With the invention of Newcomen's atmospheric engine for pumping water in the early eighteenth century, humans could direct 3,750 watts to performing work by burning fuel. A modest start, but hydrocarbon fueled machines would take off. James Watt's biggest steam engine, in 1800, delivered 100kW. A steam turbine in 1900 delivered 1MW. By 1970 a gas turbine powering a pipeline compressor would produce 10MW. In 2022, Siemens Energy's SGT6-9000HL gas turbine, the world's most powerful gas turbine, generates 410.9MW.

A horse can produce around 750 watts of power, and an elite cyclist can produce around 400W for a period of about an hour. The Ford Model-T at full speed produced 14.9kW in 1908. A modern compact car like the Kia Picanto produces around 45kW. The world's most powerful sports car, the Rimac Nevera, produces more than 1.4MW of power. By 1890, a large steam locomotive would run at full

96 Smil, Vaclav. 2017. *Energy and Civilization: A History*. Cambridge, MA: MIT Press.

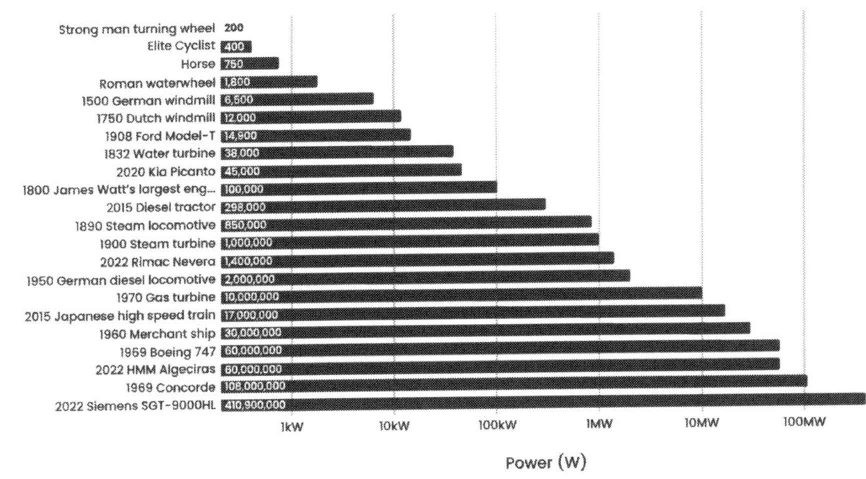

Figure 9. Maximum power over the past 3,000 years

speed on 850kW. By 1950, a powerful German diesel locomotive would run at 2MW, and in 2015, a high-velocity Japanese train ran at 17MW. By 1960, A Japanese diesel-powered merchant ship would run on 30MW, while in 1969, a Boeing 747 would run on 60MW, while a supersonic Concorde's four engines would produce 108MW at a cruising speed of 2,400 km/h. The HMM Algeciras' engine delivers 60MW. From the horse to the HMM Algeciras and Boeing 747, humanity has seen an 80,000-fold increase in the power it can bring to transportation.

Smil also compares the maximum power in field work across time. Whereas a peasant hoeing a cabbage field would produce 50W, a farmer plowing with two small horses would have 1,000W at his disposal. With a small tractor, in 1950, a farmer could harvest with 50kW of power at his disposal. And in 2015, with a large diesel tractor, a farmer could have 298kW of power at his disposal. In three centuries of technological progress, the amount of power at the disposal of a farmer has increased 6,000-fold.

Before hydrocarbons, humanity was only able to access limited amounts of usable power, and only near waterwheels and windmills. With hydrocarbons, large amounts of power can be conjured anywhere at any time, allowing for growing population centers, growing trade link between these population centers, and higher labor productivity.

Alex Epstein makes a compelling case for how hydrocarbon fuels are the root of modern prosperity.[97] Until the sixteenth century, life everywhere primarily relied on burning wood for the provision of energy. Compared to modern hydrocarbons, wood contains much less energy per unit of weight. After the utilization of coal started in the sixteenth century, later followed by oil and gas, the amount of energy available per person expanded enormously, and with it, our quality of life. To visualize the true benefit of energy to our lives, Epstein invites us to imagine the energy we consume today in terms of the energy consumption of humans performing tasks for us. By that measure, he finds that the average American has 186,000 calories at his service daily, or the energy equivalent of 93 humans. Before modern fuels, this amount of energy was rarely ever available to anyone. Only the richest kings could dream of having as much energy at their daily disposal, either in the form of combustible wood or enslaved humans.

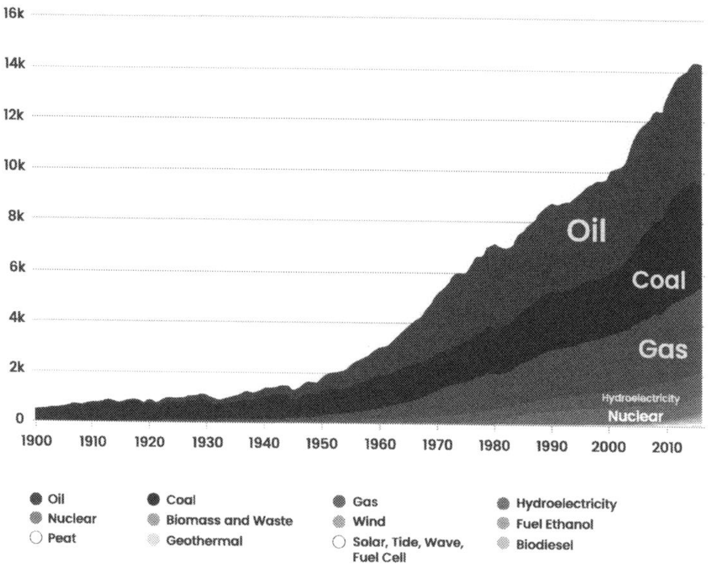

Figure 10. Global primary energy consumption[98]

97 Epstein, Alex. *The Moral Case for Fossil Fuels*. Portfolio Penguin, 2014.

98 "World Primary Energy Production." *The Shift Dataportal*, The Shift Project, 2020.

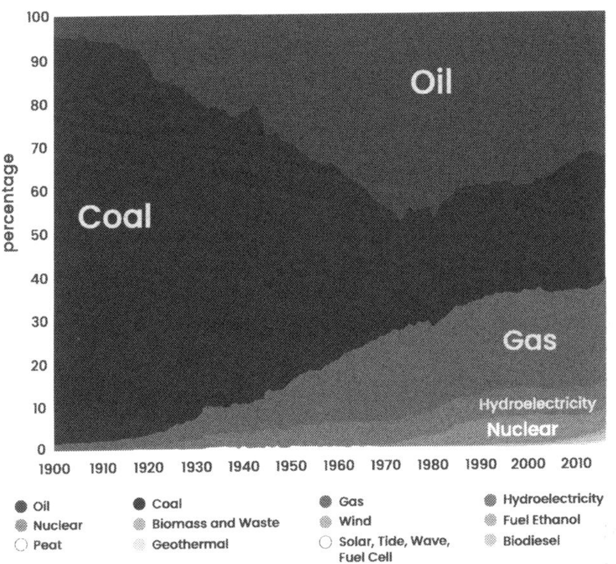

Figure 11. Global primary energy consumption, in percentage terms[99]

The Industrial Revolution, which transformed standards of living worldwide, was inextricably linked to the invention of the steam engine and the mass deployment of coal power to raise worker productivity. Coal was the predominant source of power until the turn of the twentieth century, when the invention of the internal combustion engine allowed for the mass utilization of oil, which has a higher amount of energy per weight, and is thus more efficient to transport and use in transportation. The twentieth century witnessed a rapid rise in the deployment of oil worldwide, and in the second half of the twentieth century, the use of gas power grew the fastest. Currently, around 80% of the world's energy consumption comes from these three hydrocarbon fuels.

As technology advances and standards of living improve, one would expect more of a shift to natural gas for energy generation, since it produces the least pollution among hydrocarbon fuels. However, there will realistically still be enormous demand for coal power because the only practical alternatives to coal power for many people around the world are low-power energy sources, which are intermittent and unreliable. Coal is cheap, and the technologies used

99 Ibid.

to generate energy from it have been perfected over decades, and modern clean coal technology drastically reduces the amount of harmful emissions generated by its consumption. The benefits of reliable power have proven acceptable to the vast majority of people who have moved to areas with coal plants and reliable power, and away from areas with no coal plants and no reliable power.

In 1802 Richard Trevithick built the first working railway steam locomotive, which burned coal to run train cars. Around the same time, the steamboat was invented, operating on the same principle. The automobile was invented in 1885, and the airplane in 1902. For more than two centuries, these technologies reduced the cost of transportation and increased its availability. Moving goods today costs a tiny fraction of what it cost before hydrocarbon energy, and as a result our capacity for trade has expanded significantly, and the extent of the global division of labor has grown enormously, further increasing human productivity.

Modern capitalism and the global division of labor that emerged in the nineteenth century would simply have been impossible had it not been for the introduction of hydrocarbon energy sources, which increased labor productivity significantly and raised living standards. Without these energy sources powering modern engines and machinery, labor productivity would not have risen to the point where workers were able to produce far more value than they needed to survive, and thus had considerable resources to trade with others. Capital accumulation took off in a fundamentally different way after these fuels allowed humans to use rapidly growing quantities of power.

Comparisons across the world today, and across time, can vividly illustrate the enormous value that access to high power entails. Our modern world is largely the product of the development of technologies that give us regular access to increasing quantities of energy. Modern civilization and most of its achievements would not be possible without levels of energy consumption that are complete outliers by historical standards.

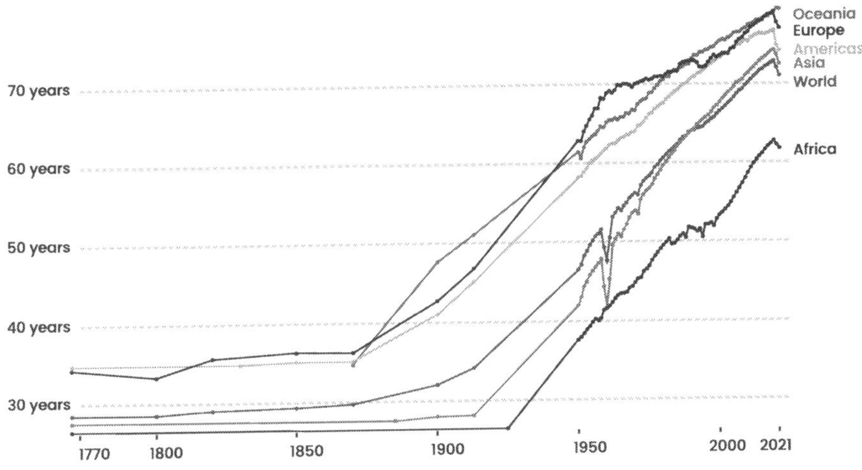

Figure 12. Global life expectancy, 1770-2021

Data from 118 countries with populations larger than four million in 2005 shows the correlation of energy consumption per capita with improved water access, life expectancy, infant mortality, mean years of schooling, electrification, and gross national income.[100] The relationships are very clear: The more a society is able to harness and consume energy, the more it is able to provide itself with the basic needs of modern life.

100 Pasten, Cesar and Juan Santamarina. "Energy and Quality of Life." *Energy Policy*, vol. 49, Elsevier, 2012, pp. 468-76.

Taking a closer look at GDP, the relationship is very clear and has been for a very long time: Greater power consumption is strongly correlated with greater economic production, and consequently, better standards of living, as is apparent in Figure 13.

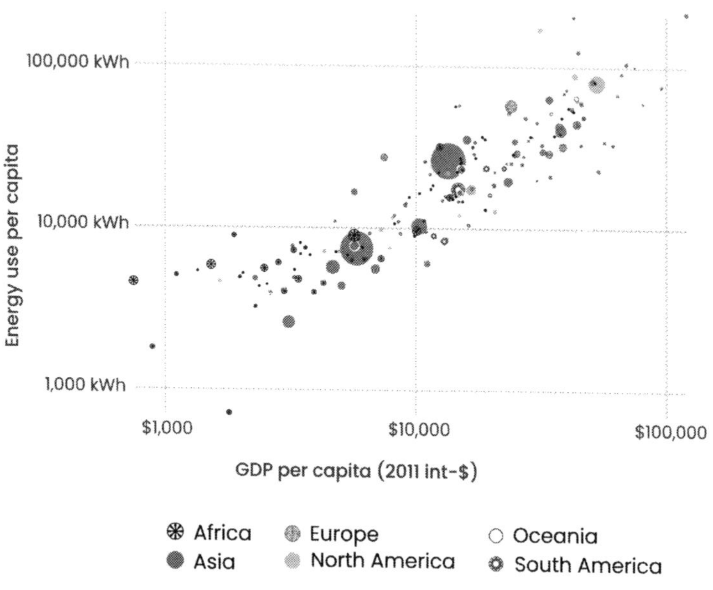

Source: International Energy Agency (IEA) via The World Bank
OurWorldInData.org/energy-production-and-changing-energy-sources/ • CC BY-SA

Figure 13. Energy use per capita vs. GDP, 2015[101]

Figure 14 shows the relationship between energy consumption per capita and the share of the population living in extreme poverty. No country that eliminated extreme poverty consumes less than 10,000 kWh/capita/year, and no country that has more than 20% of its population in extreme poverty consumes more than 10,000 kWh/capita/year.

---

101 Ritchie, Hannah et al. "Energy." *Our World In Data,* 2022.

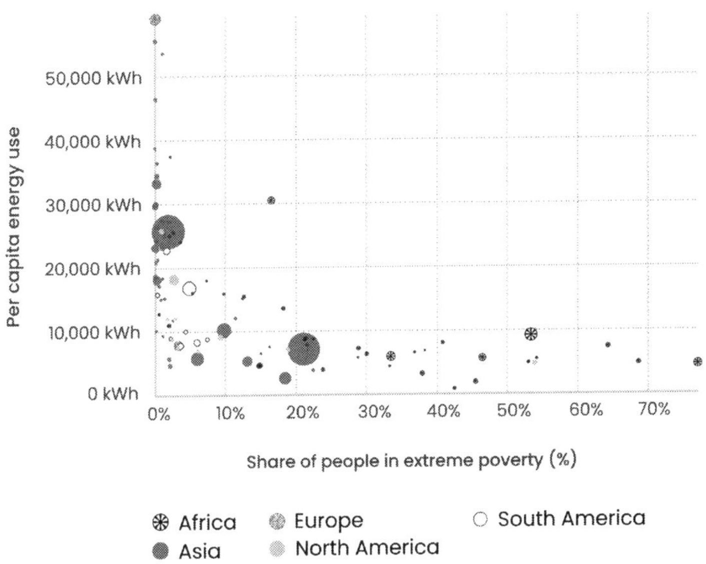

Source: International Energy Agency (IEA) via The World Bank
OurWorldInData.org/energy-production-and-changing-energy-sources/ • CC BY-SA

Figure 14. Energy use per capita vs. share of population in extreme poverty[102]

The progress of humanity has been driven by technological advancements that unlock the energy latent in hydrocarbon fuels. The fact that most humans today live protected from most of nature's harms, can stay warm in the winter, and can travel faster than their running speed is the result of Industrial Revolution innovations that gave us various forms of engines to access the energy present in the three main hydrocarbon fuels: coal, oil, and gas. As John Cross put it:

> The history of economic development is the history of the amount of energy brought under human control. Economic historians have observed the close relationship between economic growth and energy consumption as we put more energy to work for us. American economist Deirdre McCloskey called the surge in energy use that began around 1800 "the Great Enrichment." The benefits to mankind have been enormous, extending life

102 Ibid.

expectancy, increasing food output to sustain burgeoning populations, and lifting the standard of living for most people to levels not even royalty could aspire to just a few centuries ago.

The late Italian economic historian Carlo Cipolla attributed both the Agricultural Revolution thousands of years ago and the Industrial Revolution starting in the late eighteenth century to people harnessing energy power. In the Agricultural Revolution, humans evolved from hunters and gatherers to cultivate and tame the energy in plants and animals, even if most plants and animals are not very efficient converters of energy. Fire, wind and water also increased the energy at the disposal of humans. Over time, people became more efficient at using all these energy sources, through rudimentary farm tools, irrigation, fireplaces, water-powered mills and sailing boats.

Fossil fuels played a negligible role in supplying energy until the Industrial Revolution. While everything on the planet is a possible source of energy, fossil fuels proved especially efficient and convenient in meeting the energy demands of industrialization. In Cipolla's words, the Industrial Revolution "can be regarded as the process whereby the large-scale exploitation of new sources of energy by means of inanimate converters was set on foot." Coal was the first widespread source of inanimate energy, rising from 10 percent of Britain's energy supply in 1560 to 60 percent by 1750, in the process ending Britain's deforestation. This began a cumulative process, where a rising supply of energy stimulated more economic growth, which boosted education that led to the discovery of new sources of energy, notably other fossil fuels.

The first commercial use of hydrocarbon fuels was kerosene to generate light and end our perpetual plunge into darkness after sundown. (This stopped the widespread slaughter of whales, whose oil until then was the main source of indoor light.) The U.S. pioneered the exploitation of oil in the 19th century, a mantle it is reclaiming today thanks to innovative technologies to develop shale deposits. By 1860, the oil age had begun in earnest due to the development of drilling technology in Pennsylvania.[103]

---

103 Cross, Philip. "In Praise of Fossil Fuels." *C2C Journal*, 17 Dec 2015.

As humans continue to discover new technologies for utilizing power to meet our ends, we continuously reduce the cost of power in real terms. In a study of energy prices in the UK in the seven centuries between 1300 and 2000, Fouquet estimates that heating costs declined by more than 80%, the cost of power declined by 94%, transport of freight by 95%, transport of passengers by 91%, and the cost of lighting declined by 99.98%. These declines are illustrated in Figures 15 and 16.[104]

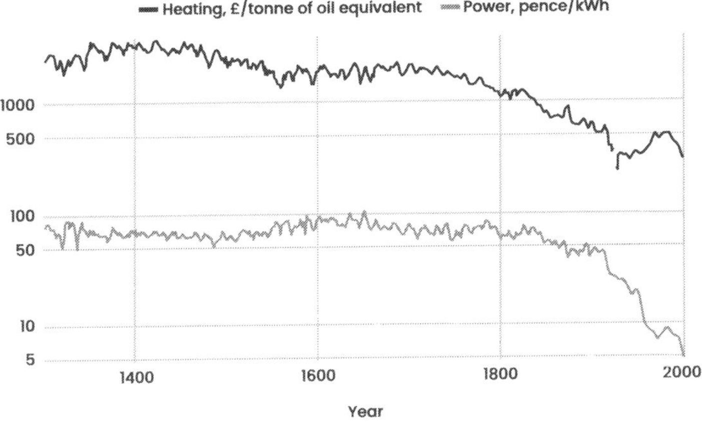

Figure 15. Cost of heating and power in UK, 1300–2000

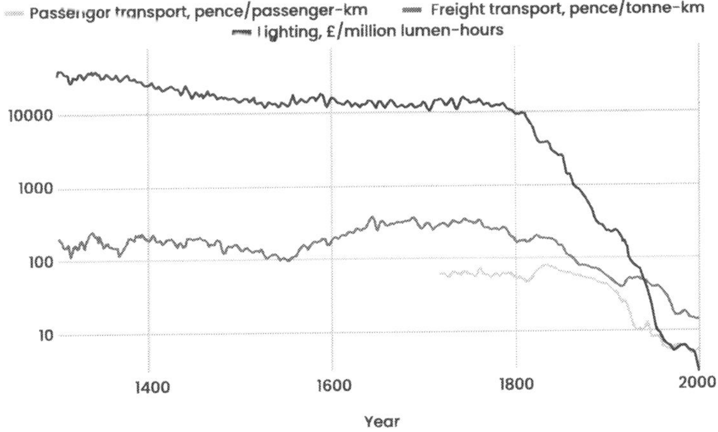

Figure 16. Cost of lighting and transport in UK, 1300–2000

104 Fouquet, Roger. "Divergences in Long Run Trends in the Prices of Energy and Energy Services." *Review of Environmental Economics and Policy*, vol. 5, no. 2, 2011, pp. 196-218. (All figures calculated for year 2000 sterling pound equivalent.)

Power of Hydrocarbon Alternatives

In spite of the amazing and undeniable benefits that high-power hydrocarbons have brought to our world, a majority of economists and the public believe they should, and will, be replaced with alternative energy sources. This animosity was initially based on the increase in the prices of hydrocarbon fuels in the 1970s, caused by inflationary monetary policy, and popularizing the doomsday cultists to prophesize that we are on the cusp of running out of these incredibly abundant fuels. As production continued to increase for decades while proven reserves increased even more, this particular hysteria has died down, but anti-hydrocarbon hysteria has found a new rationale. Incoherent and untestable pseudoscientific superstitions about greenhouse gas emissions being the control knob for Earth's weather are now the reason why we must get rid of hydrocarbons and move to "sustainable" alternatives, such as wind, solar, and biofuels. In *The Fiat Standard*, I argue the hostility of modern government-funded science to hydrocarbon fuels has its roots in inflationary monetary policy, which at once raises the prices of these essential fuels and allows the government to finance and dictate science. The government would like to promote fuel-free alternatives because they are less sensitive to monetary inflation than high-power fuels mass-produced on a global market.

It is common for promoters of wind and solar energy to argue they are cheaper than hydrocarbons because their fuel is free, since there is no charge for sunshine and wind. But this is a good example of faulty economic reasoning, because it does not analyze decisions at the margins. Marginal analysis can help us understand the irreparable problem with wind and solar energy as alternatives to hydrocarbons. Energy is not purchased in the aggregate or abstract; it is purchased at the margin, in specific quantities at particular intensities over time. Energy is not the economic good; *power* is. High-productivity machinery that makes modern civilization possible requires power to be provided at specific controlled intensities on-demand. Power from windmills and solar panels is intermittent and unpredictable, since it is only available when the wind blows and the sun shines. By contrast, hydrocarbon power sources are easily transportable and storable, allowing them to be present in large quantities when and where they are to be needed. Once the modern machinery and infrastructure have been constructed, hydrocarbon power becomes available on demand at the precise intensity needed, at a very small marginal cost.

Whether it is the electric grid, hospitals, baby incubators, refrigerators, heating and cooling, internet servers, countless online services, airports, or numerous forms of modern infrastructure, modern civilization needs its machines to operate continuously regardless of the condition of the weather. No modern company can have its factories, servers, or offices operate at the whims of the weather. For high-productivity machinery to function, it does not just require a low marginal cost of energy; it requires a low marginal cost of energy *at all times*. While the marginal cost of renewable energy fuel is indeed free when the sun is shining and the wind is blowing, when they are not, the marginal cost is infinite. No amount of capital investment will make the sun shine and the wind blow perpetually and whenever a machine is needed. When the sun is not shining, the marginal cost of solar power is infinite, and when the wind is not blowing, the marginal cost of wind power is infinite. If wind and solar power were indeed used as an alternative to hydrocarbons, a modern industrial society would no longer be possible.

As government policies have promoted wind and solar power with heavy subsidies, their use has grown, but reliance on them has come at catastrophic consequences, as it reduces the predictable load peak for any particular utility, since peak demand can now come at a time when some of the fuels are unavailable. Hydrocarbons must be relied upon to provide the entire peak load capacity, making investment in expensive wind and solar infrastructure almost superfluous. While it can indeed reduce consumption of hydrocarbon fuels, its intermittency and unpredictability make the management and maintenance of the hydrocarbon plants and grids more expensive, largely negating the consequences. It is for this reason that power generation from wind and solar only exists to the extent that it is subsidized through government spending.

As humans economize, they continuously seek ways of increasing their productivity. In the context of energy, this has constantly come in the form of increasing the energy density of the sources of power we apply to meet our ends, measured in terms of MJ/kg. To make solar and wind power suitable for modern life would require using battery technology, which has an abysmally low energy per weight, in the range of 0.5 MJ/kg, which is roughly 1% of the energy density of oil or natural gas. Batteries are also very expensive, and so their use is primarily in areas where engines are not practical.

Energy and Freedom

When human productivity was very low, and technology was primitive, there were very few ways for humans to get work done to meet their ends beyond performing their own labor. One of the most effective sources of energy was the labor of other humans. But if man had very low productivity, he needed his own labor for his survival, which meant he could rarely afford to pay others to work for him, and others could rarely afford to pay him. Opportunities for mutually beneficial employment would be scarce in such a setting. If one man wanted to procure the energy of another to serve his needs, he would likely have had to coerce the other person into providing his energy at the expense of his own needs. Slavery as an institution was more common in a world of primitive energy sources because having the energy of another human at your service meant a very substantial increase, almost a doubling, in the total amount of energy available to meet your needs. Low productivity makes survival a critical and uncertain ordeal, and the labor of others becomes enormously valuable, making enslavement profitable.

As productivity increases through the development of technology and increases in nonhuman energy sources, it becomes possible for humans to secure their needs through the deployment of increasing quantities of energy-intensive capital rather than the slave labor of others. The pressing need for the labor of others that could drive one to enslave them declines.

Machines can do much of the work of the slave, and they cause fewer problems than a human with a constant desire to break free. Because machines increase the productivity of a worker, it is possible for him to satisfy his own needs and those of an employer who provides the capital. As the machinery becomes more expensive, and a more integral part of the economic production process, the worker's importance and responsibility increases, and slavery becomes a wholly unsuitable avenue for accomplishing the work. Slave laborers employed in high-productivity tasks using expensive machinery are unlikely to be motivated to use it productively, and they may very likely engage in sabotage. As machines and energy raised the productivity of labor, they increased the likelihood of workers being hired voluntarily rather than coercively.

In the context of energy poverty, having another human being provide you with their energy was extremely significant. But in the modern context of energy abundance, where an individual in a rich, industrialized, developed country uses the energy of 100 humans every day, adding an extra human as a slave contributes very little power at the margin. As energy sources invaded human life, increasing our productivity and standard of living, the marginal benefit of enslaving a human shrunk significantly. Further, as capital accumulation and modern machinery became more central to the production process, the worker's ability to maintain the machinery and not damage it became far more valuable than the power his hands provide. A slave's dedication of their energy to their master was no longer valuable when a machine could cheaply provide many multiples of the energy needed for grunt work. The intelligence and integrity of workers in managing and maintaining machines became far more valuable than their brute force. It is no coincidence that the abolition of slavery spread across the world with the spread of industrialization. Britain led the world in the abolition of slavery precisely because it led the world in industrialization. Wherever the steam engine and the electric generator went, slavery quickly disappeared. To the extent slavery survives today, it does so in industrially primitive societies with little capital accumulation and energy consumption. The economics of machinery make slavery far less workable economically. It makes the hard labor slavery provided available at a very low cost, and increases the productivity and value of a worker's time to the point where his voluntary cooperation is more valuable than any slave labor they may perform.

High-powered machines are also an underappreciated driver of the liberation of women. In a primitive economy with little high-power machinery, human strength was an extremely valuable commodity, and the strongest humans were the most productive. Given that men are, on average, stronger than women, with bigger bodies and greater muscle mass, men's labor was more valuable than women's labor, and women were heavily dependent on men for survival and protection. When modern energy-intensive machinery took over the most physically demanding tasks, like transporting, lifting, pumping, tilling, and protection from nature and animals, the importance of physical strength declined in comparison to the need for cognitive strength, reducing the advantage that men's strength gave them over women. In a modern, energy-rich economy, the most productive and highly rewarded jobs no longer require physical strength. The strongest and most powerful individuals in society are no longer the ones able to secure the most resources. Machines perform the grunt work, and the highest rewards go to those whose cognitive skills can manage these machines. Women are far more likely to be able to support themselves independently in an industrial and informational economy than in a primitive economy. It is no coincidence that female liberation has come about with industrialization. The richest and most industrialized societies are the ones with the highest achieving and most independent women, while the preindustrial societies continue to witness widespread female repression.

PART III

The Market Order

Chapter 9

Trade

> The fundamental facts that brought about cooperation, society, and civilization and transformed the animal man into a human being are the facts that work performed under the division of labor is more productive than isolated work and that man's reason is capable of recognizing this truth.[105]
>
> —Ludwig von Mises

The previous chapters discussed economizing acts and exchanges which are performed in isolation. Labor, capital accumulation, and technological ideas for production are all tasks which humans can use to improve their well-being, without needing to interact with others, by exchanging labor for leisure, immediate gratification for delayed gratification, and new technologies for old ones. But humans are social animals; born into a family and extended social order, they spend their lives interacting with others. Exchange with others is an instinctive and natural part of life, something children perform at a young age. The most economically notable way in which people can interact is through trade or free exchange. This chapter examines and explains the rationale for and benefits of free exchange. The following chapters build on this one to develop a more complete picture of impersonal exchange in the monetary market order.

---

105 Mises, Ludwig von. *Human Action: The Scholar's Edition*. Ludwig von Mises Institute, 1998, p. 144.

Exchanging goods with others brings an important complexity to economic decision-making, which is the idea that the other individual in an economic interaction has his or her own will. When carrying out economizing acts with material goods, such as production, consumption, and capital accumulation, the individual is only dealing with inanimate objects that have no will or consciousness of their own. But when dealing with others, the individual is confronted with another will, one with its own desires, preferences, ends, and actions.

There are only two modes of interaction between people: consensual and coercive. With consent, all involved individuals are partaking in an activity that is agreeable to them all. They willingly choose to partake in the act, without engaging in violence, or the threat of violence, against one another. Trade, or free exchange, is a prime example of a consensual arrangement; both individuals willingly agree to exchange goods because they identify that they can benefit from the exchange. The mere fact of two individuals choosing to exchange goods with one another willingly allows us to necessarily deduce that they both expect to benefit from the arrangement. Had they not favored the outcome of the exchange, they would not have engaged in it in the first place. This is why trade is often referred to as a positive-sum game: The total gain accruing to each participant in trade is necessarily positive. Otherwise, they would not have engaged in it.

Exchange implies the ability of two individuals to use their reason to arrive at an arrangement that benefits them both and hurts neither of them. Only reason allows two people to interact in a way that is beneficial to both because it allows them to foresee the benefits of cooperation and how cooperating will improve their situations.

The only alternative to consent is coercion, which is the imposition, through violence or the threat of violence, of one party's will on the other. Whenever coercion is involved in a human interaction, it can necessarily be concluded that one of the parties in the interaction is worse off than they would have been had the interaction not taken place. Were this not the case, employing coercion to force him to agree to the interaction would not have been necessary; he would have taken part willingly. Coercion can be thought of as a zero-sum game, but it is more likely a negative-sum game. In the case of theft, the thief can take some of the victim's property, increasing his own well-being at the victim's expense. While quantitative economists might refer to this as a zero-sum interaction, this is based on the faulty premise that value is objective and the thief's gain is equal to the victim's loss. But since value can only be understood as a subjective phenomenon, we cannot assume both individuals value the good equally.

A family heirloom the thief values at pennies may have extraordinary subjective value for the owner. But because the thief has not purchased the item from the victim in a negotiated exchange, the value of the item to the victim has not been expressed. The thief has not offered something of sufficient value in exchange, nor even learned what that might be. So it is perhaps more likely that the value gained by the thief is less than the value lost to the victim.

Further, in the case of violence, physical damage could happen to either or both the aggressor and the aggressed, causing them to both suffer. Violence is destructive and the damage from inflicting it can in fact be larger than the loot gained. Moreover, the initiation of violence always brings with it the threat of retaliation. Further, engaging in violence against others results in a marginal increase in the normalization of violence and the likelihood of the perpetrator becoming a victim.

No matter how attractive the spoils of coercion may be, they will always pale in comparison to the rewards possible from cooperation. Man's animal instinct elicits fear of the other, but man's reason can also identify the benefits of cooperation, in effect creating a civilized society. This can be illustrated using the example of Robinson Crusoe encountering another man, Friday, on what he thought was a deserted island.

When confronted with Friday, Crusoe faces two options: coercion or consent. Coercion may seem instinctively tempting: Crusoe could try to enforce his will on Friday, subjugate him and enslave him, or murder him and take his property. Each of these entails a gain for Crusoe, but being unbearable to Friday, they would very likely lead to a violent confrontation between the two men, and the outcome would be uncertain for both. Crusoe could be defeated, enslaved, or killed himself, or he could get hurt even while triumphing. If he does triumph, he may be able to acquire all of Friday's possessions and slave labor, but he would not be able to secure Friday's enthusiastic cooperation to work productively, since Friday knows his output would be primarily for Crusoe's benefit. Crusoe would never be able to trust Friday, who could always seek to harm him any time he could. Conflict and violence leading to death are the expected outcome of this path.

On the other hand, if the two men decided to cooperate with each other and only engage each other on terms acceptable to both, they would likely both be much better off in the long run. Whatever material possessions Friday currently owns, which Crusoe could take, pale in comparison to the goods he could produce if he were to remain alive and free to work, be as productive as he could, and participate with Crusoe in a division of labor.

If Crusoe and Friday both willingly respect each other's sovereignty and property, the two of them are able to produce securely and then exchange the goods they produce. The benefits that are open to them by cooperating are far larger than anything they could secure if they remain hostile and combative. For all of the amazing benefits one can secure through labor, capital accumulation, and technological innovation alone, a far larger world of possibilities is open to humans if they engage in exchange with others. There are several mental tools and constructs developed by economists over the centuries to help us understand the significance of trade and its enormously beneficial potential. The rest of this chapter elucidates these tools to illustrate how the possibilities of cooperation are far better for all involved than conflict.

Subjective Valuation

The foundation for understanding the economic phenomenon of trade is the concept on which all economic reasoning is based: subjective valuation. Only by understanding that value is subjective does the concept of trade become possible. If value were objective, what would people gain from engaging in trade? Why would they want to exchange something for something else when they value both goods equally? Marginal utilities of exchanged goods must increase for both parties. Each party gains higher satisfaction from the thing they acquire than from the thing they give up.

People are able to exchange objects with one another because they place different valuations on the same objects. Value is not something inherent to objects, nor is it a property objects acquire in certain definitive quantities. Value is assigned by the human mind, and valuation is made at the margin. Individuals assign value to objects based on how much they value them at the specific time and place they make their valuation. This depends on a range of factors, prime among them is the existing quantity of these goods they hold.

It is therefore entirely possible for Crusoe to value an apple more than an orange, while Friday values an orange more than an apple. If Crusoe owns an orange while Friday owns an apple, they would both benefit from exchanging their fruit. We can understand this by thinking about their actions, and what we know about the way humans act. If Friday willingly proposes the trade, and Crusoe willingly agrees, we can only conclude that the trade improves their respective well-being: Since Friday values the orange more than his apple and Crusoe values the apple more than his orange, they both gain from the exchange.

Another way to understand why trade happens is by considering the implications of the law of diminishing marginal utility in the context of interpersonal interaction. Since the marginal utility of each unit of a good declines with the increasing quantity of the good, it will naturally follow that individuals will find opportunities for trade by exchanging the goods they have a lot of for the goods they have only a few of. If Crusoe has an apple tree and Friday has an orange tree, they will likely each have large quantities of their own fruit and none of the other's fruit. They would likely value the marginal fruit from their individual trees far less than the first fruit they are able to get from the other person's tree. Crusoe's orange tree gives him more oranges than he can eat, and after having eaten the majority of the tree's produce, the last few oranges have very little value to him. He may not even want to eat them. But having eaten no apples before he meets Friday, the marginal valuation he places on the first apple he can obtain from Friday will be relatively high. Friday, in turn, places very little value on the last few apples produced by his tree and would value an orange from Crusoe's tree much more dearly. Trade allows them both to give up something they do not value highly to obtain something they value more in return.

One common misconception in economics involves confusing value and price. The mere fact that humans willingly choose to engage in exchange shows that this notion is untenable. If a person pays $10 for a good, she is not valuing it at $10, she is valuing it at more than $10 because she willingly gives up $10 in exchange for the good. The seller, on the other hand, clearly values the good at less than $10, as he willingly gives it up for that amount.

While differing subjective valuation explains the rationale for trade, it does not fully capture its benefits and implications because it focuses on the decisions made about the final goods. The more powerful potential implication for trade becomes apparent when we consider the effect trade has on the production process. Two important approaches to understanding human action in interpersonal exchange are the concepts of absolute advantage and comparative advantage.

Absolute Advantage

Trade arises from differences in the subjective valuation of final goods, but it is also an expression of differences in the cost of producing different goods. Even in a primitive setting with no market prices to compare goods, individuals are able to discern the differences in the economic value of different goods, and find opportunities to improve their subjective well-being in transactions where each party gives up things for which they have a lower cost of production to acquire things for which they have a higher cost of production.

Imagine a situation in which Crusoe and Friday subdue their hostile first instincts and instead approach each other peacefully. Crusoe finds that Friday has an abundance of rabbit skins in his cave because he is very good at hunting rabbits, whereas Crusoe is skilled at catching fish. Seeing the abundance of rabbit skins, Crusoe realizes that he desires the rabbit meat and asks Friday if he would be interested in exchanging a fish for a rabbit. Having eaten nothing but rabbit meat for months, Friday accepts the offer enthusiastically. He can barely fish, and every time he tries, he wastes a lot of time and fails to catch enough fish to satisfy his hunger. But now Crusoe is offering him a fish in exchange for a rabbit, which is very easy for Friday to secure. Friday might even be thinking he is taking advantage of Crusoe, who is giving away a precious fish for a rabbit that's easy to secure, but Crusoe is likely thinking the same thing. He is finally able to secure an elusive rabbit, and all he needs to do to get one is to provide one of the many fish he is easily able to catch. In this situation, both men give up something they can produce at a low cost to acquire something they value much more. In a sense, they are both taking advantage of each other.

This situation can be illustrated with a hypothetical numerical example. We can present the production possibilities graphically using a **production possibilities frontier**—a line that illustrates all the possible combinations of both goods that can be produced. Imagine that in a day's work, Friday can catch 8 rabbits or 2 fish, while Crusoe can catch 2 rabbits or 10 fish. If they work independently and do not cooperate, these amounts would represent the respective limits on how much they could each consume daily. Friday could consume either the 8 rabbits or the 2 fish he can catch, and Crusoe could consume either the 2 rabbits or 10 fish he is able to catch. If, in isolation, they both decided to split their workday equally between fishing and hunting, Friday would end the day with 4 rabbits and 1 fish, while Crusoe would have 1 rabbit and 5 fish, as shown in points I in Figure 17. The sum for both would be 5 rabbits and 6 fish.

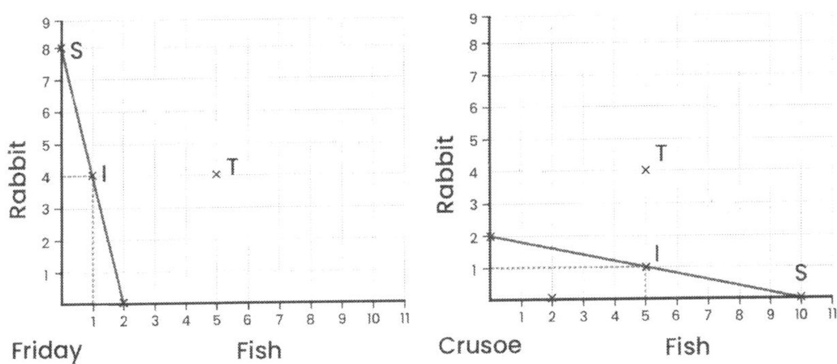

Figure 17. Production possibilities in isolation and trade

If Crusoe were to attack Friday and try to rob him, he might be able to take all the food Friday had, but that would cause Friday to starve to death, leaving Crusoe with nothing but his own production, as in his original state. But if they decided to cooperate, they could both benefit from the differences in their catches. Because Crusoe notices that Friday has an abundance of rabbits but not many fish, he suggests trading some of his rabbits for Crusoe's fish. Rabbits are abundant for Friday but fish are not, so exchanging a fish for a rabbit is a winning trade for Friday, and the opposite is true for Crusoe.

The exchange illustrates to Friday that the best way for him to obtain fish is to actually hunt rabbits and exchange them for fish, while Crusoe realizes that he can obtain more rabbits by fishing and exchanging the fish for rabbits than he would by hunting rabbits. The end result is that it makes sense for them to each specialize in the good they can produce more cheaply. If they specialize, and Crusoe produces only fish and Friday only rabbits, as shown in point S in Figure 17, their combined daily production would be 8 rabbits and 10 fish, which is 3 rabbits and 4 fish more than they would have had if they had remained hostile. If they split their harvest in half, they each end up with 4 rabbits and 5 fish, as shown in the point T.

By simply specializing in the production of the cheaper good, they have both produced more fish and rabbits than if they had each split their time and effort between producing both. This result almost seems like a magic trick: both work the same number of hours, and yet they both end up with more rabbits and fish to eat, and are both better off. This is not a one-off benefit like the loot from aggression, but a sustainable improvement in both their lives that can continue for as long as they continue to trade amicably with one another. In effect, every morning, they both wake up facing a choice: Cooperate and eat more or be hostile and eat less. By allowing each person to dedicate their time to the production of the good that is less expensive for them, trade increases the productivity of both parties. Had one of them killed the other, the "winner" would never gain as much as he would gain from cooperating voluntarily with the other.

Comparative Advantage

The rationale behind absolute advantage is intuitive and easy to understand. Each person specializes in what they can produce at a lower cost, leading to more production of all goods. But the concept of comparative advantage is a more general and powerful explanation of the benefits from trade as a consequence of differences in the opportunity cost of goods, irrespective of the nature and magnitude of the differences in productivity between participants. Trade can be mutually beneficial even if one individual is more productive in the production of both goods than the other person, because of the differences in the opportunity cost of goods for both individuals. The fact that human time is the ultimate scarce resource means that cooperation between two people is beneficial to both of them, even if one is more productive at generating both goods, because their cooperation allows them to dedicate their scarce time where it is most productive.

Imagine if, in the example above, Crusoe were more productive at both fishing and hunting, and he could produce 6 rabbits or 12 fish per day, while Friday could only produce 4 rabbits or 2 fish. This does not mean the 2 cannot benefit from the division of labor. Had the 2 men produced and consumed in isolation, and each spent half their day hunting and the other half fishing, Crusoe would have 3 rabbits and 6 fish, while Friday would have 2 rabbits and 1 fish, for a total of 5 rabbits and 7 fish. If they cooperate and specialize, Friday catches 4 rabbits and Crusoe catches 12 fish, as shown in point S. If they prefer to have more rabbits, Crusoe could spend a part of his day fishing, and they would end up with 5 rabbits and 10 fish, as shown in point S2. In this case, they would have added 3 fish to their daily consumption by specializing. There are various other combinations of fish and rabbits that they could produce, depending on their taste and preference for both. As long as the specialization allows each producer to focus on the good with the lower opportunity cost, they would have more subjectively valuable production than they would in isolation.

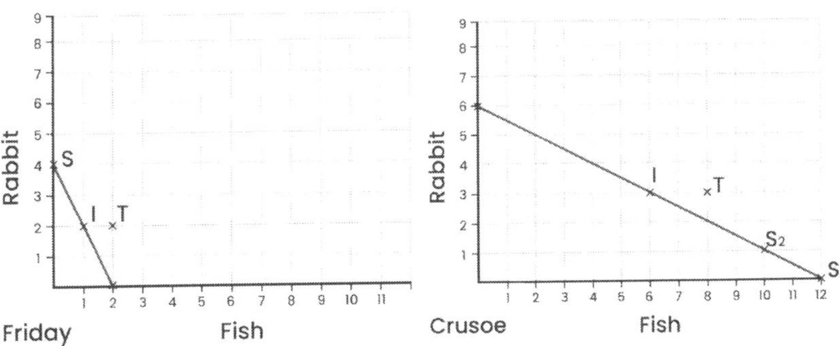

Figure 18. Production possibilities in isolation and comparative advantage trade

Both Crusoe and Friday would work the exact same number of hours, and yet they would be able to produce more output than they had before, even though Crusoe is more productive at both hunting and fishing. The fact that the two men have a different opportunity cost for the two goods means that they can improve the quantity they produce by each spending more time producing the good for which they have the lower opportunity cost. Because each person spends their time producing the good with the lower opportunity cost, they produce more of the final products they both want.

The specialization in this example happens because the opportunity cost of a rabbit for Crusoe is 2 fish, whereas for Friday, it is half a fish. This opportunity cost is expressed graphically as the slope of the production possibilities frontier curve. In isolation, for every time period in which Crusoe needs to secure 1 rabbit, he needs to give up the time necessary to secure 2 fish. But Friday has a different opportunity cost. He can produce twice as many rabbits as fish in any particular time period, so he needs to give up only half a fish to obtain an extra rabbit. If someone were to offer Friday a whole fish in exchange for 1 rabbit, he would be very happy to take it. Similarly, if Friday offered a rabbit to Crusoe in exchange for a fish, Crusoe would be happy to accept the offer, as this is a cheaper way for Crusoe to obtain the rabbit than producing it himself.

Crusoe has two options for securing an extra rabbit: 1) Reduce the time spent fishing and give up 2 fish in order to have enough time to hunt 1 rabbit, or 2) give Friday anything more than half a fish to get him to part with one of his rabbits. The first method costs Crusoe 2 fish, whereas the second costs him a sum larger than half a fish. In support of his own self-interest, Crusoe chooses to cooperate with Friday, and the same reasoning compels Friday to cooperate with Crusoe. The mere existence of differences in opportunity cost between the two means that they can coordinate to allocate their own labor in a way that maximizes the total output they can share based on terms that they agree on initially. The difference in opportunity cost is the advertisement for the trading opportunity. It signifies to each person that the other can provide what they want at a lower cost and that optimizing one's production to accommodate the possibility of trading with someone increases the productivity of both parties.

No matter the difference in productivity between the two, the difference in opportunity cost means that trading will change the allocation of labor between them to create increased output. These opportunities for trade emerge in the real world without economists having to study them and elaborate them to trading individuals. As humans interact, they notice the differing valuation of different goods between people. These differences present opportunities for exchange that benefit both parties. The logic applies at the level of individuals in a family, village, city, country, or across countries. Differences in the opportunity cost of production present opportunities for specialization and people are constantly seeking to take advantage of them.

The differences in preferences and productivity are the drivers for the universally pervasive phenomenon of trade. The mathematical examples are helpful in this regard, but they have been overemphasized in modern economic education, to the point where courses on international trade contain little economic understanding and instead focus on, and test for, mathematical operations tangentially related to these points. The profound insights into the benefits of trade are usually covered only briefly in the early chapters of most textbooks, while the needlessly complex mathematical models take center stage. The mathematical sophistry makes for easier standardized testing, and also transforms these textbooks into a series of elaborate half-baked rationales for government intervention in trade. While the average trade textbook begins by singing the praises of free trade, it quickly degenerates into recycling ancient mercantilist nonsense by slipping it in through irrelevant mathematical models.

Specialization and the Division of Labor

> The existence and possibilities of exchange open up for producers the avenue of producing for a "market" rather than for themselves. Instead of attempting to maximize his product in isolation by producing goods solely for his own use, each person can now produce goods in anticipation of their exchange value, and exchange these goods for others that are more valuable to him. It is evident that since this opens a new avenue for the utility of goods, it becomes possible for each person to increase his productivity.[106]
>
> —Murray Rothbard

The motivations for trade can be derived from differences in taste and valuation, as mentioned above, but in an extended market order, they are driven ultimately by differences in the cost of production and intensified by specialization.

Whereas in isolation, man produces what he needs, in a social system, man produces based on what he expects others to need. He need not meet the full diversity of all his needs through his own labor and can instead direct his labor to the areas of production in which he can excel most at serving others. By specializing in producing a good for a market, rather than producing for your own consumption, it becomes possible to dedicate labor toward the place where it is most productive, not where it is merely necessary. In a market economy, your needs are best met indirectly, by using your abilities to specialize in what you do best and exchanging it for the goods and services produced by others. Specialization is therefore another way of increasing productivity. Beyond just an increase in productivity, trade leads to social cooperation and civilized behavior, as the benefits of being able to engage with society peacefully in a division of labor are very high.

In *Human Action*, Mises explains that specialization is driven by differences in abilities and nature-given factors. In *Man, Economy, and State*, Rothbard argues that specialization is driven by (a) differences in suitability and yield of

---

106 Rothbard, Murray. *Man, Economy, and State with Power and Market*. Ludwig von Mises Institute, 1962, p. 89.

the nature-given factors; (b) differences in given capital and durable consumer goods; and (c) differences in skill and in the desirability of different types of labor.

Rothbard's explanation here is more comprehensive than Mises', and one can go even further than Rothbard and argue that it really is predominantly the accumulation of capital that drives specialization, particularly in the modern economy.

In the above examples, we took it as a given that there were large differences in the productivity of hunting and fishing between Crusoe and Friday. But in the real world, these differences will most likely be driven by differences in capital stock. Crusoe will have a higher productivity when catching fish because he invested in constructing a fishing rod and a fishing boat, while Friday will be better at catching rabbits because he invested in building traps and spears. The differences in productivity are unlikely to be very large without differences in capital stocks. As technological progress and capital accumulation have advanced over time, they have become increasingly detached from the natural conditions, and as such, productivity and comparative advantage in these industries are primarily driven by the extent of physical and human capital accumulation.

It is reasonable to expect geographic and natural factors to go a long way in determining comparative advantage in agricultural and natural products. Finland will likely never specialize in producing tropical fruits like mangoes, and the Sahara Desert is unlikely to export bottled water. But in a modern industrialized economy, such natural and agricultural products have become a progressively less significant part of economic activity, and of an individual's expenditure, compared to services and industrial goods. In the modern economy, the driver of specialization is largely the investment of capital in an industry. Places that have invested in car manufacturing over decades have developed the physical and human capital suited to car production, and will likely continue to have an advantage in car production. Places that invest in the infrastructure for the textile industry will likewise develop that advantage. The more sophisticated the economy, and the longer the production structures, the more comparative advantage is the result of differences in capital accumulation, and less the result of differences in natural factors.

The industry with the highest productivity in the modern world is probably the computer and telecommunications industry, which continues to achieve enormous increases in productivity as it enters and invades all industries, making them much more efficient. Competitiveness in this industry is almost entirely separate from natural and geographic factors. The software engineers and programmers in this industry only need the capital infrastructure to be able to produce, regardless of whether they are doing so on a tropical island like Singapore or a frozen Arctic landscape like the north of Sweden. This is another reason I believe modern economics does not focus enough on the importance of capital accumulation and ascribes too much importance to trade and division of labor in isolation. Without extensive accumulation of capital, there would be little scope for the increase in productivity that drives the differences in opportunity cost, which necessitate specialization.

Trade is a phenomenon that emerges naturally whenever humans interact and realize their valuation of different goods differs. As they start to realize they can meet more of their needs by producing for the market than by producing for their needs directly, people become more attuned to the needs of the market and start directing their productive capacities to meet the needs of society. This leads to a society-wide division of labor, wherein jobs are divided among the population. The more individuals can specialize in the production of a good, the more they will improve their productivity over time.

Extent of the Market

> Every step forward on the way to a more developed mode of the division of labor serves the interests of all participants ... The factor that brought about primitive society and daily works toward its progressive intensification is human action that is animated by the insight into the higher productivity of labor achieved under the division of labor.[107]
>
> —Ludwig von Mises

107 Mises, Ludwig von. *Human Action: The Scholar's Edition*. Ludwig von Mises Institute, 1998, p. 160.

In the previous sections, we looked at the example of two men on an isolated island benefiting from trading with one another and specializing in the production of the goods for which they have the lowest opportunity cost. This simple example illustrates the rationale for trade and the drivers of gains from trade, but the same logic applies as the number of trading partners increases over time, and the gains only increase as the number of partners increases, as this allows for deeper specialization, more capital accumulation, and increased productivity.

In the one-man economy, Crusoe has to meet all his needs himself. Between hunting, building a home, building weapons to fight off predators, and making his own clothes, he barely has any time to accomplish all of the necessary tasks. He has very little scope for specialization and very little time to develop capital goods in one particular avenue of production because he has to divide his time between many tasks. With another man on the island, both can specialize in half the tasks and trade their products. Only one of them needs to fish, while the other focuses on hunting. The hunter can now dedicate twice as much time to developing spears and traps, while the fisherman can dedicate twice as much time to building fishing rods and boats. As they now each have half as many tasks to complete, they are both able to dedicate more time to each mission, thus becoming better at it, as well as accumulating more capital for it. The extent of capital accumulation and specialization only increases as more people take part in the market and trade with one another.

If Crusoe and Friday were to come across another 20 people living on the island, the scope for specialization would increase even further. Now, only one person would specialize in home building, while another focused on farming, another on clothing, another on hunting, another on building the fishing rods, and another on building spears for hunting. The same logic of increased production that we saw applied to Crusoe and Friday can now be applied to this larger group, with continuously increasing productivity.

Increasing the extent of the market not only increases the productivity of workers, it also increases the number and variety of goods available to members of society. As the number of people in the market increases, and the productivity of individual producers increases, each producer is able to produce from each good enough to cover the needs of an increasing number of people. This effectively frees up workers to pursue production of newer, innovative goods which go beyond the most basic needs.

As the circle within which a person's trades grows, the productivity and quantity of available goods increase. This observation of the size of the market is a very powerful tool with which to explain economic phenomena. It helps to explain the economic incentive for immigration from rural areas to big cities. A worker in an isolated rural area produces for a small circle of potential buyers, and buys from a small circle of producers. He has to meet a lot of his own needs because there are not professional providers of these services. He has to spend part of his workday producing things for which there are no specialists in his area, in which he is not specialized, and in which his productivity is relatively low. If he were a shoemaker, for instance, he would be responsible for all stages of the production of the shoe, including the design and manufacture, as well as the sole, laces, and cushioning. But if he moves to a large city, he can specialize in whichever of these stages he finds himself most skillful, where his productivity is highest, and he can rely on others for the other stages. He could focus on the assembly of the shoe, while utilizing the designs of specialized and highly productive designers, buying the laces and soles from specialists who make them at a much lower cost than he could make them himself. The shoemaker can earn more, and be more productive living in a large city than he can in a small isolated rural town.

In a world divided into isolated economies of 1,000 people each, there can be no cars, computers, or smartphones. The 1,000 people would be preoccupied with producing their basic survival needs. If these isolated communities start to trade with one another, the extent of specialization increases and capital accumulation in each production process can increase, freeing up more people from basic survival labor so they can pursue the production of capital goods that do not yield immediate consumption goods. As the extent of the market grows, the rewards from specialization increase, because its products can be sold to larger groups of people. The current world market is the largest single market to have ever existed, and it allows for the highest level of productivity ever attained.

The technologically advanced products we use today would simply not be possible in a world with 1% of the current population, or a world of small markets isolated from one another. For a modern car factory to be able to produce the number of cars it does, at the price it can produce them, requires a large number of people specialize in increasingly specific and arcane tasks, which are only possible when the output is large and can be sold to larger markets. A modern carmaker has engineers who spend many years training and focusing on very minor aspects of the production of the car, such as the windshield. Without the ability for the carmaker to sell cars to large markets, the degree of specialization would necessarily decline, and along with it, the sophistication and value of the product, and the productivity of the workers.

It is truly a marvel to think of the degree of specialization of tasks required to make modern products. In a famous essay, Leonard Read attempts to outline the degree of cooperation needed to produce a modern pencil.[108] Even though a factory assembled and produced the pencil, there is no single human who knows how to produce the pencil from scratch. The factory that assembled it was merely one stage of a long production process involving countless specialized individuals worldwide. From the cutting of the wood, to the processing of the rubber that goes into the eraser, to the metals that go into the holder of the eraser, countless individuals had to cooperate to secure each of these materials in their raw form, transport them to the plants where they were processed, and turn them into the product that the pencil factory can assemble. This division of labor only becomes possible because of the large market in which these producers trade. Should all these people decide to not trade with the world, all their days would be spent on basic survival. By cooperating and trading, they are able to specialize in the production of highly sophisticated goods, with a high productivity, and to consume the products of the specialization of others at a very low cost. The extremely complex production of pencils is arranged, across the world, without a single central planner aware of all its details. The output is tens of billions of pencils produced each year, and available for increasingly cheap prices.

---

108 Read, Leonard. "I, Pencil: My Family Tree as Told to Leonard E. Read." *The Freeman*, Dec 1958.

As the market with which an individual is able to trade increases in size, the individual is able to select from a growing number of producers and sell to a growing number of consumers. He can specialize in increasingly specific tasks, which allows for an increase in the division of labor and the development of more sophisticated products. He is able to accumulate increasing quantities of capital to perform his task and thus achieve increasing productivity performing it. The best market with which an individual can trade is the largest market possible: the entire world. Individuals who live in countries with no or low trade tariffs are able to increase their productivity by specializing in very specific tasks they can sell to the highest bidder in the world, and they are able to increase their living standards by choosing the best and most affordable products for themselves from producers worldwide.

This insight also helps us understand why productivity, income, and quality of life rise as a society becomes better integrated into global trade. The tiny island of Saint Helena is located in the South Atlantic Ocean, 1,950 kilometers west of Cape Town and 4,000 kilometers east of Rio de Janeiro, and has a population of around 6,000 people. Trading with the rest of the world is very expensive for Saint Helenians, as it involves very high transportation costs. All capital imported to Saint Helena will be very expensive, making domestic production more expensive than better-integrated locations. Imported consumer goods for Saint Helenians are expensive because of the cost of trade, and their exports will be expensive to the rest of the world.

We can observe a similar pattern when government officials implement policies that effectively make their countries similar to Saint Helena in its isolation, namely trade restrictions. By imposing tariffs on trade, governments increase the cost of trading with the rest of the world, effectively reducing the extent of the market for individuals in their country. The world's goods become more expensive, and the possibilities for specializing are reduced. Among the most isolated economies on Earth are North Korea, Cuba, Eritrea, and Venezuela. Unsurprisingly, productivity and living standards in these economies are very low. In the past, when Venezuela was a free-market economy open to the world, it had one of the world's highest standards of living.

At the other extreme from Saint Helena and the isolationist economies stand the world's freest trading economies, whose citizens are able to trade with a very large global market regardless of the size of their own economies. The citizens of Hong Kong, Singapore, New Zealand, and Switzerland face the fewest impediments to trade with the rest of the world, and as a result, the productivity and living standards of their residents are among the highest in the world. When a citizen of an isolated economy wants to buy a good, she is only able to obtain it from domestic producers. When the citizen of an open economy wants to buy the same good, he is able to choose products from the entire planet. Citizens of the open economy can be far more productive because they can engage in production processes that sell to the entire planet, generating more revenue, and allowing for more investment in lengthening the production process and increasing its sophistication.

The absence of trade restrictions between the early American states significantly boosted the economic rise of the U.S. Free trade in North America allowed a very large population to trade among itself with increasing specialization, on top of having relatively low tariffs on international trade. By the end of the nineteenth century, the U.S. was the largest country in terms of population of all the western economies that industrialized in the nineteenth century, giving it a significant economic advantage and facilitating greater specialization and increased productivity. Had there been trade barriers erected between different states, it is highly unlikely the U.S. would have advanced as much economically.

Economics, as a field of study, attempts to explain the universal pervasiveness of trade. It is no wonder that humans are constantly attempting to engage in trade with one another, and trade encourages humans to moderate their aggressive and hostile instincts toward others and seek productive cooperation instead. The ability of strangers who are not connected by bonds of family or kinship to arrive at a mutually beneficial exchange is one of the basic building blocks of human civilization. The extent to which strangers can expect to deal peacefully with one another, respecting each other's bodies, property, and will, is the extent to which they live in a civilized human society.

Chapter 10

Money

> The services money renders are conditioned by the height of its purchasing power. Nobody wants to have in his cash holding a definite number of pieces of money or a definite weight of money; he wants to keep a cash holding of a definite amount of purchasing power. As the operation of the market tends to determine the final state of money's purchasing power at a height at which the supply of and the demand for money coincide, there can never be an excess or a deficiency of money.[109]
>
> —Ludwig von Mises

The Problem Money Solves

People who benefit from trade have an incentive to pursue more trade. But the main impediment to the expansion of trade between people is the problem of lack of coincidence of wants. When humans try to find solutions to this problem, their actions naturally lead to the emergence of money, which is defined as a general medium of exchange. By understanding how the problem of coincidence of wants is solved using money, we can discern the properties that matter for money to operate successfully, and as a result, understand the properties that make for good money that emerges freely on the market.

In large families or small tribes, trade is likely to be straightforward and

109 Mises, Ludwig von. *Human Action: The Scholar's Edition.* Ludwig von Mises Institute, 1998, p. 418.

direct. This is because everyone knows everyone else, the degree of specialization in production is very low, and there are a small number of goods and services available. In such a primitive setting, there is not much need for the emergence of money. With only a few goods available, individuals can trade these goods with one another directly. The hunter can just exchange his extra rabbits for fish from the fisherman, at whatever exchange rate the two find agreeable, in a transaction called **barter**. Because strong bonds exist between the people in a small group, individuals do not even need to provide present goods for immediate exchange; it is possible to exchange a present good for a promise of a good in the future. The hunter can give a farmer rabbits today in exchange for some of the farmer's grain crop in harvest season in a few months. Receiving a good today and promising repayment in the future is a transaction called **debt**.

Barter and debt are two ways of conducting trade, but they are only practical in specific, and increasingly rare, circumstances. Barter happens on the rare occasion in which a person wants to exchange a good for another good whose owner wants the first good. This is what is referred to as the **coincidence of wants**: Both parties to a transaction want exactly what the other party has to offer. The fisherman needs to find a hunter who is looking for fish, and the hunter needs to find a fisherman looking for rabbits. If rabbits and fish are the only goods in this economy, they are far more likely to find each other than if there were millions of other goods and services, as is the case in a modern economy. The more people in a society, and the larger the number of possible goods and products, the less likely it is for these two people to find one another for the trade to take place. In an economy in which there are only 100 people and 10 goods in total, everyone will be employed in the production of one of these goods, and everyone will need to obtain a supply of these goods. The odds of finding a trading partner whose wants coincide with yours decline drastically as the number of people in an economy, and the number of goods and services available, increases.

In the modern world, where a large variety of goods and services exist, barter is practically nonexistent. Siblings and friends might, by virtue of their proximity, identify occasions for direct exchange and engage in it. But nobody in their right mind wakes up thinking of how to find a way to exchange goods and services for one another directly. The search costs would likely exceed the gains from the exchange. No group larger than a small tribe with very few goods can ever have an economy built on barter.

The same analysis applies to the use of debt as a medium of exchange. In a small society where individuals have strong bonds and depend on repeated interaction with one another for survival, it is possible to use debt to facilitate trade. But as the size of society increases, and as interactions begin to take place between strangers who are highly unlikely to have repeated interactions with one another, the use of debt becomes unworkable. As an economy grows, trusting a trade partner becomes a more risky proposition. There is no good reason for someone to accept a promise of payment from a stranger they may never see again, as there is no good reason to believe that a stranger cares about his reputation with someone he might not meet again.

As more individuals enter an economy and the number of goods multiplies, the coincidence-of-wants problem becomes more pronounced. Human reason can find a solution to the problem by engaging in **indirect exchange**: Selling goods for a good whose only purpose is to be exchanged for the desired good. In indirect exchange, an individual will acquire a good not because she wants it, but because she wants to exchange it for something she actually wants. When the fisherman discovers that a hunter with a rabbit he wants is not interested in fish but is looking for grain, the fisherman can exchange his fish for grain and give the grain to the hunter in exchange for rabbits. Grain, to the fisherman, is not a consumer good, it is a **medium of exchange**: It is a good acquired not for the sake of its own utility, but for the sake of exchanging it for the good the holder actually desires.

Man's ability to reason makes it inevitable that these indirect exchange transactions would emerge to solve the problem of coincidence of wants. Man's actions, however, have consequences that extend beyond the aims of direct reason. As the scope of markets expands and humans increasingly resort to indirect exchange, it is only natural that some goods will perform that function better than others, with important consequences to the parties involved. "Salability" is the term Carl Menger gave to the property that makes a money desirable, and the more salable a good is, the more successful it is as a money. Understanding the function of medium of exchange allows us to understand the properties that make a specific type of money desirable.

Salability

Menger defines **salability** as the ease with which a good can be sold in a market at any convenient time at current prevalent prices. The more salable a good, the more likely the owner is to obtain a prevalent and undiscounted market price in exchange for his good when he chooses to sell it. A good with low salability is a good whose owner would expect to offer a significant discount on the price of the good if he wanted to sell it quickly. A highly salable good is one with significant market depth and liquidity, making it possible for the holder to obtain the prevailing market price whenever they want to sell it.

A great example of a highly salable good today is the one-hundred-dollar bill, accepted worldwide by merchants and currency exchange shops more frequently than any other physical monetary medium. A holder of a hundred-dollar bill who is looking to exchange it for goods and services will rarely ever need to sell it for something else to provide to a seller he is conducting a transaction with, nor will anyone with a hundred-dollar bill ever need to sell it at a discount. The holder will usually find someone to take it off their hands quickly and at face value. By contrast, a good with low salability is one for which demand on the market is intermittent and varied, making it difficult to sell the good quickly and requiring its owner to offer a discount in order to do it quickly. A great example of this is a house, car, or other forms of durable consumer goods. Selling a house is much harder than selling a one-hundred-dollar bill because it involves viewings and significant transaction costs, as well as waiting for the right buyer who values the house at the seller's asking price. The seller might need to offer a significant discount to sell the house quickly. In capital markets, the most salable instruments are U.S. Treasury bonds, which at the time of writing are collectively worth around $28 trillion. Most large and institutional investors use U.S. government bonds as their store of value and treasury reserve asset because it is easy to liquidate large quantities without causing large movements in the market.

Central to Menger's analysis of salability is the measure of the spread between the bid and ask prices for assets. The bid is the maximum price a buyer is willing to pay, and the ask is the minimum price a seller is willing to take. Bringing large quantities of a good to market would cause the spread between the bid and ask prices to widen because, as the marginal utility of the good declines with increased quantities, potential buyers begin to offer lower prices. The more a good's marginal utility declines with rising quantities, the less suited it is to the role of money. The smaller the decline in a good's marginal utility, the less the bid-ask spread will widen as larger quantities are brought to the market, the more salable the good is, and the more suitable it is for use as money.

We can also understand this process from the perspective of traders and merchants buying goods to sell later. For them, growing stockpiles of a good reduce the chance of each marginal good being sold and increase the risk of price declines hurting the seller. Thus, they will bid at lower levels for increasing quantities of a good. The faster the spread between the bid and ask grows, the less salable the good. Goods for which the spread rises slowly are more salable goods, and these goods are more likely to be hoarded by anyone looking to transfer wealth across space or time. In other words, the most salable goods will fluctuate the least in relation to the quantity brought to a given market.

Many factors, discussed below, can affect the salability of goods, resulting in a wide variety of degrees of salability. The goods with the highest salability are the ones whose marginal utility declines the least with increasing stockpiles, since increasing stockpiles can be easily exchanged for other goods. Menger defines money as the most salable good. During the natural course of market transactions, some goods will emerge to have a lower diminishing marginal utility and a higher salability than other goods, encouraging people to hold them more, which leads to increased liquidity of the good and further increases in salability. This process will naturally amplify the salability of the most salable goods, thereby concentrating the monetary role in the most salable goods. Eventually, this monetary role will concentrate in one good alone, the most salable good, the generalized medium of exchange: money, the good whose marginal utility declines the least.

The numerical example below can help us understand the salability of money. For simplicity, it is assumed that the market price of each apple, orange, and banana is the same as one monetary unit, and the utility is expressed in cardinal terms, though it should be well understood that humans only understand utility in ordinal terms, as discussed above.

Good	Apple	Orange	Banana	Money
1st unit utility	100	90	85	100 (1st apple)
2nd unit utility	80	70	65	90 (1st orange)
3rd unit utility	60	50	45	85 (1st banana)
4th unit utility	40	30	25	80 (2nd apple)
5th unit utility	20	10	5	70 (2nd orange)
6th unit utility	0	0	0	65 (2nd banana)

Table 1. Money's diminishing utility

As the marginal utility of each good declines, the marginal utility of the monetary units declines less than the utility of the good declines. Being the most salable good, money is the easiest good to exchange for consumer goods, and this makes it a more desirable option for accepting payment. For this individual, accepting money as payment is a superior option to accepting apples, oranges, or bananas, because the money is easily exchangeable for whichever of these consumer goods the individual will value the most at any future point in time. Some economic goods are more suitable than others to fulfill the role of medium of exchange. The more suitable a good is to use for exchange, the more marketable or salable it is.

Understanding the problem money solves can help us identify the properties that characterize a good solution—in other words, they help us identify what makes something a good money. The lack of coincidence of wants is the problem money solves, and it manifests across several dimensions. There is the lack of coincidence of wants in the goods themselves, as discussed in the fish, rabbits, and grains example above. Beyond that, there is the lack of coincidence of wants across space. That is, a person might want to sell something in one location and obtain a good in exchange for it in another location. Trading your apples for a car would be hard enough in most scenarios, but it would still be harder if you needed to lug your apples 1,000 miles in order to conduct the transaction.

The third dimension to the coincidence of wants is the lack of a coincidence of wants across scales. When individuals want to directly exchange goods of different sizes and values, a partial exchange is not always possible. The person who wants to sell apples cannot exchange each apple for a small part of a car from someone and then assemble the parts into one car. It would be impractical and inefficient to engage in trade with such different goods. Reason suggests some other, more divisible medium of exchange will solve the problem.

In addition to the dimensions of the good, space, and scale, there is a fourth dimension to the coincidence of wants: The lack of coincidence of time frames for trading, since a person might either want to sell an object today or over a period of time in order to obtain another good in the future. A person might want to sell apples over a three-year period in order to buy a car. It is not possible to accumulate three years' worth of apples to exchange for a car, as the apples will spoil. Man's reason naturally leads him to see the convenience of exchanging apples to accumulate a medium of exchange—one that will not rot or be eaten by worms—with which to purchase a car in the future.

By examining the different axes along which the problem of coincidence of wants emerges, it becomes possible to identify the properties that make for a good monetary medium. The characteristics that make something a good medium of exchange are what make it a good solution to the coincidence-of-wants problem in its four dimensions. As Murray Rothbard put it: "Tending to increase the marketability of a commodity are its demand for use by more people, its divisibility into small units without loss of value, its durability, and its transportability over large distances."[110]

---

110 Rothbard, Murray. *Man, Economy, and State, with Power and Market.* Ludwig von Mises Institute, 1962, p. 190.

Lack of coincidence of wants across	Description	Monetary property that solves it
Goods	I want to buy a good whose seller doesn't want what I have	Concentration into as few media as possible
Space	I want to sell something in one location and buy something elsewhere	Transportable
Scale	I want to sell something large and buy something small	Homogeneous, divisible & groupable
Time	I want to sell something today so I could buy something in the future	Durable, hard to make

Table 2. Dimensions of the problem of coincidence of wants

The third facet of the problem of coincidence of wants helps us understand why metals were naturally a superior choice of monetary medium to artifacts and other consumer goods. Because metals are made up of a homogenous substance, large quantities of metal can be divided into smaller denominations, while small quantities can be combined into larger pieces without significant loss of economic value or a change in the metal's physical properties. Metal, then, is highly divisible and groupable. This is not a property of artifact monies like seashells, cattle, and glass beads.

The second facet of the problem of coincidence of wants, salability across space, helps us understand the ancient suitability of casting gold and silver in a monetary role, and the modern limitations that prevent these metals from playing this role today. Being inert, silver and gold do not rot, ruin, rust, or disintegrate. These metals can be transported relatively easily, with little fear that transportation will alter their properties or compromise their integrity. As they can condense large amounts of economic value into small weights, these metals were particularly economical to move around compared with other monetary media. But as modern telecommunication and transportation industries grew more sophisticated with the arrival of the Industrial Revolution in the nineteenth century, the world became far more interconnected, and the scope of global trade began to expand across space. With increasingly global and long-distance trade, the movement of physical gold and silver was no longer an economical method of conducting trade. Credit based on these metals emerged as a medium of exchange in its own right, and eventually, government capture of banking institutions allowed government credit to effectively displace gold and silver in World War I, as discussed in more detail in *The Fiat Standard*.

Historically, silver and gold had a dual monetary role as they complemented each other in terms of salability across scales. Gold, being more valuable, was difficult to divide into very small pieces for transactions of small value, while silver, being less valuable, was not very suitable for large transactions. Historically, copper also served as a monetary medium used for smaller units of value than silver. Over time, copper and silver lost their monetary roles for reasons pertaining to salability across time, as discussed below. With the globalization of markets and an unprecedented degree of international trade at the end of the nineteenth century, the global economy settled on one money, gold, as the solution to the problem of coincidence of wants.

Salability across Time

The fourth facet of the coincidence-of-wants problem pertains to the ability to exchange value across time. To preserve or exchange value over time requires a medium of exchange that can hold its value across time without much loss. The better a medium of exchange is at holding its value across time, the more suitable and desirable it is as a medium of exchange. This helps us understand why metals would have a monetary role, as they are generally durable, and why precious metals—like gold and silver in particular—would have a more prominent, long-lasting monetary role than base metals like iron and copper. Being inert and indestructible gave precious metals a significant advantage over metals that disintegrate over time. But the real advantage of these metals lies not merely in their durability, but in the effect of this durability on their supply dynamics. The major feature distinguishing precious metals from all other forms of money is the relative magnitude of their stockpiles to their annual production. As these metals do not corrode or ruin, their stockpiles continue to grow over time, and rarely ever become depleted. As technology advances and humans find more ingenious ways of increasing the supply of these metals, the stockpiles continue to grow, and existing production continues to be a small fraction of total liquid stockpiles.

This property is known as hardness, meaning the difficulty of increasing the existing liquid stockpiles of a good. And we can quantify hardness using a simple metric, the stock-to-flow ratio, wherein stock refers to the total above-ground liquid stockpiles that can be used in a monetary role, while flow refers to new annual mining output. This metric is simply the inverse of the annual supply growth rate, and theoretical reasoning as well as historical evidence indicate that this metric matters enormously when determining monetary status. All metals that can corrode are constantly being consumed in industrial processes, which alter their chemical properties and eliminate them from stockpiles used to store value. For all these metals, existing liquid stockpiles are of the same order of magnitude as the annual production of the metal. There are very few stockpiles of copper, nickel, brass, and other metals for use as a liquid store of value. To the extent such stockpiles exist, they are held in reserve for producers who use large quantities of them and need them to hedge against potential supply problems stalling their production. The production of these metals is constantly being deployed for industrial use, so the stockpiles do not increase significantly. New production is thus significant compared to existing stockpiles, making the price of the metal highly vulnerable to supply shocks. Such metals are unsuited to playing a monetary role, since their salability across time can be compromised by supply shocks, and their employment as a monetary medium will necessarily bring about the supply shocks that destroy their monetary role.

To understand why, we must first distinguish between **market demand** for a good, where consumers demand the good in order to hold it or consume it for its own sake and properties, and **monetary demand** for a good, where consumers hold the good merely as a monetary medium, with the aim of exchanging it later for other goods and services. A person can choose any good as their store of value and medium of exchange and with that choice, she adds monetary demand on top of its market demand, resulting in an increase in its market price. This will naturally lead to an increase in the quantity of resources, capital, and labor dedicated to its production. This is where the stock-to-flow matters. If the good has a low stock-to-flow ratio, the portion of the liquid supply on the market that is produced by miners will be very high, and increases in mining output will correspond to large increases in liquid market supply, thus bringing the price down and punishing the savers. The market is highly responsive to miners' increases in production because the daily liquidity on the market arises primarily from miners' new production, and not from the stockpiles held by consumers, as consumers predominantly hold the good to deploy it in market production and not to resell it. The predominantly industrial nature of these metals means that anyone using them as money is simply donating their wealth to miners in a process we could describe as the easy-money trap. Storing value in a good with a low stock-to-flow ratio simply causes that value to be captured by the producers of the good.

In order for a commodity to resist the easy-money trap, and have good salability across time, its liquid stockpiles must be significantly larger than annual mining production, so when its monetary demand increases, increases in mining production will have little impact on market conditions, since mining output is only a small fraction of the liquid supply being traded. With a high stock-to-flow ratio, increases in monetary demand translate to increases in price, but when the stock-to-flow ratio is low, these increases translate to increased miner profits.

Hard money is money whose stockpiles are hard to increase significantly, no matter what its producers do, since the producers' output is a tiny fraction of the existing stockpiles. Easy money is money whose liquid stockpiles are easy to increase. This term applies equally to commodity monies and to national currencies. Easy money is common vernacular across the world, particularly in countries cursed with bad monetary policies, where citizens understand full well the desirability of relatively hard national currencies like the dollar and the euro on the one hand, and the lack of desirability of their local currency, which is easy for the local government and central banking cartel to produce in increasing quantities.

The stock-to-flow metric has a value close to 1 for all metals, except gold and silver. As base metals' production is constantly being consumed in industrial applications, existing liquid stockpiles are never significantly higher than annual production. Because these metals also rust and corrode in various ways, there is little incentive to store large quantities for the long term. The 3 main exchange warehouses for copper consistently hold less than 1,000,000 tons of copper between them, whereas annual copper production is around 25,000,000 tons.[111] Even if global copper warehouses contained 20 times more copper than the 3 main ones, that would still not suffice to raise copper's stock-to-flow above 1. In September 2020, zinc stockpiles at the 3 main exchanges totaled 133,300 tons, while annual production was around 13,000,000 tons, around 100 times larger than the stockpile, giving zinc a stock-to-flow ratio of 0.01.[112]

Because gold cannot be consumed or altered as a metal, it is mainly acquired to be held as a liquid monetary asset, so existing stockpiles are usually many orders of magnitude larger than annual production. Even as annual production increases with increased efficiency, stockpiles also continue to increase, ensuring that the stock-to-flow ratio remains significantly higher than 1. Examining the data over the last century shows that gold's stock-to-flow ratio has remained consistently around 60, translating to an annual supply growth rate of around 1.5%. Even as annual production of gold continues to increase over time, stockpiles also increase, and the ratio remains roughly constant, as can be seen in Figure 6.

Silver is similar to gold in having a stock-to-flow ratio higher than 1, but historically, its stock-to-flow ratio has declined as increasing quantities of silver used in industrial applications are effectively taken out of the liquid stockpiles. If one were to measure the silver stock-to-flow ratio based on the

---

111 These are the stockpiles held by the London Metals Exchange, Shanghai Futures Exchange, and COMEX.

112 Lutter Sina, and Heinz Jürgen Büchner. "Short Term Commodity Outlook September: Aluminum & Zinc." *Euroguss*, NürnbergMesse, 8 Sep 2022.

total stock of above-ground silver, then its stock-to-flow ratio is between 30 and 60.[113] But the silver deployed in industrial applications cannot be counted as part of the liquid stockpile since it cannot play a monetary role, nor can it be used to settle trade and debt. The price of electronics, machinery, cutlery, or jewelry that contains silver is not a function of the monetary price of the silver it contains, which usually represents a tiny fraction of the total price, but of the consumer valuation of the good itself—as a consumer or capital good, not as a monetary good. Trying to extract the silver from these goods to convert it into a monetary asset, in the shape of bars or coins, is a costly process no different from extracting silver from the crust of Earth. When the measure of stockpiles used refers only to monetary stockpiles, in the form of silver bars, coins, and investment products, then the stock-to-flow ratio is closer to 4. This is still significantly higher than nonmonetary metals whose stock-to-flow ratio is a fraction of 1, but nowhere near high enough to hold on to value well enough to maintain a monetary role. That is why, as silver's market value has declined relative to gold over the past century and a half, its nonmonetary uses have grown to consume the majority of its existing stockpiles.

If one were to consider all the silver deployed in industrial applications as part of the silver stockpile, then silver's stock-to-flow ratio would be significantly higher. As nonmonetary uses of silver have grown, they have effectively consumed the stockpile of monetary silver and brought silver's stock-to-flow ratio down. Concomitantly, silver's market value has declined in real terms.

Silver's demonetization arguably has its roots in the metal's lower stock-to-flow ratio and the advancement of modern banking. As modern banking and telecommunication technology advanced in the nineteenth century, people could transact with financial instruments such as paper money, checks, and letters of credit backed by gold held by banks and central banks. This made gold transactions possible at any scale, thus obviating silver's monetary role,

---

113 See: Nieuwenhuijs, Jan. "How Much Silver Is Above Ground?" *Voima Gold*, 2 Dec 2019. Nieuwenhuijs considers jewelry and industrial silver a part of the monetary stockpile, which he estimates at 1,750,000 tons, compared to an annual production of approximately 27,000 tons. But removing jewelry and industrial-use silver from the monetary stockpile reduces drastically, to around 108,000 tons, giving silver a stock-to-flow ratio of 4.

which was primarily geared to small transactions, and allowing everyone to hold the assets with the highest stock-to-flow and the greatest likelihood of appreciating.

Silver's demonetization took off in earnest in 1871, after the end of the Franco-Prussian war. Germany, which was then the largest economy still on a silver standard, asked for its indemnity from France in gold and used the indemnity to switch to a gold standard. As Germany's demand for silver declined and its demand for gold rose, the value of silver began to decline from its ratio to gold of around 15:1, causing economic losses for silver holders and countries on a silver standard, encouraging them to drop their silver in exchange for gold. Since then, the ratio of gold price to silver price has just been rising; it is currently around 80, or more than 5 times its ratio 150 years ago. Countries that were late to abandon the silver standard, such as India and China, experienced severe economic hardships from the decline in the value of their currency.

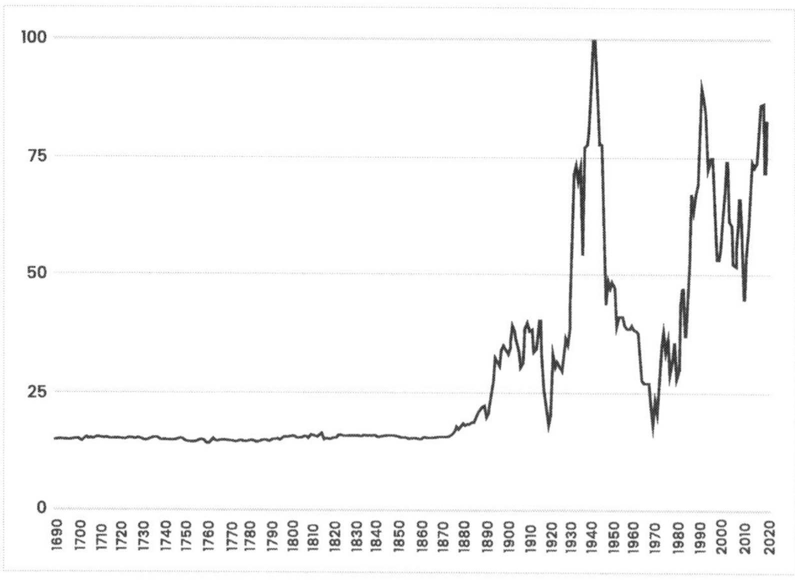

Figure 19. Gold/silver ratio

The high stock-to-flow ratio of gold destined it to play a monetary role, because it gives it the best salability across time. As the production of gold adds only small increments to the stockpile of the metal, it makes it hold its value better over time, causing a growth in the market value stored in it over time, through its appreciation against other commodities. This increase in the value of balances held in a medium corresponds to an increase in the liquidity of the market, a decline in the bid-ask spread, and therefore an increase in the marketability of the commodity. This trend is only amplified as people become more aware of it, allocating their cash balances to the good with the best expectation of future value and the smallest bid-ask spread.

The framework of salability across time and stock-to-flow ratio are particularly interesting tools to use to analyze the rise of bitcoin, a new monetary phenomenon with a pre-programmed supply schedule and a stock-to-flow ratio that constantly increases until it reaches infinity. This analytical framework forms the foundation of my first book, *The Bitcoin Standard.*

Why One Money?

Increased monetary demand for the most salable commodity will further increase its price and value, thus enhancing its salability across time even further and amplifying the size of its liquidity. As wealth will naturally concentrate in the most salable commodities, this further amplifies their salability. Holders of the most salable commodity will have a larger market and a larger amount of liquidity with which to trade. Increasing use as money further enhances a good's value as money, thus amplifying the incentive to use it as money, resulting in a winner-take-all dynamic in the market for money. The historical record shows this to be the case. The entire planet had converged on gold as money by the end of the nineteenth century, even as many thousands of different goods had been used for this role across the planet. The survival of silver's monetary role into the nineteenth century was a result of its superior salability at small scales, but as modern banking obviated this, gold became the world's money. Something similar is happening in the modern global market for government monies, where there appears to be an insatiable demand for the most marketable government money, the U.S. dollar. Not only are large numbers of non-Americans seeking to hold the U.S. dollar as opposed to their national currency, virtually all national currencies are backed by dollars, as their central banks hold large quantities of dollars they use for international trade.

The more common the medium of exchange, the more salable it is and the larger the potential market its holder can sell to. Individuals will naturally gravitate toward the most salable goods, and that in turn will amplify their salability, attracting more individuals to use them. Rothbard explained the process as follows: "As the more marketable commodities in any society begin to be picked by individuals as media of exchange, their choices will quickly focus on the few most marketable commodities available."[114]

The fundamental problem of coincidence of wants involves the coincidence of desires for goods. As the size of an economy grows, so does the degree of specialization and the number of goods that can be produced, thus complicating the possibilities for direct exchange. The only possible solution to this problem, and the only way a market's extent can grow, is to employ indirect exchange, wherein people acquire goods purely for the purpose of later exchanging them for other goods. As humans indirectly exchange various goods, it is only natural that some goods will play the role of medium of exchange better than others, rewarding those who employ them and punishing those who employ media of exchange that are unsuited for this role. As time goes by, the benefits of employing the suitable media of exchange become more pronounced, as do the harms from employing bad media of exchange. People who adopt nondurable, non-homogenous, non-divisible, and non-transportable goods will witness their wealth decline over time, while those who adopt durable, homogenous, highly divisible, transportable goods will witness it increase. As time goes by, primitive and unsuitable monetary media are discarded and ignored as their users lose their wealth, and in the long run, the most important metric in determining monetary status becomes the metric of hardness, or stock-to-flow ratio.

---

114 Rothbard, Murray. *Man, Economy, and State, with Power and Market*. Ludwig von Mises Institute, 1962, p. 191.

The process of monetary competition is driven both by human action and the brute physical, chemical, and geological realities governing the production of different goods. Intelligent individuals will use their reason to try to arrive at the best form of money to use, but even if no one were to think of this, economic reality would impose itself to produce a similar outcome. Those who use the best monies will accumulate more wealth, whereas those who use unsuitable monies will lose their wealth, and over time, the majority of wealth will end up concentrated with those who use suitable monies, whether they consciously desired this outcome or not.

The above analysis explains the emergence of money through its suitability to perform the quintessential function of money: To act as a medium of exchange. Rothbard defined money as a commodity that comes into general use as a medium of exchange. While the concept of a medium of exchange is a precise one, the concept of a "general medium of exchange" is not. It is easy to identify something that is functioning as a medium of exchange, but identifying it as a *general* medium of exchange is a matter of subjective judgment.

Money and the State

The Austrian approach to economics as the study of human action can help us understand and identify the goods likely to earn a monetary role just by analyzing the way humans act to solve the problems of exchange. Even before humans could record their actions, they engaged in direct and indirect exchange. And as humans seek to satisfy their desires through indirect exchange, some goods begin to play that role better than others, and those who employ these media of exchange benefit from using them. Others copy them, and the successful solutions become more widespread. If they do not copy the successful solutions, they lose wealth to those who do. The better solutions impose themselves as economic reality always does, by rewarding those who adopt them and punishing those who do not. There is no need for a central authority to decree a medium of exchange and compel everyone to accept it. Money emerges from the market, out of the actions of humans, and not as a result of any central-planning government.

As Carl Menger explained: "Money is not an invention of the state. It is not the product of a legislative act. Even the sanction of political authority is not necessary for its existence. Certain commodities came to be money quite naturally, as the result of economic relationships that were independent of the power of the state."[115] Certain goods will naturally succeed at playing the role of money better than others, and the market process will bring these to the fore and cause their adoption as money to grow. The process is no different from the selection of particular commodities for the production of a consumer good: Like leather is used for shoes, gasoline for car propulsion, and silicon for electronics, the market process results in the selection of the most salable goods as money.

Mises went further than Menger in explaining how the choice of money can emerge purely on the market through his **regression theorem**, which explained how a normal market good can develop into a monetary good when it acquires monetary demand, thus raising its value and increasing its salability. As the good acquires increasing monetary demand, its price increases beyond its market demand price.

The process of monetary emergence and selection by the market can be understood entirely with reference to human action. There is no need to invoke any coercive authority to select or manufacture a monetary medium. Money, like all goods, emerges on the market because it offers a utility that makes individuals give value to it. The historical and empirical record supports this contention, as it clearly shows that monetary media predate government monetary mandates. Gold's global monetary role was not conferred by some government authority. It won its monetary role on the market, and government authorities had to accept gold as money on the market if they wanted to operate successfully. Gold did not become money because it was minted into government coins. Government coins became money because they were minted from gold.

History shows no single example of a good or asset gaining its monetary role through government mandate. Modern government money is referred to

---

115 Menger, Carl. *Principles of Economics*. Ludwig von Mises Institute, 2007, p. 261-2.

as fiat money, based on the Latin word *fiat*, which denotes the decree of authority. Yet, it did not become money by fiat. All existing government monies originally acquired their monetary role through the free market's choice for money, gold. Only by hitching their monetary wagons to the market's choice could government "fiat" be accepted as money in the first place, and only by fraudulently revoking their money's redemption for gold did "fiat" money come into existence, not by pure fiat. The eventual severing of gold redemption does not alter the fact that no money ever gained its monetary role by fiat. Further, the continued need for governments to impose monopolies on banking and legal tender laws illustrates that their imposition of money cannot survive free-market competition. Governments could not decree monetary value away from gold; they confiscated it by force and accumulated it. And still, more than a century after the end of the gold standard, the world's central banks continue to stockpile ever-increasing quantities of gold.

Another powerful refutation of the statist theories of money comes from the emergence of bitcoin, which in the last 14 years has grown from nothing to become one of the world's 20 largest currencies, all without a single legal authority promoting or decreeing its use. El Salvador announced bitcoin as legal tender in 2021, but that came after bitcoin had already grown to become one of the world's 10 largest currencies in total valuation. As with gold, silver, and all forms of money, statist recognition follows economic reality; it does not predate or dictate it. Had money been an invention of the state, and had it needed state sanction to operate, bitcoin could not have functioned as successfully as it has.

Value of Money

Like the previous methods of economizing, money is a tool humans use to increase the quantity and value of the time they have on Earth. The introduction of money to an economy will reinforce all three drivers of economic growth and progress. We can understand the economic significance of money with reference to the three main functions it performs: Medium of exchange, store of value, and unit of account.

1- Increase the division of labor

As money eliminates the problem of coincidence of wants, it allows for a larger scope of trade between strangers who do not need to trust each other or be part of political and economic structures that protect them. The establishment of a money on the market increases the scope for **specialization and division of labor**, immensely widening the market for every consumer and every product. The more effective a monetary medium is at holding its value across space, and the more commonly it is held by others, the more potential trading opportunities it offers to its holder and the larger the extent of the market. As individuals realize they can meet an increasing number of their needs by exchanging goods with others, they are more likely to seek cooperation and peace with strangers they will never interact with twice. With money, human labor, capital accumulation, technological innovations, and trade take place in a large extended system of impersonal exchange. People who do not know each other, and who do not coordinate with one another directly, nonetheless manage to collaborate to produce highly sophisticated products over complex production structures. Money is an essential tool for human civilization, and its destruction has always coincided with the destruction of society and civilized living.

2- Allow for economic calculation

An important implication of the use of money is that all prices are expressed in terms of one good. In an economy with money, money is one half of every transaction. A barter economy with 10 goods would require 45 different prices, each expressing one good in terms of another (number of individual prices = *n(n-1)/2, where n=number of goods*). In contrast, a money economy with 10 goods (including the monetary good) would require only 9 prices (number of individual prices = *n-1*). The number of prices in a barter economy increases exponentially with the number of goods whereas the relationship between the number of prices and goods in a money economy is linear. We can see that a barter economy with 100 goods would require 4,450 different prices whereas a money economy with 100 goods would only require 99 prices. A barter economy with 1,000,000 goods would require 500 billion different prices but a money economy with 1,000,000 goods would require only 999,999 prices. The introduction of money to an economy thereby drastically reduces the number of prices required for exchange, bringing extraordinary efficiency to trade and markets.

Expressing the price of all goods in terms of the quantity of one good allows individuals to perform the enormously important process of economic calculation, which will be the focus of Chapter 12. With all prices in one unit, the entrepreneur is able to carefully calculate the costs and revenues expected from an undertaking. With calculation around the common denominator that is money, individuals can "construct an ever-expanding edifice of remote stages of production to arrive at desired goods because money allows for sophisticated calculation," as Rothbard put it.[116]

The degree of specialization that exists in the modern global economy is only possible with the use of money. Individuals are able to produce goods with absolutely no regard for their own consumption of the goods, knowing they can exchange them on the market for the most salable good, which they can then exchange for whatever goods they want. Complex processes of production and long supply chains are only possible thanks to the specialization allowed by money.

3- Lower time preference

Money, as a medium of exchanging value, allows its holders to preserve and transfer value to the future more efficiently than they would otherwise. Money, as explained above, will have higher salability than other market goods and will naturally end up being a good with high salability across time; it will therefore hold value better than most other market goods. As its salability allows for increasing provision for the future, the uncertainty of the future decreases, and individuals' discounting of the future decreases. The decline in the discounting of the future is simply the lowering of time preference discussed in chapters 3 and 13.

---

116 Rothbard, Murray. *Man, Economy, and State, with Power and Market.* Ludwig von Mises Institute, 1962, p. 193.

Money can thus be understood as an important technology for the lowering of human time preference, as it is an extremely powerful tool for providing for the future, reducing the uncertainty around it, and allowing its holder to plan for it. Hedging against uncertainty is one of the main functions of money,[117] and it is the reason that people prefer to hold some money rather than just holding capital goods, even though the latter produce a yield whereas the former does not. Investments are less salable and involve entrepreneurial risk. Money, at least in a free market, is the good with the most salability and least risk; it is the good that can always be converted to other goods with the smallest loss of its economic value. Money may not have a yield, but it is still held because it has the least uncertainty of all assets.[118] Time preference is a measure of the discounting of the future, and uncertainty is a major contributor to the discounting of the future. Access to money, and in particular good and hard money, is a way to mitigate this uncertainty.

Hans-Hermann Hoppe said that the lowering of time preference initiates the process of civilization.[119] Money plays a central role in that, and the harder the money is, the better it is at holding its value into the future and the less uncertain the future will be. And the more humans can plan for their future and thrive in the long run, the more money will cause time preference to decline and civilization to thrive.

Money's Uniqueness

Money as a good is distinct from other goods in several ways. The first distinction is that money is neither a consumption good nor a capital good. Consumption goods are acquired to be consumed because they serve to satisfy human needs. Capital goods, on the other hand, do not satisfy human needs directly, but they are acquired because they can be used to produce goods that

---

117 Hoppe, Hans-Hermann. ""The Yield From Money Held" Reconsidered." Ludwig von Mises Institute, 14 May 2009.

118 Ibid.

119 Hoppe, Hans-Hermann. *Democracy: The God That Failed.* Transaction Publishers, 2001, p. 7.

satisfy human needs. Money, however, is neither of these things. It is not acquired because it satisfies human needs, nor can it be used for the production of other goods; it is acquired purely to be exchanged in the future for other goods, be they consumption or capital goods.

Use as a medium of exchange is the quintessential function of money, and this means it requires no direct utility for humans to value it. The utility of money is derived from the utility of the goods it can be exchanged for. Money, like all goods, will have a diminishing marginal utility, but its marginal utility declines less than the marginal utility of all other goods, since each successive unit of money can be used to buy a unit from the next most valuable unit of any good and not just the next most valuable unit of the same good. For example, in an economy with money and only three goods, bananas, apples, and oranges, the utility of money will decline less than the utility of apples, oranges, and bananas each declines. Being liquid and easily exchangeable for other goods makes money a more useful thing to hold than other goods because it can easily be exchanged for whichever good the individual happens to value most at any time. This salability is the reason people prefer to be paid in money rather than in objects of limited salability. The high salability gives money the utility of whatever good happens to be most valuable to the holder of money at any time.

How Much Money Should There Be?

Perhaps the single most important monetary distinction between mainstream and Austrian economists is that Austrians think the absolute quantity of money is unimportant, and consequently, the money supply does not need to grow to satisfy the needs of a growing economy. Any supply of money is enough for any economy, as long as it is divisible. Money is unique from all economic goods in that it is the one good whose absolute quantity does not matter to its holder. Money does not offer any services to the holder except the ability to exchange it for other goods, making its own quantity irrelevant to the holder. The only aspect of money that matters to the holder is its purchasing power. The economic value of money lies in its ability to be exchanged for other goods, and so the value of money comes from its purchasing power, not from its quantity. Any supply of any money can be enough for any economy provided it can be divided up into small enough units.

As Rothbard explains:

> [M]oney is fundamentally different from consumers' and producers' goods in at least one vital respect. Other things being equal, an increase in the supply of consumers' goods benefits society since one or more consumers will be better off. The same is true of an increase in the supply of producers' goods, which will be eventually transformed into an increased supply of consumers' goods; for production itself is the process of transforming natural resources into new forms and locations desired by consumers for direct use. But money is very different: money is not used directly in consumption or production but is exchanged for such directly usable goods. Yet, once any commodity or object is established as a money, it performs the maximum exchange work of which it is capable. An increase in the supply of money causes no increase whatever in the exchange service of money; all that happens is that the purchasing power of each unit of money is diluted by the increased supply of units. Hence there is never a social need for increasing the supply of money, either because of an increased supply of goods or because of an increase in population. People can acquire an increased proportion of cash balances with a fixed supply of money by spending less and thereby increasing the purchasing power of their cash balances, thus raising their real cash balances overall.[120]

Rothbard follows up by quoting Mises:

> The services money renders are conditioned by the height of its purchasing power. Nobody wants to have in his cash holding a definite number of pieces of money or a definite weight of money; he wants to keep a cash holding of a definite amount of purchasing power. As the operation of the

120 Rothbard, Murray. *Economic Controversies*. Ludwig von Mises Institute, 2011, p. 698-9.

> market tends to determine the final state of money's purchasing power at a height at which the supply of and the demand for money coincide, there can never be an excess or a deficiency of money. Each individual and all individuals together always enjoy fully the advantages which they can derive from indirect exchange and the use of money, no matter whether the total quantity of money is great or small. Changes in money's purchasing power generate changes in the disposition of wealth among the various members of society. From the point of view of people eager to be enriched by such changes, the supply of money may be called insufficient or excessive, and the appetite for such gains may result in policies designed to bring about cash-induced alterations in purchasing power. However, the services which money renders can be neither improved nor repaired by changing the supply of money. There may appear an excess or a deficiency of money in an individual's cash holding. But such a condition can be remedied by increasing or decreasing consumption or investment. (Of course, one must not fall prey to the popular confusion between the demand for money for cash holding and the appetite for more wealth.) The quantity of money available in the whole economy is always sufficient to secure for everybody all that money does and can do.[121]

Rothbard adds:

> A world of constant money supply would be one similar to that of much of the eighteenth and nineteenth centuries, marked by the successful flowering of the Industrial Revolution with increased capital investment increasing the supply of goods and with falling prices for those goods as well as falling costs of production.[122]

According to the Austrian view, if the money supply is fixed, then economic growth will cause prices of real goods and services to drop, allowing people

---

121 Mises, Ludwig von. *Human Action: The Scholar's Edition*. Ludwig von Mises Institute, 1998, p. 418.

122 Rothbard, Murray. *Economic Controversies*. Ludwig von Mises Institute, 2011, p. 699.

to purchase increasing quantities of goods and services with their money in the future. Such a world would indeed discourage immediate consumption, just like the Keynesians fear it would, but it would also encourage saving and investment for the future, when more consumption can happen. Since Keynesian economists exhibit little understanding of the concept of capital and marginal analysis, they imagine a decline in consumption as a calamity. If aggregate spending declines in high-time preference Keynesian economic models, workers will be laid off, which will in turn result in even less spending, which results in more workers getting laid off, and a continuous downward spiral that ends in destitution. Only active central governments spending liberally can forestall the Keynesians' nightmare.

But to non-Keynesians—that is, to economists familiar with the concept of capital—a decline in spending is not just harmless, it is the basic bedrock of civilized society. It is only by reducing consumption and increasing saving that the deployment of capital is possible, as discussed in Chapter 6. To economists familiar with marginal analysis, a decline in the propensity to spend will cause a decline in spending at the margin, and not a complete suspension of consumption. Time preference is positive, as discussed in Chapter 3, and individuals always prefer consumption in the present to the future. Consumption in the present is necessary for survival. Individuals do not need to have the value of their money destroyed in order to consume; nature compels them to consume to survive. As saving for the future becomes more reliable, they may reduce their consumption at the margin, but they cannot abstain from consumption completely. This marginal reduction in consumption can result in a decline in marginal employment in the production of consumer goods, but not a complete collapse in employment. On the other hand, the decline in consumption of resources frees them from being used as consumer goods, and allows them to be utilized as capital goods. Saving money corresponds to saving economic resources from consumption, thus creating more opportunities for work to be directed at the earlier stages of economic production. A society which constantly defers consumption will actually end up being a society that consumes more in the long run than a low-savings society, since the low-time-preference society invests more, thus producing more income for its members. Even with a larger percentage of their income going to savings, the low-time-preference societies will end up having higher levels of consumption in the long run, as well as a larger capital stock. Far from bringing about destitution, the reduction of consumption is the only path to abundance.

Chapter 11

Markets

> The market economy is the social system of the division of labor under private ownership of the means of production. Everybody acts on his own behalf; but everybody's actions aim at the satisfaction of other people's needs as well as at the satisfaction of his own. Everybody in acting serves his fellow citizens. Everybody, on the other hand, is served by his fellow citizens. Everybody is both a means and an end in himself, an ultimate end for himself and a means to other people in their endeavors to attain their own ends.[123]
>
> —Ludwig von Mises

Money allows for specialization and the division of labor, which in turn encourages the emergence and growth of a market economy. **A market economy is a social order in which people are able to cooperate in very large numbers on economic production, providing goods and services for one another to the benefit of all involved, voluntarily, without a coercive authority dictating and coordinating their actions.**

To appreciate the enormous benefits of a market economy, imagine the impact on your life, in terms of your chances of survival, the quantity of time you have, and the quality of your time, if you were to live in isolation from the

123 Mises, Ludwig von. *Human Action: The Scholar's Edition*. Ludwig von Mises Institute, 1998, p. 258.

world or in a small tribe with no trade with the rest of the world. The range of goods available to you would be tiny, and your ability to protect yourself from nature would be very limited. Specializing in, say, welding or painting would be impossible because all your waking hours would be spent economizing the basest of tasks required to avoid starving or freezing to death. People are drawn to partake in the market economy because of the compelling and unrivaled benefits it provides to participants, as opposed to the desperately miserable alternatives.

In a market economy, individuals do not need to think about their own production with regard to their own consumption needs. The growing specialization and division of labor allow each individual to focus on the avenues of production that offer him the best returns for his effort in monetary terms, which would then allow him to maximize the goods he acquires for his own needs. Rather than produce for himself the goods he needs, a participant in the market economy specializes in providing the goods he produces best for other people and relies on other people for procuring the goods he himself needs. Profoundly, the capitalist market system makes people specialize in what they do best and focus on how to provide value for others, rather than focusing on what they value. People choose to serve others in a capitalist system because it is far more productive and efficient than working for yourself alone in isolation from the division of labor.

The underrated marvel of the market economy is how it enables cooperation between people without the need for coercion, central direction, or social ties to compel them. What coordinates the activities of producers in the division of labor is their ability to perform economic calculations on the best uses of the resources they own, using one denominator, the monetary price. As an economy grows to an extent where all economic goods can be purchased and sold on a market in exchange for one good, economic actors can calculate the different costs and benefits of any course of action and compare them to their own preferences and to the available alternatives. The freedom of all to express their preferences through economic actions gives everyone the self-interested incentive to act in ways that satisfy the desires of others. It is not authority or violence that commands people's actions, but their desire to meet their own needs, according to the calculations they perform based on prices that express the preferences of other participants in the market. As Mises put it:

> Market exchange and monetary calculation are inseparably linked together. A market in which there is direct exchange only is merely an imaginary construction. On the other hand, money and monetary calculation are conditioned by the existence of the market.[124]

When the market price of all goods is measured in terms of one good, individuals are able to compare prices, both to other prices and their own subjective valuations, and make consumption and production decisions. Value, as discussed in the first chapter of the book, is subjective. It cannot be measured objectively, as there is no constant unit against which it can be measured. But when an individual makes his own choices in a market, he is weighing economic choices against his subjective valuations. The values may not be measurable with a constant unit, but they are comparable to one constant frame of reference: the individual making the valuation. Knowing his own preferences allows man to order different options according to a scale of preference. While we cannot attach cardinal numerical valuations to different options, we can order them in terms of preference. This chapter explains a mathematical graphic model for thinking about how these decisions are made in the context of a market economy.

Consumer Good Markets

Economic actors acquire consumer goods to satisfy their needs and wants, and they pay a monetary price in exchange for them. Individuals perform economic calculations to weigh the market price of goods as opposed to the valuation they personally place on these goods. As prices change, the quantity

124 Mises, Ludwig von. *Human Action: The Scholar's Edition*. Ludwig von Mises Institute, 1998, p. 235.

of a good they would purchase changes naturally. Valuation is subjective and ordinal, not cardinal. In other words, individuals value goods by ranking them in relation to other goods. People do not attach a numerical valuation to objects, they instead compare their utility and order them in terms of their preference, as evidenced by the market choices they make.

We can think of this economic choice as being achieved through individuals producing a value scale: A ranking of goods in terms of individual preference. For any particular good, the value scale reflects the valuation of certain quantities of the good compared to monetary units.

Take as an example a man considering his daily demand for beef. The first pound of beef he eats in a day is extremely valuable for him, and he would be willing to pay a significant price to ensure that he can get it because without it, he would be malnourished and hungry. Given his own income, wealth, and preferences for beef, he would not be willing to pay $31 for a pound of beef. But he would be willing to pay $30 for the first pound of beef of the day, which means he values the first pound of beef more than $30. Once he has secured that pound, the second pound of beef is slightly less valuable to him, and the cash balance he has left becomes more valuable to him, having been reduced by paying for one pound already. At that point, he would be willing to pay up to $16 for the second pound of beef since he values it a little more than this amount. When considering whether to buy a third pound of beef, he would pay the cost only if the price were $12 or lower. And he would buy the fourth only if the price were $8 or lower. As the price declines, he demands more units, and at a prevalent market price of $4, he would consume his fifth pound of beef per day. If the price of beef were $2, he would consume 6 pounds in a day. If the price of beef were $1, he would consume 7 pounds in a day. At a price of $0, in a world in which he is offered unlimited beef for free, the man would consume only 8 pounds of beef in a day.

Based on these subjective decisions, the man can rank his valuation of different quantities of beef and dollars, ordinally:

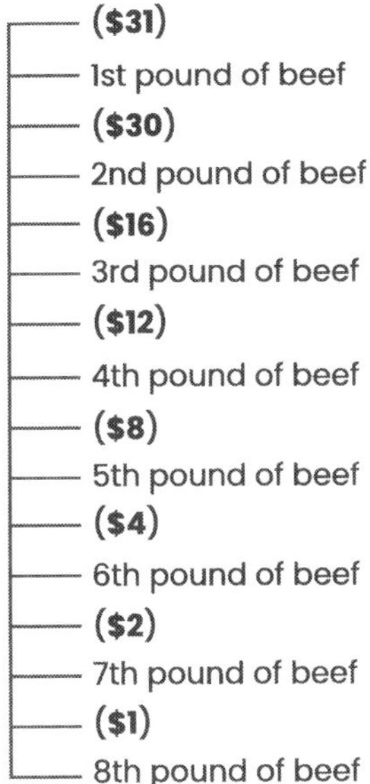

Figure 20. Ordinal consumer valuation scale

The ordinal ranking of goods is a conceptual tool economists use to understand the thought process that goes into making purchasing decisions. The ordinal value scale can be understood as the subconscious foundation of that choice, but in the real world, the buyer is confronted only with one price, and he will decide the quantity he will buy at that price. We can deduce the quantities he would purchase at each price. From this ordinal ranking of beef against monetary units, it is possible to derive a **demand schedule: A table that shows the quantity demanded at each price level**.

Market Price, $	Quantity Demanded, in pounds of beef
$31	0
$30	1
$20	1
$16	2
$12	3
$8	4
$4	5
$2	6
$1	7
$0	8

Table 3. Demand schedule

This demand schedule can then be presented in graphical form to visualize the quantities demanded at each level. In economics, the convention has it that the quantity is plotted on the x-axis, while the price is plotted on the y-axis. This can appear counterintuitive to anyone coming from the natural sciences, since convention there is that the dependent variable is placed on the y-axis, whereas the independent variable is placed on the x-axis. Nonetheless, in economics, the quantity demanded is a function of the price.

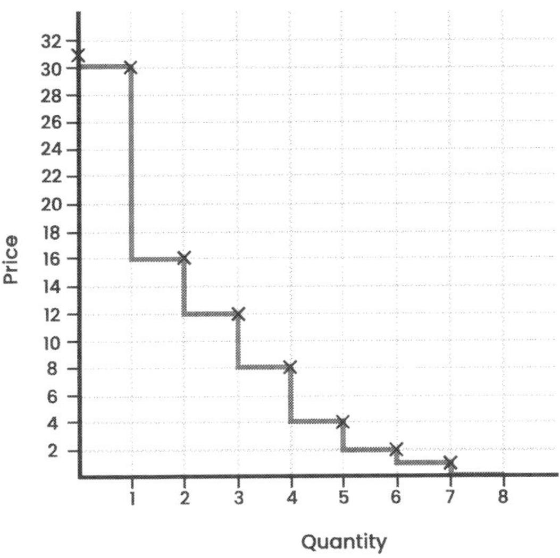

Figure 21. Demand curve

As explained in Chapter 2, individuals value the first unit of a good more than all other subsequent units, and the valuation declines the more units they acquire. On the other hand, spending money on the units causes the buyer's cash balance to decline, raising the marginal utility of money. With each increased unit of the good, the marginal price that the buyer would pay declines, which implies **the law of demand: As the price increases, the quantity demanded declines. Demand curves always slope downward, or are vertical, but they cannot slope upward because the quantity demanded of a good cannot increase as the price increases.**

This analysis was conducted for one individual, but it can be applied to all individuals in a market for a good. By adding the quantities demanded for each person at each price point, we can get a curve showing the total market demand at a particular point. For simplicity, let us assume that this market is made up of 100 consumers whose average is represented by the consumer discussed above, so that the quantity demanded is 100 times the values shown in the individual demand schedule. Because the numbers grow, and individual preferences vary slightly, we will also get a more granular distribution of quantities, rather than the clear-cut step function of the individual demand curve shown above.

Market Price, $	Quantity Demanded, in pounds of beef
$31	0
$30	100
$20	140
$16	200
$12	300
$8	400
$4	500
$2	600
$1	700
$0	800

Table 4. Market demand schedule

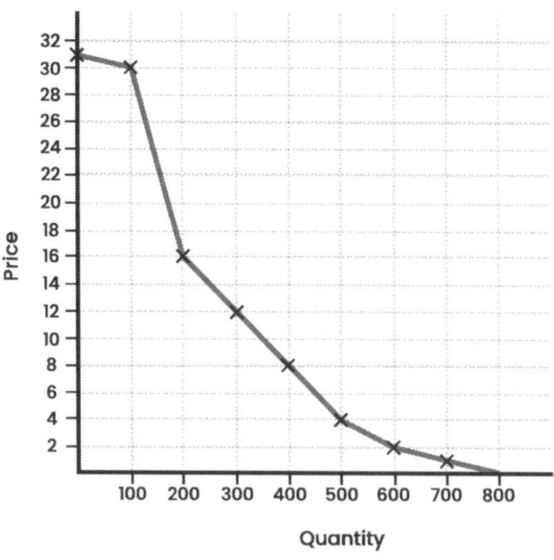

Figure 22. Market demand curve

On the supply side, producers perform a similar mental calculus with the goods they sell. Producers' personal preferences can be expressed as a value scale that results in an ordinal ranking of quantities of the good against different quantities of money. In a market economy where producers produce to sell, and not for their own consumption, the cost of producing the goods is the prime determinant of the ordinal producer's ordinal value scale. The higher the market price, the higher the expected return on sales, and the more resources that can be dedicated to producing more units of the final good.

As an illustrative example, consider a butcher selling beef to the consumers above. At a price of $0 or $1 per pound, the butcher will not sell any beef, as the price does not cover the cost of providing the beef, so he prefers to either keep his beef for himself or not butcher it at all. Only at a price of $2/lb is the butcher able to begin producing, and he can provide 10 pounds of beef, a small quantity he can provide with a basic set up he can afford to operate at that low price by procuring beef from the closest farms. At a price of $3/lb, he can hire a worker and provide 30 lb. If he can expect a price of $4 per pound of beef, he can hire another worker and provide 50 lb. At a price of $5, he can provide 60 lb of beef, and at $6, he can provide 70 lb of beef, which is the maximum he is able to provide. Further increases in price cannot increase his capacity past 70 lb of beef.

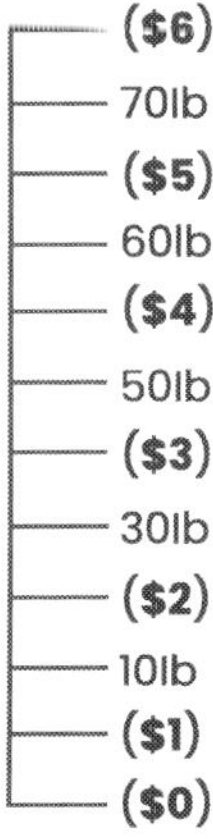

Figure 23. Ordinal producer value scale

This valuation scale can also be converted to a demand schedule and curve, which show the quantity the producer would supply at every price level.

Market Price, $	Quantity Demanded, in pounds of beef
$7	70
$6	70
$5	60
$4	50
$3	30
$2	10
$1	0
$0	0

Table 5. Producer supply schedule

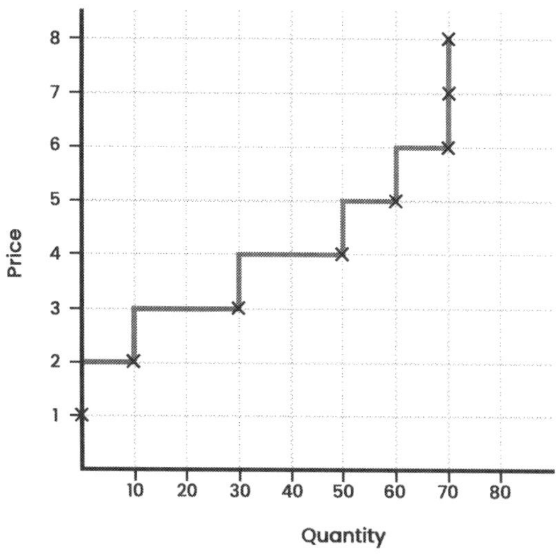

Figure 24. Producer supply Curve

The law of supply states that as the price goes up, owners of an economic good become more willing and able to sell larger quantities. As a consequence, supply curves slope upward only. This can be understood with reference to individuals' preference for owning goods, which decreases as the price they can get in return for their money increases. It can also be understood for the case of producers on the market; increased prices increase producers' incentive to produce more and allow greater investment in securing raw materials and laborers, resulting in larger quantities supplied.

For a good with several producers, the supply schedules and curves of all producers can be aggregated into one market supply curve. The market demand curve shows the quantity that would be produced by all producers of the good at every given price level. For this example, let us assume there are ten producers and that the above example represents their average.

Market Price, $	Quantity Demanded, in pounds of beef
$7	700
$6	700
$5	600
$4	500
$3	300
$2	100
$1	0
$0	0

Table 6. Market supply schedule

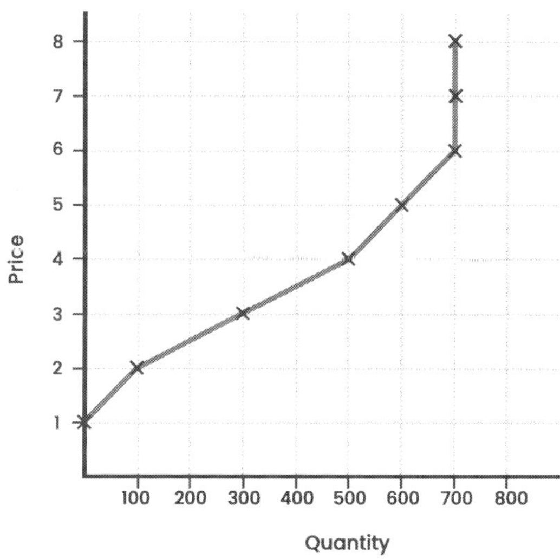

Figure 25. Market supply curve

Equilibrium

At a price of zero, the quantity demanded is very large, while the quantity supplied is likely zero. As the price rises from zero, the quantity demanded decreases, while the quantity supplied increases. There is, at most, one price point at which the quantities demanded and supplied are equal, and that is referred to as the **equilibrium price**. This price point functions like a magnet to buyers and sellers, drawing them to always transact around it.

If prices are set higher than the equilibrium price, the sellers supply a quantity of the good larger than the quantity demanded by the buyers, resulting in a **surplus**. Sellers would naturally want to drop the price in order to encourage more buyers to buy their surplus goods, drawing the price to the equilibrium price. If, on the other hand, prices were set lower than the equilibrium price, consumers would demand a quantity larger than that provided by sellers, resulting in a **shortage**, which would incentivize sellers to raise their prices to ration the supply and maximize their profits. They can keep raising their prices until the equilibrium price, after which point, any further price increases would result in fewer buyers and a surplus. The dynamics of the market would always draw the price to the equilibrium price.

We can see the market equilibrium from the previous example by superimposing the supply and demand curves on one chart. Because the demand curve slopes downward, while the supply curve only rises, the 2 curves can only intersect at 1 point, if at all. In this market, the ten producers of beef would produce 400 pounds of beef to sell at a price of $4, and the 100 consumers would buy all these at a price of $4. There are no surpluses or shortages. As changes occur in individual value scales, the supply and demand curves will adjust to reflect these changes, and the equilibrium will shift, but it will continue to attract buyers and sellers.

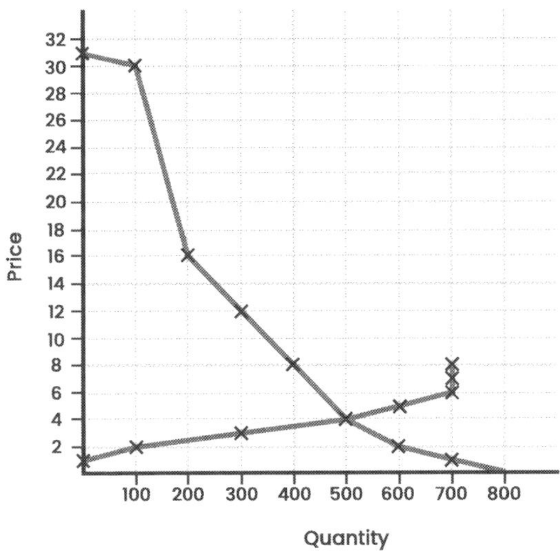

Figure 26. Market equilibrium

All participants in the market act in ways that benefit themselves. They agree to take part in these transactions because they expect to benefit, and they choose which transactions to take part in because they think they are getting the best deal possible. The concept of equilibrium is very powerful for understanding how voluntary market interactions arrive at prices without coercive authority or decree. Yet it is more productive to think of markets as equilibrating processes, rather than to imagine that markets arrive at a rigid set of equilibrium prices for all goods. The world of human action is constantly changing, and supply and demand conditions are constantly being affected by various factors. As their own individual conditions change, the realities of the market change. Equilibrium, then, is not a final state at which markets arrive. Instead, markets are constant processes of discovery where supply and demand conditions are always equilibrating toward the prices that help produce the most value for the actors involved.

Changes in price result in a change in the quantity that individuals demand, graphically expressed as movement along their demand curves. But changes in other factors pertaining to demand cause the reformulation of the price-demand relationship, with a new quantity demanded at each price, and thus a shift in the entire demand curve. Factors that could shift the demand curve include changing preferences, changes in income and wealth, or changing prices of other goods and services. If the buyer's income or wealth increases, they are likely to demand more of most goods and the demand curves for goods would shift to the right, increasing the quantity demanded at all price levels. But for inferior goods, an increase in income or wealth would cause the opposite effect, reducing the quantity demanded at all price levels, shifting the demand curve to the left, as people are able to afford superior alternatives. Beans are an example of such an inferior good: As incomes rise around the world, people are likely to reduce their demand for beans and increase their demand for beef.

A good's demand curve can also be affected by changes in the prices of other goods. A rise in the price of a good causes the quantity demanded to decline and causes the quantity demanded of a good complementary to it to decline at all price points, shifting its demand curve to the left. If that same good declines in price, the quantity demanded will rise, while the quantity demanded of the complementary good will rise at all price levels, shifting its demand curve to the right. The opposite holds when the good is a substitute good.

Other than price, market supply is also affected by the cost of production and the prices of related products that can be produced with the same factors of production. As producers' costs of production rise, they are able to supply lower quantities of their product at each price level, shifting the supply cost to the left. On the other hand, if the producer realizes he is able to make better returns by shifting his productive factors to producing another good whose price is rising, that would shift the supply curve for the original good to the left, reducing the quantity supplied at all price levels.

This graphical framework helps explain how a free market would react to changes in supply and demand conditions over time. In industries where technological innovation allows producers to produce increasing quantities of a good at a given price, the result is a shift in the market supply curve to the right. The consequence of this shift is that the equilibrium price will drop, and the quantity sold will increase. This trend can be seen in the high-tech industry, where prices and quantities are constantly increasing due to increased productivity and technological innovation.

Graphically, this can be illustrated with the shift from S1 to S2 in Figure 27.

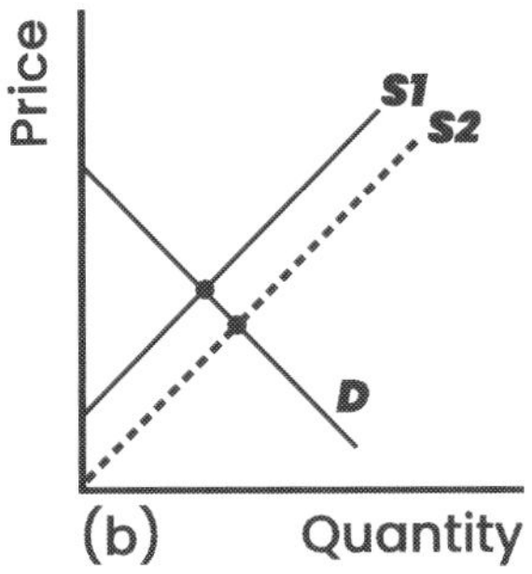

Figure 27. Shifts in the supply curve

If the opposite were to happen, and a supply chain problem negatively affected the production of the good, producers would be able to provide a smaller quantity of the good at any given price level, effectively shifting the supply curve to the left. In this situation, the new equilibrium with the demand curve would emerge at a higher price and a lower quantity. A natural disaster is an extreme example of this, in which the available quantities of a good decline enormously, while the prices rise. This is reflected graphically in the shift from S2 to S1 in Figure 27.

We can apply the same analysis to shifts in the demand curve. Factors that cause increases in consumer demand at all prices, such as an increased consumer preference for the good at all prices, or an increase in the price of substitute goods, or a drop in the price of complementary goods, would cause the demand curve to shift to the right, graphically illustrated as the move from curve D1 to curve D2 in Figure 28. A decrease in consumer demand for the good at all prices, or an increase in the price of complementary goods, or a drop in the price of a substitute good would shift the demand curve to the left. Graphically, this is shown by the move from curve D2 to D1 in Figure 28.

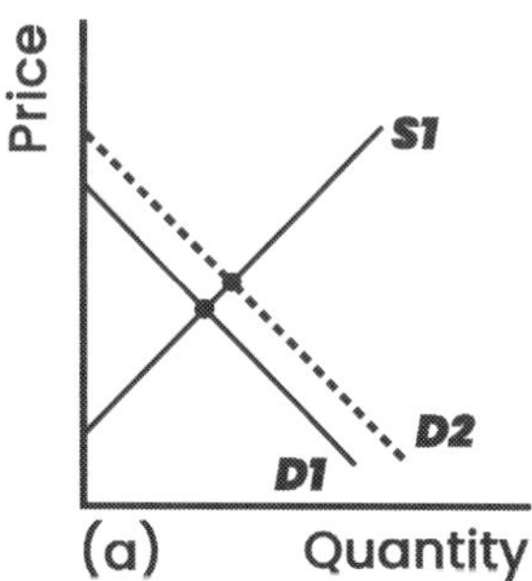

Figure 28. Shifts in the demand curve

Producer Good Markets

When making their production decisions, producers also base their decisions on the utility provided to them by different courses of action. The difference between consumer choice and producer choice lies in the fact that the producers are not deriving personal utility from the factors that they employ; they are purely employing them in order to maximize the monetary profit they can achieve from their business. Consumer sovereignty means the producer is basing all his business decisions on the wants and needs of the consumer.

The production process consists of turning production factors into final goods and services to be sold to consumers. The quantity of each factor of production employed is determined by comparing its cost to the revenue it contributes to business operations, at the margin. Each additional unit of labor or capital employed in production will result in a marginal increase in the quantity of final goods produced. Employers will keep hiring factors of production as long as the expected marginal revenue of the employed factor exceeds the cost of employing it. The prices of these factors of production will in turn be determined by how well they satisfy consumer demand. If hiring an additional worker for a day is expected to add $10 of revenue to a business, that business will only hire an additional worker if their wage demand is less than $10 per day. If an entrepreneur is considering buying a machine that costs $1,000, he will buy it only if the expected discounted marginal value product it produces over its lifetime is greater than $1,000. Ultimately, therefore, it is the consumers' valuation of final goods that gives value to factors of production. The function of the entrepreneur is to make judgments about the future desires of consumers, invest in the factors of production before production has taken place, and assume the risk that he is wrong about what consumers will value after production.

It is futile to complain about wages or returns on capital. These are vital signals from the market telling individuals how valuable their labor, land, and capital are. Entrepreneurs cannot simply decide wages for themselves; they are beholden to the subjective valuations of consumers. If an entrepreneur decides to pay too much for wages, he will lose his profitability and be replaced by entrepreneurs who pay a more appropriate price. If the entrepreneur decides to pay a lower wage, he will lose his workers to others willing to pay a higher price. In order to remain an entrepreneur in a particular line of business, the entrepreneur has no choice but to pay workers for their marginal productivity. Under a free-market system, capitalists and entrepreneurs cannot oppress workers, because the workers have the freedom to leave and work elsewhere and because the consumers have the freedom to buy their products elsewhere. Only by carefully and correctly walking the tightrope between workers and consumers can entrepreneurs continue to operate.

Economizing in the Market Order

We can think of the market system as the larger framework in which all the previously discussed acts of economizing can be practiced with the greatest increase in productivity. Labor, capital, technology, power, trade, and money are all tools that can be employed far more productively in the context of free and impersonal exchange on the market. As a result, the market economy has steadily increased the real wages of workers, because the market economy is constantly finding new ways of increasing the value of human time, by using it most productively to satisfy the needs of other humans.

Market participants communicate their changing preferences and conditions to each other through their actions in buying or not buying at particular prices. This process of mutual cooperation allows all market participants to act in their own best interest, while coordinating their actions to better benefit one another. All preferences of consumers are expressed to other market participants in terms of their choices to buy or not buy at a particular price, giving producers valuable knowledge on which to base their production decisions. As Mises put it:

> The market process is the adjustment of the individual actions of the various members of the market society to the requirements of mutual cooperation. The market prices tell the producers what to produce, how to produce, and in what quantity. The market is the focal point to which the activities of the individuals converge.[125]

Mises further adds:

> In nature there prevail irreconcilable conflicts of interests. The means of subsistence are scarce. Proliferation tends to outrun subsistence. Only the fittest plants and animals survive. The antagonism between an animal starving to death and another that snatches the food away from it is implacable. Social cooperation under the division of labor removes such antagonisms. It substitutes partnership and mutuality for hostility. The members of society are united in a common venture.[126]

Consumer Sovereignty

The careful analysis of the market process illustrates why in a free market, the consumer is king. Individuals are sovereign in a market economy in their capacity as consumers, because the producers have no way of forcing them to purchase their goods, except by producing goods that meet the needs and desires of the consumer at a price they can afford. Producers invest their capital resources in

---

125 Mises, Ludwig von. *Human Action: The Scholar's Edition*. Ludwig von Mises Institute, 1998, p. 259.

126 Ibid. 273-4.

the production process and are reliant on consumers liking their product for their investment to not go to waste. Producers are in no position to dictate terms or exploit consumers, who have full choice. As Mises explains:

> If they were not intent upon buying in the cheapest market and arranging their processing of the factors of production so as to fill the demands of the consumers in the best and cheapest way, they would be forced to go out of business. More efficient men who succeeded better in buying and processing the factors of production would supplant them. The consumer is in a position to give free rein to his caprices and fancies. The entrepreneurs, capitalists, and farmers have their hands tied; they are bound to comply in their operations with the orders of the buying public. Every deviation from the lines prescribed by the demand of the consumers debits their account. The slightest deviation, whether willfully brought about or caused by error, bad judgment, or inefficiency, restricts their profits or makes them disappear. A more serious deviation results in losses and thus impairs or entirely absorbs their wealth. Capitalists, entrepreneurs, and landowners can only preserve and increase their wealth by filling best the orders of the consumers.[127]

Mises further compares the power of consumers in the market to the democratic process, showing how it is superior, because it caters to the needs of all, whereas democracy only caters to the need of the winning majority:

> With every penny spent the consumers determine the direction of all production processes and the details of the organization of all business activities. This state of affairs has been described by calling the market a democracy in which every penny gives a right to cast a ballot. It would be more correct to say that a democratic constitution is a scheme to assign to the citizens in the conduct of government the same supremacy the market economy gives them in their capacity as consumers. However, the comparison is imperfect. In the political democracy, only the votes cast for the

127 Ibid. 271.

> majority candidate or the majority plan are effective in shaping the course of affairs. The votes polled by the minority do not directly influence policies. But on the market no vote is cast in vain. Every penny spent has the power to work upon the production processes. The publishers cater not only to the majority by publishing detective stories, but also to the minority reading lyrical poetry and philosophical tracts. The bakeries bake bread not only for healthy people, but also for the sick on special diets. The decision of a consumer is carried into effect with the full momentum he gives it through his readiness to spend a definite amount of money.[128]

A Contrast of Approaches

For as long as governments have existed, the urge to set prices by decree has existed and has resulted in a slew of terrible and predictable consequences.[129] But the many and various futile attempts by central governments to fix prices have had one positive consequence: They have made a lot of people understand economics as a product of human action, even though they may not quite articulate it in these Misesean terms. By contrasting the analysis of the politician imposing the price control and the economist, we can clearly see the power of the economic way of thinking.

The politician who is unhappy about a market price and seeks to alter it is thinking of the price as something arbitrary, which he can set. He is not thinking in the economic way because he does not view prices as the result of human action, reflecting human choice. He ignores the element of individual and personal choice that goes into determining prices and instead focuses on the political and social implications of these prices. He compares the current reality to a hypothetical reality in which the price is lower and the quantity consumed is higher, while everything else remains the same.

Most political leaders do not get to their positions through the strength of their understanding of economics. Arguably, understanding economics is

---

128 Ibid. 271-2.

129 Schuettinger, Robert L., and Eamonn F. Butler. *Forty Centuries of Wage and Price Controls: How Not to Fight Inflation*. Heritage Foundation, 1978.

a significant hindrance to success in politics. Politicians consider the prices of economic goods and services purely as a measure of their affordability, and they know that the lower the prices, the happier the population. Without understanding prices as the emergent outcome of human action in response to economic reality, the politician thinks he can manage prices to achieve his desired outcomes, and so he will pass laws that mandate maximum prices for specific goods. The faulty reasoning assumes that if the price of a good is set by law, then buyers and sellers will have no choice but to buy and sell at that price.

Should the political leader seek to consult an economist, he is likely to prefer the advice of quantitative economists who can produce seemingly valid rationales for these policies. A quantitative economist can mathematically model the effect of prices on economic activity and find a theoretical quantitative relationship between the price of a good, the level of spending in the economy, and economic growth. It is possible to hypothesize a causal mechanism, based on real-world data, in which lowering the price of an essential good causes an increase in the living standard of a large section of the population, resulting in more savings and investment and faster economic growth. With the quantitative observation of the magnitudes and untestable assumptions about the flow of causality, the quantitative economist can provide the government with a seemingly scientific formula for improving the state of the economy by mandating critical prices by law. Without a constant unit of measurement, these equations cannot be accurate, so any result desired can be arranged.

From the perspective of the sound economist, however, price is more than just a measure of the affordability of a good. It is a product of voluntary human action and choice and the solution to a calculation problem for the producer and consumer. Should the government impose a different price for the good, there is no guarantee that the individuals involved would perform the same actions they had performed otherwise, nor that they can satisfy each other in the same way.

Prices are not arbitrary numbers placed by merchants, they are arrived at through a complex interplay of humans acting and affecting market supply and demand. A market transaction taking place at a particular price indicates that both the buyer and seller chose to accept this price. Both of them would obviously prefer other prices; the buyer would have preferred a lower price, and the seller would have preferred a higher price, but the actual price was clearly acceptable for both, since they traded. If a politician were to intervene and force the price to change by law, there is no reason to assume the buyer and seller would make the same decisions as before. And from the perspective of an economist, such a law would be far more destructive than whatever prices had emerged on the market, no matter how distasteful they were to the leaders.

What a market price for a good tells us is that the seller is happy to sell this good at this price, and the buyer is buying it. Should buyers refuse to buy this good at that price, then the producer would have to drop his prices. Should he be unable to drop his price to meet the consumers' valuation, then the good does not get produced. In order for the business to sell any particular good, the price needs to compensate the producer for the entire cost and opportunity costs incurred to make the product available. When price controls set a maximum price for a good that is below the cost of the producer, then the producer will simply stop selling it, leading to shortages.

Producers, being self-interested humans, will not sell a good for a price that does not cover their entire cost of production. They would rather go out of business and stay home than work in a business that loses them money. So trying to mandate lower prices simply results in the destruction of the human incentive to produce a good, resulting in higher prices and even lower supplies. The other inevitable consequence of price controls is the emergence of black markets where the seller and buyer can transact at rates suitable to both of them, but without the attention of the government.

Chapter 12

Capitalism

> If historical experience could teach us anything, it would be that private property is inextricably linked with civilization.[130]
>
> —Ludwig von Mises

A market economy, as discussed in the previous chapter, is a social order in which individuals act economically in their self-interest to the benefit of everyone involved. All methods of individual economizing, labor, capital accumulation, technological innovation, trade, and modern power production are performed voluntarily by individuals using monetary media to expand the scope of their production and significantly increase their material satisfaction over what they could achieve individually. The extended monetary market economy is what allows for the emergence of capitalism, the system of private ownership of capital goods in which individuals can buy and sell capital freely, and decide how to employ their capital, reaping the rewards of using it productively and bearing the losses of using it unproductively.

In *The End of Socialism and the Calculation Debate Revisited*, Rothbard explains Mises' criteria for what makes a market economy:

130 Mises, Ludwig von. *Human Action: The Scholar's Edition*. Ludwig von Mises Institute, 1998, p. 254.

> One time, during Mises' seminar at New York University, I asked him whether, considering the broad spectrum of economies from a purely free market economy to pure totalitarianism, he could single out one criterion according to which he could say that an economy was essentially "socialist" or whether it was a market economy. Somewhat to my surprise, he replied readily: "'Yes, the key is whether the economy has a stock market." That is, if the economy has a full-scale market in titles to land and capital goods. In short: Is the allocation of capital basically determined by government or by private owners?[131]

For Mises and the Austrians, the presence of a stock market is an effective litmus test of capitalism because it is the unmistakable mark of a free market in producer goods, open to all members of society, allowing capital to be allocated to those who use it most productively. Companies traded publicly on stock markets will own a significant portion of a society's productive capital, which is available for anyone to buy and sell as they see fit. Any individual who thinks they can use capital goods more productively than their owner is able to purchase them by paying the going price for share ownership. Anyone can allocate their own savings to a production process they expect to be more beneficial than holding cash. Those who succeed in allocating their capital productively benefit by accruing profits, giving them the ability to command more capital resources. Those who allocate their capital resources unproductively will suffer losses that make their ownership of capital an untenable and expensive mistake, encouraging them to sell their capital resources to buyers who are willing to pay a higher price because they expect to use these resources more productively. With a stock market and a free market in capital, there are no mechanisms to protect capital owners who misuse their capital goods. They will either sell to those who use them better, or they will continue to accumulate losses until their entire capital base has been consumed. Either way, capital is always part of a process of relocating to more productive and more capable

---

131 Rothbard, Murray. "The End of Socialism and the Calculation Debate Revisited." *The Review of Austrian Economics*, vol. 5, no. 2, 1991, p. 59.

hands. By definition, no privileges or mandates can override this inexorable march toward more productive use of capital in a free-market system.

By basing the definition and explanation of capitalism within the context of human action, Austrian school economists provide the most comprehensive and coherent definition and treatment of capitalism—a powerful and practical analytical tool for understanding real-world economic issues and the workings of a capitalist system. This stands in stark contrast to superficial treatment of the topic offered by other schools. Marxist economists think of capital as a force for evil that allows capital owners to exploit and enslave other members of society, and they have little regard for the benefits it provides workers in terms of increased productivity, the cost incurred by owning it in terms of opportunity cost, and the responsibilities and risks associated with ownership. Meanwhile, most mainstream economists today think of capital as an aggregate quantity—a homogenous self-perpetuating blob that is used for production. Neither treatment discusses the importance of private property for the growth of capital and the importance of a free market for allocating capital to its most productive users. With the essential function of capital markets ignored, both schools of economics allow their followers to imagine that capitalist economic production can be carried out even in a compromised system of private ownership and free exchange of the means of production that is its lifeblood.

The value of capital goods is subjective and depends on individuals valuing them; it is not inherent or intrinsic. Whether something is a capital good or not is entirely the consequence of the judgment and action of the person in command of it. A computer used for playing games is a consumer good, but the same computer used for professional graphic design is a capital good. Without the ability to command capital goods for profit, there is little incentive for anyone to accumulate and maintain capital in the first place. Without the ability to trade capital for monetary gain, there is no mechanism to ensure capital is allocated for productive uses and is not monopolized by those who misuse and degrade it. Capital is not a lump of machines, but a mental construct that survives, like a living organism, in an ecosystem where it is constantly valued and traded by acting individuals. It thus makes little sense to speak of a societal capital stock outside of the ability of individuals to freely value and command these capital goods, use them in production, and benefit from their use. Capital outside a market economy is like a fish out of water—a limp, lifeless shell of its former vivid self.

Capital Markets

It is very common to hear laypeople, politicians, and mainstream economists refer to various countries as socialist or capitalist without having a clear definition to inform these designations. But Mises' criteria provide us with a very powerful litmus test for understanding what constitutes a capitalist economy and what constitutes a socialist economy.

An economy that has not developed a stock market is not a capitalist market economy, as it has not developed the level of economic specialization and the lengthening of capital structure of production necessary to develop a market for capital. An economy that has its stock market forcibly closed by government will be a socialist economy, as its capital has been removed from the realm of market competition and placed in the hands of bureaucrats who do not own it, cannot legitimately profit from it, and cannot perform economic calculation to decide the best production avenues and methods to utilize it. Mises' criterion allows us to divide economies into three categories: pre-capitalist, capitalist, and socialist. History for most of the world's countries has been the positive development from pre-capitalism to capitalism, interrupted by calamitous forays into socialist devastation.

Russia's stock market was established by an edict of Peter the Great in the early eighteenth century, at which point Russia could be said to have developed from an agrarian economy into a capitalist economy. The stock markets continued operation until the Bolshevik coup of 1917, when Russia had a socialist economic system. As the Bolshevik coup came to an end, the stock market resumed operations in 1991, returning the country to being a capitalist economy. The devastating impact of socialism on Russia coincided exactly with the years in which the stock market was shuttered.

Germany provides another useful example of the power of Mises' criteria. Several exchange markets were founded as early as the sixteenth century in

Hamburg, Frankfurt, and other German cities. In 1815, the Hamburg stock exchange began to offer trading in company stocks, arguably marking Germany's development into a modern capitalist economy. Stock markets in Germany continued operating until Adolf Hitler's National Socialist Party came to power in 1933, when all companies were forced to join cartels, and their capital was placed at the command of the Nazi regime.

The Deutsche Börse Group describes this episode: "With the Nazi takeover in 1933, overall economic policy was incorporated into the general government and war policy. Stock exchange supervision was taken away from the states and made the domain of the central government, with the number of stock exchanges reduced from 21 to 9. The Frankfurt stock exchange incorporated the Mannheim stock exchange in 1935. The merged institution was called the Rhine-Main Stock Exchange. Although the Frankfurt Stock Exchange continued to function as a 'domestic stock exchange,' it had, in reality, no major function. Nazi economic controls constricted the development of the free-market and stock-market trading. By and large, potential capital assets were only supposed to benefit the war economy and could no longer be invested in larger bonds or shares."[132]

After the defeat of the Nazi regime, the west of Germany became a capitalist economy as its stock markets returned to normal free-market operation, while the east of the country remained a socialist economy with no functional stock markets until German reunification in 1990.

Poland provides yet another instructive example. The first mercantile exchange in Poland, established in 1817, started trading company shares in the 1840s and remained operational until 1915, when it was shut down due to the breakdown of the Polish economy in World War I. The stock market resumed operation in 1919, reestablishing Poland as a capitalist economy until 1939, when the Nazi-Soviet alliance jointly invaded, and control of the country was divided between Germany and Russia. The defeat of the Nazis in 1945 placed the entirety of Poland, still without a stock market, under Soviet control, plunging the country into socialist poverty and dysfunction until 1991, when

132 "History of the Frankfurt Stock Exchange." Deutsche Börse Group.

the Polish socialist economic system collapsed, and a free-market economic system was reinstated. The stock market reopened in April of 1991.[133]

In all three countries, the existence of a stock market is a reliable indicator of an economy transitioning between pre-capitalist, capitalist, and socialist forms of economic organization. It is no coincidence that the absence of a stock market in all of these countries coincided with poverty, war, and mass destruction of capital resources.

It is common today to hear politicians, particularly in the United States and third-world countries, hold up Scandinavian countries as examples of successful socialist regimes. But the stock markets of all Scandinavian countries have been open and operational without interruption for more than a century. Denmark's stock market has been functioning since 1808, Sweden's since 1863, Norway's since 1881, and Finland's since 1912.[134] Not once has a Scandinavian stock market been taken over by a government, meaning capital allocation and ownership in all of these economies have always been directed by the preferences and actions of freely acting individuals and not the coercive commands of a central government authority. In contrast to the incoherent and emotional popular discussions of this topic, Mises provides clear criteria for determining what a socialist economic system is.

Capitalism Is Entrepreneurial, Not Managerial

The importance of private ownership of the means of production to the economic system derives from, and illustrates, Mises' explanation of capitalism as an entrepreneurial system as opposed to a managerial system. This subtle distinction's confusion is at the root of all attempts to override the market economy and replace it with central planning. In a capitalist economy, the division of labor comes down to the process of investment itself, dividing the act of investment into three distinct roles: the capitalist, the entrepreneur, and the manager. The process of investment begins with the capitalist, who chooses to defer

133 "About the Company." *GPW Main Market.*

134 "About Us." *Nasdaq OMX Nordic.*

consumption of economic resources and instead saves them to invest later. Lowering the time preference to allow for saving is the first step in investment, and in a modern capitalist economy, the investor can place their money in the financial markets to be allocated to various lines of production and businesses. The investor could allocate the money himself, or he could give it to a professional investor who allocates the capital to different economic uses. Allocating this capital is the entrepreneurial function of markets. Once the money is allocated to different businesses, it is the role of the managers of these businesses to use it for production of the final goods and services. With the separation of ownership, allocation, and management, the capitalist system can channel large amounts of capital from savers across society, who can specialize in their own jobs and not think about capital allocation or its management.

A free market in capital goods forces each capital owner to either use capital productively or lose it to those who can. The function of financial markets, and their myriad financial instruments, is to channel wealth from those who are willing to risk their savings, the capitalists, to entrepreneurs who exercise their judgment about how to allocate the capital to achieve the highest productivity. The entrepreneurs in turn entrust investment to professional managers who specialize in putting capital and labor into productive work.

As important as the function of the manager is, it is distinct from the function of the capitalist who provides the capital and the entrepreneur who allocates it, even if these roles may overlap in the same individual in certain contexts. The entrepreneur brings economic calculation to capital markets, choosing the most productive deployment of capital stock. The manager performs economic calculation on the deployed capital goods and decides how best to utilize them in the line of production chosen by the entrepreneur.

The function of the entrepreneur in a market economy is to determine the allocation of capital to different lines of production and different industries. The entrepreneur decides which products to produce and which lines of production need to be introduced, expanded, contracted, or shut down. Once these foundations have been laid, the entrepreneur entrusts the manager to supervise the day-to-day operation of these production processes. The manager is not the one responsible for dedicating capital to production processes but merely managing it once it has been allocated. As Mises put it: "Those who confuse entrepreneurship and management close their eyes to the economic problem. ... The capitalist system is not a managerial system; it is an entrepreneurial system."[135] For academics and scholars who have never engaged in entrepreneurship, this distinction is not obvious, which results in their belief that private ownership of capital can be curtailed without affecting the production process, as in their models, the workers and managers can capably handle the entire production process, the capitalists do not contribute anything, and the entrepreneur is an inconsequential detail.

But in the real world, the action of management and labor are determined and dictated by entrepreneurial allocation of capital. The correct costs and benefits of actions cannot be calculated unless the capital goods involved are owned by someone who can use them in any way he likes. Having all options available to the owner allows the owner to choose the option that serves society best and would generate the most profit for him. Without ownership and full command over capital goods, which entails reaping profits and suffering losses, there is no scope for rational calculation of profit and loss.

Profit and Loss

Entrepreneurs speculate on production processes being profitable and apply the factors of production (labor, capital, and land) to them. They incur the upfront costs and risks and collect the revenues and rewards. The use of money as a medium of exchange means it constitutes one-half of every economic transaction in a market economy; this allows money to serve as a tool for entrepreneurs calculating profits and losses by denominating all their costs and revenues in the same medium of exchange. When entrepreneurs calculate that their incomes in one line of business exceed their expenditures, they realize they are making a profit. This profit implies that the market valuation for all revenues received by the entrepreneur exceeds the market valuation for all the expenditures he allocated

135 Mises, Ludwig von. *Human Action: The Scholar's Edition*. Ludwig von Mises Institute, 1998, p. 704.

to inputs to the production process. The subjective valuations placed by other market participants on the outputs of the production process are larger than those placed on the inputs. By turning a profit, entrepreneurs are serving society. They productively convert labor, land, capital, and raw materials into finished products which society values more, and for that, they are rewarded with profits, allowing them to engage in more entrepreneurial allocation.

When the entrepreneur's income is less than his expenditure, he is incurring a loss because the prevalent market price of his inputs exceeds the price of his outputs. The entrepreneur is converting scarce, valuable resources into less valuable final goods, thus impoverishing the society around him. For that, he suffers a loss that reduces the capital available to him and incentivizes him to change his methods of production, shift to another line of business, or stop being an entrepreneur. The scorecard in the game of capitalism is the entrepreneur's own wealth and prosperity, and without this very personal and consequential involvement, there can be no rational calculation of the best uses for capital and no market process for constantly ensuring capital is managed by the most capable. Economists who imagined market production could be replicated without private property, profit, and loss are engaging in cargo cult science, like primitive tribes who encountered airplanes for the first time and imagined that replicating their shape with wood sticks would produce a functioning airplane.

The discussion of scarcity in the early chapters of the book is essential to understanding why economic calculation can only work in the context of private property rights. Unless the person making the allocation has to make real choices involving trade-offs between different options over scarce resources, they will not be able to consider the true costs involved. Capitalism works precisely because the stakes are always high for participants: "one cannot play speculation and investment. The speculators and investors expose their own wealth, their own destiny. This fact makes them responsible to the consumers, the ultimate bosses of the capitalist economy. If one relieves them of this responsibility, one deprives them of their very character."[136] This is the process of economic calculation, and it is the essential role of the entrepreneur. One

136 Ibid. 705.

of Mises' most enduring and significant contributions is the explication of the central role of the process of calculation in a capitalist economy.

The Economic Calculation Problem

When discussing the resounding failure of socialist economic systems, most laymen and modern economists will attribute these failures to the problem of incentives. Under a system in which property rights are curtailed and payment is determined by central planners, there is little financial incentive to excel at work. There is also little incentive to take on the least pleasant and hardest jobs. If living standards were equal, why would anyone want to collect garbage or spend decades training to become a brain surgeon? Why work at all if the government guarantees everyone a decent living? While this is indeed a problem for socialist economic systems, it is not the fundamental economic problem of socialism. Most socialist regimes have found a satisfactory answer to the incentive problem through violence: If you refused to take out the trash or follow strict orders, you could be killed or sent to a labor camp. The incentive to avoid death is arguably more pressing and motivating for humans than the incentive to get rich. Accounts of the collapse of socialist economies show that the problem was not absenteeism. The inmates in the gulags had no choice but to show up, and other workers generally showed up to their regular jobs out of fear of being sent to the gulags. Yet socialist regimes still failed.

Mises goes even further. He argues that even if the socialists had succeeded in building a society composed entirely of the fabled new socialist man, who was utterly selfless in his dedication to the cause, socialism would still fail. As Rothbard explains, "What exactly would those planners tell this army to do? How would they know what products to order their eager slaves to produce, at what stage of production, how much of the product at each stage, what techniques or raw materials to use in that production and how much of each, and where specifically to locate all this production? How would they know their costs, or what process of production is or is not efficient?"[137]

---

137 Rothbard, Murray. "The End of Socialism and the Calculation Debate Revisited." *The Review of Austrian Economics*, vol. 5, no. 2, 1991, p. 52.

In his analysis of socialism in 1922, when most economists were taken by this popular new idea sweeping the globe, Mises correctly identified the Achilles heel of socialist economic systems as the inability to perform calculations to allocate capital goods without considering the private property rights associated with them. There is no rational means of ascertaining how to allocate resources without property, prices, and a market for entrepreneurs and consumers to conduct economic calculation. To quote Rothbard:

> Mises demonstrated that, in any economy more complex than the Crusoe or primitive family level, the socialist planning board would simply not know what to do, or how to answer any of these vital questions. Developing the momentous concept of calculation, Mises pointed out that the planning board could not answer these questions because socialism would lack the indispensable tool that private entrepreneurs use to appraise and calculate: the existence of a market in the means of production, a market that brings about money prices based on genuine profit-seeking exchanges by private owners of these means of production. Since the very essence of socialism is collective ownership of the means of production, the planning board would not be able to plan, or to make any sort of rational economic decisions. Its decisions would necessarily be completely arbitrary and chaotic, and therefore the existence of a socialist planned economy is literally "impossible."
>
> ...
>
> Mises concludes that, in the socialist economy "in place of the economy of the 'anarchic' method of production, recourse will be had to the senseless output of an absurd apparatus. The wheels will turn, but will run to no effect."[138]

How can planners know if a given stockpile of steel is better used in cars or

138 Ibid. 52-3.

trains? If there is no market for cars or trains, the cars and trains are assigned by the government to citizens, and planners have no mechanism for ascertaining how much citizens value them in relation to one another. On what basis should a central planner determine the allocation? Under a market system, consumers buy cars and train tickets based on their preference for either of the two, and private producers of cars and trains receive money that allows them to bid on capital goods. The highest bidder will be the capitalist who can use the resources most productively. The steel goes where it is needed the most.

Several socialist economists (if you will excuse the oxymoron) accepted Mises' critique and reformulated their economic systems in ways that they thought would address it. They would move beyond the silly faith that expropriating capital from owners would produce infinite goods, enough to allow everyone to take all that they needed. They would also move beyond the nonsensical ideas of an economy operating without money or prices, or one where prices are expressed according to the labor theory of value. Instead, socialists like Oskar Lange, Abba Lerner, and Fred Taylor argued that a socialist central-planning board would order managers to assign prices to goods, observe the reactions of buyers, and use trial and error to arrive at proper prices in the same way capitalists would: They would react to a surplus by lowering the price, while reacting to a shortage by raising prices. With this seemingly clever trick, socialist central planners could implement what they saw as the only important part of the market economy, and ensure the operation of their socialist plans.

Lange was a Polish socialist economist and friend of Joseph Stalin whose harebrained schemes were at the forefront of the destruction of Poland's economy. While internalizing Mises' critique and believing he adapted socialism to it, he even wrote of the debt of gratitude the future socialist utopia would owe Mises for being the only person to draw their attention to the most critical aspects of a market economy, which their childish model has ignored.

> Socialists have certainly good reason to be grateful to Professor Mises, the great advocatus diaboli of their cause. For it was his powerful challenge that forced socialists to recognize the importance of an adequate system

> of economic accounting ... the merit of having caused the socialists to approach this problem systematically belongs entirely to Professor Mises.[139]

The socialist detachment from reality was so severe Lange suggested building a statue of Mises in the Central Planning Board of the successful socialist state! Unfortunately, the socialists had not learned Mises' lessons properly or they would not have been so comically sure of their impending success. The socialist central planners' managers were not entrepreneurs. They did not have secure property in the goods they managed, and they could not calculate the profits and losses associated with different lines of production. Even if they did have a market for consumer goods, the government would maintain ownership of capital goods, as that is the definition of socialism. Rational economic calculation cannot happen based purely on a market in final goods. Capitalists need to bid for capital competitively for its most productive uses to emerge, rewarding the successful capitalists and entrepreneurs with more capital and punishing the unsuccessful with less capital. If all capital is owned by one entity, and that entity assigns it without using market prices and calculations of profit and loss as a guide, capital cannot be allocated rationally. As Mises concludes:

> But the characteristic mark of the socialist system is that the producers' goods are controlled by one agency only in whose name the director acts, that they are neither bought nor sold, and that there are no prices for them. Thus there cannot be any question of comparing input and output by the methods of arithmetic.[140]

Socialists have attempted various other tweaks to their system to address the fatal flaw Mises identified. One such choice involved using consumer surveys to understand what consumers would want as a way to inform the

---

139 Lange, Oskar. "On the Economic Theory of Socialism: Part One." *The Review of Economic Studies*, vol. 4, no. 1, Oxford University Press, 1936, p. 53.

140 Mises, Ludwig von. *Human Action: The Scholar's Edition*. Ludwig von Mises Institute, 1998, p. 701.

decisions of planners. But survey questions in the abstract can in no way substitute for market decisions based on real-world prices and scarcity. When asked what car they most desire, people are likely to respond that they want Ferraris, Lamborghinis, and models produced by the most expensive car makers. Yet, in the real world, the vast majority of people make do with Toyotas, Hondas, Kias, and the affordable options that meet their needs and their budget constraints. With no concept of opportunity cost, demands have no limit and trade-offs do not exist.

The notion that market allocation can be arrived at by having managers treat the capital under their command as if it were their own property and having consumers express their preferences in surveys is so absurd it serves only to communicate the utter lack of comprehension of what a market economy is and how it functions. Economic decisions are made only in the context of scarcity, when each decision will carry with it a real cost and benefit that the decision-maker will experience in the real world. Without property, opportunity cost, and real-life consequences, socialist pretend-markets bear no resemblance to the real thing. As Mises puts it:

> What these neosocialists suggest is really paradoxical. They want to abolish private control of the means of production, market exchange, market prices, and competition. But at the same time they want to organize the socialist utopia in such a way that people could act as if these things were still present. They want people to play market as children play war, railroad, or school. They do not comprehend how such childish play differs from the real thing it tries to imitate.[141]

Modern Economics and Calculation

The idea that central planners could perform economic calculation without taking private property into account is also untenable when one understands the dynamic and ever-changing nature of a market economy. The allocation

141 Ibid. 702-3.

of resources and capital for production is not a one-off decision that central planners need to get right once so that their economy will be able to run on autopilot. The world is dynamic and ever-changing, entrepreneurs are constantly discovering new ways of creating products, and consumers are constantly discovering new preferences for new products. The world is constantly changing, and uncertainty is ever-present. The capitalist entrepreneur is the most important actor in the economic system, as he stakes his own property on his ability to anticipate changes correctly. He is the force that affects change and creates economic reality. The general equilibrium models of modern economics are essentially worthless because they cannot accommodate the role of the entrepreneur, the one who shapes and creates economic reality. These models take economic reality as it is, ignoring how it came about, allowing no room for the process that will inevitably change it.

Modern mainstream economists have astonishingly managed to completely ignore Mises' critique of socialism, and to continue operating in the realm of Walrasian general equilibrium modeling of economic activity, a genre of literature that is a better fit for fiction shelves than those set aside for economics. Under this economic fiction framework, all economic data is known to all participants in the market, from tastes and value scales to technologies and available resources; a state of perfect competition exists between producers; and all managers have full knowledge of all prices. There are no entrepreneurs in the Misesian sense, only managers, and capital allocation is considered given. In such a static and totally unrealistic world, socialist and Keynesian economists find that economic central planning can work. Rather than a damning indictment of this entire approach to economics, somehow, economists find redemption for socialism in these entirely absurd models.

General equilibrium is a mental construct that abstracts from the real world to allow us to analyze it. It is purely theoretical. Of course, calculation by a central planner can work in the general equilibrium theoretical model; that is what these models are made for. But that does not translate to calculation being possible in reality, as the real world is very different from theory. In attempting to project their irrelevant and simplistic models on reality, modern economists are similar to navigators walking around a map and concluding that they could also walk around the territory represented by the map in the same time it takes them to walk around the map itself.

It is only by understanding the absurdity of the fetishism surrounding Walrasian general equilibrium that one can understand the hilarious and scandalous track record of modern western economists praising the economy of the Soviet Union. Paul Samuelson wrote the most popular economic textbook of the twentieth century, which has been used to miseducate millions worldwide to believe in a socialist-Keynesian hodgepodge of confusion. The astonishing details can be found in "Soviet Growth and American Textbooks," a paper by David Levy and Sandra Peart.[142] Levy and Peart studied the different versions of Samuelson's textbook and found that he repeatedly presented the Soviet economic model as being more conducive to economic growth, predicting in the fourth edition in 1961 that the Soviet Union's economy would overtake that of the United States sometime between 1984 and 1997. These forecasts for the Soviets overtaking the United States continued with increasing confidence through seven editions of the textbook, until the eleventh edition in 1980, with varying estimates for when the overtaking would occur. In the thirteenth edition, published in 1989, which hit the desks of university students as the Soviet Union was beginning to unravel, Samuelson and his then-coauthor William Nordhaus write, "The Soviet economy is proof that, contrary to what many skeptics had earlier believed, a socialist command economy can function and even thrive."[143] Nor was this confined to one textbook, as Levy and Peart show that such insights were common in the many editions of what is probably the second most popular economics textbook, *McConnell's Economics: Principles, Policies and Problems*, and several other textbooks.[144] Any university student who learned economics in the postwar period following an American curriculum (essentially the majority of

---

142 Levy, David, and Sandra Peart. "Soviet Growth and American Textbooks: An Endogenous Past." *Journal of Economic Behavior & Organization*, vol. 78, iss. 1-2, Elsevier, Apr. 2011, pp. 110-25.

143 Samuelson, Paul, and William Nordhaus. *Economics*. 13th ed., McGraw-Hill, 1989.

144 McConnell, Campbell, Stanley Brue, and Sean Flynn. *Economics: Principles, Problems, and Policies*. McGraw-Hill, 2009.

the world's students) learned that the Soviet model is a more efficient way of organizing economic activity. Even after the collapse and utter failure of the Soviet Union, the same textbooks continued to be taught in the same universities, with the newer editions removing the grandiose proclamations about Soviet success without questioning the rest of their economic worldview and methodological tools.[145]

The Effects of Entrepreneurial Investment

Economic calculation in an entrepreneurial market economy has several important economic consequences. The most obvious and notable is that it increases the productivity of capital investments. Entrepreneurship brings the benefits of specialization and division of labor to the process of capital allocation and use. It allows savers to become capitalists by delegating the entrepreneurial and managerial functions of capitalism to others, thus encouraging more saving and more investment and lowering interest rates. This increase in saving and investment results in an increase in the lengths of the processes of production by making capital available for progressively longer periods. Increased capital spurs invention and innovation, multiplying the range of goods and services available to all market participants. Economic calculation in entrepreneurial investment also leads to increased productivity to investment by constantly rewarding the most productive and punishing the least productive.

The benefits of capitalist entrepreneurship in a market order extend beyond just the entrepreneur and investor. Capitalist entrepreneurship leads to sustained increases in real wages, as more capital and more efficient capital allocation increase the productivity of labor. While wages will increase in real terms, they are likely to decline in the long run in nominal terms, as increased production of all goods will likely result in a drop in their nominal prices, compared to money, which the market selects as a good that is hardest to produce.

Entrepreneurs and capitalists profit from their entrepreneurship, but their profits are generally fleeting, as they are subject to competition from other

145 This paragraph draws heavily on the text of *The Bitcoin Standard*, p. 159.

entrepreneurs who can bid up the price of factors of production. Capitalists do not necessarily benefit from capital accumulation, which, as discussed in Chapter 6, comes at a high cost. There is always a risk of loss. And if there is a profit, the market will quickly start to eat away at it. Higher profits will inevitably accrue to the workers and landowners, whose wages and rents will continue to rise to match their increasing productivity. Entrepreneurship is not all fun and games; it involves far more uncertainty than labor. It is entirely understandable that a large number of people prefer labor to entrepreneurship. Labor in a large market with a highly productive division of labor can be very rewarding and involves far less risk.

Beyond just the economic benefits of capitalism, the social implication of capitalism is that it encourages behaviors that are conducive to peaceful societal coexistence. Being able to behave in a civilized manner allows a person to enter into economic networks that involve a growing number of people, and a high degree of specialization.

PART IV

Monetary Economics

Chapter 13

Time Preference

> [No] matter what a person's original time-preference rate or what the original distribution of such rates within a given population, once it is low enough to allow for any savings and capital or durable consumer-goods formation at all, a tendency toward a fall in the rate of time preference is set in motion, accompanied by a "process of civilization."[146]
>
> —Hans-Hermann Hoppe

Whereas Chapter 10 discussed money conceptually, this chapter and the next two will take a closer look at the operation of money in a capitalist market economic order, as discussed in Chapters 11 and 12. This chapter begins with a discussion of time preference, and its role in determining interest rates on the market. The next chapter introduces the topic of banking, and Chapter 15 explains how the distortion of the market for money results in the business cycle. This is a topic of extreme importance in economics because one cannot understand the economic calamities that have befallen the world in the past century except as a consequence of the disruption of the workings of the market for money and capital. The standard state-sponsored economics textbook views economic crises as a normal, inevitable, and inexplicable part of the market process. In this view, the business cycle is like the

146 Hoppe, Hans-Hermann. *Democracy: The God That Failed.* Transaction Publishers, 2001, p. 6.

weather or a natural disaster, an unstoppable act of nature that must be managed and alleviated by central governments through wise fiscal and monetary policy. The closely related Marxist economists imagine economic breakdown to be the inevitable consequence of a capitalist economic system, and the precursor to workers' inevitable revolt against capitalism.

But applying the economic way of thinking and the tools of economic analysis to the question of money can explain how and why crises happen, how they can be avoided, and the problems of state-sponsored economics textbooks. Perhaps in no area of economic analysis are the implications of the Austrian method more significant than this. The reason the Austrians are so vilified and excluded from mainstream academia is not because their ideas are egregiously wrong. It is because they offer a coherent explanation of the emergence of money on the free market and the devastating consequences of subjecting this enormously important technology to government monopoly control. It is possible for money to exist without the state, and it is possible for the topic of money to be studied without resorting to the ridiculous quasi-religious faith that modern economic textbooks place in the omnipotent and omniscient monetary central planners. The Austrians are vilified because their accurate understanding of economics poses a threat to all who benefit from strong central governments controlling money.

For the majority of its history, the Austrian school has had to explain its theories in the terms laid out by state-sponsored economists. This book approaches the question of money from the perspective of the Austrian school itself and builds the case from the first principles. In order to explain money as a market phenomenon, we must begin the treatment from an understanding of time preference.

The scarcity of time is the starting point for all economic choices. The scarcity of time forces man to choose between alternatives at all points in his life, and it means that every decision has an opportunity cost. Even with no restraint on the quantity of resources available, an individual's choice of how to spend his time results in the elimination of all other choices for which he could have used the time.

Economizing time is unique because time passes and cannot be stopped or reversed. When he is born, man's life clock begins ticking; it continues ticking relentlessly, and it only stops when he dies. There is no knowing when this clock will stop, and there is no restarting it after it stops. Man gets one uninterrupted shot at life, and he never knows when it will end.

Time is not a normal commodity for which man can choose the quantity he would prefer. There is no market choice between different quantities of time, and time cannot be traded directly. The way an individual values time is subjective and variable, but some regularities exist. The nearer the period of time to the present, the more valuable it will appear to an individual. The present is certain, as it is already here, but the future is always uncertain, as it may never come. The future can only come through successfully securing survival in the present, which makes the needs of the present always more pressing and important. The present is where all senses experience life and its pleasures and pains. Future pains and pleasures are hypothetical, but those of the present are real and visceral. Hunger felt in the present is far more pressing than hunger anticipated in the future, which makes food more valuable in the present than the future. The danger in the present is far more pressing than future danger, and tools that secure safety today are thus more valuable today than in the future. Given a choice between obtaining a physical good in the present, or the same good in the future, man chooses the present.

The higher valuation of present goods is a permanent fixture of human action. That humans choose to consume rather than just accumulate more of the goods they value, including money, confirms this preference. Their choice to consume in the present implies they place a higher valuation on a present good than the same good in the future. Time preference is the degree to which present goods are preferred over future goods. It is always positive because humans always prefer present goods over future goods, but its magnitude varies from person to person and for each person across his life according to his situation. A high time preference indicates a heavy discounting of the future in favor of the present and greater present orientation, while a low time preference implies a lower discounting of the future and greater future orientation.

An endless variety of factors can affect an individual's rate of time preference, and Hoppe distinguishes between external, biological, and social or institutional factors. External events influence an individual's expectations of the future, and thus influence the degree to which they prioritize the future. The biological realities of life also shape an individual's time preference. As Hoppe explains:

> It is a given that man is born as a child, that he grows up to be an adult, that he is capable of procreation during part of his life, and that he ages and dies. These biological facts have a direct bearing on time preference. Because of biological constraints on their cognitive development, children have an extremely high time-preference rate. They do not possess a clear concept of a personal life expectancy extending over a lengthy period of time, and they lack full comprehension of production as a mode of indirect consumption. Accordingly, present goods and immediate gratification are highly preferred to future goods and delayed gratification. Savings-investment activities are rare, and the periods of production and provision seldom extend beyond the most immediate future. Children live from day to day and from one immediate gratification to the next.
>
> In the course of becoming an adult, an actor's initially extremely high time-preference rate tends to fall. With the recognition of one's life expectancy and the potentialities of production as a means of indirect consumption, the marginal utility of future goods rises. Saving and investment are stimulated, and the periods of production and provision are lengthened.
>
> Finally, becoming old and approaching the end of one's life, one's time-preference rate tends to rise. The marginal utility of future goods falls because there is less of a future left. Savings and investments will decrease, and consumption—including the nonreplacement of capital and durable consumer goods—will increase. This old-age effect may be counteracted and suspended, however. Owing to the biological fact of procreation, an actor may extend his period of provision beyond the duration of his own life. If and insofar as this is the case, his time-preference rate can remain at its adult-level until his death.[147]

147 Hoppe, Hans-Hermann. *Democracy: The God That Failed.* Transaction Publishers, 2001, pp. 4-5.

Numerous social and institutional factors affect an individual's time preference. Perhaps most important among them is the security of property, which would provide man with a very effective way of providing for his future. Acquiring durable goods is arguably the initiation of the process of the decline of time preference for humanity. A man who commands a valuable good that can be used in the future reduces the uncertainty that surrounds his future and becomes likely to discount it less. As the concept of property rights becomes widely accepted in a society, as discussed in Chapter 5, it leads to a widespread decline in time preference as individuals begin to increase their valuation of their increasingly secure future. The security of property rights strongly influences time preferences. As a property owner's certainty of their command of a good increases into the future, he is likely to maintain the good in good shape and more likely to act with the future in mind.

Time Preference and Money

Providing for the future suffers from the problem of coincidence of wants discussed in the context of trade in Chapter 9. The future is unknowable and uncertain, and no individual can know for sure what goods they will require in the future. In the same way that money solves the problem of coincidence of wants in trade, it solves it for future provision. By saving money, the most liquid good and the generalized medium of exchange, the saver is able to exchange it in the future for the most valuable goods available, and to do so at the time of their choosing. Money is thus held precisely because of uncertainty. In a future that is perfectly predictable, individuals could arrange all their future financial inflows to go directly to the providers of the goods they would need at the time they need them, and would not need to hold any money. But in the real world, where the future is unpredictable, money is the best tool for providing for the future, as its liquidity allows it to be converted to whatever goods are desired in the future. As the most salable good, money can be most cheaply converted into whatever good has the highest marginal utility to the holder in the future. As human society develops money as a good, humans find it a very convenient and powerful tool for transferring value into the future, and this allows them to lower their time preference and to engage in more saving and future provision. Money supercharges our ability to save over just holding the consumer goods for the long term, as their utility in the future is more uncertain, and they are not as salable.

As humans use money to conduct trade, the technology used for money improves and becomes more efficient at carrying out its task as a medium of exchange, both in the present between individuals, and between a present individual and his future self. Money is a technology, and the proliferation of users leads to a proliferation of choices competing against each other. Better ideas and technologies win out and drive out the inferior ones. In money, the productivity of the technology pertains to how well it performs its function as a medium of exchange, or its salability, as discussed in Chapter 10.

A monetary medium that is easy to produce in excessive quantities in response to demand increases will likely experience substantial increases in its supply and a reduction in the economic value held in it over the long term. On the other hand, monetary media that are difficult to produce in increasing quantities in response to demand increases are likely to witness their supply expand to a limited extent, which causes their price to rise to meet increasing demand, making them better at preserving value. Those who store their wealth in the harder monies witness the preservation and appreciation of their wealth, while those who store it in easy money witness its dissipation. They may learn this lesson before it is too late, moving their wealth to the harder money, or they may not. In both cases, the end result is the same: The majority of the wealth will accrue to the hardest money.

This process explains the demonetization of seashells, glass beads, iron, copper, and other primitive monies in favor of gold and silver all over the world. It also explains the demonetization of silver in the nineteenth century and the precipitous decline in its value compared to gold, the undisputed winner of the global market for money at the end of the nineteenth century. As the vast majority of the planet converged on the one commodity which had the reliably lowest annual supply growth rate, secure savings into the future became ubiquitous, encouraging people around the world to save for their future, thus lowering their time preference. This made plenty of savings available for capital investment, increased labor productivity, incentivized investment in technological innovations, and increased prosperity.

As humanity progresses toward using monetary media that are harder to produce, our ability to provide for our future increases. The efficiency of transacting with our future selves increases, and the uncertainty of the future declines. The security of money as a medium of saving has allowed countless people to escape the ravages of war and disaster with wealth they can easily transport worldwide. As the uncertainty of the future declines, and the expected wealth we are able to transfer to it increases, the discounting of the future decreases and the rate of time preference declines. For any society and at all times, the hardness of monetary technologies available to people is inextricably connected to time preference, for good or for ill.

Time Preference and Saving

Economic goods can be used in three ways: They can be consumed, held for future consumption, or invested in order to produce more economic goods. The same is true for money, which is an economic good optimized for holding value into the future. Money is always used in one of three ways: It is exchanged for consumer goods, saved in a cash balance, or exchanged for capital goods, which means it is invested in the production process of other goods, in the hope it will generate a return higher than holding a cash balance.

The important distinction between savings and investment has been largely lost in modern economics, where the two terms can be used interchangeably at times. This is thanks in no small part to the many students who have suffered the misfortune of learning these concepts in the nonsensical way the Keynesian framework teaches them. For the Keynesian, saving and investment are levers that government policy dictates, completely separate from any notion of opportunity cost. While central planning bureaucrats adore this, mostly because it justifies their salaries, reality is quite different.

The distinction between saving and investment lies in the salability and risk in each category. Saving specifically refers to accumulating money in cash balances. The rationale behind holding cash is to hedge against future uncertainty. If man lives in a world in which everything is certain and perfectly predictable, he has no reason to hold any cash. With the perfectly predictable timing of all future income and expenditure flows, he can hold all his wealth in investments that earn a return, and only liquidate them at the times in which he needs to spend. But because life is uncertain, and man never knows when he will need to spend, he prefers to hold a balance of cash to take advantage of its high salability, even if it earns nothing. Investment, while it can earn you returns, is less salable, harder to liquidate, and involves the risk of losses. When man needs to liquidate his investment to spend it, he risks being unable to find someone willing to pay the price he wants at the time he wants. Further, in times of systemic crises, when everyone wants to liquidate investments for cash, the reduction in the market price from what the owner expected would be large. In contrast, money's value rises in times of crisis as individuals reduce expenses and liquidate investments for cash.

Cash allows its holders, be they individuals or businesses, to protect themselves against unexpected negative economic shocks, and to take advantage of positive economic opportunities. Should the money holder get into an accident and require medical treatment, he can spend the cash rather than liquidate an investment. Should he come across a good business opportunity, if he is holding cash, he can allocate to it quickly. If he has his money tied up in other investments, he may not be able to. The grandmother's wisdom of always keeping savings on you is quite common across the world. Value investment, at least in a world where cash is not penalized through inflation, encourages investors to maintain a large amount of cash as "dry powder" so they are able to move very quickly on good investment opportunities. Investing all your cash in whatever opportunities are available is a sure way to miss out on the best opportunities, which emerge unexpectedly and are snapped up quickly.

Money is acquired for one property only: Its marketability or salability, the ease with which it can be sold without a significant loss in its value. Cash salability is helped by its widespread use, its divisibility, durability, transportability, and the expectation that it can resist inflation in the future. Cash savings are held not to chase a return on investment, but for their liquidity and low risk of reduction in their value. A gold coin or a U.S. dollar bill is highly salable worldwide in our current day. Should you hold one and need to liquidate it, there will likely be no shortage of willing buyers to take it at a price close to the prevalent value on the market. A house, a car, a stake in a business, or a fine painting, on the other hand, have far lower salability. Should one need to sell these, it would likely take some time to find the right buyer willing to pay the prevalent market price for these goods. A house that's worth 10 bitcoins will not fetch these 10 bitcoins immediately after being put on the market. Many people will want to see the house, examine it, and think about it before buying. You may not be able to quickly find someone whose requirements for a house are exactly those of the house you have, so you will only get bids from people who don't value your house highly, offering a lower price. If you have no choice but to sell, you will be forced to sell at a significant loss. When you want to sell a house, you would much rather it not be a time-sensitive sale so you can wait until the right buyer who properly values your home comes along. For time-sensitive unexpected expenditures, you want to have highly salable liquid cash stashed away.

Unlike saving, investing necessitates relinquishing control of your capital so that it can be employed in production. You give up on the salability and reliability of having a cash balance in order to employ the capital in a productive process, hoping it will generate a profit. The investor sacrifices liquidity of cash and takes on the risk of loss in exchange for a return on investing. There is no investment without risk, as there is always the risk of partial or complete loss of capital.

Time preference can be understood as the driver of savings and investment. Once an individual can lower their time preference to engage in activities that do not offer immediate rewards, they can choose to sacrifice present time in exchange for the future. Once they decide to forgo consumption of present goods in order to save them for the future, they are lowering their time preference further.

Conceptually and chronologically, saving can only be understood as the precursor and prerequisite of investment. No matter the capital good, it can also be consumed or exchanged for goods that can be consumed in the present. Before one can invest capital, one must first defer its consumption by saving it. No matter how short the period between earning wealth and investing it, that period is a period of saving. This is the logic of grandmothers and present-day money managers worldwide: Reduce your expenditures to be able to save a certain sum you need as a cash balance, to protect you from a rainy day or an accident, and once you have reached that amount, start investing your excess savings in productive businesses.

One does not need to choose between savings and investment in the absolute, and each has their place in a person's portfolio. The choice between these two is decided at the margin, and it depends on the quantity of each already held. Young people with little wealth will likely prefer to secure some cash balance free from risk before they can take risks in capital markets. Those who accumulate significant savings are more likely to invest in capital markets.

As a man starts accumulating his cash balance from zero, the marginal utility of holding cash is very high, since he has very little of it. At this point, the utility of a cash balance is likely larger than any investment, since all investments have risk and low salability, and with a small amount of wealth, salability is prized, while risk is undesirable. As he accumulates larger cash balances, the marginal utility of adding to these balances declines, until it drops below the expected return of the best investment opportunity available to him. The more cash the man has, the more he is able to withstand the riskiness of the investment. A bad investment will not ruin him because he will still have his cash balance.

The lowering of time preference is what drives individuals to accumulate cash balances and to invest. The lower the time preference, the less they consume, and the more resources they will have to save and to invest. Each person keeps in cash a balance they would like to have with certainty, and takes risk with their investment in search of returns. Under a hard money standard, such as gold, the hard money itself would be held as savings, as its relative scarcity makes it appreciate slightly every year. In a modern easy-money economy, "cash is trash," as every investment manager knows. People instead hold the equivalent of their savings in government bonds or low-risk investment stocks, and take more risks with the rest of their portfolio.

Saving and investment are not competitors; investment follows saving. Both are driven by, and must be preceded by, a lowering of time preference and a delaying of gratification. When money is expected to appreciate, people are more likely to defer consumption to save in hard money. When savings increase, the possibility of investing increases. When cash balances can be held with confidence in their value, individuals have the freedom to take on more risks with their investments. In a world of hard money, the only investments that would make sense would be ones that offer positive real rates of return, unlike the scenario under easy money, where investments that offer positive nominal returns but negative real returns can be undertaken, leading to capital destruction in real terms. Contrary to Keynesian propaganda, inflation does not promote investment, it misallocates it. In Chapter 6, we saw how the Keynesian model posits the baseless claim that savings need to be equal to investments at equilibrium. From that perspective, a surplus of savings over investment results in unemployment and recession. But in reality, investments follow savings, and tend to rise as savings rise. The choice to allocate between consumption, savings, and investment is faced at the margin, and is shaped by time preference. As time preference declines, economic resources shift from consumption to savings. As savings increase, the marginal valuation placed on added units of savings declines, making investment risk more tolerable.

The more time preference declines, the more likely individuals are to defer consumption, and the more cash they have on hand, the more they are willing to invest and lend. The abundance of loanable funds allows for the financing of an increasing number of productive enterprises, at progressively lower interest rates. As more capital is available, productivity of labor increases, and with it income and living standards. The increase in income, in turn, allows for more capital accumulation, in a virtuous cycle of improving material well-being. This is the process of civilization.

Time Preference and Civilization

As individuals lower their time preference and accumulate more capital, their productivity increases, and as a result, they are incentivized to lower their time preference further. In *The History of Interest Rates,* Homer and Sylla show a 5,000-year process of decline in interest rates, intertwined with significant increases during periods of war, disease, and catastrophe.[148] The move toward

---

148 Homer, Sidney, and Richard Sylla. *A History of Interest Rates*. John Wiley & Sons, Inc., 2005.

harder monies with better salability across space and time can be viewed as a contributor to the epochal decline in time preference by allowing humans better savings technology, making the future less uncertain for them, and thus making them discount it less. This results in more savings, and thus more capital available at lower interest rates.

For as long as individuals are able to accumulate capital and reasonably expect it to remain theirs after they invest in it, this process is likely to continue, generating a higher stock of capital and a lower interest rate. This process, however, can be interrupted and reversed through various factors. Natural disasters destroy property and capital, lower living standards, and endanger survival, leading to a higher discounting of the future and a need to consume more available resources in the present, reducing capital accumulation, and raising time preference. But man-made disasters are an equal, perhaps more common threat to property.

Violations of property rights are the most important social and institutional factor affecting time preference. Theft, vandalism, and other forms of crime have a similar effect to natural disasters in that they reduce the stock of capital and goods available to an individual, forcing them to consume a larger fraction of their resources in the present, and increasing their uncertainty about the future. The increased occurrence of crime further leads to the expenditure of increasing resources on protection from crime, taking resources away from other productive enterprises. The more prevalent crime becomes, the more resources need to be dedicated to protection, which produces no increase in wealth.

Far more significant than individual crime is institutional or organized crime in the form of predatory government policies, which arguably extends to all forms of coercively imposed regulation, as discussed by Per Bylund in *The Seen, The Unseen, and the Unrealized.*[149] Whereas it is possible to purchase protection from random individual criminals, government violations of property rights are systemic, recurring, and inescapable. Because they are considered legitimate, it is much more difficult to defend against government

149 Bylund, Per. *The Seen, the Unseen, and the Unrealized: How Regulations Affect Our Everyday Lives*. Lexington Books, 2016.

violations of property rights than individual crime. Taxation implies a reduction in future income and a reduction in the return on investment.

The devaluation of the currency is one violation of property rights that is highly destructive of future orientation and the process of the lowering of time preference. The process of lowering time preference is inextricably linked to money. Having money allows man to delay consumption in exchange for something that can hold value well and be exchanged easily. Without money, delaying consumption and saving would be more difficult, because the goods could lose their value over time. You could store grains to grow, but the chance of them spoiling before the next season is higher than the chance of a gold coin being ruined. If you can sell the grain for gold, you are able to exchange it back for grain whenever you need to, and you can use it to purchase something else in the meantime. Money naturally increases the expected future value of deferring consumption, compared to a world with no money. This incentivizes future provision. The better the money is at holding on to its value into the future, the more reliably individuals can use this money to provide for their future selves, and the less uncertainty they will have about their future lives.

Salt, cattle, glass beads, limestones, seashells, iron, copper, and silver have all been used as money in various times and places, but by the end of the nineteenth century, practically the entire globe was on a gold standard. With the gold standard of the late nineteenth century, the majority of the world had access to a form of money that could hold its value well into the future while also being increasingly easy to transfer across space. Saving for the future became increasingly reliable for more and more of the world's population. With the ability to save in hard money, everyone is constantly enticed to save, lower their time preference, and reap future rewards. They see the benefits around them every day in terms of falling prices and the increased wealth of savers. Economic reality is constantly teaching everyone the high opportunity cost of present spending in terms of future happiness.

The twentieth century's shift to an easier monetary medium has reversed this millennia-old process of progressively lowering time preference. Rather than a world in which almost everyone had access to a store of value whose supply could only be increased by around 2% a year, the twentieth century gave us a hodgepodge of government-provided abominations of currencies growing at 6%–7% in only the best examples, usually achieving double-digit percentage growth and occasionally, triple-digit growth. The numerical average for the growth of all national currencies' broad supply during the period between 1960 and 2020 is 30% per year. Calculating the average weighted by currency size shows us roughly a 14% annual increase in the market supply of all fiat currencies, which can be viewed as the average money supply increase experienced by the average citizen of the fiat nations of the late twentieth and early twenty-first centuries.[150]

Rather than expecting money to appreciate and thus reliably retain value into the future, fiat returned humans of the twentieth century to far more primitive times, when retaining value into the future was far less certain, and the value of their wealth was expected to be reduced in the future, if it survived at all. The future is hazier with easy money, and the difficulty in providing for the future makes it less certain. This increased uncertainty leads to a higher discounting of the future and thus a higher time preference. Fiat money effectively taxes future provisions, leading to a higher discounting of the future and an increase in basic present-oriented behavior among individuals. Why delay consumption today when your savings will buy you less tomorrow? In this way, fiat monetary systems distort natural economic incentives and warp human behavior, often in ways that stymie human flourishing and undermine well-being, as I discuss in more detail in *The Fiat Standard.*

The extreme of this process can be seen when observing the effects of hyperinflation, i.e., the move to a very easy and rapidly devaluing currency. A look at the modern economies of Lebanon, Zimbabwe, or Venezuela through their recent hyperinflationary episodes provides a good case study, as do the dozens of examples of hyperinflation in the twentieth century. Adam Ferguson's *When Money Dies* provides a good overview of the effects of hyperinflation in interwar Germany, a society that was one of the world's most advanced a few years earlier.[151]

---

150 Ammous, Saifedean. *The Fiat Standard: The Debt Slavery Alternative to Human Civilization*. Saif House, 2021, p. 90.

151 Ferguson, Adam. *When Money Dies: The Nightmare of Deficit Spending, Devaluation, and Hyperinflation in Weimar Germany*. Perseus Books, 2010.

In each of these hyperinflationary scenarios, as the value of money was destroyed, so too was a concern for the future. Attention turns instead to the short-term quest for survival. Saving becomes unthinkable, and people seek to spend whatever money they have as soon as they secure it. People begin to discount all things that have value in the long run, and capital is used for immediate consumption. In hyperinflationary economies, fruit-bearing trees are chopped down for firewood in winter and businesses are liquidated to finance expenditure—the proverbial seed corn is eaten. Human and physical capital leave the country to go where savers can afford to maintain and operate them productively. With the future so heavily discounted, there is less incentive to be civil, prudent, or law-abiding, and more incentive to be reckless, criminal, or dangerous. Crime and violence become exceedingly common as everyone feels robbed and seeks to take it out on whoever owns anything. Families break down under the financial strain. While more extreme in the cases of hyperinflation, these trends are nonetheless ever-present, in milder forms, under the yoke of the slow fiat inflationary bleed.

The most immediate effect of the decline in the ability of money to maintain its value over time is an increase in consumption and a reduction in saving. Deferring consumption and delaying gratification require one to give up immediate pleasure in exchange for future reward. The less reliable the medium of exchange is for transforming value into future reward, the lower the expected value of the future reward, the more expensive the initial sacrifice becomes, and the less likely people are to defer consumption. The extreme of this phenomenon can be observed at the beginning of the month in supermarkets in countries witnessing very fast inflation. People who get their paycheck will rush to the supermarket to immediately convert it into groceries and essentials, knowing that the quantities they can acquire by the end of the month will be far smaller due to the destruction of the value of the currency. Fiat's low and steady inflation does something similar, but it is more subtle.

The culture of conspicuous mass consumption that pervades our planet today cannot be understood except through the distorted incentives fiat creates around consumption. With the money constantly losing its value, deferring consumption and saving will likely have a negative expected value. This pushes unsavvy savers to consider investing in securities. But finding the right investments is difficult, requires active management and supervision, and entails risk. The path of least resistance, the path permeating the entire culture of fiat society, is to consume all your income, living paycheck to paycheck.

When money is hard and can appreciate, individuals are likely to be very discerning about what they spend it on, as the opportunity cost appreciates over time. Why buy a shoddy table, shirt, or home when you can wait a little while and watch your savings appreciate to allow you to buy a better one. By contrast, with cash burning a hole in their pockets, consumers are less picky about the quality of what they buy. The shoddy table, home, or shirt becomes a reasonable proposition when the alternative is to hold money that depreciates over time, allowing them to acquire an even lower-quality product. Even shoddy tables will hold their value better than a depreciating fiat currency.

The uncertainty of fiat extends to all property. With the government emboldened by its ability to create money from thin air, it grows increasingly omnipotent over all citizens' property, able to decree how they can use it, or to confiscate it altogether. In *The Great Fiction*, Hoppe likens fiat property to the sword of Damocles hanging over the head of all property owners, who can have their property confiscated at any point in time, increasing their future uncertainty and reducing their provision for the future.[152]

Another way to understand the destructive impact of inflation on capital accumulation is that the threat of inflation encourages savers to invest in anything they expect will offer a better return than holding cash. In other words, inflation decreases the perceived value of discernment. When cash holds its value and appreciates, an acceptable investment will return a positive nominal return, which will also be a positive real return. Potential investors can be discerning, holding on to their cash while they wait to find a better opportunity to invest in the future. But when money is losing its value, savers have a strong impetus to avoid the devaluation of savings by investing, and so they become frantic to preserve their wealth. They are less discriminating. Investments that offer a positive nominal return could nonetheless yield a negative real return.

152 Hoppe, Hans-Hermann. *The Great Fiction*. Ludwig von Mises Institute, 2021.

Business activities that destroy economic value and consume capital appear economical when measured against the debasing monetary unit and can continue to subsist, find investors, and destroy capital. The destruction of wealth in savings does not magically create more productive opportunities in society, as Keynesian fantasists want to believe; it reallocates that wealth into destructive and failed business opportunities. It also creates a massive investment management industry to sell people what the gold standard offered them by default for free: appreciating savings. This is a negative-sum game: The value lost to inflation to finance wasteful government spending cannot be acquired back by all victims of inflation. Only a fraction will be able to invest to beat inflation, but the financial industry, with its monopoly central banking privileges, can be relied upon to come out on top. This is also a deeply regressive tax: Those most likely to beat inflation with their investment, are likely the rich who can afford to invest resources in researching markets, not the poor.

The manners and mores that make human society possible also suffer when time preference rises, as broad discounting of the future leads to increased interpersonal conflict. Trade, social cooperation, and the ability of humans to live in close contact with one another in permanent settlements are dependent upon them learning to control their basest, hostile animal instincts and responses, and substituting them with reason and a long-term orientation. Religious, civic, and social norms all encourage people to moderate their immediate impulses in exchange for the long-term benefits of living in a society, cooperating with others, and enjoying the benefits of the division of labor and specialization. When these long-term benefits seem far away, the incentive to sacrifice for them becomes weaker. When individuals witness their wealth dissipate, they rightly feel robbed. The supposed social contract appears to have been torn up, and they question the utility of living in a society and respecting its mores. Rather than a way to ensure more prosperity for all, society appears to be a mechanism for an elite few to rob the majority. Under inflation, crime rates soar and more conflict emerges.[153] Those who feel robbed by the wealthy

153 Fischer, David Hackett. 1996. *The Great Wave: Price Revolutions and the Rhythm of History*. Oxford University Press. • Rosenfeld, Richard. "Crime and Inflation in Cross-National Perspective." *Crime and Justice*, vol. 43, no. 1, 2014, pp. 341-66. • Tang, Chor, and Hooi Lean. "Will Inflation Increase Crime Rate?: New Evidence From Bounds and Modified Wald Tests." *Global Crime*, vol. 8, no. 4, Nov 2007, pp. 311-23.

elite of society will find it relatively easier to justify aggression against others' property. Diminished hope for the future weakens the incentive to be civil and respectful of clients, employers, and acquaintances. As the ability to provide for the future is compromised, the desire to account for it declines. The less certain the future appears to an individual, the more likely they are to engage in reckless behavior that could reward them in the short term while endangering them in the long term. The long-term downside risk of these activities, such as imprisonment, death, or mutilation, is discounted more heavily compared to the immediate reward of securing life's basic needs.[154]

Time Preference and Bitcoin

The emergence of bitcoin represents a fascinating opportunity to understand the effect of money on time preference, as well as to reverse the global trend of rising time preference presented by fiat. Bitcoin is free and open-source software for operating a peer-to-peer payment network with its own native currency. The two most important features of bitcoin are that its native currency has a strictly fixed supply that is completely unresponsive to demand, making it the hardest money ever invented, and that it allows for cross-border payments without needing any political authority to supervise the transaction. These two properties—hardness and censorship-resistance—arguably give bitcoin the capability to be the most salable good across time and space. Its scarcity means that its supply cannot be diluted unexpectedly, ensuring it is likely to hold on to its value in the future. And its automated processing of payments, secured by a truly decentralized network, means it can travel worldwide, and no single authority has the power to censor or confiscate it.

Bitcoin is pretty basic, and it simply allows you to hold and transfer ownership of currency units. In practice, the most prevalent use case for bitcoin

154 For more on the social, cultural, and moral implications of inflation, see Salerno, Joseph. "Hyperinflation and The Destruction of Human Personality." *Studia Humana*, vol. 2, no. 1, 2013, pp. 15-27. • Hülsmann, Jörg Guido. *The Ethics of Money Production*. Ludwig Von Mises Institute, 2008. • Hülsmann, Jörg Guido. *Deflation and Liberty*. Ludwig Von Mises Institute, 2008.

has been its use as a store of value, or a savings account replacement. Millions of people worldwide have used bitcoin as a savings account, and they have profited from this immensely as bitcoin's price has appreciated significantly in the long term.

This offers us a very interesting insight into the importance of money to time preference. Democracy, inflation, government predation, wars, the Keynesian managerial state, and the vast majority of modern factors causing an increase in time preference are still there, and they are usually getting worse. Yet for a small but growing minority of the world's population, bitcoin represents an escape hatch from monetary inflation. Unlike the vast majority of humans in the past century, bitcoiners today are able to save for the future in a monetary medium protected from debasement; they can expect, with relatively low uncertainty, to have their savings available in the future and to have their purchasing power increase. If money is important for time preference, we would expect to see these people differentiate themselves from their fiat peers by having a lower time preference. My personal experience from years of discussing this with bitcoiners has provided me with compelling evidence for this.

The story of bitcoin leading to increased savings is one I have come across very frequently. Before bitcoin, many people simply had no conception of saving and delayed gratification. They spent all the money they earned, and when they had major expenses, they went into debt to pay for them. They continued to work and pay off debts indefinitely. To the extent most people invest, they do so through their work retirement funds. People who do invest are mostly those who spend considerable time studying the markets and trading, making it almost a job. The notion of saving passively while earning money from a job was very rare. After bitcoin, it became increasingly common.

As it is expected to lose its value over time, easy money is not a reliable way of providing for the future; this increases future uncertainty, encouraging heavier discounting of the future, or a higher time preference, as observed in the twentieth century under the fiat standard. Because it can be expected to hold on to its value into the future, hard money increases the potential payoff from saving and delaying gratification, reducing the uncertainty of the future, and encouraging more saving and more future-oriented behavior, as was the case under the gold standard, and in the nascent bitcoin standard. Bitcoin could be the free market's solution to the problem of rising time preference. It is the technological solution that allows anyone to rejoin the process of lowering time preference, saving, capital accumulation, and civilization. It requires no political permission, it obviates politics and monetary policy, it is unstoppable, and it is hugely rewarding for everyone who adopts it.

Chapter 14

Credit and Banking

> Every kind of human arrangement is connected in some way or other with money payments. And, therefore if you destroy the monetary system of a country or of the whole world, you are destroying much more than simply one aspect. When you destroy the monetary system, you are destroying in some regards the basis of all interhuman relations. If one talks of money, one talks about a field in which governments were doing the very worst thing which could be done, destroying the market, destroying human cooperation, destroying all peaceful relations between men.[155]

— Ludwig von Mises

Banking

As time preference declines, individuals save more, and consequently, invest more, which tends to lead to an increase in productivity and, in turn, increases the amount of savings available for them. As savings increase and the division of labor becomes more complex, the management of money itself becomes a service provided on the market by specialized professionals. The development of the division of labor leads to increases in specialization across all goods and services, and money is no different. As with food, clothes, or houses, specialization increases the productivity with which a good is provided on the

155 Greaves, Bettina Bien. 2010. *Ludwig von Mises on Money and Inflation: A Synthesis of Several Lectures.* Ludwig von Mises Institute.

market. Banking is the industry that specializes in the management of money, and it has two essential functions: managing deposits and investments.

On an individual level, we can see how lower time preference leads to delayed gratification and increased savings, investment, productivity, and economic abundance. At the level of the market economy, with the division of labor occurring on a large impersonal scale, and the use of money as a common medium of exchange and saving, the banking industry increases the productivity of saving and investment, allowing for greater capital accumulation and higher productivity. Members of society benefit from others lowering their time preference in this way. That is to say, other people's savings increase the productivity of your labor.

The first job of banking is to help savers maintain the wealth they have accrued and protect it from theft and ruin. As individuals' homes are optimized for location, comfort, and various other characteristics, they are not optimized for resisting theft. An increasingly specialized economy will provide individuals and firms with the opportunity to store their wealth in facilities specializing in secure storage. Banks would accept deposits and charge their owners for the privilege of using the facilities. Building a facility specializing in securing savings allows its building to be optimized for security and safety from theft or ruin. By charging a small fee to many wealth holders, bank owners finance the construction and operation of safe facilities that are less likely to be robbed than individual homes or workplaces. In its basic form, when done safely, sanely, and honestly, deposit banking is a boring and largely uninteresting market good that does not merit much economic analysis. It is only when deposit banking is abused that the interesting and tragic consequences unfold. Unfortunately for savers, deposit banking is so commonly abused that safe and boring banking has become a thing of the past.

Credit

The first function of banking is to hold savings on behalf of their owners. The second function is to invest these savings in pursuit of profits that increase them while taking the risk of losing them. Extending credit allows the saver to make a return on their savings by deploying it in the service of an entrepreneur who has a business engaged in economic production. By abstaining from consuming and by abstaining from saving money, the saver becomes an investor, and she makes her savings available to purchase inputs for a production process. The factors of production are then combined to produce the outputs, which are sold on the market, ideally at a revenue that exceeds costs, rewarding the entrepreneur and the capitalists with profit. Should the business fail to make a profit, the creditors stand to lose their savings.

Whereas a capitalist lends her own money to an entrepreneur, a bank lends the money of savers, effectively specializing in the allocation of investments while leaving the savers to specialize in whatever it is that earns them their income. The introduction of specialization and division of labor into the job of capital investment allows its productivity to increase. It allows individuals to invest amounts of money they would otherwise have no obvious use for investing in their own line of work. Their ability to invest becomes no longer contingent on the ability of their own business to grow. By investing in lines of production unrelated to their own industry, investors are able to hedge against the failure of their business or disruptions to their industry.

The task of bankers is to act as the intermediary between the saver and the entrepreneur. They perform due diligence on a large number of potential investments and make an entrepreneurial judgment on which projects are worthy of financing with savers' savings. The job of the investment banker allows the savers to delegate the selection of investments to professionals and allows entrepreneurs to seek the savings they require from the bank rather than attempt to gather them from unspecialized individuals.

Not all bank credit is the same. Mises makes an important distinction between two different types of banking credit: Commodity credit and circulation credit.[156] The rest of this chapter discusses commodity credit, while the next chapter will focus on circulation credit.

---

156 Mises, Ludwig von. *Human Action: The Scholar's Edition*. Ludwig von Mises Institute, 1998, p. 568-72.

Commodity Credit

Mises uses the term commodity credit to refer to the credit which is borrowed by banks and granted to entrepreneurs, making banks mere intermediaries profiting from the difference between the interest rate they pay their lenders and the rate they charge their borrowers. This difference arises from the expectation that the bank's specialization will allow them superior returns over the lender attempting to find counterparties all by themselves. For a bank to be an intermediary granting commodity credit, its lending must follow the golden rule, which is according to Mises: "The credit that the bank grants must correspond quantitatively and qualitatively to the credit that it takes up. More exactly expressed, 'the date on which the bank's obligations fall due must not precede the date on which its corresponding claims can be realized.' "[157] In other words, it is essential that the quantity of the credit that the bank extends does not exceed the quantity of savings that savers have lent to the bank. Further, the date at which any particular loan is granted by the bank must be no later than the date at which the credit was granted to the bank by savers. According to the golden rule, the bank cannot grant a saver's 1-year deposit to an entrepreneur for 2 years, counting on the fact that they will be able to find another lender in a year to make an equivalent deposit, which they can use to repay the depositor.

Should there be a discrepancy between the quantity of credit the bank borrows and the quantity it lends, or should there be a discrepancy between the maturity dates, then the bank is no longer engaged in lending of commodity credit, but in circulation credit. In this case, the bank is not merely transferring the money of savers to entrepreneurs; it is issuing credit that is being used as money, effectively inflating the money supply, with substantial consequences discussed in the next chapter.

The distinguishing feature of commodity credit is that it involves a sacrifice on the part of the lender. Someone has to forgo access to monetary

157 Mises, Ludwig von. *The Theory of Money and Credit*. 2nd ed., Foundation for Economic Education, 1971, p. 363.

instruments equal to the full value of the loan for its entire duration in order for the loan to be issued. The lender forgoes the money in the present in the expectation of receiving a larger payout in the future. The borrower, on the other hand, gains access to the money in the present but pays an added cost when repaying the loan. The interest rate at which the loan takes place illustrates the differing valuations placed on time by each party. The lender has a lower time preference, which makes the value of the principal and interest in the future higher than the principal today for her, making lending at that rate profitable. In turn, the borrower has a higher time preference, and so the principal and interest repayment in the future are worth less to him than the principal today. The difference in time preference between the two is what creates the opportunity for them to agree on an exchange.

Interest Rates

In mainstream economics, interest rates are viewed as the determinants of savings rates, as individuals compare their time preference to interest rates and decide if they will save. But that is only tenable in a centrally planned world where interest rates are set by the government. In a free market, what would determine the interest rate? It would be determined by people's time preferences. It cannot be determined by the productivity of projects funded since there are projects at all levels of productivity. What determines which projects are funded and which are not is not their productivity, but the availability of capital, which is a function of time preference. Time preference makes the capital available, and entrepreneurial judgment attempts to allocate it to the projects with the highest expected returns.

> The capitalists' function is thus a time function, and their income is precisely an income representing the agio of present as compared to future goods. ***This interest income, then, is not derived from the concrete, heterogeneous capital goods, but from the generalized investment of time.*** It comes from a willingness to sacrifice present goods for the purchase of future goods (the factor services). As a result of the purchases, the

> owners of factors obtain their money in the present for a product that matures only in the future.[158]

The ratio of the value assigned to a present good and the value assigned to an identical future good is called the originary interest. Originary interest measures the percentage discounting on the valuation of a good an individual requires to receive the good in the future. For instance, a person who expects to receive a shipment of 10 bushels of corn today would have to be offered a certain premium to delay acceptance by a year. The percentage increase in the quantity that needs to be offered to that individual to delay their consumption is the originary interest rate.

From the perspective of Austrian economics, all economic phenomena have their root in human action, and interest is no different. Time preference is what creates the phenomenon of originary interest. The ingrained time preference of individuals is inevitably reflected in a premium for present goods over future goods; this is in turn reflected in the market for money, which is a market good no different from all others. Assuming the value of the currency remains constant, a person who is owed a payment of $100 today would need to be offered a premium on it in order to delay accepting the payment by a year, in the same way, they would need to be offered a premium on the bushels of corn. The existence of time preference is itself the determinant and originant of monetary interest.

The presence of money allows originary interest to be harmonized across goods and individuals. This happens through the emergence of a credit market, in which future obligations of money are traded for present payments, establishing a general discount rate of the future, or an interest rate. Deviations of discount rates for particular goods from the prevalent market interest rate for money will create opportunities for profitable arbitrage in these goods, bringing the interest rate on all goods into a narrow range, reflected on the market as the market interest rate. Hoppe describes this market-determined interest rate as

158 Rothbard, Murray. *Man, Economy, and State, with Power and Market.* Ludwig von Mises Institute, 1962, p. 355.

"the aggregate sum of all individual time-preference rates reflecting the social rate of time preference and equilibrating social savings (i.e., the supply of present goods offered for exchange against future goods) and social investment (i.e., the demand for present goods thought capable of yielding future returns)."[159]

While individual capital goods have their own markets in which they are traded, in a modern monetary economy, capital is traded as an abstract good through the borrowing and investment of sums of money. Societal monetary savings are made available to financial institutions who lend them to entrepreneurs who use them to purchase capital goods. The demand for investing and purchasing capital goods is practically infinite, as coming up with entrepreneurial ideas is far easier and less costly than deferring the consumption of present resources. The limiting factor on the quantity of investment is the quantity of cash saved, and that in turn is restricted by the desire and need to consume—by time preference being positive. The existence of capital goods, and capital markets in general, is entirely contingent on individuals lowering their time preference enough to provide the capital needed. The demand is for investable funds, and the borrowers' expected rates of return do not determine interest rates, as there are projects expected to offer a very wide range of returns. Time preference determines the quantity of loanable funds, which will then go to fund the projects with the highest expected returns, whose borrowers are willing to pay the highest interest rates. The more funds are saved, the lower the interest rate, the more projects can be funded, and the lower the expected rate of return on the marginal project. More saving also results in a growing diversity of funding mechanisms, increasing the liquidity of the market for capital and its options.

By deferring consumption to provide capital for investors, the capitalist incurs the cost of the operation in terms of time. The capitalist invests the time in the enterprise by sacrificing present goods for future goods. This sacrifice is what allows the workers and the providers of the input goods for the process of production to get paid before production is concluded and the goods are sold on the market. In the same way that a fisherman living in isolation needs to

159 Ibid. 2.

sacrifice time spent catching fish in order to build a fishing rod, someone must defer consumption of resources for any production process to take place. The entrepreneur uses the resources and sacrifice of the capitalist to pay the workers, landowners, and capital good sellers in the present. The process of production takes place over time, and the entrepreneur sells the final goods. Only then is the capitalist paid the agreed-upon interest rate. The workers and the sellers of input goods get paid as they perform the service, not as the product is sold, because they are not contributing their time to the endeavor, and they are not deferring consumption. The capitalist is the one who defers consumption, and in doing so, contributes the time for the resource goods to mature into final products. Time is an essential input into the process of production, no different from labor, land, and capital, and the capitalist receives compensation for it from the entrepreneur in the form of the prevalent market interest rate.

Should the revenue from selling the final output of the production process exceed the costs paid to the providers of the labor, land, capital, and time, the business is profitable. It is important here to distinguish between the interest and the profit. The profit is derived from the difference between the market valuation of the input goods and the market valuation of the final goods. The interest is merely the payment for the time input provided to the production process by the capitalist. The profit or loss is the difference in market valuation of the inputs and outputs.

In the market for capital, individuals have value scales ranking present goods against future goods. Present goods are more valuable than identical future goods; humans effectively place a discount on future goods. Individuals compare their own discount rate for goods to the market interest rate. If a person's personal discount rate is higher than the market interest rate, she would demand to borrow from the market, since she would value the repayment of the principal and interest in the future less than the principal in the present. If, on the other hand, her personal discount rate is lower than that of the market, she would lend her cash savings on the capital market, as she would value the repayment of the principal and interest higher than holding the present cash savings. The larger the disparity between personal time preference and market interest rate, the larger the quantity of borrowing and lending demanded.

We can illustrate this relationship graphically: An individual has a "time market" curve, which determines the quantity of money she would like to borrow or lend at any given interest rate. For a saver who places a 5% annual discount on the future, a 5% market interest rate leaves her not wanting to borrow or lend, as the market has the same discount level as she does. If the market interest rate were to rise 7%, she is now offered a tempting opportunity: If she forgoes enjoying a certain sum of money today, she could lend it and receive it along with a 7% interest rate in a year's time. Since she discounts next year's money at a rate of 5%, this loan would give her a return of 2%. If, on the other hand, the interest rate were to drop to 3%, then she would have the incentive to borrow from the capital market. Borrowing at 3% means she has to repay in a year 103% of the principal, and since he discounts the future at 5%, her repayment is lower than the value of the loan to her today. Naturally, as the interest rate rises, the demand for borrowing declines while the demand for lending increases.

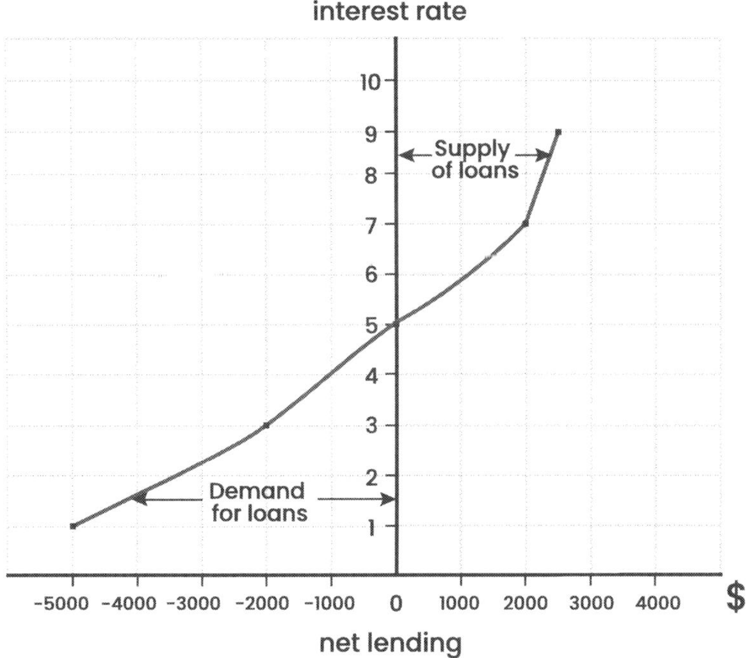

Figure 29. Individual time market

At the capital market level, all of the individual time preference and money demand and supply curves are effectively aggregated into economy-wide supply and demand curves for loanable funds. At any given interest rate, there is a total amount of capital that is available for lending and demanded for borrowing. Since the capital available for lending increases as interest rates rise, while the capital demanded for borrowing decreases as interest rates rise, the two quantities must only meet once, at the interest rate which clears the market capital, where the quantity of loans is equal to the quantity of capital saved from consumption and made available to borrowers.

It is important here to reemphasize that time preference and future discounting are subjective phenomena and they are not measured by interest rates. What exists in acting humans' minds is an ordinal ranking of future and present goods, and it is by being exposed to an offer of an interest rate that they are able to ordinally compare the implied discounting available on the market to their personal discounting, and decide between the two. Further, there is no such thing as a prevalent market interest rate, only individual interest rates, which are affected by the individual projects and the individuals involved. It is useful to think of the market interest rate, as with the market equilibrium price, as a tool to help understand these economic concepts. While the tools of mathematical analysis are useful to communicate an understanding of market phenomenon, it is important to not fall into the trap of treating them as scientific units based on accurate measurement of constants.

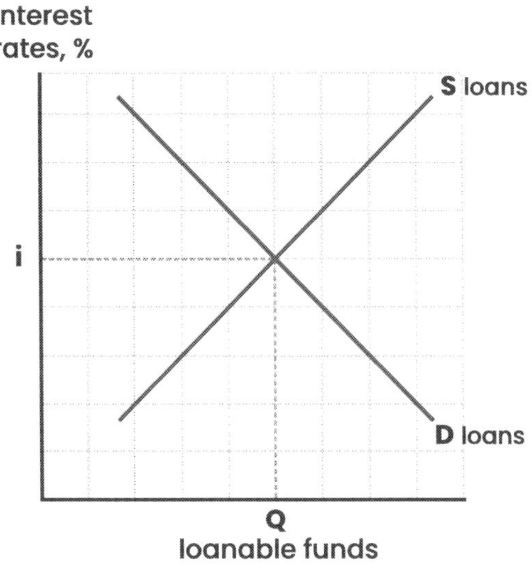

Figure 30. The market for loanable funds

As capital is allocated to economic production, productivity increases and incomes rise. With secure property rights and increased certainty of the future, time preference would be expected to continue to decline further, making individuals more likely to defer consumption, more likely to save, more likely to lend, and less likely to borrow. The abundance of loanable funds allows for the financing of an increasing number of productive enterprises at progressively lower interest rates. Unless interrupted by war, pestilence, depredation, the perverse regulatory burdens of centralized governments, or violently imposed easy fiat money, this virtuous cycle of improving material well-being continues, which can be understood as the process of civilization. But how far can this process go? How low can interest rates go?

Can Interest Be Eliminated?

The topic of interest lending is a historically, politically, and religiously charged one. Interest lending has been forbidden by many religions and is still viewed as immoral by many people worldwide to this day, even in a monetary system that relies heavily on credit creation. Mises and the Austrian economists have gone to great lengths to explain it as an inextricable part of a market economy and to make a case for why it is a productive institution in the market economy. From the Austrian perspective, interest is not an alien invention imposed on society by leaders. Like all economic phenomena, interest has its root in human action and in the time preference that is positive in each individual. As Mises explains:

> We cannot even think of a world in which originary interest would not exist as an inexorable element in every kind of action[160] ... If there were no originary interest, capital goods would not be devoted to immediate consumption and capital would not be consumed. On the contrary, under such an unthinkable and unimaginable state of affairs there would be no consumption at all, but only saving, accumulation of capital, and investment. Not the impossible disappearance of originary interest, but the abolition of payment of interest to the owners of capital, would result in capital consumption. The capitalists would consume their capital goods and their capital precisely because there is originary interest and present want satisfaction is preferred to later satisfaction.[161]

Attempting to abolish interest, according to Mises, would not lead to the elimination of interest-rate lending and would instead lead to the consumption of capital stocks as savers have less of an incentive to preserve their capital when they cannot make a return on it. Banning individuals from trading financial assets based on their time preference will not eliminate their time preference, which will continue to direct their consumption and production decisions. Capital owners with a positive time preference who no longer have access to the option of lending at interest find themselves with a stronger incentive to consume their capital stock. Banning interest then leaves the borrowers worse off by not allowing them access to much-needed funds. It also

---

160 Mises, Ludwig von. *Human Action: The Scholar's Edition*. Ludwig von Mises Institute, 1998, p. 524.

161 Ibid. 529.

leaves the lenders worse off since it forbids them from gaining a return on savings. And it hurts society overall by reducing the incentive to save and thus resulting in less capital accumulation. A society without interest lending is less productive, less innovative, and less prosperous.

From the Austrian perspective, it is difficult to argue that interest is exploitative of the borrower. There is no coercion in the loan contract, and both parties willingly choose to enter it, so there is no legal or moral justification for calling it illegal or for an outside party to attempt to violently prevent both parties from transacting.

> Therefore there cannot be any question of abolishing interest by any institutions, laws, or devices of bank manipulation. He who wants to "abolish" interest will have to induce people to value an apple available in a hundred years no less than a present apple. What can be abolished by laws and decrees is merely the right of the capitalists to receive interest. But such decrees would bring about capital consumption and would very soon throw mankind back into the original state of natural poverty.[162]

This book's biggest break from Austrian orthodoxy is to present the case for why the interest rate may, in fact, be eliminated from a purely free market and not through official abolition or edict. As discussed in the previous section and explained in detail by Hoppe in *Democracy*, the process of civilization is initiated with the lowering of time preference, which results in capital accumulation, increased productivity, and improved living standards, in turn encouraging further reductions in time preference in a continuously amplifying spiral. Wars, diseases, natural disasters, increased future uncertainty, and growing uncertainty over property rights can forestall this process by causing increases in time preference and forcing people to increasingly prioritize the present at the expense of the future.

The historical empirical record supports this contention. As discussed in the previous chapter, the history of interest rates, and as detailed in the encyclopedic

162 Ibid.

study on the topic by Homer and Sylla,[163] humanity has seen a steady, long-term decline in interest rates over the past 5,000 years, interrupted by the aforementioned calamities. Hoppe summarizes the history of interest rate declines:

> In fact, a tendency toward falling interest rates characterizes mankind's suprasecular trend of development. Minimum interest rates on "normal safe loans" were around 16 percent at the beginning of Greek financial history in the sixth century B.C., and fell to 6 percent during the Hellenistic period. In Rome, minimum interest rates fell from more than 8 percent during the earliest period of the Republic to 4 percent during the first century of the Empire. In thirteenth-century Europe, the lowest interest rates on "safe" loans were 8 percent. In the fourteenth century they came down to about 5 percent. In the fifteenth century they fell to 4 percent. In the seventeenth century they went down to 3 percent. And at the end of the nineteenth century minimum interest rates had further declined to less than 2.5 percent.[164]

Yet this trend of declining interest rates was reversed in the twentieth century. The move to fiat money likely played a major role in this shift, along with many other factors that are discussed at length in Hoppe's *Democracy*. The hypothetical thought experiment worth asking here is: What would have happened to interest rates had they continued their decline in the twentieth century? What would have happened had the world remained on a gold standard, and people maintained the ability to save for the future, capital continued to become more abundant, and productivity increased? How low would interest rates go?

We may accept Mises' contention that originary interest may never drop to zero and yet still arrive at a market interest rate of zero. The key is to consider that money, like all goods, has a carrying cost. Whatever form it takes, money requires safekeeping and storage, and this will always involve a nonzero cost and will always involve a nonzero risk of theft, loss, or ruin. The cost could be

---

163 Homer, Sidney, and Richard Sylla. *A History of Interest Rates*. John Wiley & Sons, 2005.

164 Hoppe, Hans-Hermann. *Democracy: The God That Failed.* Transaction Publishers, 2001, p. 63.

paid in many forms, such as purchasing a safe or storage facility, paying for a deposit account at a bank, or paying for insurance on the sum. Or it could be paid in the form of theft and loss, which is a risk that always exists. Some nonzero costs must be paid to hold money. For the lender, the opportunity cost of lending lies not in maintaining their nominal wealth in full. Instead, not lending means witnessing a slow decline in the value of the money due to the nonzero cost of keeping it safe.

As time preference continues to decline, and originary interest declines along with it, the implied market interest rate may eventually become lower than the carrying cost of money. In such a situation, the lender would be happy to lend at a nominal interest rate of 0% because it is a better return than simply holding the money, which would have a negative return. Rather than requiring abolition by decree, the continued process of civilization, capital accumulation, and lowering of time preference could naturally eliminate lending with interest entirely.

A decline in time preference increases the abundance of capital, and as the abundance grows, the price of capital, as interest, declines. A continuously advancing civilization would witness its time preference decline, leading to more future provision and more moral concern for future generations, which results in capital being widely abundant. As people own larger quantities of capital, the demand for borrowing declines as well. At a sufficient level of abundance, the return on lending becomes lower than the cost of carrying the money, at which point a borrower can secure a loan from the many lenders available by simply promising to pay it back in full because he would be saving the lender the cost of storage and insurance or the risk of theft and loss.

As interest rates decline with time preference, the asymmetry of the loan deal becomes increasingly unappealing to the lender. Why take on the risk of losing all the capital in exchange for such a measly return? The loan contract limits the upside benefit to the lender, but there is no force that can truly guarantee that the lender will get their money back. Risk exists, and the risk of complete and catastrophic loss can never be legislated away. In the modern fiat-based economic system, the risk of bank insolvency has been severely alleviated by being transferred to the national currency. Loans are effectively guaranteed through the central bank's ability to monetize them and make the lenders whole on any defaults on their portfolio. This is why the FDIC is able to guarantee bank accounts in the modern world, but this is not something that you would expect to exist in the hypothetical society of this scenario, where capital accumulation and dropping time preference could not have reached some advanced stages with inflationary fiat money which the central bank can use to bail out banks, because such money would discourage saving and would not allow time preference and interest rates to decline. We would only expect to arrive at such a point with a hard monetary standard that encourages savings and allows for no bailouts for banks and no protection for lenders from bankruptcies. In such a world of lowtime preference, hard money, and no bailouts, lending for interest becomes unlikely. Lenders would get a very small return while sharing in the full downside. If they are taking the full downside, they would prefer to also get full exposure to the upside through an equity investment.

In a world of high capital abundance and negligibly low interest rates, or a world of zero nominal interest rates, people who are credit-worthy will have no problem securing capital from friends and family for emergency expenses or hardship. Lending at zero interest would save the money owner from needing to spend on storage and relieve him from taking the risk of loss. At a very low time preference, lending to a trusted borrower would thus be preferable to holding money. But for business investments, it is highly likely that the market would be predominantly based on equity. Such a world would see banking get neatly divided into two categories: investment equity banking and deposit banking.

Mises' golden rule discussed above stipulates that commodity credit is backed fully by savings that match the full maturity of the loan. But without a lender of last resort, and at zero nominal interest rates, the rule would have an added stipulation: The lender gets a preset share of the profit of the enterprise. In other words, there would be no lender with a loan but an investor with equity.

Understanding the time preference theory of interest rates from the Austrian perspective can help explain the historical and religious case against interest. The world of the zero nominal interest rate is the world where time preference is so low that originary interest is lower than the carrying cost of money. Religious mandates against interest can be understood as prescriptions for members of the religion to lower their time preference to the point where interest lending no longer forms an attraction to them. Belief in the afterlife could be understood as conducive to the lowering of time preference. Believers expect to live in the afterlife for eternity, and so expect to face infinite rewards and punishment for their actions, leading to infinitely low discounting of future consequences.

While religions and traditions seek to impose this reality on their believers through dictates, the modern market economy, through constant capital accumulation, division of labor, technological advancement, and lowering time preference, is the tool that drives us toward this reality in practice. In other words, if the processes of the market and civilization are uninterrupted, future discounting declines to the point where market interest lending is eliminated, resulting in a system free of usury, similar to those embodied by traditional Christian and Islamic banking.

Joseph Schumpeter provides a good summary of the work of Eugene Böhm-Bawerk, the Austrian economist who did the most to develop the Austrian theory of interest rates.

> [Interest] is, so to speak, the brake, or governor, which prevents individuals from exceeding the economically admissible lengthening of the period of production, and enforces provision for present wants—which, in effect, brings their pressure to the attention of entrepreneurs. And this is why it reflects the relative intensity with which in every economy future and present interests make themselves felt and thus also a people's intelligence and moral strength—the higher these are, the lower will be the rate of interest. This is why the rate of interest mirrors the cultural level of a nation; for the higher this level, the larger will be the available stock of consumers' goods, the longer will be the period of production, the smaller will be, according to the law of roundaboutness, the surplus return which further extension of the period of production would yield, and thus the lower will be the rate of interest. And here we have Böhm-Bawerk's law of the decreasing rate of interest, his solution to this ancient problem which had tried the best minds of our science and found them wanting.[165]

165 Schumpeter, Joseph. *Ten Great Economists: From Marx to Keynes*. Routledge, 1997, p. 182.

Whether a continued decline in time preference would bring down interest rates to a nominal zero rate is a separate question from the economic efficacy of banning interest coercively. Without the requisite low time preference, prohibiting interest lending would likely lead to more consumption, less saving and lending, and likely less investment overall. It might be the case that interest lending is the only thing that abolishes interest lending. By incentivizing saving and increasing capital accumulation, interest lending leads to a decline in time preference and interest rates, until they disappear entirely.

Chapter 15

Monetary Expansion

> [The] expansion of credit cannot form a substitute for capital.[166]
> —Ludwig von Mises

Circulation Credit

The previous chapter explained the working of commodity credit, which Mises defines as credit extended by banks with perfect correspondence between the quantity and maturity of the loan from the savers to the bank and from the bank to investors. In other words, commodity credit is a credit transaction where the bank is a mere intermediary facilitating the matching between savers and investors. In each commodity credit transaction, the amount of the capital invested induces an equivalent sacrifice of consumption by the owners of the savings invested, meaning interest rates reflect lender time preference. This chapter discusses credit arrangements where investment does not elicit a reduction in consumption on the part of lenders. In what Mises terms circulation credit, lending effectively creates new money.

The most common way in which circulation credit comes into existence is

---

166 Mises, Ludwig von. *The Theory of Money and Credit*. 2nd ed., Foundation for Economic Education, 1971, p. 22.

when financial institutions lend out money which they also promise to make available for the depositor on demand. This practice is known as **fractional reserve banking**. The lender, in this case, the bank's depositor, does not have to defer consuming his deposit while it is being lent out as credit to an entrepreneur, as is the case in full reserve, maturity-matched commodity credit, where the depositor forsakes the deposit for the entire duration of the entrepreneur's loan.

Another way in which a bank can generate circulation credit is by mismatching the maturities of its loans and deposits. If the bank only lends out credit equal to its deposits but lends at a longer maturity than it borrowed, then it is also effectively engaging in the creation of circulation credit. The loan effectively assumes the bank's ability to find depositors willing to deposit money for a rate of return lower than the rate it is offering the entrepreneur. Circulation credit is thus generated every time the golden rule discussed in Chapter 14 is broken.

A third way in which circulation credit can be created is through the practice of rehypothecation of lending collateral—the reuse of collateral for more than one loan. If the collateral had been previously pledged to a loan, then the second loan would also not entail the deferral of consumption on the part of the lender.

In all of these three ways, credit is generated without commensurate sacrifice on the part of the lender, and it is issued as **fiduciary media**: Notes and bank balances that are redeemable for money but do not have an equivalent amount of money available in the bank on demand to be paid for their bearer for the entire duration of the deposit.

Money, as discussed in Chapter 10, is unique in that it is the one good that is obtained purely to be exchanged for something else. It is not consumed, like consumer goods, nor is it used in the production of other goods, as capital goods are. Since its sole purpose is to be passed on, and it performs no physical function to its owner, a claim on it, or a substitute for it, is capable of playing its role in a way that cannot be played by any substitute or claim on another consumer or capital good. A voucher for a steak cannot be eaten, a receipt for a machine cannot produce the goods that the machine produces, and an airplane ticket cannot make you fly. But a claim on money can perform the essential function of money: It can be exchanged for other goods. As Mises puts it:

> The peculiar attitude of individuals toward transactions involving circulation credit is explained by the circumstance that the claims in which it is expressed can be used in every connection instead of money. He who requires money, in order to lend it, or to buy something, or to liquidate debts, or to pay taxes, is not first obliged to convert the claims to money (notes or bank balances) into money; he can also use the claims themselves directly as means of payment. For everybody they therefore are really money-substitutes; they perform the monetary function in the same way as money; they are "ready money" to him, i.e., present, not future, money.[167]
>
> A person who has a thousand loaves of bread at his immediate disposal will not dare to issue more than a thousand tickets each of which gives its holder the right to demand at any time the delivery of a loaf of bread. It is otherwise with money. Since nobody wants money except in order to get rid of it again ... it is quite possible for claims to be employed in its stead ... and it's quite possible for these claims to pass from hand to hand without any attempt being made to enforce the right that they embody.[168]

Because of this peculiar nature of money, monetary substitutes like fiduciary media can be used as money by people, acquired and spent as payment for goods or services, without having to be redeemed for money at the issuing bank. The banknotes or bank accounts that the bank issues as fiduciary media are themselves the medium of exchange without having to be redeemed for money. Note here that fiduciary media are distinctly different from banknotes issued with full reserve money available on demand at the bank in one very important respect: The issuance of fiduciary media involves no sacrifice on behalf of the issuing party. Therefore, when banknotes are issued with 100% money on reserve, there

167 Ibid. 266.
168 Ibid. 267.

is no impact on the total supply of money. On the other hand, when fiduciary media are issued, they are an addition to the existing money stock. Whereas mining gold is an expensive and uncertain venture whose cost usually approximates the expected sale value of the gold, the issuance of fiduciary media increases the money supply without requiring any substantial cost on the part of the issuing financial institution. The increase in money supply naturally affects the market value of money, with substantial consequences, which the Austrian school has worked diligently to analyze over more than a century, to be discussed below.

Mises' Typology of Money

The peculiar nature of money, as a good that does not get consumed, allows money substitutes and fiduciary media to play a monetary role as well as money, which can create confusion about what exactly is referred to by the term "money." Important distinctions exist, and it is useful to follow the typology laid out by Mises in *The Theory of Money and Credit* and explained in *Mises: The Last Knight of Liberalism,*[169] Jörg Guido Hülsmann's intellectual biography of Mises:

> Mises developed a comprehensive typology of monetary objects—that is, in Mengerian language, of all the things generally accepted as media of exchange. On the most fundamental level, he distinguished several types of "money in the narrower sense" from several types of "money surrogates" or substitutes. Money in the narrower sense is a good in its own right. In contrast, money substitutes were legal titles to money in the narrower sense. They were typically issued by banks and were redeemable in real money at the counters of the issuing bank.
>
> In establishing this fundamental distinction between money and money titles, he applied crucial insights of Böhm-Bawerk's pioneering work on the economics of legal entities. He stressed: "Claims are not goods; they are

169 Hülsmann, Jörg Guido. *Mises: The Last Knight of Liberalism*. Ludwig von Mises Institute, 2007, p. 216.

> means of obtaining disposal over goods. This determines their whole nature and economic significance." As his exposition in later parts of the book would show, these distinctions have great importance, both for the integration of monetary theory within the framework of Menger's theory of value and prices, and for the analysis of the role of banking within the monetary system. At the heart of his theory of banking is a comparative analysis of the economic significance of two very different types of money substitutes. Mises observed that money substitutes could be either covered by a corresponding amount of money, in which case they were "money certificates," or they could lack such coverage, in which case they were fiduciary media—Umlaufsmittel. Mises devotes the entire last third of his book to an analysis of the economic consequences of the use of Umlaufsmittel.[170]

The term "money" is broadly used to refer to money and money substitutes. Mises clarifies the distinction in a way that helps explain the Austrian analysis of the business cycle. Money, in the narrower sense, can come in three forms:

Commodity money: A general medium of exchange that is also an economic good that is exchangeable with goods of the same type. It is sold on an open market with many producers and consumers. Historical examples are mainly precious metals, but more recently, bitcoin can be added as a new form of non-metal digital commodity.

170 Hülsmann's footnote here is worth including in full: "Regrettably, this comparative focus of his analysis was lost in the English translation of the title of the book: Theory of Money and Credit. The term Umlaufsmittel, which literally translates into "means of circulation," was rendered in the English text as "fiduciary media." Consequently, the title of the book should have been Theory of Money and Fiduciary Media, but the publisher decided that the unusual terminology would irritate readers and thus opted for the smoother but toothless Theory of Money and Credit, failing to honor the fact that even in the original German version the expression was unusual. Mises was hostile to innovations in language that were not justified by the analysis of hitherto neglected phenomena. But the difference between money certificates on the one hand and *Umlaufsmittel* on the other was such a neglected phenomenon to the point that established scientific terminology even lacked the means for expressing this difference. Mises thus introduced the expression *Umlaufsmittel* for this purpose and even used it in the title of his book to highlight its importance.

Credit money: A future financial claim on an entity that is used as a medium of exchange. What distinguishes credit money from credit is that the recipient accepts it with the intent of passing it on to another recipient, not because they want to collect the financial claim.

Fiat money: A medium of exchange accepted because of the legal decree of an authority. "The deciding factor is the stamp, and it is not the material bearing the stamp that constitutes the money, but the stamp itself."[171] Fiat money can take the form of paper money, bank deposits, or token coins.

Money substitutes are frequently confused for money, but they are distinct.

Money substitutes: Physical or financial instruments that are legal titles to money in the narrow sense. They can be redeemed for money on demand and are used as a medium of exchange in transactions. Money substitutes come in two forms:

Money certificates: A financial instrument or piece of paper redeemable in full for money on demand. (Value is 100% covered by the issuing authority.) Examples include a dollar bill redeemable in gold under a strict gold standard, or a bank account based on gold-backed dollars. In the realm of bitcoin, we can think of bitcoin on the lightning network as being a unique type of money certificate, because its operation is entirely in the hands of the money holder, and redemption does not depend on any third parties. Tradable receipts for bitcoin held in custody would also constitute money substitutes. And while these would have an issuing counterparty, they would still be relatively cheaply and easily redeemable for bitcoin, since access to the network is not easy to censor.

Fiduciary media: Money substitutes not backed by money holdings. When a financial institution issues money substitutes but does not have the money

171 Mises, Ludwig von. *The Theory of Money and Credit*. 2nd ed., Foundation for Economic Education, 1971, p. 62.

to redeem all substitutes, the difference is fiduciary media. This is a key term in Mises' explanation of the business cycle, as it is precisely the creation of these media that sets in motion the boom-bust cycle. In the digital realm, these would be the equivalent of bitcoin-denominated credit issued without equivalent bitcoin backing.

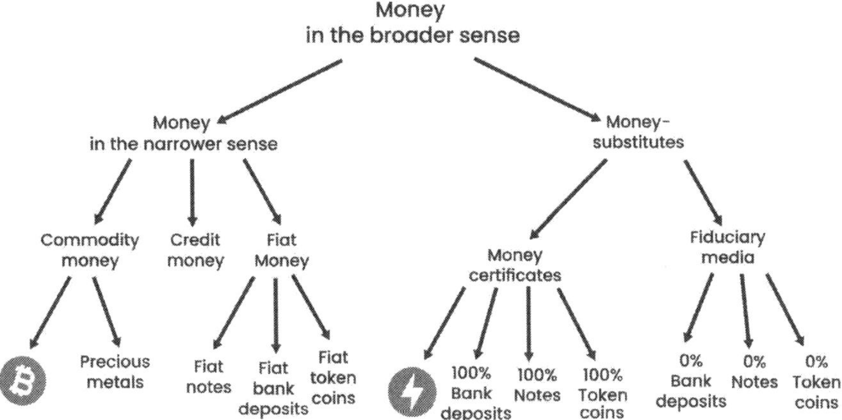

Figure 31. Money typology[172]

According to Mises' typology, the function of money is orthogonal to its physical form. Bank deposits take the form of money certificates when redeemable in full for money, fiduciary media when issued by banks without money backing them, or fiat money if decreed by government authority. Similarly, paper money can be a 100% money certificate, in which case it is redeemable for commodity money at face value, as in the gold standard; if it is issued by a bank and not redeemable for money, it is fiduciary media; and it is fiat money if printed by a government without redeemability. Physical coins can be made from commodity money, such as gold and silver coins; as fiduciary media if issued by a bank; as a money certificate if redeemable for money; or as fiat money if issued out of a base metal and having its value decreed by an authority independent of its metal content. By stepping away from the physical

172 Image courtesy of @Conza, adapting Guido Hülsmann's interpretation.

forms of the money and explaining the difference between fiduciary media and money certificates, Mises could provide an explanation of business cycles grounded in human action.

Money certificates have an equivalent sum of money in the narrow sense placed on demand for the holder at the issuing institution; their issuance does not cause an increase in the monetary media in circulation. At any point in time, when the money certificate is used for payment, the money behind it is idle in a bank vault, but effectively changes ownership. It is not possible for that narrow money to settle monetary transactions while the money certificates are in circulation. Once the money certificate is redeemed for that narrow money, the money can be spent, but the certificate cannot. Money certificates do not increase the supply of money, in the broader sense. The introduction of money substitutes in the form of fiduciary media, on the other hand, does result in an increase in the total supply of money and money substitutes in circulation.

In the past, kings would enrich themselves at the expense of their subjects by collecting coins from their subjects and minting them into new coins with some base metals mixed in to lower the content of the precious metal. By introducing base metals into the mix, the king was able to produce more coins than the amount of the precious metal he had, benefiting the king with increased purchasing power at the expense of the holders of the original currency. Over time, the price of goods would rise to reflect the drop in their metal content, and a part of everyone's real wealth would be transferred to the king.

Although modern centralized governments no longer debase their physical coins, they nonetheless achieve something very similar by using legislation, the threat of violence, and monopoly power to force people to accept money certificates that are no longer redeemable in money as if they were money. With their redeemability suspended, money certificates become fiduciary media, which increases the overall supply of money. In the same way that kings profited by mixing base metals with precious metals, modern governments benefit by mixing fiduciary media with money. The consequences in both cases extend beyond just enriching the government at the expense of society. Introducing a cheap supplement to money does not enhance its function; it compromises it. Money is unique from other goods in that its absolute quantity does not matter to its holder, only its purchasing power. Increasing the quantity of money does not increase wealth, nor does it make money more effective; instead, it devalues existing holders' wealth, transfers it to the recipients of the new money, and alters the prices of goods, causing economic miscalculations.

Business Cycles

Mainstream schools of economics have done a terrific job in treading carefully around the question of what causes business cycles, and for very good reason. As modern economics is largely funded by central banks to inform policy-making, it is highly unlikely to offer a successful career strategy for any person whose conclusions are not flattering to central banks.[173] Mainstream economics research has mainly focused on discussing how to escape recessions, with very little focus on what causes recessions. It is childish impudence to attempt to solve a problem without caring to understand its causes, but fiat money allows central banks to attempt to create their own reality by financing research that focuses on finding solutions and marginalizing scholars critical of central banks. This approach was best exemplified in Krugman's introduction to a recent reprint of Keynes' *General Theory*, in which Krugman extols Keynes' inability to offer an explanation for the causes of the business cycle:

> Rather than getting bogged down in an attempt to explain the dynamics of the business cycle—a subject that remains contentious to this day—Keynes focused on a question that could be answered. And that ... most needed an answer: given that overall demand is depressed—never mind why—how can we create more employment?[174]

Success in modern fiat academia is primarily a function of fealty to central banks rather than coherence or value of ideas, and as a result, the business

173 White, Lawrence H. "The Federal Reserve System's Influence on Research in Monetary Economics." *Econ Journal Watch*, vol 2, no. 2, 2005, pp. 325-54.

174 Krugman, Paul. Introduction. *The General Theory of Employment, Interest, and Money*, by John Maynard Keynes, Palgrave Macmillan, 2018, p. xxxiii.

cycle continues to be presented as a normal, inevitable part of the workings of a modern capitalist economy, as inevitable as night turning into day and seasons changing.

In stark contrast, the Austrian economists, and their causal realist framework for understanding the world, offer a coherent explanation for why business cycles happen and how they can be prevented. Unburdened by having to toe the central bankers' line to secure funding, Austrians are able to offer more than the dubious Keynesian recommendations for exiting the depression: They can offer an explanation for how to avoid a depression in the first place.

The Austrian theory of the business cycle is founded on, and is a natural extension of, the Austrian theory of money and the aforementioned discussion delineating the difference between fiduciary media and money. The basic premise of the theory is the simple dictum that economic resources cannot be conjured by creating unbacked claims for them. That may sound like common sense, but for most modern economists, it is a radical concept. Governments and banks attempting to pass off unbacked claims for economic resources as equivalent to the resources or backed claims to them results in an increase in the supply of money, manifesting as an increased amount of financial capital in the hands of entrepreneurs. The increased financial capital causes entrepreneurs to engage in investments for which they do not have sufficient resources, something which only becomes apparent after they begin spending their financial capital, causing an unanticipated rise in the price of their input goods, preventing them from completing the projects.

In an economy with only commodity credit, the interest rate is determined by the interaction of individuals' preferences for borrowing and lending at different interest rates. The preferences of these individuals for holding money, borrowing it, or lending it are determined by the quantities of money at their disposal as well as their economic conditions and desires. In a world of only commodity credit, all loans must come from a saver deciding to forgo consumption in favor of earning a positive return on lending.

The saving and consumption decisions concerning financial capital correspond directly to consumption and saving decisions for physical capital. The individuals who forgo consumption of financial capital do so by forgoing the consumption of the economic goods and services they could have bought with the financial capital. These resources that were not consumed can instead be directed toward the process of production; now, they are invested in productive enterprises.

As an obvious example, the consumer who decides to forgo eating corn allows it to be used as seed grain. As a more elaborate example from a complex economy, the consumer who decides to forgo going to a beach resort reduces the demand for staff at the resort and decreases the likelihood that the resort will purchase a new plot of land to expand. The holiday abstainer deposits the money he would have spent on the trip into a saving deposit at his bank, so the bank can now lend this money to a carmaker, which is now more likely to afford the marginal worker who was not hired by the beach resort as well as the piece of land that the resort has given up. By choosing to forgo the immediate gratification of a vacation and offering his financial assets to entrepreneurs instead, the saver has spared resources from meeting the demand for consuming holidays and allowed them to be used in the long-term production of cars.

Scarcity is the fundamental starting point of economics; money and financial institutions are tools we use to economize, increase our productivity and efficiency, and battle scarcity, but they cannot eliminate the scarcity of resources. There is a limited amount of workers, office space, equipment, computers, land, and resources, and trading them with money is the way we allocate them. As long as an economy operates on commodity credit, financial resources map onto real resources, and consumption decisions reflect real individual preferences pertaining to real-world resources, as expressed through their prices.

This process is distorted by the introduction of fiduciary media, which circulate like money but are unbacked by money. When a financial institution makes a loan without money backing it, they are issuing credit without a corresponding deferral of consumption by a consumer. The bank has issued a fiduciary note to the farmer to buy seed corn that has already been eaten. The total amount of loans issued to buy seed corn exceeds the market value of all the seed corn left from last year's harvest at the current price. The bank has issued the car manufacturer the money to purchase land and hire workers when the holidaymaker had spent his money in the resort, allowing the resort to hire the same workers and buy the same land.

When the fiduciary media are created as a loan to entrepreneurs, it may not be clear to anyone (except Misesian economists) that this loan has created more claims than there are resources. At current corn prices, the quantity of corn which farmers plan to purchase exceeds the quantity of seed corn available on the market. But once it is planting season and the farmers go to buy the seed corn, they quickly bid the price up. Those who buy it early might manage to get all the quantity they had planned to get, but the majority will get a smaller amount. This miscalculation will be an expensive error for farmers, who will have overinvested in land, labor, and capital relative to the amount of seeds they expected to have available.

The resort and the car factory both expect their holdings of money and fiduciary media to be sufficient to secure them the land and the workers they need. But once they set out to actually hire the workers and purchase the land, the increased fiduciary media will lead to a decline in the value of money relative to the input goods, causing their prices to rise. As the landowner receives bids from the resort and the car plant, he initiates a bidding war between them and can charge a higher price. As workers find opportunities at both businesses, their wages also rise. With fiduciary media giving banks and entrepreneurs an exaggerated assessment of the reality of resources available to them by lowering interest rates, many business opportunities begin to appear profitable in entrepreneurs' calculations when the actual resources available are not sufficient to complete them.

With the cost of the land, labor, and capital goods escalating, the two entrepreneurs' plans are ruined. They had performed all their economic calculations based on the prices prevalent before the fiduciary media had entered circulation. But as the prices of input goods increase, their previous calculations are rendered useless. Their profitability is reduced or eliminated. Either or both of them might be liquidated, causing their work and investment to go to waste.

A business opportunity expected to offer a 4% rate of return would not attract capital from lenders when the prevalent market interest rate is 6%. But if the introduction of fiduciary media results in the interest rate declining to 3%, then it will attract capital. The same business, with the same capital stock, in the same market, goes from being unprofitable to profitable simply through the introduction of fiduciary media, which can be produced at a negligible cost. The absurdity of the situation should be obvious: Money is a good that offers no value in itself, and it is acquired to be passed on. Its quantity does not matter, only its purchasing power. Making more monetary units cannot change the economic reality of businesses whose inputs and outputs are capital and consumer goods, and if they suddenly appear profitable, then that can only be due to the defective nature of the money used.

The insolvency of these unprofitable businesses begins to become exposed when they bid up the prices of their input goods and have to revisit their profit calculations. An additional infusion of fiduciary media at this point can serve to delay the day of reckoning by providing businesses with more fiduciary media that improve their profitability, on paper, before they start spending it and prices rise again. For the boom to continue, credit creation needs to proceed at an accelerating pace. But it cannot continue forever, as the currency will collapse eventually.

The Business Cycle Graphically

The introduction of fiduciary media into the credit market can be expressed as a shift in the supply curve for loanable funds to the right: An increase in the quantity of loanable funds available at any interest rate, as opposed to the world in which only commodity credit is available. The result is not just an increase in the amount of credit extended in the economy but also a decline in the interest rate, which lets borrowers secure debt at a lower interest rate than they would without fiduciary media. Equivalently, lenders receive a lower interest rate on their loans, which, therefore, encourages them to save less. The increased expectations of profit make matters worse by encouraging people to spend more.

This decline in interest rates is distinct from the decline brought about by the decrease in time preference leading to more abundant savings and causing the borrowing rate to decline. This decline in interest rates is created purely by monetary manipulation, not by the sacrifice of present consumption, and that is what makes it unsustainable. The introduction of fiduciary media at once leads to an increase in lending and consumption and a decline in savings, thus creating a gap between the real economic sources available to entrepreneurs and their expectations of these resources.

In *Time and Money*, Roger Garrison presents a graphical framework for explaining the Austrian business cycle theory and for demonstrating the difference between it and sustainable economic growth. Garrison uses the production possibilities frontier, a graph showing the maximum combinations of investment and consumption possible for an individual or society.[175] The PPF illustrates the trade-off between consumption and investment. On the PPF, moving toward more investment requires sacrificing current consumption, and vice versa, and the slope of the curve at any point shows the price of capital in terms of consumption. Over time, if economic growth takes place, the curve will shift outward, allowing more abundant combinations of capital and consumption, whereas economic contraction will shift the curve inward, allowing lesser combinations of consumption and capital goods.

The second graph shows the market for loanable funds, where borrowers have a demand curve showing the quantity of borrowing they would undertake at all given interest rates, while lenders have a supply curve showing the quantity of lending they would provide at each price level. These two curves meet at the interest rate that equalizes the demand and supply of loans. Finally, Garrison uses the intertemporal structure of production triangles, based on Hayek's work on business cycles.[176] While simple, this triangle is essential in communicating the intertemporal nature of economic production, and the sequential interdependence of production stages, a point woefully missing from Keynesian analysis. The horizontal axis of the triangle represents time, in the

---

175 Garrison, Roger. *Time and Money: The Macroeconomics of Capital Structure*. Routledge, 2001.

176 Hayek, Friedrich von. *Prices and Production and Other Works: F.A. Hayek on Money, the Business Cycle, and the Gold Standard*. Ludwig von Mises Institute, 2008. • Hayek, Friedrich von. *Monetary Theory and the Trade Cycle*. Martino Pub, 2012.

successive stages of economic production, while the vertical axis represents the market price of economic goods through the production process, which increases with each stage of production until it reaches the final output.

The horizontal axis of the triangle represents the sum of consumer goods produced in an economy, corresponding to the x-axis in the production possibility frontier. The y-axis of the production possibility frontier represents the total quantity of investment and corresponds to the y-axis of the market for the loanable funds. The three graphs can be plotted next to each other to demonstrate the dynamics of economic growth and contraction, as well as the business cycle.

In the case of a lowering of time preference, individuals defer the consumption of final goods and invest in earlier stages of production, lengthening the stages of production, as was discussed in the examples of the fisherman in Chapter 6. When the fisherman forgoes catching a few fish in a day in order to spend time building a boat to increase his productivity, he is reducing the height of the triangle by reducing his consumption, but extending its base by lengthening the process of production. This corresponds to a move down the production possibility frontier, as consumption declines and investment increases. The same process takes place in a modern capitalist market economy as the deferral of consumption is reflected in the loanable market funds with a rightward shift in the supply curve for loanable funds, resulting in a decline in the interest rate and an increase in the quantity of loans available.

Should the investment succeed, and there is no guarantee it will, the product of the consumption will exceed the forgone initial consumption, reflected in a shift in the production possibility frontier outward, a rise in the height of the stages of production triangle, and the same level of investment maintained. As humanity has advanced in its production of fish through the stages of catching fish by hand to modern fishing boats, this process continues with more investment, consumption, and ever-longer stages of production, as shown in Figure 32. This process continues through the development of banking and the loanable funds market allowing for a larger, more specialized market in the allocation of capital, allowing savers and borrowers to transact without even having to know each other. It continues, that is, as long as the monetary instruments that are used are money certificates.

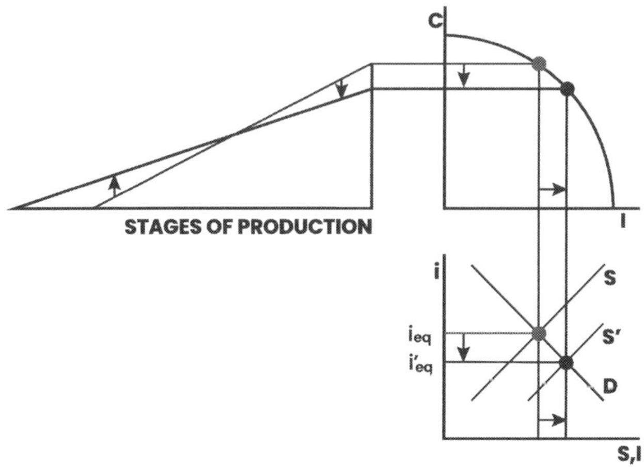

Figure 32. Economic growth through investment and deferral of consumption

Pure 100%-backed money certificates cause no increase in the money supply. Every money certificate issued as a loan corresponds to a set quantity of a market good being held by the certificate issuer. An actual market good, money, is taken out of the hands of savers and placed at the disposal of the borrower, holding its receipt. That sacrifice is what frees up economic resources to be used in the early stages of production, rather than in consumption goods.

Things look very different when fiduciary media are issued instead of money certificates. Fiduciary media are issued with no corresponding money held on hand by the bank. They involve no sacrifice of economic goods on the part of anyone. Graphically, credit expansion via fiduciary media allows borrowers to attempt to lengthen the stages of production without the requisite reduction in consumption. Borrowing entrepreneurs attempt a move beyond the production possibilities frontier with a quantity of investing and consumption, which exceeds the total resources available. In the loanable funds market, it shifts the supply curve artificially by increasing the loanable funds, and in doing so, brings the interest rate down. But the reduction in the interest does not correspond to an increase in savings to finance the increased investment. On the contrary, lower interest rates encourage less saving.

The quantity of funds invested in this example, I2, is much larger than the quantity of resources saved, S2, in Figure 33. The monetary expansion not only makes entrepreneurs think they have more resources than they actually do; it also makes fewer resources available by discouraging saving and encouraging increased consumption. The difference between I2 and S2 in this graph is the capital that went to finance what Mises terms **malinvestments**—investments that would not have been undertaken without distortions in the capital market and whose completion is not possible once the distortions are exposed.[177] The failure of the investment to produce the desired output results in the contraction of the production possibilities frontier, as the quantity of resources available declines. The stages of production triangle get shorter, and the stages of production contract.

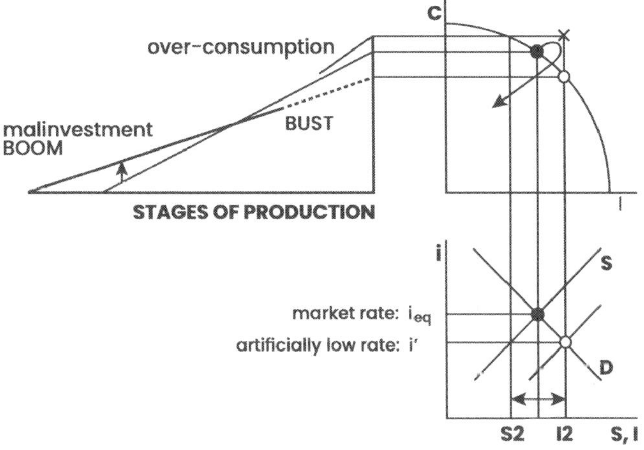

Figure 33. Credit expansion with fiduciary media and the business cycle

In the capital market, the opportunity cost of capital is forgone consumption, and the opportunity cost of consumption is forgone capital investment. The interest rate is the price that regulates this relationship: As people demand more investments, the interest rate rises, incentivizing more savers to set

177 Mises, Ludwig von. *Human Action: The Scholar's Edition*. Ludwig von Mises Institute, 1998, p. 574.

aside more of their money for savings. As the interest rate drops, it incentivizes investors to engage in more investments and invest in more technologically advanced methods of production with a longer time horizon. A lower interest rate, then, allows for the engagement of longer structures of production with high productivity: Society moves from fishing with rods to fishing on large oil-powered boats.

As an economy advances and becomes increasingly sophisticated, the connection between physical capital and the loanable funds market does not change in reality, but it does get obfuscated in the minds of people. A modern economy with a central bank is built on ignoring this fundamental trade-off and assuming that banks can finance investment with new money without consumers having to forgo consumption. The link between savings and loanable funds is severed to the point where it is not even taught in economics textbooks anymore. A standard textbook portrays the supply curve for loanable funds as a straight vertical line whose magnitude is determined by policymakers. In the Keynesian alternative universe, central banks simply determine the money supply and interest rate, and it is assumed that the physical resources will materialize to fulfill the bank's nominal monetary fantasies.

But real resources cannot be manifested by monetary policy, so artificially lowering the interest rate inevitably creates a discrepancy between savings and loanable funds. At these artificially low interest rates, businesses take on more debt to start projects than savers put aside to finance these investments. In other words, the value of consumption deferred is less than the value of the capital borrowed. Without enough consumption deferred, there will not be enough capital, land, and labor resources diverted away from consumption goods toward higher-order capital goods at the earliest stages of production. There is no free lunch, after all, and if consumers save less, there will have to be less capital available for investors.

This shortage of capital is not immediately apparent because banks and the central bank can issue enough fiduciary media for all borrowers. Creating new pieces of paper and digital entries on paper over the deficiency in savings does not magically increase society's physical capital stock. Instead, it devalues the existing money supply and distorts prices, causing producers to begin production processes requiring more capital resources than are actually available. As more and more producers are bidding for fewer capital goods and resources than they expect there to be, the natural outcome is a rise in the price of the capital goods during the production process. This is the point when the manipulation is exposed, leading to the simultaneous collapse of several capital investments, which suddenly become unprofitable at the new capital good prices; the ***malinvestments***. The central bank's intervention in the capital market allows for more projects to be undertaken because of the distortion of prices that causes investors to miscalculate. In other words, central bank intervention *causes* malinvestment. However, the central bank's intervention cannot increase the amount of actual capital available, so reality eventually imposes on the projects leading to their suspension. As a result, what actual capital was deployed in the project is unnecessarily wasted. The suspension of these projects at the same time causes a rise in unemployment across the economy, as a large number of people in many industries witness their business fail or have to readjust. This economy-wide simultaneous failure of overextended businesses is what is referred to as a **recession**.

Only with an understanding of the capital structure and how interest rate manipulation destroys the incentive for capital accumulation can one understand the causes of recessions and the swings of the business cycle. The business cycle is the logical result of the manipulation of the interest rate distorting the market for capital by making investors imagine they can attain more capital than is available with the unsound money they have been given by the banks. Contrary to Keynesian animist mythology, business cycles are not mystic phenomena caused by flagging "animal spirits" whose cause is, in turn, to be ignored as central bankers seek to try to engineer a recovery. Economic logic clearly shows how recessions are the inevitable outcome of interest rate manipulation in the same way shortages are the inevitable outcome of price ceilings. Keynesian economics creates the business cycle and then sells Keynesianism as the cure.

An analogy can be borrowed from Mises' work (and embellished) to illustrate the point: Imagine the capital stock of a society as building bricks and the central bank as a contractor responsible for assembling them to build houses.

Each house requires 10,000 bricks to build, and the developer is looking for a contractor who will be able to build 100 houses, requiring a total of 1 million bricks. But a Keynesian contractor, eager to win the contract, realizes his chances of winning the contract will be enhanced if he can submit an offer promising to build 120 of the same house while only requiring 800,000 bricks. This is the equivalent of the interest rate manipulation: It reduces the supply of capital while increasing the demand for it. In reality, 120 houses will require 1.2 million bricks, but there are only 800,000 available. The 800,000 bricks are sufficient to begin the construction of the 120 houses, but they are not sufficient to complete them. As the construction begins, the developer is very happy to see 20% more houses for 80% of the cost, thanks to the wonders of Keynesian engineering, which leads him to spend 20% of the cost saved on buying a new yacht.

But the ruse cannot last as it will eventually become apparent that the houses cannot be completed and the construction must come to a halt. Not only has the contractor failed to deliver 120 houses, but he will also have failed to deliver any houses whatsoever, and instead, he has left the developer with 120 unfinished houses, effectively useless piles of bricks with no roofs. The contractor's ruse reduced the capital spent by the developer and resulted in the construction of fewer houses than would have been possible with accurate price signals. The developer would have had 100 houses if he had gone with an honest contractor. By going with a Keynesian contractor who distorts the numbers, the developer continues to waste his capital for as long as the capital is being allocated according to a plan with no basis in reality. If the contractor realizes the mistake early on, the capital wasted on starting 120 houses might be very little, and a new contractor will be able to take the remaining bricks and use them to produce 90 houses. If the developer remains ignorant of the reality until the capital runs out, he will end up with 120 unfinished homes that are worthless, as nobody will pay to live in a roofless house.

When the central bank manipulates the interest rate lower than the market clearing price by directing banks to create more money by lending, they are at once reducing the amount of savings available in society and increasing the quantity demanded by borrowers while also directing the borrowed capital toward projects which cannot be completed. Whenever a government has started on the path of inflating the money supply, there is no escaping the negative consequences. If the central bank stops the inflation, interest rates rise and a recession follows, as many of the projects that were started are exposed as unprofitable and have to be abandoned, exposing the misallocation of resources and capital. If the central bank were to continue its inflationary process indefinitely, it would just increase the scale of misallocations in the economy, wasting even more capital and making the inevitable recession even more painful. There is no escape from paying a hefty bill for the supposed free lunch that Keynesian cranks foisted upon us.

Friedrich Hayek likened credit expansion to catching a tiger by the tail. Once you have held on to the tiger's tail, he begins to run, and there are no good options moving forward.

> We now have a tiger by the tail: how long can this inflation continue? If the tiger (of inflation) is freed he will eat us up; yet if he runs faster and faster while we desperately hold on, we are still finished! I'm glad I won't be here to see the final outcome.[178]

Capital Market Central Planning

Fiduciary media are financial products that could emerge naturally on a free market, but it is entirely unlikely they would survive for long. They could emerge on the market due to the unique nature of money as a good whose only purpose is to be exchanged for something else, which makes a claim on money seemingly as good as money since both can be exchanged for goods. Fiduciary media would not be likely to survive long on a free market, however, because their existence leaves their issuer at risk of insolvency should a certain percentage of their creditors seek to redeem their fiduciary media for money.

Under the gold standard, fiduciary media were widely used, but they led to periodic financial crises in which large amounts would be wiped out

178 Hayek, Friedrich von. *A Tiger By The Tail: The Keynesian Legacy of Inflation*. Ludwig von Mises Institute, 1972, p. 126.

or discounted heavily. Fiduciary media could survive under a gold standard since a significant amount of overall monetary holdings would remain in the bank at all times, and many money holders preferred to keep their money in the bank, where it could have been used for settling payments at a far lower cost than moving physical gold. Paying in person with physical gold was prohibitively expensive outside of one's whereabouts, and the advancement of transportation and telecommunication technology meant more and more of an individual's transactions took place across long distances, so an increasingly large percentage of gold cash balances had to stay in banks to increase its salability across space. Any time a holder of a banknote chose to cash it out for physical gold, they forwent a large decrease in the salability of their money across space. This allowed banks a margin of error with issuing fiduciary media, knowing not all their customers would ask for redemption at the same time.

But this margin of safety is self-defeating: The more secure the bank is, the more fiduciary media it issues, then the less secure it becomes and the more susceptible it is to a bank run. These bank runs would come periodically and would be disastrous for many people involved. A free market in money and banking would have likely continued to wipe out banks and customers engaging in the issuance of unbacked credit until such a practice was eliminated. The marginal cost of producing fiduciary media for a bank approaches zero, and a free market in banking would supply fiduciary media until their price is equal to their cost of production, which effectively means the fiduciary media will be discounted until they become money certificates, with their face value equal to whatever backing exists to redeem them.

In the nineteenth-century United States, monopoly state banking licenses prevented free-market competition from doing away with fiduciary media. So long as entry into the banking industry was restricted, it was profitable for the incumbents to produce fiduciary media, even though these media would still have caused periodic crises and collapses. Periodic government interventions in the banking system and the establishment of the first and second U.S. central banks would help protect banks from the free-market consequences of unbacked credit expansion. In 1907, a large financial crisis crystallized the attention of financial industry leaders on the need to establish a third monopoly central bank to stand ready to bail out banking institutions in times of financial crises. In 1913, the U.S. Federal Reserve Act was passed, and the new central bank was given the inherently contradictory dual mandate of protecting the value of the currency while also rescuing banks from financial crises, which can only be achieved by debauching the currency. Over the past century, the cost of protecting unbacked credit from just market assessment has been the constant debasement of the currency. Whereas in the nineteenth century, fiduciary media issuance would cause financial crises and distress, this would be relatively contained and restricted to people willingly involved with these financial institutions. Gold holders had nothing to fear since the market price of their money was largely unaffected. In the twentieth century, financial crises were almost always ameliorated and resolved through the devaluation of the currency held by people uninvolved with insolvent institutions.

Rather than offering a way to increase investment and productivity, credit expansion unbacked by real savings has proven to be a recipe for financial crises in the nineteenth century and the cause of the destruction of sound money in the twentieth century. In order to protect financial institutions from the consequences of unbacked lending, a socialist central-planning board was placed in charge of the market for money and capital, the most important market and the one integral part of all markets.

While most people imagine that socialist societies are a thing of the past and that market systems rule capitalist economies, the reality is that a capitalist system cannot function without a free market in capital, where the price of capital emerges through the interaction of supply and demand and the decisions of capitalists are driven by accurate price signals. Recessions and financial crises are best understood as the failures of capital markets when central planning restricts monetary freedom. Monopoly central banks' meddling in the capital market is the root of recessions and financial crises. Yet the majority of politicians, journalists, and academics invariably blame these centrally planned disasters on capitalism.

The form of failure that capital market central planning takes is the boom-and-bust cycle, as explained in Austrian business cycle theory. It is thus no wonder that this dysfunction is treated as a normal part of market economies because, after all, in the minds of modern economists, a central bank controlling interest rates is a normal part of a modern market economy. But a central bank is as normal a part of a capital market as a monopoly potato bureau is a normal part of potato markets.

Austrian authors have meticulously documented monetary history in some highly recommended reads, which use Austrian theory to illuminate our understanding of history, which is so often blinded by government historians' need to embellish the actions of the state and its monetary disasters. Hayek's *Monetary Nationalism and International Stability*, Rothbard's *America's Great Depression* and *A History of Money and Banking in the United States*, and Ferdinand Lips' *Gold Wars* are particularly good examples. This history points to some unfortunate, disastrous, and regular patterns in the development of modern banking and governments.

In the short term, governments and central bank administrators believe they can achieve their goals by debasing money to finance credit creation and spending on important causes. Governments may believe they are boosting the economy, or protecting people from the consequences of free markets, but by debasing the money to achieve these goals, they are creating malinvestments and sowing the seeds of great long-term harm. Attempting to rescue the economy from the inevitable resulting crises results in further credit creation and bailouts encouraging irresponsible behavior, rewarding the wasteful and punishing the prudent. In that way, central banks all but ensure the boom-and-bust cycle will become a permanent fixture of an economy, and their power over the market grows. Over time, the result is the destruction of capital, money, the ability to save, and the division of labor itself. Placing money in the hands of government monopoly is far from a panacea; it is destroying the foundations on which human society and modern capitalist civilization are built.

PART V

Civilization

Chapter 16

Violence

All the economizing human actions this book has discussed so far have been voluntary. Part II discussed voluntary economizing actions individuals undertake on their own to improve the quality and quantity of their time. Part III explained the market system that emerges from social interactions individuals voluntarily undertake to improve the quality and quantity of their time. In each section, the individuals involved acted of their will and volition, whether individually or in concert with others. But that is not the only way for humans to interact. They can also improve the quality and quantity of their time on Earth by employing violence and the threat of violence against others. They may aggress against the body and property of others, with the aim of acquiring their property and possibly even their body. Violence and the threat of violence result in **coercion**: the imposition of one's will on another.

Non-Aggression Principle

Economics does not assume violence and coercion away, nor does it wish they were irrelevant. They are studied as a form of human action whose consequences are examined and contrasted alongside the consequences of voluntary exchanges. The fundamental difference between voluntary and involuntary interaction is that all participants in a voluntary interaction expect to benefit from it, whereas someone must expect to suffer negative consequences in an involuntary interaction (otherwise, they would not have needed to be coerced into it). A voluntary exchange may not always succeed in achieving the intended results of the actors. Coercion, on the other hand, guarantees that one party will suffer undesirable consequences. People who do not benefit from consensual interactions can readjust their erroneous expectations and refrain from partaking in them or can adjust their methods and hope for better results. But victims of violent coercions have no such ability, as their will is overruled by violence or the threat of violence. Coercive interactions can continue when the perpetrator does not suffer the negative consequences of their aggression.

In terms of undesirability, the negative impacts of coercive aggression can be likened to natural disasters or attacks by animals. And like natural disasters and animal attacks, humans have long sought ways of protecting themselves from such calamities. In the same way humans work, accumulate capital, trade, and innovate, they also learn to defend themselves and develop increasingly elaborate and effective mechanisms for protecting their body and property from the aggression of others. Chapter 17 details various defense strategies against aggression. The rest of this chapter examines one specific kind of aggression: government aggression.

In ethical and economic terms, there is a very important distinction between violence and the initiation of violence. Initiating violence violates the victim's ownership of his body or property, leading to hostility and likely retribution on the part of the victim or the shunning of the perpetrator by others. This makes peaceful cooperation more difficult and prevents the growth of the extent of the market and the division of labor. The extent to which groups of individuals, small or large, agree to reject the initiation of violence is the extent to which they can live in a peaceful extended market order and benefit from the division of labor. The extent to which the initiation of violence is accepted by some members of a group is the extent to which conflict emerges and undermines the cooperation necessary for the market order. Aggression being legitimate for one individual or group but not others is not a moral standard that can be consistently applied across society.

Violence, on the other hand, can be considered ethically acceptable when deployed in self-defense to repel or punish initiators of aggression. Legitimate self-defense can also be considered compatible with an extended market order. Members of a market order can all cooperate in an extended market order if they all agree to one universal rule applicable to them all: the illegitimacy of initiating aggression and the legitimacy of self-defense. This asymmetry between violence and initiation of violence, and the implications for a market order, are the basis for the **Non-Aggression Principle**, which Rothbard defines as:

> No one may threaten or commit violence ("aggress") against another man's person or property. Violence may be employed only against the man who commits such violence; that is, only defensively against the aggressive violence of another. In short, no violence may be employed against a non-aggressor.[179]

The non-aggression principle is formulated and popularized by Rothbard and Austrian economists, but it has historical origins throughout history and across civilizations, as documented in a paper by Edward Fuller:

> [A] large and diverse group of history's most eminent thinkers have expressed ideas very similar to the non-aggression principle. The rudiments of the principle were known to the ancient Egyptians around 2000 BC, the ancient Hindus around 1500 BC, and the ancient Hebrews around

179 Rothbard, Murray. *A Libertarian Analysis: War Peace and the State*. The Libertarian Forum, 1962. • Rothbard, Murray. *Egalitarianism As a Revolt against Nature and Other Essays*. 2nd ed. Ludwig von Mises Institute, 2000.

> 1000 BC. Around 500 BC, the ancient Chinese and Greek philosophers expressed the underlying logic of the principle. Cicero came close to articulating the principle in its modern form. Thomas Aquinas reasserted something strikingly similar to non-aggression after the Dark Ages, and the scholastic philosophers carried the idea into the early modern period. During the seventeenth century, the non-aggression principle rose to the pinnacle of Western philosophy.[180]

Many economics textbooks, including this one, use the story of Robinson Crusoe on a deserted island to illustrate the realities of economic production and the benefit of peaceful cooperation. The origin of the story comes from a fictional novel, *Hayy Ibn Yaqdhan,* which is the work of Arab philosopher Ibn Tufayl, who used the premise of the story to explain how a human being can develop an understanding of morality, even if born alone in isolation from humanity.

Government Coercion

Most mainstream schools of economics and politics present government as society's solution to the problem of aggression. Since violence and aggression are ever-present, the only way to establish a civilized and peaceful social order in any territory is for an entity to establish a monopoly on violence. When all inhabitants of the territory accept the legitimacy of the monopolist (willingly or otherwise), acts of violence committed by any other entity are considered illegal and punishable by the monopolist.

The political and intellectual debates of the nineteenth and twentieth centuries mainly revolved around the proper role of the state in society and not its legitimacy or necessity. Mises and the classical liberals viewed the proper role of government as consisting of securing its people and their property and ensuring their safety from aggression and theft.

---

180 Fuller, Edward W. "The Non-Aggression Principle: A Short History." *Revista Procesos de Mercado*, vol. 16, no. 1, 2019, pp. 31-88.

> Government ought to do all the things for which it is needed and for which it was established. Government ought to protect the individuals within the country against the violent and fraudulent attacks of gangsters, and it should defend the country against foreign enemies. These are the functions of government within a free system, within the system of the market economy.
>
> Under socialism, of course, the government is totalitarian, and there is nothing outside its sphere and its jurisdiction. But in the market economy, the main task of the government is to protect the smooth functioning of the market economy against fraud or violence from within and from outside the country.[181]

By ensuring the security of property, the government would allow individuals to plan for the future, lower their time preference, accumulate capital, increase productivity, and improve their lives. But classical liberals argued that if a government failed to restrict its mandate to the preservation of property and enforcement of law and order, it would do more harm than good. Its interventions in the market economy would fail to bring about the intended ends, primarily because of the problem of economic calculation without clearly defined property rights (discussed in Chapter 12). If the government is the owner of the capital resources, then there is no market for these resources and no possibility of performing economic calculation on the alternative uses of these resources or determining how they can be allocated. When government bureaucrats make coercive decisions about resources owned by others, they do so blindly without knowledge of the most important factor that determines the allocation of resources: the subjective preferences of the individuals involved. Economic calculation without property rights results in the misallocation of resources, waste, and destruction of capital.

A staggering number of works have been written on the failures of

---

181 Mises, Ludwig von. *Economic Policy: Thoughts for Today and Tomorrow*. Free Market Books, 1995.

government intervention in economic affairs,[182] both by economists in the Austrian tradition and mainstream statist economists. The rest of this chapter will refer to several of the failure modes of some of the most common and popular forms of government intervention in individual decision-making in the capitalist economy. By using the lens of human action and understanding the properties of the emergent market order, we can identify the economic impacts of particular forms of government coercion.

Imposing price controls is arguably the most popular form of government intervention in the economy. It is a tempting solution to real problems that can have enormous implications, to the benefit of some and at the expense of many others. The rationale seems simple and compelling: If the price of a good is too high, the government can mandate a price ceiling, making it illegal to sell at a high price while forcing sellers to sell at a lower price. This way, people who are unable to pay the higher price can get the lower-priced goods. In *Forty Centuries of Wage and Price Control: How Not to Fight Inflation*, Robert Schuettinger and Eamonn Butler provide a highly informative historical account of the failures of price controls across four millennia and countless locales. A startling number of governments throughout history have taken this very course of action to deal with the prices of an endless array of goods, from foodstuffs to rent. There is no record of price controls succeeding in bringing prices down; instead, they only ever lead to shortages, black markets, and the emergence of highly wasteful methods of rationing the limited supply.

If price controls have any effect whatsoever, it is that they stop people from trading at a particular price they would have willingly traded at. When trade is prohibited at the market price, the producer will invariably become less able to produce the good. And without the revenue from the higher price, the producer will be unable to secure enough of the resources necessary to produce the good. Government coercion can force the producer to not sell under the minimum price, but it cannot force him to sell at the minimum price, as he can

---

182 See Block, Walter. *Defending the Undefendable*. Ludwig von Mises Institute, 2018. • Krueger, Anne O. "Government Failures in Development." *Journal of Economic Perspectives*, vol. 4, no. 3, 9-23, 1990. • Tullock, Gordon, Gordon Brady, and Arthur Seldon. *Government Failure: A Primer in Public Choice*. Cato Institute, 2002.

simply choose to stop producing. The effect of this intervention will invariably be reducing the supply of the good on the market.

Another likely effect is the emergence of a black market, where goods are sold illegally at higher prices. The black market helps secure the good for those who need it and it navigates around the damage caused by government intervention. But it also imposes waste on transacting parties. Rather than dedicate scarce resources to producing the desired good, producers must incur costs to arrange for the illicit sale and distribution of their good, and they must risk prosecution, confiscation, and imprisonment. Alternatively, dedicated organizations will emerge to arrange for the sale of the good, and a large part of the profits will be captured by these organizations, instead of being dedicated to investment in capital goods to produce more of the limited good. Price control does not magically alter the economic valuation of goods and their cost of production. It only makes it criminal to exchange the goods at the prices the producers are asking for. That constitutes a subsidy to the criminal sector in the economy. For people who are used to operating beyond the law, this is a lucrative business. Resources that could have gone to the producers to allow them more investment, will instead go to crime.

As shortages inevitably appear after price controls, the demand for the good will exceed the supply, necessitating new mechanisms for rationing supply among consumers. Queuing is one common mechanism wherein consumers spend time waiting in line until the good becomes available. Because time is scarce, queuing simply transfers the cost of the good from money to time. So, consumers will now pay for the good with the time they wasted, which cannot be captured by the producer to make more of the good.

For some other economic goods, violent government intervention will seek to impose a higher price on the market than the price emerging from voluntary exchange. This is most commonly exercised in the case of wages, where governments have long sought to mandate higher wages for workers. The failure of the minimum wage is explained in detail in Chapters 1 and 4.

The problem of prices almost always has its roots in inflation, which is a result of coercive government meddling in market money. As discussed in Chapter 10, money emerges on the market as the good with the best salability across time—the good most likely to hold on to its value over time. Since its supply can be reliably expected to increase at the lowest rate among all other market commodities, the value of money tends to appreciate over time, as relatively more of all other goods are produced than money. In such a world, prices of all goods would tend to fall in terms of money, while wages would increase in real terms even if they stay constant or decline in nominal terms. But with coercive intervention in the market for money, the value of money declines over time, forcing sellers to raise prices and depreciating the wages of workers. The story of inflation has long been the same, even when its mechanisms differ: From Roman emperors reducing the gold or silver content of their coins and replacing it with copper and other base metals, through modern governments printing large quantities of paper money to manipulating interest rates down to allow for the creation of credit beyond the savings of society.[183] Inflation takes real wealth from savers, devaluing their money and raising the prices of the goods they purchase while allowing the government to spend with little constraint.

Mainstream schools of economics may admit to the problems of monetary inflation to money holders and the economy at large, but they view government spending as a good thing that can ameliorate these problems and help achieve better societal goals. They fail to properly consider the cost. Understanding opportunity cost, the subjective nature of economics, and the problems of economic calculation lead to the opposite conclusion. Any spending performed by the government must be financed by money taken from productive members of the market economy at the cost of their own spending. Individuals direct their spending to meet their needs best. Coercively taxing their income to spend the money on other uses cannot increase their well-being, as they would have chosen to spend that money elsewhere themselves. No government spending can be seen as voluntary as long as inflation and taxation are not voluntary. Thus, government spending is best understood as consumption spending for the people in government institutions; it is not an investment.

183 See Rothbard, Murray. *What Has Government Done to Our Money? And the Case for a 100 Percent Gold Dollar*. Ludwig von Mises Institute, 2005. • Hayek, Friedrich. *Denationalisation of Money: The Argument Refined*. Institute of Economic Affairs, 1976.

Another common government intervention is the dispensation of subsidies to people or the purchase of specific goods for them. The simplistic view here is to assume that government spending is costless and that governments can direct subsidies to improve the well-being of citizens. But economic analysis quickly dispels this. Government subsidies distort the market, influencing people's decisions away from where their incentives and economic calculations would lead them. Subsidies lead to the overproduction and overconsumption of goods away from what people would freely choose when able to freely calculate. When subsidies are given to individuals based on their economic situation, they create a stronger incentive for people to choose the condition that makes them eligible for those subsidies. Welfare encourages those with low income to stay on a low income. Subsidies for the unemployed create an incentive for unemployment. Worse, by being financed at the expense of the employed, they also lead to the erosion of the incentive to work.

Government provision of goods and services is often presented as a solution to the problem of their lack of availability or affordability. Whereas private sector providers are concerned with profitability, government could do a better job, it is argued, by focusing on inclusion instead. This rationale is presented in favor of government provision of many goods and services, such as education, water, and healthcare, but it also misunderstands the basics of capitalist economic production. Profits are not just a mechanism for greedy people to get rich—they are what coordinates the entire structure of market production, allowing producers to calculate the costs and benefits of their various options while searching for a way to serve others the most and produce optimal gains for themselves. Eliminating the profit motive from economic production does not lead to selfless, abundant, and affordable production; it leads to a failure of economic calculation, causing large amounts of waste. Products might be undesirable, thus constituting a waste of resources. Or, if they are desirable, the absence of a free-market price will lead to overuse of the resources and problems with allowing users access to said resources. For instance, government-provided free roads end up packed with traffic, causing large delays for travelers that likely are more expensive than what they would pay to build private roads. And government-provided healthcare in places like Canada is notorious for making patients wait for very long periods before they can be seen by a doctor. Tellingly, as Canada has a free-market healthcare system for animals, it is astonishing that a sick Canadian pet will get seen by a doctor faster than its owner.[184]

Government spending, beyond just being damaging to the economy by disrupting individuals' private calculations of profit and loss, is destructive because it must be financed by taxation either directly or through inflation. Taxing producers to finance government spending penalizes economic production, thus, reducing the incentive to engage in it. The depreciation of savings reduces the incentive to save, and the taxation of capital gains reduces the incentive to invest. By making a person less able to provide for his or her future, governments counteract the process of lowering time preference, which is the driving force of human civilization.

Whether it be in price controls or crop subsidies or taxation, all government interventions involve the coercive perversion of some humans' actions away from how they would be taken freely. Left to their own devices, victims of government coercion would spend their time and wealth on the ends they find most valuable, whether that be producing for themselves or others. Since economic value is itself subjective, perverting a human's action away from his chosen course must be less subjectively preferred by him.

To their credit, most mainstream economists, particularly since the end of the Soviet Union, have demonstrated some understanding of the problems of government intervention in the economic system and its distorted impacts. Even the Samuelsonian textbook now incorporates a discussion of the problems of government intervention in markets. But the rationalization for interventionism continues unabated—only now it is presented in terms of governments solving for "market failures," a term mainstream economists use to denote an outcome of free human interaction they do not favor.

184 Righton, Barbara and Nicholas Köhler. "Veterinary Care Faster Than Health Care for Humans." *The Canadian Encyclopedia*, 16 December 2013, Historica Canada.

Rationales for Government Violence

The modern rationales for government intervention are usually presented in the language of market failure: Left to their own devices, free individuals will produce outcomes that are inferior and suboptimal. The initial flaw of this approach is that the market is presented as an agent who failed to deliver on some desired outcome. But in reality, the market is an umbrella term humans use to refer to the actions of individuals enacting their own will to maximize their own satisfaction in life. The term "market failure" posits an omniscient central planner capable of deciding what would be the optimum outcome of individuals' free interactions, then denouncing the actions of free individuals as inferior and in need of change. While couched in terms of the public good, methodologically, this approach simply consists of a central planner declaring their will to supersede the will of all freely acting individuals.

The conveyor belt of mainstream economists and their highly rewarded, unreadable papers published over the past few decades contains an inordinate amount of government propaganda masquerading as economic analysis. Their thinking all follows the same predictable script: An economist performs a large amount of theoretical or mathematical or experimental make-work, then concludes that freely acting individuals are producing something suboptimal to society as a whole, which they, in turn, call a "market failure." They conveniently skip over the question of what allows an academic—who has to write government research grants to eat—to pass judgment on the ultimate ends of every other person's actions and what goal they should meet. The collectivist methodology of this approach to economics presumes that valuations are objective and knowable to an impartial central planner. It also disenfranchises individuals by depriving them of the right to make their own decisions with regard to their property, capital, and consumption. By presenting economics as an objective mathematical function, when economic value itself has no unit with which it can be measured, government-funded economists can conjure any numbers needed to justify any form of aggression against the individual property.

The root of market failure analysis comes from the standard model of neoclassical economics, which tried to model the market process mathematically.

Rather than follow the Austrian school method of individual action as the basis of understanding economics, modern economists, in a bold display of cargo cult science, attempted to copy physics. Most economics, since the 1930s government takeover of academia, has largely focused on trying to apply concepts borrowed from physics to John Maynard Keynes' ideas to arrive at rationalizations of government and central bank policies. Mathematical economists attempted to impose a mathematical model from physics on economic reality, and whenever they were confronted with any of the countless insurmountable obstacles to mathematizing human action, they made a simplified assumption of a flattened economic reality in order to make it more pliable for math. Some of the most notable of these assumptions are 1) that all agents in a market system must possess complete knowledge; 2) that they are rationally self-interested; and 3) that there is a state of perfect competition, with an infinite number of buyers and sellers for each market. These assumptions obviously do not hold in the real world, but mainstream economists have treated the assumptions' inaccuracy as proof that markets fail rather than simply realizing that such mathematical models are useless!

With the "market failure" established, the economists then posit, without any evidence or analysis, that government intervention can correct this perceived market inefficiency. They then publish this nonsense in highly regarded journals, get jobs teaching it at a university, and collect accolades and prizes for providing the pretexts for government coercive intervention and aggression against private property. There is no cost to being wrong in fiat academia, and there is plenty of reward for being wrong in support of government power.[185] The entirety of fiat economics can be likened to an elaborate scam of building up straw men, tearing them down, and using their demise to claim the land on which they stood as ownerless before taking it over.

Information Asymmetry

Among the more fashionable rationales for economic intervention in recent decades has been the fallacy of "information asymmetry." According to this

---

185 See Fiat Science, Chapter 9 in *The Fiat Standard.*

enormous school of unreadable research, individuals who take part in a transaction do not possess complete knowledge of everything pertaining to the transaction, which often results in bad outcomes. This is a completely trivial statement of the obvious: It is impossible for a person to know everything the other knows. But this thought is presented as proof in support of coercive government intervention to allow trades to take place. Yet billions of market transactions take place each day worldwide, and the vast majority of them are to the satisfaction of both parties. One does not need to know everything to know what constitutes a beneficial trade—one simply needs to know their own preference for the traded goods. And, of course, this rationale ignores the problem of how the coercive regulatory authority happens to secure knowledge that is not available to both parties, and how an authority can use that knowledge to enforce, with the threat of violence, a superior solution to both parties. How, if the parties themselves do not have sufficient information, would a regulatory body in charge of all transactions in a society have the information for each transaction? And whose interest will this central planner be optimizing?

To the extent that information asymmetry is a problem in markets, it is a problem that is best resolved through voluntary means. Fiat economists' favorite example of information asymmetry is the market for used cars—and yet a large industry of used car information has developed around the car industry to solve this problem. Car buyers prefer to buy cars with a car history report. Car owners, in turn, voluntarily choose to sign up for these services to increase the value of their car to potential purchasers. Thus, the market solves the supposed market failure in a completely voluntary manner. A multitude of product information services has emerged in all such industries to allow consumers access to the information about products: movie reviews, restaurant reviews, electronics reviews, and so on. Were these industries stymied from growing because of government intervention and regulation under the pretext of imperfect information, then how would that have benefited consumers and producers?

Irrationality

Among the newly emergent pseudoscience of behavioral economics, "irrationality" is another highly popular cluster of fallacies used to justify government coercion. Behavioral economists posit arbitrary and irrelevant criteria for what constitutes rational behavior and then test their university's undergraduate students—as human lab rats and stand-ins for all of humanity—to see whether these criteria are fulfilled by humans. After the undergrads fail to give the researcher a result that meets his criteria of rationality, he smugly denounces the human race as irrational. Finally, he concludes that the only way to correct this behavior is through the coercive intervention of the government.

Economic rationality, though, cannot be studied in the context of a lab experiment, as it is inherently subjective and marginal. It pertains to individuals' decisions at the time and place where these decisions need to be made, and in a lab setting, all decisions pertain to the lab, not to the real world. After all, the world is full of enormous complexity and countless factors that cannot be transferred to a lab. There is no reason to accept behavioral economists' completely contrived experiments as an accurate reflection of the real world and the incentives of an experimental subject as being equivalent to real-world incentives. But even if one were to accept them, the bigger question remains: How can humans be irrational, but behavioral economists rational? If human biases distort rationality, why would behavioral economists be exempt? More significantly, why would the regulators who intervene in these markets be immune from this irrationality? And how much more destructive would it be if the irrationality is imposed at a coercive macroscale rather than restricted to them and the people who willingly and voluntarily choose to deal with them?

Imperfect Competition

As the neoclassical economic model assumes perfect competition, another way in which markets fail is imperfect competition: The failure of markets to have an *infinite* number of suppliers and demanders for each market. Obviously, that is an impossible bar to clear. As long as the number of buyers and sellers is not infinite in any market—which, of course, it never is—then the market can be denounced as suffering from imperfect competition or monopolization.

This situation can only be remedied, according to statist economists, by having a monopoly on violence that forces all market participants to obey its edicts on how to operate in a market free of monopolies.

But markets do not tend toward monopolies, except through the use of coercive violence. Quite simply, individual producers who charge exorbitant prices cannot stop competitors from undercutting them—unless they resort to force. In decades of examining this question, I have never come across a single example of a monopoly provider whose monopoly status was secured on the market peacefully rather than through coercive intervention. It is always government rules and regulations that create monopolies, as they are the only barrier that can stop peaceful private enterprise. The irony here is that government mandates turn specific industries into monopolies, which then normalizes the idea that this industry inevitably can only function as a monopoly, making it a "natural monopoly." But there is nothing natural about monopolies, and government regulation of monopolies is a problem masquerading as its solution, as Thomas DiLorenzo explains in an article that thoroughly refutes the basis of monopoly as a justification for government coercion:[186]

> It is a myth that natural-monopoly theory was developed first by economists, and then used by legislators to "justify" franchise monopolies. The truth is that the monopolies were created decades before the theory was formalized by intervention-minded economists, who then used the theory as an ex-post rationale for government intervention. At the time when the first government franchise monopolies were being granted, the large majority of economists understood that large-scale, capital-intensive production did not lead to monopoly, but was an absolutely desirable aspect of the competitive process.

Certain examples of monopolies often presented by economists refer to producers who managed to grow their share of the market by offering a vastly

186 DiLorenzo, Thomas. "The Myth of Natural Monopoly." *The Review of Austrian* Economics, 1996, pp. 43-58.

improved product to their competitors at a lower price. In this case, monopoly laws do not protect the consumer from a monopolist producer; they simply protect inefficient producers from more efficient ones. And they allow the inefficient to remain profitable without having to upgrade to the most efficient production mechanisms adopted by the market leader.

Externalities and Public Goods

Some of the most common rationales for government coercion are the fallacies of "externalities" and "public goods," which are presented as unique goods that, by their very nature, can only be provided satisfactorily through government coercion. Most mainstream economic textbooks will concede that free-market capitalism is the best societal organization principle for the production and allocation of private goods. But these textbooks present "public goods" as a special kind of good for which markets are inadequate.

Externalities are positive or negative economic implications accruing to a person as a result of another person's consumption or production decisions. Negative externalities can take the form of pollution or economic losses. Positive externalities can take the form of benefiting economically from activities others undertake, such as a hotel or restaurant enjoying outsized revenues thanks to a sports event taking place near their location. Or a real estate development agency witnessing a rise in the prices of its properties because a public park was opened on nearby land, making the properties more attractive to buyers. The use of externalities as a justification for government coercion is inadequate. Externalities are either violations of property rights, in which case they can be resolved by arbitration or an inevitable consequence of living in a society that offers no rationale for initiating violence. An example of the former is pollution. If a factory starts to release waste into neighboring properties, it is simply violating the property of its neighbors. The polluting act is the initiation of aggression, and the landowner who is its victim can resort to taking a legal action against the factory. In the same vein, virtually every economic activity in the market economy impacts others. Your buying the last piece of cake at your local bakery means others are unable to buy it. Your looking presentable and acting civil—as opposed to you looking and smelling awful—has a positive impact on people who deal with you. Any person can take an interest in any other person's decisions and thus develop positive or negative utility from them, but never does that justify the initiation of aggression.[187] Chapter 5 explained the rationale for private property and how it is the only consistent moral standard by which a society can function peacefully and productively. Participating in the market economy means economically interacting with a very large number of people and incurring countless externalities every day from their private decisions. The only way this economic and social system can operate peacefully is if all members exercise their sovereignty over their own property and accept the sovereignty of others over their own property. If the property owner does not violate the property of others, then the emotional state of people who do not own a good cannot possibly constitute legitimate grounds for the initiation of violence against the owner. This is a moral standard that can be enforced universally. A moral standard where people can control the property of non-aggressors will inevitably lead to interminable conflict and the unraveling of the foundation upon which civilized society rests: private property.

Public goods are defined as goods that are non-excludable and non-rival—terms closely intertwined with the concept of externality. Non-excludable is a term used to refer to the fact that it is not possible to prevent someone from benefiting from the good if someone *else* pays for it. In other words, the benefits of the good would accrue to the person who paid for it as well as to the person who did not pay for it, which would encourage everyone to not pay for the good, resulting in suboptimal production, i.e., underproduction. With government coercion forcing everyone to pay for the good, it can be provided to everyone in the necessary quantity. The fatal, unmentionable assumption here is that the economist and central planners can determine the optimal production of a good for society overall. They make the decision on behalf of everyone, fully cognizant of the trade-offs involved and the opportunity cost incurred for every single other person. But economic calculation can only be performed when

187 Hoppe, Hans-Hermann. "Fallacies of the Public Goods Theory and the Production of Security." *The Journal of Libertarian Studies*, vol. 9, no. 1, Winter, 1989.

capital resources are privately traded, so their prices can act as reliable signals for the market. Public goods are provided at the margin, and they require the dedication of labor and capital resources based on economic calculation. Abstract considerations about their value are immaterial if they cannot be translated into price through the free action of individuals as workers and capitalists.

A mainstream economics textbook presents the military and police, public parks, roads, lighthouses, fire brigades, and police as examples of non-excludable goods. If you were to move to a city in which you did not pay a single cent to produce these goods, you would still benefit from them. The army would still keep you and everyone in the town safe, and you could enjoy the parks and roads without paying a cent. Your goods would arrive on boats benefiting from lighthouses that you did not contribute to building. The fire brigade would extinguish a fire in your house, while the police would arrest criminals in your neighborhood, making it safer for you. Since society cannot exclude you from benefiting from these goods, the free rider problem emerges—everyone would like to benefit from these goods without contributing to their provision. Hence, mainstream economists conclude without government coercion to force people to pay for these goods, they would be underprovided.

And yet history is full of examples of these goods being successfully provided voluntarily as well as examples of these goods being provided wastefully and inadequately through violent government intervention. A voluntary provision does not always have to be provided through profit-seeking organizations. Countless forms of charity or voluntary associations can provide crucial goods without resorting to violent coercion. Countless public parks have been donated by landowners to their hometowns. Private parks also abound in many areas, where private organizations manage biodiversity and beautiful areas and protect them from the revenues generated from entrance fees and various experiences and products. These privately owned natural areas cover approximately 200,000 km^2 in South Africa—roughly a sixth of the entire country's area.[188] There, fees are paid to enjoy natural areas. The historical

188 Jacobsen, Tanya. "Private Game Reserves Are Vital for Conservation." *Africa Geographic*, 24 July 2021.

record is full of lighthouses built by private entities that operate ports and financed through the fees charged to docking boats.[189] The fact that some boats passing by the port can benefit from seeing the light without contributing to its construction is no impediment to its building, as it can still be economically useful enough for port users to pay for. In a pinch, operators of lighthouses can also turn the light off when free riders are benefiting from them to force them to arrange payments.[190]

The fundamental problem with the externality argument is that it ignores the reality of how marginal economic decisions are taken. When deciding whether to purchase a good, a man decides by economically calculating the costs and benefits of this marginal purchase. If the benefits outweigh the costs, he purchases the good. It is immaterial to him whether others will manage to benefit from it or not. As long as the product does not involve violating the property of others, then the decision-maker has no reason to calculate other people's benefits or losses from it. He will not choose to inconvenience himself just to ensure that others will not benefit. If the lighthouse is beneficial to the port owner, then docking boats will pay more for using it than it costs to build it, so he will likely build it.

Public roads worldwide suffer from congestion and degradation. The governments that build them can confiscate land and pay the price they deem necessary to owners, so central planners do not face an accurate cost accounting for the main resource they plan, meaning they do not have to pay the full market price for it. The result is an overproduction of roads that leads to the consumption of large amounts of land for roads, reduces the usable space of a city, and forces people to have to drive increasingly more as the city spreads out. Contrary to well-worn statist tropes, a world where governments do not provide roads would not be a world with no roads. It would simply mean that the providers of roads would have to pay the full cost for them, and the return from using the road to consumers and from repurposing the land for alternative uses would have

---

189 Coase, Ronald. "The Lighthouse in Economics." *Journal of Law and Economics*, vol. 17, no. 2, October 1974, pp. 357-76.

190 Barnett, William, and Walter Block. "Coase and Van Zandt on Lighthouses." *Public Finance Review*, vol. 35, no. 6, 2016, pp. 710–33.

to be high enough to justify paying that cost. No such calculation is possible when governments can confiscate land to build roads or impose a selling price on landowners. At the margin, such a policy will allow governments to acquire land at a cost lower than its market price. Further, the economic calculation is performed by people with a vested interest in more projects taking place, as that entails more funding in their hands. When no entity can buy land at a price it decrees, then the land will be allocated to economic uses and will not be overused in one particular avenue. Many roads are built privately, and by charging their users directly, the roads end up being far more functional, as they eliminate the costs of congestion on users by charging a price that keeps the road flowing with traffic. Walter Block's work on the economics of roads is very useful here.[191] The next chapter examines security and defense and why they are regular economic goods that do not require special provisions.

Non-rivalry refers to goods whose consumption by one person does not reduce the benefit accruing to other consumers. These are goods that can be provided to society as a whole or to nobody. A lighthouse, streetlights, and national defense are classic examples. A lighthouse benefits all boats passing by a seaport, even if the boat is not docking in the port and paying a docking fee to its owners. Boats passing by the lighthouse can all see its light and benefit from it, and they do not reduce the light for each other. Similarly, all pedestrians on a road benefit from streetlights, and their benefiting does not take the light from others. An army that protects the country from foreign invaders protects all members of society, and adding an extra member to society does not reduce the safety and security of other members. The military either stops foreign armies from invading for the good of all citizens or it does not.

On closer inspection, however, this also proves a faulty rationale for the initiation of aggression. If a good is truly non-rival, it would be a non-economic good. Rivalry is always present in economic goods, and the solution to that problem is property rights and the principle of non-aggression. Streetlights are simply part of the street, belonging to its owner, who charges for

---

191 Block, Walter. *The Privatization of Roads and Highways: Human and Economic Factors*. Ludwig von Mises Institute, 2009.

them as part of charging for access to the street. Even in the case of common streets—in urban areas that are owned by nobody—individuals who live on the street benefit from its light most, as do customers and visitors. For them, if the benefit of street lighting is worth investing in, they can invest, individually or collectively, through voluntary forms of association. The fact that they might not be able to stop passersby from benefiting is no justification for aggressing against all members of society in order to finance the streetlights. If one street's residents can expect the rest of society to finance their streets, then all streets' residents will expect the same. Rather than voluntarily deciding whether the costs outweigh the benefits individually, the collectivist solution places a central planner in charge of making that decision for all of society. Giving some people lights for which they pay very little and forcing others to pay for lights they do not use if their street is deemed unworthy of lighting. Ultimately, with property rights, nothing is non-rival. There is a limit to the number of people who can use a road and benefit from its lighting, and this rivalry is what motivates the road owner to optimize the infrastructure of the road. Doing so benefits him *and* the users he wants to have on the road.

It is also fallacious to assume national defense is non-rival. Defense from aggression and security are private goods, and each individual's security adds to the burden of the security provider. The more territory that must be secured, the higher the cost of security. The more people live in the territory, the more possible targets of attack for enemies, and the more security risks come from the behavior of each added individual, whose actions can endanger the security of others.

In all of these examples, sloppy economic reasoning has its root in ignoring marginal analysis. It is tempting to speak of national defense, justice, roads, light, and the like in absolute and aggregate terms, but in economic reality, there are only marginal items, and individuals making the decision about the employment of capital resources to produce these goods at the margin. Whether it is a soldier, policeman, judge, road, or lamppost, there are only individual units being deployed, with an economic cost and benefit. Only through economic calculation with property rights can these resources be deployed productively and rationally.

Rationality in Economics

The root of market failure analysis comes from the standard model of neoclassical economics, which, as I have noted, tried to model the market process mathematically. To do so, economists made some ridiculous assumptions: That all agents in a market system must possess complete knowledge and be rationally self-interested; and that there is a state of perfect competition, with an infinite number of buyers and sellers for each market. The past seventy years of economics have primarily consisted of supposed geniuses receiving government paychecks to poke holes through this ridiculous mathematical model and then concluding that they have disproved the possibility of markets working.

A good metaphor here is to imagine that an economist is creating a mathematical model for the flight of a bird. To make the model computable, he makes simplifying assumptions, such as the weight of the bird is uniformly distributed across its body. With this assumption, some sort of simplified model of bird flight can be constructed and made conducive for exam questions. Market failure economists would then elaborately dispute the assumption and proudly proclaim that they have proven that ... birds do not fly! They do not simply reject this model of bird flight as inaccurate—they reject the real-world phenomenon that the model is inaccurately conveying, even though they can see flying birds every day. Just as it does not matter that birds can actually fly, it also does not matter that billions of people worldwide partake in satisfying, mutually beneficial market exchanges daily. For the fiat academic, truth is decreed by the interests that conjure their fiat paycheck from thin air, not by reflecting reality. As long as an economist can point out a flaw in the ridiculous mathematical models of other economists, all the mainstream textbooks will faithfully regurgitate the holy mantras: "Markets fail!" and "The government fixes this!"

This becomes clear after reading Vernon Smith's fascinating book, *Rationality in Economics*.[192] An experimental economist who tested economic models in

192 Smith, Vernon L. *Rationality in Economics: Constructivist and Ecological Forms*. Cambridge University Press, 2008. For a concise statement of the most important findings of Professor Smith's long career, see his speech in acceptance of the Bank of Sweden Prize in Economics.

classrooms, Smith was definitely not an Austrian economist—at least not for most of his long career. But as he experimented with economic decision-makers, Smith arrived at the same conclusions that the Austrian economists had arrived at decades earlier. Even in artificial laboratory settings, Smith's subjects could conduct beneficial trades and discover prices. And they did so without needing to meet the assumptions of the neoclassical model and without needing a benevolent central planner to dictate terms to them. Thus, markets do not need to meet the assumptions of the neoclassical model of economics to work; rather, it is the neoclassical model that needs *these assumptions* to compute. Real-world markets need these models as much as the sun needs astronomy to rise.

This realization led Vernon Smith to build on the work of Friedrich Hayek to distinguish between the results of human design and human action and how each can be understood to be rational in its own way.[193] "Constructive rationality" is the term Smith uses to designate things that are designed consciously by human reason—an example being the design of a car or airplane. Engineers drew out every single detail of their design and manufactured it accordingly. By contrast, Smith uses the term "ecological rationality" to refer to phenomena that emerge out of human action and interaction—through an evolutionary process of variation and selection—without a specific designer decreeing the contours of the design. An example would be airplane routes, which are not designed by a planner from above, but instead, emerge out of an extensive process of variation and selection. In this case, countless airlines try many different routes and plans for connecting flights, but consumer choice ultimately decides which routes are profitable and which are not. Airlines then utilize market feedback—building new airports, launching new lines, optimizing for particular connections—to produce the highly sophisticated global web of airplane routes that blanket our planet. Hayek introduced the concept of spontaneous order to refer to these phenomena, which appear as the complex outputs of a designer's work, but in reality, are the product of human action and interaction under a set of agreed-upon, abstract rules.

---

193 See Chapters 5 and 6 from Hayek, Friedrich von. *Studies in Philosophy, Politics and Economics*. University of Chicago Press, 1967.

Hayek's powerful insight is that so much of the order in our life, and the institutions on which we rely for our survival, is a spontaneously emergent product of human interaction—not the product of conscious human design. Language is perhaps the best example of this. While some modern languages, such as Esperanto, are constructed rationally, the vast majority of the world's languages have no designer or founder. These languages emerged and developed over thousands of years, with generations of people learning them and making small additions and alterations, some of which survived while others were discarded. Hayek, the Austrians, and Smith contend that the capitalist market economy is also not the product of any one person's design but the complex emergent phenomenon evolving from the actions of humans functioning under a set of abstract rules. Nobody designs markets or brings them into existence by fiat; they emerge in a world in which individuals are free to engage in the economizing acts discussed in the second part of this book. In a social order in which humans have justly acquired property and maintain ownership of their bodies, they are able to work, accumulate capital, increase their utilization of energy sources to meet their needs, and improve the state of the technology they use. In a society where humans respect each other's property and reject the initiation of aggression, we can trade with one another, and from that emerges money, the division of labor, and the modern capitalist system. There is no conscious designer directing the development of a market economy; it is the spontaneous order emerging from the observance of the abstract rules that govern modern civilization.

Mainstream economists of the twentieth century completely miss this point. Instead, they imagine that markets are the products of rational design, like a car, table, or at least, something that can be improved with conscious top-down design. The fatal conceit here, to borrow Hayek's term, is that by seeking to improve and mend the market economy with top-down planning, coercive action will undo and disrupt the basic abstract rules that are the foundation of the market economy. To that end, Hayek offers the Austrian perspective on the job of the economist:

> The curious task of economics is to demonstrate to men how little they really know about what they imagine they can design. To the naive mind

> that can conceive of order only as the product of deliberate arrangement, it may seem absurd that in complex conditions order, and adaptation to the unknown, can be achieved more effectively by decentralizing decisions and that a division of authority will actually extend the possibility of overall order. Yet that decentralization actually leads to more information being taken into account.[194]

Mainstream fiat economists are quick to provide voluminous rationalizations for why markets fail, why humans are irrational, and why only coercive intervention can succeed in improving things. Yet closer inspection shows that markets function regardless of economists' objections and that the real failure of markets occurs when coercive intervention, under alluringly altruistic pretexts, is used to try to fix these markets. Perhaps it is not market participants but economists who are irrational and who refuse to see the natural order of the market even as they rely upon it for their daily survival. But that is not a fair charge, for the reality is that the modern economist's livelihood relies on attacking the market economy and rationalizing government interventions. Producing nonsensical research to justify government initiation of aggression is arguably, and unfortunately, the rational course of action for a professional economist in a world in which academia has been hijacked by the state.

194 Hayek, Friedrich von, and William Warren Bartley. *The Fatal Conceit: The Errors of Socialism*. University of Chicago Press, 1988.

Chapter 17

Defense

The previous chapter provided rationales against government intervention in economic activity and critically examined the rationales for it, finding an absurd mishmash of conflicting rationales and transparently motivated reasoning. Initiation of aggression is a crime that seeks justification, something state-sponsored economists toil very hard to provide and popularize among the population. The closer one examines these rationales, the more obvious it becomes that they are incompatible with the fundamental basis of a capitalist market economy—respect for property rights and a civilized society—rejecting the initiation of violence.

Whereas classical economists of the nineteenth and twentieth centuries went to great lengths in rejecting the initiation of aggression in the economic sphere, they did not extend their analysis to the existence of the state or the legitimacy of its provision of security, defense, and law and order. But the works of Murray Rothbard,[195] Hans-Hermann Hoppe,[196] and many other anarcho-capitalist scholars in the Austrian tradition extend the analysis of human action and non-aggression to the establishment of the state itself, the legitimacy of its monopoly on violence, and the feasibility of its provision of security, defense, and law through monopoly financed by expropriation.

The Market for Defense

It is a common misconception among state-employed economists to consider defense and violence as being outside the scope of economic analysis. But as I discussed in Chapter 1, defense from aggression has all the characteristics of an economic good. It has utility, as humans prefer to avoid death and physical harm and to actualize their own will rather than being subject to another's will. Defense from aggression is also scarce. It is not available in unlimited quantities, since aggression is an infinite series of potential threats that can arise any time, while defense consumes resources and is therefore finite and must be economized. The combination of utility and scarcity makes defense valuable. Humans can work to produce it or obtain it from others. People desire it, so they are willing to pay for it. Those who provide it can benefit from providing it to willing customers. It is a market good that people can buy, in the same way they can buy any other market good.

An important distinction needs to be made here between violence and the initiation of violence. Defense as a good may or may not involve violence, but it does not involve the initiation of violence. Defense involves preventative measures that make violence less likely and retributive measures that respond to the initiation of violence and punish the initiator or seek restitution for the victim. The initiation of violence is a coercive act whose performance cannot be freely accepted by one party in the transaction so it cannot be considered

195 See Rothbard: *The Ethics of Liberty*; *Anatomy of the State*; *Power and Market*; *For A New Liberty*.

196 See Hoppe, Hans-Hermann. *The Private Production of Defense*. Ludwig Von Mises Institute, 2009. • Hoppe, Hans-Hermann. *The Myth of National Defense: Essays on the Theory and History of Security Production*. Ludwig Von Mises Institute, Auburn University, 2003.

a market good. But defense from the initiation of aggression and retribution against it are regular market goods that can be bought and sold without initiating aggression in a voluntary market. While defense may involve violence, it is violence committed against someone who had already committed violence. This ethical distinction between different types of violence has been recognized since man first began pounding iron into swords and shields, and the same principle applies to missiles and F-35s.

The market for defense is highly developed, diverse, and sophisticated, offering a wide range of goods and services to meet people's needs for security and freedom from aggression. It includes products such as safety locks, safety alarm systems, surveillance cameras and drones, fences, personal guns, armored vehicles, security guards, and private investigators. Researchers in The Business Research Company estimate the size of the private security industry to be around $303.58 billion as of 2021.[197]

Most people are under the impression that security is the purview of the state, but this is incorrect. The startling reality is that even in today's world, with governments afforded the exorbitant privilege of using their own credit as money, and thus the ability to acquire services limitlessly for as long as their currency works, the majority of security personnel worldwide are employed privately, not by government. In 2011, China had 5 million private security workers compared to 2.69 million police officers, while India had 7 million private security workers and 1.4 million police officers. In the United States in 2016, there were one million private security officers and 800,000 police officers. In fact, this was the case for Brazil, Russia, Japan, Germany, the United Kingdom, and a total of 46 out of 81 nations for which data was available in this study. The countries of this study alone had a population of 4.9 billion, and 4.15 of them lived in countries where the majority of security guards were private. In the entire sample, there were an estimated 20 million private security workers and 10.5 million police officers.[198] A commanding majority of

---

197 "Investigation And Security Services Global Market Report 2022 by Type, Deployment Type, Application." *Research and Markets*, The Business Research Company, Feb 2022

198 Provost, Claire. "The Industry of Inequality: Why the World Is Obsessed with Private Security." *The Guardian*, 12 May 2017.

humanity lives in places where there are twice as many private security workers as police officers. This disparity has likely been amplified in the intervening years, given growing problems with police financing and recruitment, along with increases in security incidents.

Far from being an unrealistic techno-utopian dream, the existence of a market in defense and security is the reality most of the world is already living. The majority of companies with valuable inventories rely on hiring private security to secure their businesses. This arrangement suits both private contractors and the local government police, whose limited resources cannot be stretched to provide every citizen and business with all the protection they might want. The calculation problem discussed in Chapter 12 also applies to security, and its only solution is entrepreneurial calculation within the framework of clearly defined property rights. Indeed, it would be no exaggeration to observe that government security forces in many places in the world are mainly preoccupied with securing the government and not the people, who must purchase their own security on the market by arming themselves or hiring armed guards. While enemies of market's ideas often pose the question "Who will pay for the police?" as if it is some profound rebuttal, the reality is that private individuals and corporations are already finding non-governmental sources of law, order, and security in the free market for defense.

Arguably, the market for defense is much broader than the aforementioned goods and police services, and includes the world's weapons industry as well. Granted—a large fraction of weapons are used for aggression and the initiation of violence, and a much larger fraction of weapons are purchased by governments, using money acquired involuntarily, through taxation or inflation. Thus, the market for weapons is highly distorted. Nonetheless, the fact remains that weapons manufacturers are predominantly voluntary private entities, deploying accumulated capital from savers, hiring freely contracting individuals as labor, buying raw materials from global markets, and often selling their output freely on the market to the highest bidder. Of the 100 largest weapons manufacturers in the world, 68 are privately owned, 24 are government-owned, and 6 are owned jointly by private entities and government.[199] Even the government-owned firms only exist in the context of a global free-market order for all their input and most of their output goods, where they benefit from performing economic calculation using market prices for their inputs and outputs. All the raw materials that go into manufacturing weapons are sourced from global markets with an extensive division of labor and freely accumulated, privately owned capital. Without a capitalist market, the profit motive, capital accumulation, and the division of labor, nobody would produce weapons much more sophisticated than rocks, spears, bows and arrows, and primitive traps.

This conclusion is inescapable once one understands the nature of violent conflict, the impossibility of economic calculation, and an extensive impersonal division of labor without property rights. War, after all, consists of the delivery of large amounts of kinetic energy to inflict maximum damage against the enemy. Power in the military sense is power in the very literal engineering and economic sense, as discussed in Chapter 8: Delivering large quantities of energy over short bursts of time, at the margin, to meet specific objectives. Modern weaponry advances and wins wars by increasing its ability to deliver kinetic energy effectively and under the control of its wielder over short periods of time, so as to bring about physical changes to reality through the murder of enemy combatants or civilians. Capital accumulation, private property, and the division of labor have proven to be the most effective system for channeling the largest quantities of power to meet human needs. And it is only natural that this would also be the most effective system for channeling power to military conflict.

Military power is also entirely reliant on a capitalist free-market economy, which produces the raw materials and economic surplus that can be channeled for producing weapons. Without a productive modern capitalist economy financing it, even the world's strongest army would degenerate into slave labor camps, unable to defeat enemies or feed its own soldiers. The raw materials that go into weapons manufacturing are produced through extensive global supply chains and sophisticated machinery that is developed, designed, and

199 "Top 100 Defense Companies." *Defense News*, Sightline Media Group, 2022.

distributed in a global manner. It is the market economy that has produced all the most amazing innovations in weapon making, which public sector and private sector criminals use daily for violent aggression. The extent of the development of weapons systems is a function of the development of a market economy. The world's sophisticated weapons systems could never be developed without the extreme degree of specialization, division of labor, capital accumulation, and technological advancement that is only possible in a free-market economic system. The Soviet Union dedicated a very large percentage of its economic output to the production of weaponry, a percentage that was much higher than that of the United States. But by the end of the 1980s, this spending translated into enormously expensive piles of dysfunctional rust. Meanwhile, with a smaller percentage of economic output being spent on weapons, the United States' private weapons industry had produced enormous advances in its weaponry.

Soviet industrialization benefited from existing within a global capitalist system with which it traded and from which it could calculate prices. Within a few years of attempting socialism, Soviets came to grasp the enormity of the calculation problem. They realized they needed to rely on taking prices for commodities from the international market to attempt to economically calculate the allocation of resources. This was arguably a major reason their bureaucratic government survived for as long as it did. But even that was not enough. Domestic resources were all owned by the government, there was no market in them, they had no prices, and so they could not be the subject of rational economic calculation. The arms industry was no exception. By the 1980s, it became clear to Soviet leadership that continuing to operate such an enormous arsenal with a dysfunctional economic system was completely unworkable.

There is perhaps no more flattering compliment to free exchange than the fact that the vast majority of violent aggression worldwide, carried out by governments and private individuals alike, relies predominantly on the weaponry manufactured by the market order. This, in turn, relies on the deferral of consumption by private individuals to provide capital to entrepreneurs, who perform economic calculations to determine how to peacefully hire workers and try to sell their goods to the highest bidder at a price that exceeds inputs. The uncivilized and violent may take pride in their aggression and rejection of peace and cooperation, but their choice of weaponry in aggression speaks louder than their puerile words. They do not choose to live in isolation from civilized society, produce their own weapons, and use them to aggress against civilization. They choose to acquire the most advanced products of the division of labor to increase the productivity of their violence. They may not have the mental capacity to understand how peaceful division of labor is so valuable to them, but their actions do.

The Market for Law and Order

The market for security and protection from aggression arguably extends beyond the markets for weapons and police. It also includes arbitration, which serves to protect people by allowing them an avenue for restitution of stolen property, and punishment for those who aggress against them. While most of the world today has monopoly legal systems intertwined with the political system, it does not follow that arbitration and judicial review are goods that can only be provided by the state. The common law of Britain developed over centuries primarily from private courts, which were not under the command of government.[200] Private courts offered their services to any citizens who would hire them, and they had every incentive to be as fair and impartial as possible to continue to secure the business of more clients. These courts did not have monopolies over territorial jurisdictions, and their areas of operation overlapped. So, citizens could choose to go to the court they trusted rather than remain confined to their local jurisdiction. Judges in these courts were incentivized to look at precedent cases to assess their own cases, and from the centuries of precedents and rulings, the common law as a body emerged. It did *not* emerge from the top-down design of a central planner. The law merchant and admiralty law were similarly developed in private courts. This independent and freely competitive judiciary was arguably

200 Stringham, Edward. *Private Governance: Creating Order in Economic and Social Life*. Oxford University Press, 2015.

quite instrumental in the development of free markets and enterprise in Britain. It was also very conducive to the emergence of the Industrial Revolution, which transformed the entire world's economy.

Even today, most countries have growing and thriving private arbitration businesses, where individuals and corporations can take their disputes to impartial third-party judges to adjudicate. The private arbitration industry witnesses fast-growing demand because of its extremely efficient operation compared to state monopoly courts. The American Arbitration Association conducts around 40,000 arbitrations every month, and there are many other organizations in this fast-growing industry. As the U.S. court system continues to become slower, more expensive, and less efficient, many are choosing to take their court cases to private arbitration organizations. Because arbitration, like defense or apples or cars, is just another market good: scarce, offering utility, and thus given subjective value by many.

The growth of the industry and the history of independent judiciary clearly show that there is value for contracting parties to have recourse to an independent third party to which they can refer a dispute with their counterparty. A growing number of commercial contracts contain clauses for both parties to defer to independent arbitration in the case of disputes. In a 2008 survey of 26 corporations, researchers found that 77% have arbitration clauses in consumer contracts and 93% have them in employment contracts.[201] Both parties to a contract have an incentive to include arbitration clauses, as they both would like to resolve any dispute cheaply and quickly. Industry experts, lawyers, judges, and legal scholars all have a financial incentive to provide arbitration services to clients—and to provide them honestly, impartially, efficiently, and quickly. Government courts, being centrally planned and directed, are usually much more expensive than arbitration, so they are impractical for many uses. They also usually lack the capacity to provide expertise on highly complex technical or commercial issues in dispute.[202]

---

201 Eisenberg, Theodore, Geoffrey Miller, and Emily Sherwin. "Arbitration's Summer Soldiers: An Empirical Study of Arbitration Clauses in Consumer and Nonconsumer Contracts." *University of Michigan Journal of Law Reform*, vol. 41, no. 4, 2008, pp. 871-96.

202 Caplan, Bryan, and Edward Stringham. "Privatizing the Adjudication of Disputes." *Theoretical Inquiries in Law*, vol. 9, no. 2, 2008, pp. 503-28.

The growing industry of independent arbitration and the rich history of private independent courts help us see that there is nothing special about a judiciary system that makes it impossible to exist on the free market. In interactions between individuals and corporations, the possibility of dispute always exists. People would therefore prefer to have recourse to an independent third party that can be relied upon to rule justly in the case of disputes. There is no need to impose a judiciary monopoly on all contracts. Individuals and contracting parties are capable of agreeing beforehand on independent third parties to resort to in the case of disputes. In the absence of state-monopoly organizations handling law and defense, society is likely to witness a blossoming of for-profit and nonprofit organizations. These will provide law and defense to individuals with full accountability and without being able to force consumers to pay for them. In *Private Governance*, Edward Stringham offers a fascinating and highly edifying study of various types of voluntary arrangements for the provision of law and defense that do not require resorting to violent monopolies.

State Monopoly of Defense and Law

While Mises saw the "preservation of private ownership of the means of production and its protection against violent or fraudulent encroachments,"[203] he had a different conception of the state than what is prevalent today. Mises stressed the importance of the right of self-determination, making government a voluntary entity. He writes:

> The right of self-determination in regard to the question of membership in a state thus means: whenever the inhabitants of a particular territory, whether it be a single village, a whole district, or a series of adjacent districts, make it known, by a freely conducted plebiscite, that they no longer wish to remain united to the state to which they belong at the time, but

203 Mises, Ludwig von. *Human Action: The Scholar's Edition.* Ludwig von Mises Institute, 1998, p. 714.

> wish either to form an independent state or to attach themselves to some other state, their wishes are to be respected and complied with. This is the only feasible and effective way of preventing revolutions and civil and international wars. ... However, the right of self-determination of which we speak is not the right of self-determination of nations, but rather the right of self-determination of the inhabitants of every territory large enough to form an independent administrative unit. If it were in any way possible to grant this right of self-determination to every individual person, it would have to be done.[204]

With the right of secession granted, the state cannot take for granted the allegiance and revenue from its citizens and needs to work for them. Without the right to secession, government becomes a territorial coercive monopoly. If the protection of private ownership is a desirable good, why would a coercive monopoly succeed at providing it? And if it could succeed at providing this economic good, why would it not also succeed in providing other goods? Why do the problems of calculation manifest in all markets but not in the market for defense and law? Rothbard dismantles some of the most common statist justifications for a monopoly on law and order in *For a New Liberty*.[205]

Statist economists may posit that the state is needed to define property rights and that without a monopoly frame of reference for just claims on property, there is no possibility of defining property rights in a way that avoids conflict. But this is patently false. As discussed in Chapter 5, the organizing frames of reference for property are the principles of self-ownership, the ownership of natural resources found and transformed by a person's labor, and the ownership of goods acquired through consensual exchange. Outside of socialist societies, the state itself does not determine property—it merely acts to enforce these principles in disputes over property. There is no reason this enforcement, according to these well-established principles, cannot be provided by private individuals and organizations without recourse to monopoly financing.

---

204 Mises, Ludwig von. *Liberalism: The Classical Tradition*. Foundation for Economic Education, 1996, pp. 109-10.

205 Rothbard, Murray. *For a New Liberty*. Macmillan, 1973.

Another argument for a coercive monopoly on defense and law says that property is a precondition for all economic activity, and that there can be no economic activity without it. But many other goods, like food and land, are essential, and voluntary market arrangements are clearly a superior way of providing them than a coercive monopoly. Rather than an inevitability, the coercive monopoly over defense and law lies at the root of the many failures of these markets. For if defense and law are economic goods, why would not the failures of coercive monopoly provision also affect them?

If the mass of people accepts the legitimacy of coercive monopoly provision of any particular economic good, they witness a deterioration in the quality of the good they receive, shortages in supply, and increases in cost. The monopolist providers, on the other hand, usually benefit from their privileged economic position of being able to extract payment from the sellers irrespective of quality of service. This is exactly the condition of state security and defense in the majority of the world today. Individuals in positions of government benefit immensely from their monopoly privilege, while consumers suffer from a lack of defense and injustice of law. Matters are made worse by governments abusing their monopoly over money to finance extensive propaganda campaigns in schools, universities, and mass media to promote acceptance of the legitimacy of coercive monopoly over defense and law. The more time one spends examining modern state-funded schools and universities, the more one sees their entire purpose as consisting of promoting acquiescence to the state.

Chapter 8 presented the argument that modern high-power machinery has been the driving economic force behind the abolition of slavery, as it can produce more grunt labor at a much lower cost than enslaved humans. With modern machinery and high-power energy sources, the raw labor of humans becomes increasingly cheap, as their productivity rises and intellectual work—supervising machines—becomes increasingly valuable. It is no longer profitable to enslave people in the traditional sense, but that has not erased the ancient dynamics of enslavement and domination that have existed in human societies for millennia. Statism is the outlet for the ancient base animalistic desire to dominate and enslave others rather than cooperate with them in civilization. But instead of physical enslavement, statism allows for mass psychological enslavement of societies via their conditioning to believe they have no alternative but to acquiesce to, and yield before, a violent monopoly provider of security. Slaves are thus set free from the drudgery and violence of chains and grunt labor to pursue more productive means of meeting their ends. Meanwhile, the individuals who make up the state are able to extract a large chunk of the fruits of their subjects' labor by propagandizing and educating them into accepting—and paying for—one monopolist security and law provider.

When defense is treated as a good like any other, defense producers strive to deliver it as cheaply, efficiently, and effectively as possible. Private security providers are much more responsive to their clients' needs precisely because their entire business relies on their efficiency and because they do not have a monopoly. But problems arise when state propaganda convinces citizens that defense is a special good—and when humans are educated and conditioned to think they have no choice but to remain subject to the rule of the protection agency they were born under. This is where nationalism and various forms of government propaganda come in handy. The modern slave is not kept in physical chains, as his physical freedom makes him too productive to restrain. He is instead kept in mental chains of statist education, accepting inferior security while having his wealth pillaged, with no real accountability or choice. As long as a majority of the population continues to believe they are bound to receive security as a gift from a hopefully benevolent monopolist, its provision is likely to be deficient, as is the case with all market monopolies.

The struggle for civilization is the struggle for humans to deal with each other based on the principle of non-aggression, where everyone agrees to respect the property rights of everyone else in their person and justly acquired property. When this principle is overturned in favor of a violent monopolist, the exception begins to seep into all other aspects of life, for the violent monopolist will seek to control all other aspects of life. And with the population conditioned to pliably accept the legitimacy of violent coercion in the sphere of defense and law, it is not very difficult to convince them to extend it to other aspects of life, beginning with money, as in modern fiat capitalist economies, and ending with the concept of property itself, as in communist societies. Social relations cannot be arranged on the basis of respect for property rights when the enforcement of this property itself is based on an organization that by its very existence violates property rights. Government, after all, is defined as the organization that does not finance itself voluntarily and so must resort to imposing taxes coercively on its subjects. This is the original sin of government, which makes it wholly incompatible with a civilized social order of voluntary cooperation. As Hoppe explains, it is in vain to expect the protection of property to be performed by an organization whose existence depends on coercively expropriating property:

> Once the principle of government—judicial monopoly and the power to tax—is incorrectly admitted as just, any notion of restraining government power and safeguarding individual liberty and property is illusory. Instead, under monopolistic auspices the price of justice and protection will continually rise and the quality of justice and protection fall. A tax-funded protection agency is a contradiction in terms—an expropriating property protector—and will inevitably lead to more taxes and less protection. Even if, as some classical liberal statists have proposed, a government limited its activities exclusively to the protection of pre-existing private property rights, the further question of how much security to produce would arise. Motivated (like everyone) by self-interest and the disutility of labor but endowed with the unique power to tax, a government agent's response will invariably be the same: To maximize expenditures on protection—and almost all of a nation's wealth can conceivably be consumed by the cost of protection—and at the same time to minimize the production of protection. The more money one can spend and the less one must work to produce, the better off one will be.[206]

In this way, Rothbard and Hoppe exploded the contradiction at the heart of modern classical liberal thought and offered a coherent anarcho-capitalist alternative congruent with the principles of economics as the study of human action.

---

206 Hoppe, Hans-Hermann. *Democracy: The God That Failed.* Transaction Publishers, 2001, p. 230.

Rather than peaceful cooperation under the rule of law applicable to all, society under government eventually degenerates into competitive conflict and aggression between people seeking to gain control of the power to dominate others. One common statist objection to the idea of a free market in defense is that the largest, most powerful group of thugs will take over and control society. The anarchist's response is that this is merely the reality of what the state is. Statists present their own cognitive enslavement as an argument for itself. Understood correctly, the state is the largest gang of thugs, and the progress of human civilization depends on minimizing the damage from this gang, not on commandeering it for the impossible task of using its license for evil to do good. In societies where the majority of the population accepts the insane idea that the government needs to have a monopoly over the potato or electricity markets, society ends up with massively dysfunctional potato and electricity markets. Similarly, a society that accepts government monopoly over the market for defense and security will suffer from dysfunctional defense and security.

It is no surprise, then, that today a growing fraction—possibly a majority—of defense and protection is provided by private institutions on the market. Given the aggressive nature of state prosecution of crimes against the state compared to state prosecution of state crimes against common citizens, it is not an exaggeration to say the purpose of state security is to protect the state, not the people. Individuals must still work and pay to secure themselves through the various avenues of defense available on the market. A free market in security is not hypothetical. A coercive tax-funded monopoly in security provision that succeeds in providing security, on the other hand, is the hypothetical that state-sponsored scholarship treats as a given.

State Monopoly Failure Modes

When examined through the lens of human economic action, many of the security problems of the world today can be seen as resulting from the absence of a freely competitive market in the provision of defense, security, and law, and the domination of these industries and many of their vital functions by monopoly providers. In the absence of a free market for these goods, central planners have no rational way of allocating resources to best meet the desired ends of the payers, since the payers are paying involuntarily, not freely choosing. Defense is ultimately a good that cannot be provided in infinite quantities. Economically rational decisions need to be made about where to allocate particular resources and what outputs one should seek to produce. In statist rhetoric and propaganda, where marginal analysis is not comprehended, defense is presented as an on/off switch, a complete package of clearly defined goods that is delivered in a well-known way. But with the understanding of marginal analysis, we can see that defense is provided at the margin, in the form of a myriad of goods and services that are particular to the time and place in which they are provided. There are marginal economic decisions to be made about the level of security provided to every household, as well as the allocation of every policeman and weapon. Should each neighborhood get a twenty-four-hour police patrol? Or should each street? Or each household? Should police spend more time protecting rich houses and neighborhoods because they are more likely to be the target of burglary? But why should poor taxpayers pay to protect the rich? How many policemen does a certain neighborhood need? Should some people get bodyguards? Should sporting events and concerts get extra police patrols to prevent trouble, or should the organizers of these events handle their own security? These questions are very important to the people involved, and in a free market, they would be able to calculate the best allocation of resources and property to meet these needs in the best way they can. But in a world where a central monopoly is financed by taxes, these decisions will be made blindly, without resorting to prices or rational economic calculation.

Tax-funded security providers have no economic incentive to minimize human and monetary cost, as customer satisfaction is tangential to their job. They are able to take the least economic choices available, as their operation is not constrained by an operations budget or a budget for recruitment and training of manpower. Monopoly army and police can treat their members as dispensable cannon fodder since they are not being allocated by entrepreneurs who succeed or fail in their enterprise by their prowess in allocation. The startling trigger-happy nature of modern police, notorious for wasting life and endangering police and citizens alike, cannot be understood without reference to the lack of market discipline imposed on police services.

In a free market for security, private providers have no tax revenue to subsidize them, and so must economize to survive and succeed. They would aim to minimize violent conflict and, to the greatest extent possible, seek peaceful solutions because doing so is good business. Private security guards in private establishments have nowhere near the same nasty reputation as police, precisely because they operate in a free market with accountability to the customer, and they have rational market calculation motivating their decisions, training, and operation. Private security guards everywhere illustrate that it is possible to provide security without having a monopoly and without being in charge of applying and interpreting the law that governs your behavior.

The monopoly tax financing of government security and defense providers makes them practically above the law. Ultimately, in a conflict between a state agent and a citizen, the state agent has the benefit of a giant institution with unlimited access to financing, and he is motivated to implement the law in a way that is favorable to the government. When the government has a judicial monopoly, the matter is exacerbated, as justice itself becomes monopolized and suffers from the same problems. As Hoppe explains:

> Moreover, a judicial monopoly will inevitably lead to a steady deterioration in the quality of justice and protection. If no one can appeal to justice except to government, justice will be perverted in favor of the government, constitutions and supreme courts notwithstanding. Constitutions and supreme courts are state constitutions and agencies, and all limitations to state action they might contain or find are invariably decided by agents of the very institution under consideration. Predictably, the definition of property and protection will continually be altered and the range of jurisdiction expanded to the government's advantage until, ultimately, the notion of universal and immutable human rights—and in particular property rights—will disappear and be replaced by that of law as government-made legislation and rights as government-given grants.[207]

207 Ibid.

When government members are allowed to initiate violence legitimately in the eyes of the population, they are extremely likely to abuse that privilege to their own benefit. The policeman and politician can and have used their positions to enrich themselves, dominate other citizens, and get away with criminal activity. They face no market test for performing their jobs effectively and have no profit motive to do so. They derive a great deal of profit motive from abusing their position. Humans are obviously not angels, so it is no surprise that many abuse their positions. But when endowed with no special legal privileges, they must perform their jobs to the satisfaction of their customers. Their motive and financial well-being depend on satisfying customers by providing them security in a free market. In a society in which violence is legitimized for one class of citizens, their motive and financial well-being are largely irrelevant to their customer satisfaction and are strongly enhanced by abusing their privilege.

The same dynamic is arguably true for national militaries. Since the military's financing is based on monopoly government edicts and not obtained from voluntarily paying customers, there is little scope for accountability to the people financing the military. The result is perhaps most starkly visible in the United States, where the world's strongest military spends hundreds of billions of dollars of tax and inflation revenue yearly and has military bases all over the world, and yet still cannot make it safe for a child in Chicago to walk to their local grocery store. With funding secured irrespective of security, a powerful military-industrial complex has succeeded in channeling large quantities of money to itself by ensuring an endless parade of military conflicts for the U.S. to engage in, under the flimsiest of pretexts, making the U.S. less secure by fostering the enmity of billions worldwide. Without consumer choice, security is an afterthought compared to the producer's pretext for securing more revenue. The story is not much better in smaller countries with weaker militaries, where the military establishment also succeeds in living on the defense budget secured coercively, and the military often ends up being little more than a puppet for more powerful regional or global regimes.

Government monopoly provision of security is also hampered by the fact that so much of society's property is held as "public property," which means no clear property rights and no ability to enforce private law on these lands. The term public property is in itself an oxymoron, as ownership is defined by the ability of the owner to do as he pleases with his property. But the public is not one uniform entity that can decide collectively what to do. Everyone has some right to use public property, but nobody has the right to responsibly manage it like an owner, who can perform economic calculation to determine the most productive ways of securing the property, and who has the sovereign right to punish people who abuse the property or its residents.[208]

Government markets itself as a provider of defense, but in reality, it is aggression. Government aggresses against its citizens in order to finance its operation. It does not offer its "customers" the choice of not using its goods. It is aggression masquerading as protection. Government defending against aggression is a contradiction in terms. There is a reason, for example, that the U.S. Department of Defense was previously known until 1947 as the Department of War.

So, how can we have law and order in the absence of government? If you understand government as coercion, that question practically answers itself. Law is not a creation of the state any more than money or the market economy were created by the state. Natural law has been understood across civilizations, and states gain their legitimacy only by appealing to it. A society would have more law and order if it did not grant its government the legitimacy to violate natural law by initiating aggression. Crime and violence will likely always exist, and finding solutions for them is increasingly and overwhelmingly a market good. Civilized society constantly seeks technological and institutional solutions for the problem of individual aggression, which everyone understands to be illegitimate. And given civilization's ability to continuously calculate and innovate, it is likely to continue to become more effective at protecting civilized people from private and governmental predation. As Rothbard puts it:

> And, indeed, what is the State anyway but organized banditry? What is taxation but theft on a gigantic, unchecked, scale? What is war but mass

208 Barnett, Randy. "Pursuing Justice in a Free Society: Crime Prevention and the Legal Order." *Anarchy and the Law: The Political Economy of Choice*. Edited by Edward Stringham, Transaction Publishers, 2007, pp. 75-106.

> murder on a scale impossible by private police forces? What is conscription but mass enslavement? Can anyone envision a private police force getting away with a tiny fraction of what states get away with, and do habitually, year after year, century after century?[209]

A Free Market in Defense

As discussed in previous sections of this chapter, the market for defense, security, law, and arbitration already exists, and this market arguably is responsible for providing the people of the world far more defense, security, law, and order than governments at a much lower cost. Yet, the market is also heavily distorted, disfigured, and compromised by the extreme levels of government intervention and government monopoly in its provision, which likely exceed every other industry, with the possible exception of money and banking. One cannot help but wonder how a truly free market would handle security and defense in the absence of statist control, in a world where citizens understand defense and security as a private market good, and in which providers of these goods have no recourse to coercively acquire tax money, no special legal status, and no ability to operate above the law.

In examining the current state of the U.S. economy, we find that productive citizens are forced to pay large sums of money through taxes and inflation to finance a monopoly police force and a monopoly military that commits aggression both at home and abroad. Meanwhile, American cities are notoriously unsafe, particularly large ones. Four American cities are among the 50 most dangerous cities in the world, and large American cities are notorious worldwide for having extremely dangerous neighborhoods.[210] It is puzzling how few Americans, particularly economists, arrive at the very obvious conclusion: Monopoly government provision of defense is extremely expensive and highly ineffective.

---

209 Rothbard, Murray. *For a New Liberty*. Macmillan, 1973, pp. 293-4.

210 "Most Violent Cities in the World 2023." *World Population Review*.

Imagine if American citizens were saved from all the tax and inflation expenses they (and the rest of the world, thanks to the dollar) spend on U.S. police and military and foreign policy and were instead allowed to spend their money as they see fit to keep themselves safe. Imagine if the people of Chicago had all their wealth that goes to the police and army available to them to spend on security services that were responsible to them, had no monopoly, no special legal protections under the law, no right to initiate aggression, and no ability to extract tax. Imagine how superior the protection they get would be to what they have today.

A free market in defense would contain no monopolies for any defense-related goods and would not tolerate the initiation of aggression by any entity. It is difficult for most people to imagine that such a system could offer deterrence for crime. But deterrence is not only possible in such a world; it is arguably far more effectively and efficiently provided. There are 4 broad ways in which a free market would encourage peaceful, civilized conduct and discourage violence.

First, self-defense would be viewed as entirely acceptable in this context. An anarchist free market in defense is not a pacifist Garden of Eden. It is rather a place where property owners' violent retaliation against aggression is perfectly valid, socially acceptable, and even encouraged. With property owners' hands freed from the control of the state, thieves, and murderers would be reluctant to initiate aggression. The right of self-defense extends beyond just the right of property owners to enforce their rules and exact punishment. Self-defense includes the rights of any hired agents, which frees the hands of private security providers to deliver punishment on behalf of the owner.

Second, in a free market for defense, people have the freedom to choose to only engage with others under mutually agreed-upon contracts and legal frameworks, deferring to the judgment of specific authorities and courts, which would entail clear consequences for potential misconduct, contract breach, or violent aggression. You will only hire people who agree to sign the employment contract from the reputable employment court, which clearly stipulates consequences for absenteeism, theft, or sabotage on the employee's part, or non-payment on the part of the employer. You will only eat at restaurants whose owners agree to abide by specific court rulings in the case of poisoning or conflict with customers. You will only engage in business contracts with firms that agree to abide by the corporate law of reputable courts. There need be no coercive monopoly to force you to deal with any specific court; you will want to deal with the courts because they have built a reliable track record of helping people engage in mutually beneficial transactions. People will accept to enter into these arrangements that place punishment against them precisely because it will help them deal with others. With efficient private sector provision of enforcement and voluntary acceptance of the conditions, people are far more likely to behave.

Third, a free society would still be able to use reputation, ostracism, shaming, shunning, and boycotts to deter people from behaving badly. This is particularly powerful in commercial dealings, where reputations of free-market participants are enormously important to the continued success of businesses. Without government monopoly licensing boards, free associations of merchants and professionals can impose very harsh sanctions against transgressors and would have a very strong incentive to stamp out illegitimate commercial behavior. Credit ratings, expert reviews, and customer reviews are all good examples of how reputation is valuable as an economic good today. The rise of the internet has made businesses highly conscious of their performance to appease reviewers and develop a good reputation. But the role of reputation is not confined to commercial dealings; it can also apply to petty and serious crimes. If members of a community agree to shun someone and refuse to deal with him for committing a crime, this could serve as a literal death sentence, even if delivered nonviolently. If civilized people agree that the fruits of the division of labor are only available to those who respect the sanctity of others' ownership of their body and property, then aggression would leave its initiators unable to benefit from the extended division of labor and even in danger of starving to death trying to survive on the fruits of their own labor. While it is common for state-funded economists to construct arcane and unrealistic theoretical models where markets are derailed through information asymmetry, in reality, market information is itself a market good, and a free marketplace in information, reputation, and track records produces valuable information for participants. It is also a very effective deterrent against deceptive and abusive practices.

Fourth, the insurance industry would likely take on a proactive role in providing security and ensuring the survival and well-being of its clients. Humans value their time, and they will pay to give someone the incentive to prolong their time on Earth and keep them safe and healthy. With an open market in security provision, and a vested financial interest in the survival of its clients, insurance companies in a free society could take on many of the functions of the security monopolies of the state while also introducing market calculation and discipline to them. It is not difficult to see the synergies involved in the vertical integration of the services of security, justice, and property administration. Property owners would have a strong interest to engage protection agencies, which take a fee to produce a security and agree to make insurance payouts when their clients are aggrieved.

It is difficult to predict what a free market in security would look like. Imagine, for instance, trying twenty years ago to predict the structure of the computer or internet industries today. The shape of this industry is not designed by any one particular entity; it evolves over decades of entrepreneurial offerings and consumer selection, in what Vernon Smith terms "ecological rationality," as opposed to constructive rationality (discussed in the previous chapter). Something similar would take place in the market for security were the statist monopoly to be liberalized. Should a society reject the legitimacy of initiating aggression and the legitimacy of a monopoly on aggression, that would be the basic abstract rule for organizing defense and protection, which would lead to the emergence of complex emergent orders of organization.

Similarly, it is not easy to predict what laws and rules a free society would adopt. This is an extremely complex evolutionary process, which will emerge out of the actions of humans rather than their designs. Countless protection agencies will implement different forms of protection rules, and individuals will get to see the consequences of each set of rules. Individuals would be able to see the implications of having a very lenient policing approach versus a very harsh one. For instance, does lenient policing offer similar results while costing less money? Or does it result in more crime and cost more money? People can similarly freely opt in to, or out of, protection arrangements with different levels of tolerance for consumption of intoxicants. A fully liberal approach would make substance consumption completely outside the purview of the protection agency, saving protection clients from incurring the high costs of attempting to enforce their morality on other drug users. This might be the winning formula for protection agencies, but you can also see why it might not be. Users of mind-altering drugs might be more likely to commit crimes and get involved in accidents, which would be dangerous for the population and significantly raise costs for the associated protection agency and insurance company. The more secure and economical option might be to have protection agencies mandate abstention from particular drugs on their members. To ensure compliance, the agencies might perform periodic and random drug tests on users, with clear criteria for fines and punishments in case of noncompliance. Drug users would still be free to opt out of these arrangements and find protection agencies that tolerate their drugs. But these might end up costing a lot more, or they might not even exist. At this point, the drug addict is faced with the choice of continuing to use the drug, being practically excommunicated from society, as nobody would want to deal with them, or relocating. The world will likely naturally fragment geographically into areas where people have different values for what they like to consume. Perhaps a place like Las Vegas, given its multigenerational reputation for hedonism, will continue to act as a magnet for people with a liberal approach to drugs, alcohol, gambling, and prostitution. Highly conservative places like Saudi Arabia, on the other hand, might continue to be populated by conservative people who do not want to live with people who partake in these vices, and so security institutions will make it very difficult to live there and engage in these activities.

This previous example deliberately offers no concrete predictions. It serves to simply illustrate the enormous range of possibilities available for peacefully establishing defense and protection over human interactions to the satisfaction of all involved. Anything that you want your government to do for you can be provided through property rights and specialized division of labor—even the desire to live away from people who consume certain substances.

Acceptance of property rights in self and material goods are the only possible framework for establishing the extended market order described in the chapters of this book. It is the only way in which human civilization can develop peacefully and productivity. An understanding of Austrian economics, as studied in this book, would naturally incline someone toward a more libertarian outlook. To the extent that a person has any concern for the long-term sustainability and productivity of the market order on which he relies, they must favor living in a world whereas many people as possible exercise full property rights in their time and property, able to cooperate at their desired terms.

There is a naive conception of libertarianism (among critics and some adherents) as an ideology of desire indulgence and consequence denial. For this author, and I believe for the majority of economists in the Austrian tradition, libertarianism is the rejection of the initiation of violence, which does not entail any responsibility for anyone in society to accept your behavior or liberate you from its undesirable consequences. In fact, the freedom of libertarians is precisely the freedom to reap what your actions sow, whether sweet or bitter. A private law society would not seek to protect people from suffering bad consequences; it would deliver these consequences to them with a speed and efficiency that government monopolies cannot match. The thief, rapist, and murderer will be punished by his victim more effectively than under government monopoly, in the same way, the entrepreneur in the free market is rewarded more effectively when he produces goods others desire. A libertarian rejects the legitimacy of a government initiating aggression against a peaceful drug consumer, but would not reject the right of individuals to refuse to live next to, work with, or be part of the same security agency as a drug consumer.

Does it follow from this analysis that a truly free society must be stateless? It is, after all, difficult to predict how these institutions can evolve. We may well continue to have an entity similar in functions to the modern state, even in an increasingly free society. It might be that people will willingly choose to enter into associations that perform the functions of today's government, and these organizations may have exclusive right to aggress against members who agree to these terms. The extent to which the state is compatible with a free society is the extent to which it respects the right of secession, as discussed by Mises above.

In *The State in the Third Millennium*, HSH Prince Hans-Adam of Liechtenstein offers an alternative vision for the role of a state in a free society, primarily based on the respect of self-determination and secession.[211] Rather than do away entirely with the state as an organizing institution, Prince Hans-Adam argues for the right of communities, right down to the local village level, to decide to join whichever political entity they want to join or to secede and form their own. The state in this model can provide defense and law, among other services, but the beneficiaries will always reserve the right to leave their state if they do not like it, without having to move and uproot themselves and their communities. This model brings back consumer choice and sovereignty to the tasks of the government, because individual communities can opt out of any arrangements they do not like. But it also allows for the functions of defense and law to be provided by entities that have provided them for centuries and allows them the freedom to determine the way they operate. This vision of democracy focuses on giving people the right to choose their government, as opposed to the right to micromanage the decisions of a monopoly government they cannot escape.

The model is similar to the way market institutions operate and successfully serve their consumers. Consumers do not get to vote on company decisions or appoint leaders; they simply get to choose whether to buy the finished product or not. This is how all the wonders of the market economy have been delivered. The automobile, airplane, personal computer, and smartphone were not invented through a democratic voting process for every engineering decision along the way. Entrepreneurs built these products and presented them to consumers, whose ultimate choice to adopt or reject these inventions made them succeed or fail. In a world where the market economy continues to increase peaceful cooperation and living standards, this might be a reasonable way of organizing defense and law among increasingly civilized peoples. As economic activity becomes increasingly digitized, and workers become mobile, this form of competition between jurisdictions is already becoming more commonplace. An increasingly high number of people currently move to live in monarchies

211 Hans-Adam. *The State in the Third Millennium*. 1st ed., Van Eck, 2009.

like Qatar and the United Arab Emirates, offering very few political rights, along with very low taxation.

HSH Prince Hans Adam's vision of the state in the third millennium may well be compelling to a growing number of people, particularly when examining the favorable track record of the world's most successful royal ruling families. The Japanese royal family has been in power for 2,600 years and has been instrumental in the development of Japanese civilization. European, Islamic, Chinese, and countless other civilizations thrived and emerged under monarchic rule, as well. Perhaps the institution of monarchy is one of these spontaneously emergent phenomena the modern mind thinks it can easily replace with something top-down, as we saw occur with the largely tragic and bloody experiment of democratization in the twentieth century. It might be the case that the royal family, invested in its survival for the long term, is the most successful market institution for the long-term provision of defense and law.

Perhaps monarchies will be the naturally emergent outcome of this selection process if they are understood as family businesses that have provided law and order for their societies over the long term. As multigenerational businesses, monarchies can have a lower time preference than private corporations, whose ownership is likely more focused on short-term profitability. The monarch wants his descendants to rule a prosperous and rich land in the future, so he will govern with an eye for long-term outcomes. The interests of citizens as consumers are more likely to align with a multigenerational family business in charge of government than a democracy whose leaders face high levels of uncertainty. Ultimately, these leaders are exchanged every few years, incentivizing them to maximize their ability to extract wealth in the short term at the expense of the long term.[212]

---

212 Hoppe, Hans-Hermann. *Democracy: The God That Failed.* Transaction Publishers, 2001, pp. 1-43.

Chapter 18

Civilization

> The fundamental facts that brought about cooperation, society, and civilization and transformed the animal man into a human being are the facts that work performed under the division of labor is more productive than isolated work and that man's reason is capable of recognizing this truth. But for these facts men would have forever remained deadly foes of one another, irreconcilable rivals in their endeavors to secure a portion of the scarce supply of means of sustenance provided by nature. Each man would have been forced to view all other men as his enemies; his craving for the satisfaction of his own appetites would have brought him into an implacable conflict with all his neighbors. No sympathy could possibly develop under such a state of affairs.[213]
>
> —Ludwig von Mises

In this book, I have attempted to offer an overview of economics through the lens of human action, in particular, how humans act to meet their economic needs, which revolve around increasing the quantity and subjective quality of their time on Earth. Reason allows humans to recognize and appraise the benefits that can accrue to them from actions. Reason lets them orient their lives toward those actions that help them achieve their subjective ends, and away from those that do not. Actions, traits, and patterns of

---

213 Mises, Ludwig von. *Human Action: The Scholar's Edition*. Ludwig von Mises Institute, 1998, p. 144.

behavior conducive to economic progress will proliferate over time, as they confer an advantage on those who adopt them. Social systems of organization that allow strangers to interact peacefully, productively, and voluntarily will allow their members to increase their well-being significantly by engaging in larger and more sophisticated division of labor. Civilization can be understood as the extended social order that emerges from human utilization of reason, lowering time preference, and cooperating in the pursuit of improving life over time.

Civilization has many definitions.[214] They will differ between one civilization and the other, and from one period of time to another, yet the essential underlying reality to all conceptions of civilization is an improvement of material conditions. The improvement in material conditions itself may not be the most significant part of civilization to participants of civilization, but it is what makes all other parts possible by providing human society with high productivity and high life expectancy. Material conditions may not be the end of civilization, but they are the inescapable means to it. More than just material profit, civilization offers us an unparalleled method for improving our chances of survival and our quality of life. The move from barbarism to civilized society was not some accident or coincidence—there were very compelling economic reasons behind it. By settling down into a relatively more peaceful social order, humans are able to protect themselves better from nature and predators. From the first human societies, all the way to the modern, highly specialized, and technologically advanced global economy, there is a long, winding road, whose every step was taken because of its economic expediency.

Human civilization is inescapably linked to the economizing methods we have found to increase the value and quality of our time on Earth. Both require lowering time preference, capital accumulation, and the division of labor, which in turn require peaceful social cooperation and human ingenuity, which applies human reason to whatever problems it confronts and attempts to achieve the best outcomes possible. These are the three processes that elevate

---

214 Howden, David, and Joakim Kämpe. "Time Preference and the Process of Civilization." *International Journal of Social Economics*, vol. 43, no. 4, 2016, pp. 382-99.

human labor above the labor of animals, allowing us to build civilization and increasingly master our environment and surroundings.

The essential starting point of human civilization is the lowering of time preference. This shift in human thought and behavior allows us to ascend from being governed by the base instincts that govern all other animals, and instead defer to reason. Lowering time preference, and developing the capacity for delaying gratification, is the starting point for all savings, which allows for capital accumulation and an increase in productivity and living standards. Beyond just saving, lowered time preference makes people more likely to be civilized in their behavior. They become more likely to think of the consequences of their actions, and thus more conscious of the patterns of behavior that are conducive to growing the division of labor, which is another enormously powerful way of increasing human well-being. Without the division of labor, man is left alone, at the mercy of nature. With the division of labor, his productivity increases, and he can partake in societal civilization. But to do so, he first needs to be able to engage in the division of labor, the economic phenomenon that binds people together in civilization, making them interdependent and reliant upon one another. As the number of people with whom a person interacts in the division of labor grows, it becomes more imperative to develop social institutions and norms for clear and reliable ways for strangers to deal with each other: These are the civilized manners and mores. Human institutions, culture, customs, and traditions revolve around making human behavior conducive to an extended social order. The most important tenet on which social cooperation rests is the respect for property. Much of social order stems from the need to inculcate into humans the ideal that civilized society is only possible through respect for property and the adoption of civilized manners.

Society is defined by the phenomena that lead to lowering of time preference, as these are what allow society to grow, in terms of both capital accumulation and peaceful cooperation. Civilized society exists to the extent that people lower their time preference, save, engage in the division of labor peacefully, and use their reason. The more the division of labor grows, the more civilized we need to become as we deal with more people. Civilization emerges as the manifestation of lowered time preference. The lower the time preference, the more civilized we become.

To the extent that a social institution survives and thrives, it can only do so if it is conducive to human civilization. Social institutions do this by offering members civilizational benefits, meaning lower time preference, better ability to engage in the division of labor, and higher productivity. Family is an essential institution for societal development. Family allows us to discount less heavily what comes after our own life. We become concerned about a part of us that will survive us, what will happen to our children when we die lowering our time preference. By developing a concern for and strong identification with descendants, humans lengthen the period of time for which the consequences of their actions matter. Without many generations' sacrifice of present enjoyment for the sake of future generations, the world today would have a lot less capital accumulated, and we would be far more primitive. Concern for future generations is essential to maintaining civilized society, and having children is a very powerful way to lower time preference.

Humans' desire to give their children a better life might be the key motivation for engaging in human society and civilization. Without concern for children and the world after us, there is a reduced incentive for our actions to account for the consequences that come after our death. Among animals, only human reason can develop such a strong bond with its progeny. By being productive, engaging in the division of labor, accumulating capital, and lowering our discounting of the future, humans can have a good chance of providing their children with a better life. Much of what has made us human, and much of our human experience from as far back as records exist, revolves around providing our offspring with a better life. This is a powerful driving force of civilization, and a good tool for individual life, as it orients humans toward low-time-preference cooperative and reasonable behavior, which, when practiced over generations, accumulates into a priceless inheritance to which all humans are born: human civilization. The world's languages, religions, traditions, technologies, ideas, physical infrastructure, and magnificent buildings—these are the legacy of ancestors who lowered their time preference, divided their labor, and cooperated to build civilization. More than just human intelligence, it is our ability to collaborate, build civilization, and accumulate capital, physical and in the form of ideas, that allows us to conquer nature, live safely, and subdue violent animals, human or otherwise.

Civilization can be understood as the most effective way to sustainably extend and improve the value of our life on Earth. It is practiced intergenerationally. It is a long-term process—as long as humanity itself—of trying to accumulate knowledge and capital and improve the quality of life. Every civilized human spends his or her life toiling in hopes of improving their life, and if they start a family, hoping to give their child a better life. Civilizational advance can be understood as equivalent to long-term sustainable economic development—not just because it results in higher living standards, but also because it can only be attained through increased peaceful interaction among a growing number of people, lower time preference, and innovation. Civilization as a process is what happens when successive generations live better lives than their predecessors. Decivilization is what happens when successive generations have worse lives than their ancestors.

The Cost of Civilization

The fruits of civilization are enticing, and virtually all who have tasted them have become lifelong addicts. Very few people have left human civilization to live alone in nature, and for those who do, the experience is usually neither long nor pleasant. But the fruits of civilization cannot be conjured at will and out of thin air. They require significant sacrifice in terms of delayed gratification and, more generally, the curbing of human instincts and bringing them under the reign of reason. With reason, man can calculate the expected payoffs of different courses of action. And he can take the most beneficial to him, even if it may involve a negative early cost. As Mises puts it:

> Rational conduct means that man, in face of the fact that he cannot satisfy all his impulses, desires, and appetites, foregoes the satisfaction of those which he considers less urgent. In order not to endanger the working of social cooperation man is forced to abstain from satisfying those desires

> whose satisfaction would hinder the establishment of societal institutions. There is no doubt that such a renunciation is painful. However, man has made his choice. He has renounced the satisfaction of some desires incompatible with social life and has given priority to the satisfaction of those desires which can be realized only or in a more plentiful way under a system of the division of labor. He has entered upon the way toward civilization, social cooperation, and wealth.[215]

This magnificent edifice of economic cooperation spans thousands of years and incorporates the labor of tens of billions of people, and it rests on one foundation: self-ownership. If you accept the idea of self-ownership, you may interact peacefully with others in a mutually beneficial way, and you can gain from this interaction goods you could never obtain if you were to attack them instead. The incredible achievements of modern civilization were only possible because of productive free people worldwide coordinating their work through free exchange. No violent ruler could ever muster what free-market capitalism built in the modern era. No slave owner could ever get slaves to produce the marvels produced by free people who willingly choose to work. Even after decades in which millions were murdered to secure obedience, Soviet industry produced little more than painted rust, and was reliant on trading with the capitalist world to survive for as long as it did. The problem, as discussed in Chapter 12, is not the lack of incentive or any one particular mistake; the problem is the absence of a market in the means of production. Without widespread ownership of the means of production and the development of a market in capital goods, there is no rational way of allocating capital most productively. The output of a modern society is not something that can be produced by one controlling mind—it requires billions of people worldwide to *voluntarily* work in a free market, using prices to calculate the costs and benefits of alternative options to decide which is the most productive and profitable. No coercive authority could replicate this. Individuals must be free to own the fruits of their labor and suffer the consequences of their mistakes.

---

215 Ibid. 171-2.

Only then can they obtain the productivity and living standards to live in a civilized society. Without the acceptance of the concept of self-ownership, every society would devolve into violent internecine conflict, destroying productivity and life. Violence destroys, and its fruits cannot compare to the fruits of productive cooperation under the division of labor.

To partake in civilization, humans must abstain from many courses of action that are instinctively desired. The most fundamental requirement for civilization is respect for property rights. For people to willingly cooperate in an extended social order, they need to accept that other people have ownership over their own body and property. Without a widespread acceptance of the illegitimacy of initiating aggression against strangers, there is little point in partaking in civilized society. There is no use planting the tree of civilized behavior if its fruits are constantly up for grabs. The prohibition of murder, assault, and theft forms the basis of all human societies and is a main tenet of religious and political institutions.

More broadly, the customs, traditions, and moral norms that permeate civilized society can best be understood as the patterns of behavior contributing to enjoying the advantages of economic trade and civilized living in population centers. Honesty, conscientiousness, and trustworthiness make it more likely for strangers to engage in business with one another to the benefit of all involved. Sexual restraint allows for the formation of families and for their sustainability, leading to a decline in time preference and the development of civilization.[216] Immorality, on the other hand, expressed through disregard for the future, violations of the property and body of others, deceptiveness, untrustworthiness, a lack of conscientiousness, and lack of sexual restraint, makes conflict more likely, and stable long-term civilized institutions like marriages, cities, and companies more difficult.

Civilized behavior revolves around long-term satisfaction and forsaking the immediate satisfaction we would get from following our instincts. Acting impulsively on animalistic instincts compromises our long-term goals, while reasonably delaying gratification helps us achieve them. The uncivilized

216 See Unwin, Joseph Daniel. *Sex and Culture*. Oxford University Press, 1934.

barbarian, the undisciplined child inside each man, would like to immediately, violently assault anyone who bothers him, to take whatever he fancies regardless of who owns it, to lie to get his way, to force sexual intimacy on anyone he fancies. And many uncivilized and undisciplined people do indeed engage in this behavior. It takes years of education, rearing, and refinement for humans to learn to subdue these base instincts and instead defer to reason in anticipation of future gain. This is not easy, but civilization can only exist if human reason leads us to subdue our instincts and cooperate.

The Case for Civilization

Should humans bother to engage in civilization? Why, after all, would humans sacrifice their innate instinctive nature to fight strangers and acquire their property? Are the material comforts of economic growth worth giving up on living our humanity to its fullest, with its ups and downs? Mises offers a first answer:

> Biology does not provide any standard for the appraisal of changes occurring within living beings other than whether or not these changes succeeded in adjusting the individuals to the conditions of their environment and thereby in improving their chances in the struggle for survival. It is a fact that civilization, when judged from this point of view, is to be considered a benefit and not an evil. It has enabled man to hold his own in the struggle against all other living beings, both the big beasts of prey and the even more pernicious microbes; it has multiplied man's means of sustenance; it has made the average man taller, more agile, and more versatile and it has stretched his average length of life; it has given man the uncontested mastery of the earth; it has multiplied population figures and raised the standard of living to a level never dreamed of by the crude cave dwellers of prehistoric ages.[217]

---

217 Mises, Ludwig von. *Human Action: The Scholar's Edition*. Ludwig von Mises Institute, 1998, p. 170.

This is the utilitarian and consequentialist argument for civilization summarized. Civilization gives us more material comforts and allows us to live longer. That might seem like a compelling enough case for most, but it is not necessarily a definitive answer. It could be argued that a shorter and more brutal life, allowing us to express our animalistic instincts to the full, is preferable to the instinctive prison of civilized behavior. The fact that the civilized life is likely to be longer and easier does not necessarily mean it is better than the uncivilized life. Ultimately, value is subjective, and there is no objective mathematical basis for asserting that all humans will necessarily value civilization more than savagery.

Another argument for civilization comes from the concept of natural rights. Humans are born with inalienable rights and with no right to aggress on the rights of others. Civilization is simply the order that emerges from a society in which humans use their reason to discern these natural rights and then agree to respect each other's natural rights. This is an argument that is compelling to people who are already subscribed to civilizational institutions—in particular, religions—which inculcate in them a positive valuation of civilization. But this argument is not compelling to all, and most people, even those who are religious, are unable to consistently respect the natural rights of others, finding many justifications for initiating aggression when it suits them.

But rather than invoking utility math or religion, a case for civilization can be constructed from the methodology of economics and this book: Examining human action and deriving its implications and what that tells us about humans. The intellectual brain formulates sophisticated arguments and is mostly used for entertainment and rationalization purposes. Human reason is, to a point, governed and regulated by real-world consequences.

The vast majority of humans choose to live in civilization, even though the majority of Earth's surface is uncivilized wilderness. Very few people decide to truly leave civilization and forsake the products of the division of labor. Retiring to a farm does not count as forsaking civilization, as long as the equipment for the farm is the product of capital accumulation. Very few populations on Earth remain uncontacted and unwilling to establish contact with outsiders, and even these few tribes will have their own isolated civilization, capital accumulation, no matter how primitive, in the form of spears and houses, and a division of labor, no matter how embryonic.[218]

Christopher Knight, the so-called Hermit of North Pond, was one of those who abandoned society. He dropped out of his life and lived alone in the woods of Maine for more than 25 years. But even he was still dependent on civilization, as he regularly stole what he needed to survive. He did not abandon civilization, as he still needed to steal its products; he simply abandoned contributing to civilization, making him a criminal.

A majority of people likely have little understanding of the concepts of capitalism and self-ownership, and in the right context, some will find it acceptable to initiate aggression against others and violate their right to property and self-ownership. And yet capitalism and human civilization continue to survive. Their survival is not down to the intellectual understanding of the average person, but rather their self-interested reason. Beneficiaries of civilization may pay lip service to not needing others or to being fine with the initiation of aggression, but they still transact with others consensually for the vast majority of their lives. They still rely on modern technological devices only possible through a sophisticated division of labor. Even criminals and supporters of governments who claim their aggression is justified still rely for their survival on the products of the division of labor, peaceful exchange, and global capitalism. The world's weapons are not produced by the most belligerent and least peaceful people; they are produced by low-time-preference capitalists who invest their wealth for decades in extensive capital infrastructure, innovative engineers motivated by capitalists' salaries, and supply chains that incorporate the labor of millions worldwide. Relieved of the hypocrisy of using the fruits of civilization to fight civilization, the strongest and most belligerent uncivilized human, like the strongest most belligerent animal, stands no chance against any adult or child capable of pulling the trigger of a gun produced by capitalist civilization.

While modern intellectuals and authors may write elaborate treatises on the problems of civilization and human society, they nonetheless continue

218 Worrall, Simon. "Why the North Pond Hermit Hid From People For 27 Years." *National Geographic*, 9 Apr 2017.

to offer their thoughts from the confines of civilized offices and classrooms in civilized societies, through books printed by a global division of labor and transmitted globally to readers through the cooperation of countless businesses and workers. Nobody is ever forced to stay in civilization; and yet, all the people who complain about it are unable to separate from it.

But perhaps the most decisive argument for civilization and property rights is also derived from analyzing human action—specifically, the act of arguing itself.[219] The person looking for an argument for civilization is an acting human, looking to reason with another human. The mere fact of engaging in argument and seeking another opinion is a recognition of the other person's sovereign right to their body and property. If you, dear reader, have made it to a point in your life where you have managed to pick up this book—a book written, produced, printed, and distributed by countless people worldwide in a sophisticated division of labor, using highly advanced capital goods—you are taking part in a capitalist economic order, to which you contribute and from which you benefit. The mere fact that you can indulge in the act of arguing about such topics is itself a rejection of the barbarian savagery of yielding to all our base instincts and a manifestation of rational behavior. Rather than merely acting from a basic animalistic urge to attack enemies and take what is theirs, you are looking for a rational basis for supporting civilization. You have a conception of right and wrong, and so you accept that you cannot simply impose your will on the world. You acknowledge that other people have a right to their mind and thoughts, and you are seeking arguments to discuss with them to inform how you act with them.

> For one thing, no one could possibly propose anything, and no one could become convinced of any proposition by argumentative means, if a person's right to make exclusive use of his physical body were not already presupposed. It is this recognition of each other's mutually exclusive control over one's own body which explains the distinctive character of propositional

219 Hoppe, Hans-Hermann. *The Economics and Ethics of Private Property: Studies in Political Economy and Philosophy*. Kluwer Academic 1993, p. 339-45.

> exchanges that, while one may disagree about what has been said, it is still possible to agree at least on the fact that there is disagreement. It is also obvious that such a property right to one's own body must be said to be justified a priori, for anyone who tried to justify any norm whatsoever would already have to presuppose the exclusive right of control over his body as a valid norm simply in order to say, "I propose such and such." Anyone disputing such a right would become caught up in a practical contradiction since arguing so would already imply acceptance of the very norm which he was disputing.[220]

Indeed, when writing this book, it was very difficult to separate value-free economic analysis from making the case for free markets and individual sovereignty and non-aggression as the basis for civilized life. The economic arguments for individual freedom are practically inseparable from the case for civilization. The mere fact of engaging in writing a book already implies an acceptance of the right of others to determine their own thoughts.

A corollary to Hoppe's argumentation ethics is that any objection to property rights and the division of labor can only be considered if expressed without resorting to any of the fruits of the division of labor and property rights. Any argument against property rights written in a book, or spoken on TV or the internet, must rely on a very elaborate civilizational structure only possible through property rights and the division of labor. Therefore, it is fair to say that all arguments against property rights and civilization are invalid if communicated in any way other than violent grunting. The violent grunting "argument" is nothing new to civilized people. Violent grunting animals have been a permanent feature of nature, pestering human civilization since its inception, but also forcing it to adapt and evolve. These savages may inflict damage and material and human losses, but they are no match for the intelligent humans armed by self-restraint and collaboration under the civilized division of labor. Violent animals, both human and nonhuman, will likely continue to initiate aggression against civilized humans—but civilization will

220 Ibid. 342.

continue to rout them. Violent animals cannot overpower the weapons available to a member of civilization, which are produced through the cooperation of extremely large networks of highly productive workers and accumulated capital.

Finding fault with the concept of self-ownership and capitalist division of labor and civilization is not an argument. It is a glorified return to monkeys flinging their own feces at each other—merely a reversion to nonhuman animal life. The problem with being an opponent of capitalism is that you cannot do anything against capitalism that is any more complex than slinging your feces without becoming a capitalist. Any weapon more complex than your own feces requires delayed gratification and capital accumulation. Any weapon beyond what you can make with your bare hands requires participation in the global division of labor. The opponents of capitalism destroy their own ability to produce, specialize, and innovate, making themselves weaker and less impactful. Capitalist civilization continues to win because its opponents either fling their feces powerlessly at it, or engage in it to try to fight it, effectively supporting it and pushing it forward.

The Fiat Slavery Alternative to Civilization

Recorded human history contains many periods of civilizational rise and fall, but it is fair to argue that the overall trend has been the advancement of civilization. This is seen in the increase in worker productivity over time, the increase in energy consumption over the centuries, and the declining cost of energy. It is also seen in the technological advancement of the capital goods humans enjoy. And it is seen in the long-term trend of declining interest rates. Time preference is the determinant of interest rates, and as interest rates decline in the long term, as was discussed in Chapter 13, a decline in time preference has driven this process. But this civilizational process has not been a plain-sailing, linear improvement. Natural disasters, wars, and societal collapse have caused living standards to decline for long periods of time. The global market order of the Roman Empire allowed a high degree of specialization and higher productivity, but the Empire's collapse reversed this, and the ancient world's population splintered into smaller markets and experienced lower productivity for centuries. More recently, it can be argued that the last century has witnessed a reversal in the process of civilization and a rise in global time preference. Hoppe explains:

> In fact, a tendency toward falling interest rates characterizes mankind's suprasecular trend of development. Minimum interest rates on 'normal safe loans' were around 16 percent at the beginning of Greek financial history in the sixth century B.C., and fell to 6 percent during the Hellenistic period. In Rome, minimum interest rates fell from more than 8 percent during the earliest period of the Republic to 4 percent during the first century of the Empire. In thirteenth-century Europe, the lowest interest rates on "safe" loans were 8 percent. In the fourteenth century they came down to about 5 percent. In the fifteenth century they fell to 4 percent. In the seventeenth century they went down to 3 percent. And at the end of the nineteenth century minimum interest rates had further declined to less than 2.5 percent.[221]
>
> From 1815 onward, throughout Europe and the Western World minimum interest rates steadily declined to a historic low of well below 3 percent on the average at the turn of the century. With the onset of the democratic-republican age, this earlier tendency came to a halt and seems to have changed direction, revealing twentieth-century Europe and the U.S. as declining civilizations. An inspection of the lowest decennial average interest rates for Britain, France, the Netherlands, Belgium, Germany, Sweden, Switzerland, and the U.S., for instance, shows that during the entire post-World War I era interest rates in Europe were never as low as or lower than they had been during the second half of the nineteenth century. Only in the U.S., in the 1950s, did interest rates ever fall below late nineteenth-century rates. Yet this was only a short-lived phenomenon, and even then

221 Hoppe, Hans-Hermann. *Democracy: The God That Failed.* Transaction Publishers, 2001, p. 63.

> U.S. interest rates were not lower than they had been in Britain during the second half of the nineteenth century. Instead, twentieth-century rates were significantly higher than nineteenth century rates universally, and if anything they have exhibited a rising tendency.[222]

The First World War was a pivotal moment for humanity, as it can be viewed as the moment human civilizational progress began to stall and reverse. The mass death and destruction of the twentieth century were unprecedented on a historical scale, and it was arguably facilitated by the destruction of free-market money that was replaced with government debt—essentially a loyalty reward scheme for entities whose raison d'etre is the initiation of violence.[223] Beyond just leading to an increase in violence, the destruction of money has been slowly rotting the global monetary market order and human civilization itself, compromising every method of economizing humans employ, as discussed in detail in the chapters of this book. The rest of this section applies the analysis of my second book, *The Fiat Standard*, to the economizing actions and extended market order discussed in this book.

By destroying the ability of individuals to save for the future, fiat money takes away the incentive to delay gratification, reduces the creation of capital, and undermines the basic starting point of economic development and civilization. Rather than have the security of money to brace for future uncertainty, fiat makes humans become debt slaves of their government's banking cartels. As discussed in *The Fiat Standard*:

> Holders of present fiat tokens, whether in cash or bank accounts, are constantly subject to having the value of these tokens diluted by lenders who can create new present tokens by issuing credit based on future receipts of fiat tokens. It therefore makes the most sense for individuals, corporations, and governments not to hold positive balances, as they will be devalued through inflation, but to borrow. Users with negative balances, i.e., those in

222 Ibid. 64.

223 See Ammous, Saifedean. *The Bitcoin Standard*. John Wiley & Sons, Inc., 2018, pp. 145-9.

> debt, lack security and risk catastrophic loss. Financial security, in the sense of having a stable amount of liquid wealth saved for the future, is no longer available in the current system. You will either witness the dissipation of your wealth through inflation, or you will borrow and live in the insecurity of losing your collateral if you miss a few payments. Fiat has effectively destroyed savings as a financial instrument, with enormously negative consequences.[224]

With savings compromised and with the government financially emboldened to provide for more of a person's needs, the incentive to invest in a family is compromised, and the effects on society have been disastrous. Beyond the catastrophic impact on savings, the suspension of the gold standard violates the fundamental basis of civilized society: natural law. It blatantly breaks the contract between the state and money holders to redeem for gold their paper gold receipts and bank account balances. The government protects the banks that renege on their promises and redefines the law to allow them, and itself, to continue to engage in inflation through the issuance of credit. This contract involves every single member of the capitalist economy. They all have to use money to engage in the extended order of the market. When money is debased, everything is debased. When the government—which ostensibly markets itself as the enforcer of contracts and upholder of justice—breaks such a powerful contract, citizens will inevitably follow suit, becoming less trustworthy and more dishonest, thus undermining the basis of civilized society. When the contract of money is broken, every member of the capitalist economy concludes that the rule of law does not apply to all, and society shifts from attempting to adhere to natural law to trying to exploit it for personal gain. Fiat allows the state to finance itself more and more, which results in the monopolization of the defense and law industries, and their corruption away from meeting society's needs toward protecting an unproductive, parasitic ruling regime from the people they claim to serve.

---

224 Ammous, Saifedean. *The Fiat Standard: The Debt Slavery Alternative to Human Civilization*. Saif House, 2021, p. 69.

By allowing for loose money creation away from the free-market choice of hard money, fiat money destroys the monetary order of society, causing business cycles and destroying capital, as has been extremely common in the century of central banking. It further destroys the banking system, either through hyperinflation in extreme cases, or by turning it from an essential institution of the capitalist economy to a protected monopoly for speculative gambling. Gambling profits accrue to the government and banking cartel, and losses are borne by society at large.

Fiat money further undermines the capitalist economic system by distorting its essential driving process: economic calculation. As the value of money stops being determined on the market through supply and demand, economic calculation for entrepreneurs becomes an error-strewn process. As can be seen today, capital markets become little more than a reaction to monetary commissars' edicts. When the bureau setting U.S. interest rates decides to lower interest rates, all assets rise in value—only to fall when interest rates rise. Economic calculation of a business' profits and losses becomes entirely secondary, and capital allocation becomes an exercise in monetary policy tea leaf parsing instead. Entrepreneurship and innovation take a backseat to the fiat monetary casino's overlords' dictates.

Fiat also destroys money as a market good. We no longer have a money in the sense of a generalized medium of exchange with high salability across time and space, as was the case with gold before World War I. A hodgepodge of different assets now replaces the one monetary medium, defeating the point of money and returning the world to a system of partial barter, where different forms of money are traded for one another, and different forms of money are held for different salability considerations. The U.S. dollar is the most salable asset across space, thanks to the U.S. Federal Reserve's monopoly over the global banking system. Other national currencies are more salable within the confines of their local central banks' monetary plantations. Salability across time, and the ability to hold value over time, are much more complicated. Bonds, gold, real estate, art, stocks, and an endless kaleidoscope of assets compete for this worldwide, distorting their markets.

With economic calculation based on the ever-shifting quicksand of centrally planned national currencies optimized for government theft of the population, economic calculation of the benefits of trade becomes heavily distorted, and the uncertainty that arises discourages people from partaking in mutually beneficial exchange. International exchange rate oscillations can destroy a profitable business or undeservedly reward unprofitable businesses. The global foreign exchange market processes transactions worth many multiples of the global GDP, as people must acquire foreign currencies to buy goods from abroad. Local and international trade are also compromised by fiat money. As prices rise, people are constantly forced to substitute the goods they desire with inferior substitutes, and government uses its inflation privilege to finance pseudoscientists to manufacture propaganda science that argues that replacing meat with soy, bugs, and industrial sludge is better for human health.

In *The Fiat Standard*, I make the case for why fiat inflation is undermining technological progress and our ability to increase our consumption and utilization of energy sources to meet our needs. Inflation at once devalues the savings and earnings of citizens, taking away from them the ability to spend on modern energy sources. It also allows their government to spend limitlessly on propaganda to try to distract citizens from their declining living standards by blaming it on a slew of ridiculous bogeymen, the most recent of which is the insane notion that carbon dioxide—an atmospheric gas essential to all living things and existing in the tiny concentration of 0.042% in the atmosphere—is ruining Earth's weather and causing apocalyptic damage to society. The only way to fix this supposed apocalypse, conveniently and coincidentally enough, is for people to forsake the essential energy technologies that have made our modern life possible: hydrocarbons. The same energy sources whose prices are very sensitive to inflation because of their importance. Fiat also allows governments to spend incomprehensibly large amounts of resources on the insane quest to generate enough power from preindustrial energy sources to power modern industrialized society. Hundreds of trillions have been spent over the past decades, and the only thing the green energy mafia has to show for it is a continuous increase in the price and a decrease in the availability of reliable and essential energy sources.

Fiat money has also allowed for the corruption of scientific knowledge and educational institutions. Rather than continue to accumulate knowledge and advance technologically, universities have been transformed into inflation propaganda and elaborate apologia. *The Fiat Standard* discusses the corruption of economics, nutrition, and climate science as examples, but the rot is likely more widespread. There is perhaps nothing as symbolic of the degeneration of the modern academy, as well as the moral rot that fraudulent, coercive money imposes on society, than the fact that the most venerated and important economist of the twentieth century was a self-described "immoralist" who engaged in recreational child slave trafficking, as documented in *The Bitcoin Standard.* In Keynes' own words:

> We entirely repudiated a personal liability on us to obey general rules. We claimed the right to judge every individual case on its merits, and the wisdom to do so successfully. This was a very important part of our faith, violently and aggressively held, and for the outer world it was our most obvious and dangerous characteristic. We repudiated entirely customary morals, conventions and traditional wisdom. We were, that is to say, in the strict sense of the term, immoralists. The consequences of being found out had, of course, to be considered for what they were worth. But we recognized no moral obligation on us, no inner sanction, to conform or to obey. Before heaven we claimed to be our own judge in our own case.[225]

With morality becoming a bad word and a criminal immoralist elevated to genius scholar, the moral foundation for a civilized society is unraveling. One cannot understand the drivel that passes for the mainstream economic scholarship today, which consists of little more than transparent justifications for government violations of natural rights, without reference to the immoral character of its most important idol. Not only is the institution of property rights itself constantly transgressed by the government in the form of inflation and taxation, but humans' property in our own time is violated through the coercive banning of the prime technology for the preservation of

225 Keynes, John Maynard. *Two Memoirs: Dr. Melchior, a Defeated Enemy, and My Early Beliefs*. Rupert Hart-Davis, 1949.

the economic value produced by our time: money. We must constantly work harder, longer, and in increasing uncertainty about the future to make up for the theft of the fruits of our time's labor within the capitalist market order. The breakdown of the family, along with the increase in crime in major cities, are but symptoms of the deepening malaise of a global economy that is consuming its millennia-old capital in a process of decivilization.

Money is the lifeblood of an economic system, the *sine qua non* of economic calculation and coordination. By taking it from the realm of consensual interaction and placing it in the hands of a violent monopoly, the entire edifice of civilization is undermined and shaken. It is easy to become despondent about the fate of human civilization, but it is too soon to lose hope in the ingenuity of humans, their technologies, or a capitalist creative process that has survived millennia and defeated many enemies.

The Triumph of Reason

History suggests that a lot of people who come across civilization cannot preserve it for long.[226] Beneficiaries of capitalism are born into comparative affluence: They have extended periods of childhood and adolescence, in the sense of not needing to work to provide for themselves for extended periods of their lives. With the products of industrial capitalism at their disposal, families are able to provide for their children until adulthood and sometimes beyond. It becomes entirely feasible for members of capitalist societies to not perform any productive work before they are in their twenties and thirties. With such detachment from the realities of economic production, delusional anti-civilizational ideas and superstitions can easily take hold in the minds of citizens, eliminating the low-time-preference, cooperative, and capitalistic mentality required for the extended order of economic production. Can these ideas derail civilization?

Yet, the sustainability and continuation of civilization arise from the superior organizational efficiency of capitalist economic calculation, the enormous

226 Ibn Khaldun, Abd Alrahman. *Al-Muqaddima*. 1377. • Gibbon, Edward. *The Decline and Fall of the Roman Empire*. Alfred A. Knopf, 1994. • Glubb, John. *The Fate of Empires and Search for Survival*. Blackwood, 1978.

benefits of voluntary specialization, and the incessant creativity of humans. In physical war, as in all avenues of human action, the enemies of capitalism are always at a disadvantage because of their inability to organize the production and mobilization of resources in the same way capitalism can. The absence of prices and calculation also cripples their innovation, while the incentive for innovation is stymied by the limitations on profit. They cannot access a division of labor as large and productive as the largest market in the world, the world market.

You can think of the capitalist free-market economy as a very powerful machine because, in many ways, it is. All the privately owned machines and capital deployed in the process of production are acting together in one economic system: the extended order of the free-market economy. The ability to deploy billions of machines worldwide in production processes, all interrelated and interdependent, allows us to achieve much higher levels of productivity than any alternative. The extent to which humans rise above mere day-to-day survival and are able to engage in economic trade is determined by the extent to which they employ the machines of the capitalist market system in their lives. These machines carry an enormous advantage to anyone who engages in economic calculation. Productive humans who make these machines will find ways to get away from the fanatics, Luddites, and parasites who want to destroy them.

But the current enemy of capitalism is different from the Luddites of the early Industrial Revolution, the Soviet bogeyman of the twentieth century, and various other dysfunctional socialist totalitarian regimes. In contrast to explicit external enemies, the threat facing modern capitalism is internal, illicit, and seemingly inextricable. As the world economy has become increasingly globalized and integrated, it has become increasingly centralized around the U.S. dollar and the Federal Reserve System. Almost the entire world economy uses the U.S. dollar or currencies of central banks that hold the U.S. dollar in reserve. The vast majority of national banking systems use the U.S. dollar as well as the Federal Reserve's international clearance system. This means the vast majority of participants in the global market system witness the value of their money declining in order to finance U.S. government spending and the fiat banking cartel. But as inefficient, wasteful, and downright criminal as this system is, it manages to continue because its enemies are unable to tap into an alternative market economy anywhere near as large. For all of its problems, the fiat monetary system is still superior to autarky and isolation from the world economy. Violent monopoly over the money supply allows central governments to commandeer a large portion of the gains of capitalist free markets, thus benefiting from its superior productive capacity, using its gains to tighten its control on all facets of economic life, and ultimately strangling the capitalist civilization on which it depends. Capitalism has proven adept at fighting external enemies—but how can it fare against an internal parasite that controls the heart whose beat regulates its lifeblood? To survive, capitalism needs to invent and deploy an entirely independent and alternative heart to the one infested by parasites. This is a seemingly impossible task, but human reason might just be up for it. The entire process of civilization is based on the systematic application of reason to human action, and the more monetary central planning becomes a problem for civilization, the more the market provides incentives for solutions to this problem.

Capitalist economic calculation is at the root of technological innovation. What enables a technology to succeed and gain widespread adoption is its economics—its ability to offer users a positive economic return on employing it. Capitalism is a never-ending bounty program for innovations that solve problems for people. The larger a problem becomes, the larger the costs it inflicts on society, the more powerful the signals for finding a solution, and the larger the reward for its resolution. As the problems of the world's decrepit monetary system become more obvious, the most advanced technologies, engineers, and entrepreneurs will increasingly be drawn to tackling these problems. Capitalism weaponizes human reason in the service of innovations that benefit humanity, and it rewards it to the extent it succeeds. If fiat allows governments to capture the beating heart of civilization, capitalism is the brain fighting back by incentivizing reason to find a solution to this problem.

Technology is the sum of tools humanity has devised to confront the problems facing civilization. The human mind remains the last bastion of freedom, and the most advanced technology free humans can produce is software, if measured in terms of its productivity. Information in the form of letters and numbers, when conveyed in the correct way, can cause many machines worldwide to perform large amounts of work and thus create economic value for their owners. Machines perform the work of hundreds of men, but software moves thousands and millions of machines. All over the world, more and more economic production is coming to depend on software. Productivity in industry and software continues to grow, but it is hampered by the absence of a free monetary market to allow for accurate economic calculation to inform the decisions of capital owners worldwide. At a time when global information can move instantly, money continues to operate through a massively inefficient system manipulated to benefit its operators. As software is invading most of the industries of the world, and serving as a control for the world's industrial machinery, it appears inevitable it will invade and conquer the monetary market, particularly with the current violent and destructive incumbent fiat technology.

The software alternative to fiat central banking is bitcoin, a decentralized peer-to-peer payment network that uses its own native token, whose supply is capped. The significance of bitcoin lies in two main properties. First, bitcoin offers the only working alternative to central banking for the transfer of money across international borders. Second, bitcoin's supply is strictly capped, meaning there is no way to devalue the existing supply to the benefit of any entity. By offering everyone in the world the ability to save in a form of money that cannot be debased, bitcoin can stop the constant process of rising time preference. By giving everyone the ability to send and receive money internationally without resorting to their monopoly central bank, bitcoin allows everyone to partake in the global division of labor. It is precisely the central planning of these two markets—money and international transfers—that lies at the heart of the problem of global capitalism. The historical importance of bitcoin is that it is a technological solution to the problem of central banking, offering a technologically and infinitely more compelling alternative that obsoletes central banking.

In the same way, human reason moved us from using slaves to horses to cars to sophisticated supersonic jets—and moved us from using human messengers to carrier pigeons to paper mail to email to video calls—it is now moving us away from relying on monopoly central banks to reliable open-source software. Humans have reason, and it is reason that has taken us out of the caves and allowed us to conquer our environment, tame the wildest beasts, and live longer and better. The current parasitic governmental banking monopoly is just another in the long list of challenges human reason has faced, and bitcoin may prove to be the device our reason concocts for conquering it. With transparent rules available for anyone in the world to audit, and with a system built entirely on verification rather than authority, bitcoin gives the entire world a monetary market commodity that works without needing coercive political authority. It allows us to make peaceful non-aggression the basis of human economic interaction, bringing the productivity of the market system to the monetary realm, reversing the violent high time preference statist fiat detour of the last century. If it can unleash human civilization from the clasp of the state's fiat claws, bitcoin will be remembered as our age's most significant civilizational achievement.

Appendix 1

This appendix delves into Mises' contention from Chapter 1 that there are no constants in human action. It is a profound criticism of the methods of modern economics, and to illustrate it, let us examine how the natural sciences formulate quantitative relationships based on constants, using the example of the ideal gas law in thermodynamics, which states:

$$PV=nRT$$

Where P is pressure in bars, V is volume in liters, n is the number of moles (where each mole is 6.02214076 x 10e23 atoms), T is temperature in kelvin, and R is the Regnault constant of 0.083145 L.bar/mol.K.

Establishing such a relationship is possible because measurements of real physical phenomena are made in units that are *constant* and clearly defined by the International System of Units (SI), which defines seven base units on which all scientific measurements are built: the second, meter, kilogram, ampere, kelvin, mole, and candela. From these seven units, all other physically meaningful units can be derived.

The liter, for instance, is the volume of a cube with 10-centimeter (cm) sides. In the modern world, there are many measurement devices that can be used to reliably measure length and volume consistently. The bar is defined as the Earth's atmospheric pressure at an altitude of 111 meters and a temperature of 288.15 kelvin, and it is divided into 100,000 pascals of pressure. Barometers are produced according to reliable and consistent standards for measuring pressure using this unit.

In the past, the kilogram and meter, and indirectly, the kelvin, were defined in terms of specific artifacts kept in Paris. Each degree on the kelvin scale corresponds to a change in thermal energy by 1.380649x10e-23 joules. The joule is, in turn, defined as the energy transferred to an object when a force of 1 newton acts on that object in the direction of the force's motion through a distance of 1 meter. The newton is defined as the force needed to accelerate one kilogram of mass at the rate of 1 meter per second squared in the direction of the applied force.

The second was defined as one 86,400th of a day. However, in 1967, a new and more precise definition was adopted by the International System of Units, relying on the Cesium standard, the most accurate and precise time and frequency standard to be discovered so far. According to this standard, the second is defined as the duration of 9,192,631,779 periods of radiation corresponding to the transition between the 2 hyperfine levels of the ground state of the cesium-133 atom at a temperature of 0 kelvin. Since 1983, the meter has been defined as the length of the path traveled by light in vacuum during a time interval of 1/299,792,458 seconds. This measurement can be determined, demonstrated, and verified through experimentation.

In 2019, the kilogram was redefined in terms of the meter, second, and the Planck constant, which is defined as the quotient of a photon's energy divided by its frequency, and has a value of 6.62607015x10e-34 joule*second. With the redefinition of the kilogram, all the basic units are defined in terms of fixed fundamental constants of nature. Beyond just the units, scientific relationships can uncover constants of nature. The International System of Units lists 7 SI defining constants, whose values are used to derive all units: the hyperfine transition frequency of cesium, the speed of light, the Planck constant, elementary charge, the Boltzmann constant, the Avogadro constant, and luminous efficacy.

In the ideal gas law, we also find the Regnault constant, which is measured at 0.083145 L.bar/mol.K. This relationship and this constant are repeatable and demonstrable. This law posits that any person can measure the pressure, volume, temperature, and mole number of any gas in a container, and, from that, determine the Regnault constant and verify that the relationship holds. Should any person find a different relationship, with a different value for the constant, the ideal gas law would be disproven.

The existence of these reliable physical units for measurement makes it possible to engage in systematic, reproducible, and quantifiable scientific experimentation. These constants and measurements make it possible to conduct systematic experimentation with gases at different volumes, temperatures, and degrees of pressure. From these observed measurements, the relationships between these physically defined categories are established. In the case of the ideal gas law, a mathematical relationship is found between pressure, volume, and temperature. This relationship is scientific because it is objective. It is not founded on any singular or subjective experience; anyone can replicate it and test it. It has achieved the status of a scientific law only because a large and growing number of people have tested it and found it to hold. Since the relationship was first hypothesized by Benoît Paul Émile Clapeyron in 1834, no experiment has disproved it.

All these units and constants are defined in terms that are acceptable and comparable across the world, as well as being verifiable and testable by skeptics. Thanks to this uniformity, it is possible for people anywhere to engage in trade and sophisticated engineering projects. The reliability of these units is reflected in the number of workers and technicians who use the same tools and equipment with commonly agreed-upon standards. When an Argentine purchases a German-designed refrigerator manufactured in China, a large number of people all over the world had to agree on the definition of all of the scientific units detailed above in order to ensure the satisfactory production and delivery of the fridge.

These clearly defined, interpersonally and internationally agreed-upon units for measuring physical phenomena have no equivalent in economic science. There are no clearly defined units with which to measure economic value or utility, and any assessment of the metrics detailed above is subjective. Economic value can only be measured ordinally, in a way that compares the value of one good to another, and not cardinally, by assigning a mathematical value to each good. This is because the raw material of economics, value, is not measured with a physically or precisely defined quantity; it is a psychologically experienced judgment, as discussed in the second chapter of this book.

Bibliography

Go to saifedean.com/poe to access:

The book's full bibliography

Chapter-by-chapter bibliography

Links to download readings

And soon:

A study guide to this book

An online course based on this book

Index

A
absolute advantage, 166, 168
anarcho capitalist, 342, 353
Austrian economists, 3, 19, 35, 45, 203, 233, 240, 252, 282, 287, 298, 311, 317, 320, 326, 329, 337-8, 342, 364
Austrian School of Economics, 35, 135, 233, 252, 326

B
bank, 5, 21, 106, 192-3, 195, 196, 199, 251, 267, 271-4, 283, 285-7, 289-300, 303-12, 326, 359, 381-3, 387, 388-90
banknotes, 291
bankruptcy, 24, 72, 101, 106, 132, 189, 286
barter, 182-3, 200, 383
Bitcoin, 2, 46, 53, 124, 141, 195, 199, 247, 259, 268-70, 293-5, 381, 385, 389-90
bitcoiner, 269
The Bitcoin Standard, 2, 33, 124, 195, 247, 270, 381, 385
Britain, 114, 125, 127, 157, 347-8
business, 5, 23-4, 70, 72, 101, 224-5, 227, 230, 238-9, 251, 258-9, 267, 273, 278, 286, 293, 295-8, 300-3, 305, 307, 311, 321, 343-4, 347, 352, 356, 361, 366, 373, 383-4
business cycle, 5, 72, 251, 293, 295, 295-8, 301-3, 307, 311

C
capital, 4, 5, 36, 51-2, 57, 60-1, 69, 70-1, 77, 78, 82, 86, 89-109, 111-2, 115, 116-20, 122, 135, 137-8, 148, 155-7, 161-2, 164, 173-6, 178, 184, 191, 193, 200, 202-3, 205-7, 210, 224-7, 231-48, 251-2, 254, 257, 259-62, 265-7, 270, 272-3, 275, 277-90, 298-303, 305-9, 311-2, 316, 319-21, 323-5, 329, 330, 332, 335, 338, 341-2, 344-6, 352-3, 368-72, 375-7, 379, 381-9

capital accumulation, 5, 60, 91, 94, 96-109, 112, 118-9, 135, 137, 148, 157, 161-2, 164, 173-6, 200, 231, 248, 261-2, 266, 270, 272, 283, 285-8, 307, 345-6, 368-9, 375, 379
capital goods, 77, 82, 85, 90, 92-4, 96, 100, 103-4, 112, 118, 175-6, 202-3, 206, 231-4, 237-8, 241-3, 257, 275, 277, 282, 290, 300, 302, 306-7, 321, 372, 377, 379
capitalism, 5, 61, 76, 79, 107, 118, 148, 231-4, 236, 238, 247-8, 252, 311, 330, 372, 376, 379, 386-9
cash, 106, 181, 195, 204-5, 212, 215, 232, 257-61, 266, 277, 278, 310, 381
central bank, 192-3, 196, 199, 267, 275, 281, 285-6, 296-8, 306-312, 326, 383, 387-90
civilization, 3, 5-6, 60, 84-7, 103-4, 144, 148, 154-5, 161, 179, 200-2, 231, 251, 261, 164, 270, 281, 283, 285, 287, 312, 324, 338, 347, 351-2, 354, 364, 366-90
coincidence of wants, 181-3, 186-9, 196, 200, 255
coins, 193, 198, 259, 294-6, 322
comparative advantage, 166, 168-9, 172-3
credit, 5, 20, 71-2, 102, 107, 189, 193, 271-4, 276, 282, 286, 289-95, 298-9, 301, 304-5, 309-12, 322, 324, 343, 361, 381-2
crime, 262-3, 265, 267, 321, 341, 354, 358, 360-13, 386

D

decentralized, 268, 389
depression, 298, 312
digital, 123, 293, 295, 306

E

Earth, 4, 45, 46-55, 59-60, 67, 71, 81, 122, 133, 135, 138-41, 154, 178, 193, 199, 315, 362, 367-8, 371, 374-5, 384, 392
easy money, 191, 256, 260-1, 264, 269
economic, 1-5, 11-2, 14-38, 42, 45-7, 50-2, 56-62, 68, 72-90, 93, 98-9, 101-8, 111, 113-4, 116-7, 119-25, 127-30, 135, 137, 140-3, 150-4, 156-8, 161-2, 164, 166, 171, 173-4, 176, 179, 186, 188-9, 194, 197-206, 209-12, 214, 219, 228-9, 231-52, 256-8, 261, 263-4, 267, 272-3, 275-6, 280-2, 285, 287-9, 292-294, 297-304, 306-7, 316, 318-26, 328-338, 341-2, 345-7, 350-1, 353-5, 358, 361, 363-5, 367-9, 371-375, 377-8, 381, 383-391, 393-4
education, 152, 171, 323, 352, 374, 384
exchange, 16, 33-5, 59, 66, 69-70, 73, 77-8, 82, 98-9, 118, 161-6, 168, 170-2, 179, 181-7, 189, 192, 194, 196-7, 200-1, 203-5, 210-1, 225, 233-5, 238, 241, 244, 255-7, 259, 263, 265, 267, 272, 275, 277, 285, 290-4, 309, 316, 321, 336, 346, 350, 366, 372, 376, 378, 383-4
exchange rate, 33, 182, 384

F

Federal Reserve, 21, 73, 311, 383, 387
fiat, 23, 26, 72-3, 105, 154, 189, 199, 264-6, 268-9, 284-6, 294-6, 297, 326-7, 336, 338-352, 379, 381, 382-5, 388-90
fiat money, 73, 199, 264, 284, 286, 294-5, 297, 381, 383-4
fiat standard, 105, 154, 189, 264, 269, 326, 381, 382, 384, 385
fractional reserve, 290

G

GDP, 48, 150, 384
gold, 41, 49, 52, 55-6, 72, 136, 142-3, 188-9, 192-5, 198-9, 256, 258, 260, 263, 267, 270, 274, 284, 286, 290, 292, 294-5, 302, 309-12, 322, 382-3
gold coins, 258, 263

gold standard, 52, 56, 72, 136, 194, 199, 263, 267, 270, 284, 294-5, 309-10, 382
government money, 196, 198

H

hard money, 52, 191, 202, 260-1, 263, 269
Hayek, Friedrich, 18-19, 302, 309, 312, 322, 337-9
Hoppe, Hans-Hermann, 14-15, 60, 79, 82, 103, 202, 251, 253-4, 265-6, 276, 283-4, 331, 342, 353, 356, 366, 377-8, 380
human action, 2-3, 11-27, 33, 38, 41, 45, 47, 58, 65, 68, 86, 92, 102-3, 111, 113, 117, 120, 137, 161, 166, 172, 174, 181, 197-8, 205, 209, 211, 221, 226, 228-9, 231, 233, 238, 243, 253, 273, 276, 282, 296, 305, 315-6, 320, 326, 337, 342, 349, 353, 367, 374-5, 377, 387-8, 391.
hydrocarbon, 119, 138-40, 142-8, 151-2, 154-5, 384
hyperinflation, 264-5, 383

I

indirect exchange, 183, 196-7, 205
inflation, 20-1, 25, 71-3, 107, 154, 258, 261, 264-9, 286, 309, 320-1, 322, 324, 344, 357, 359, 360, 381-5
interest rates, 5, 104, 247, 251, 261-2, 275, 277, 280-1, 283-9, 298, 300-2, 304, 306, 309, 312, 322, 379, 381, 383,

K

Keynes, John Maynard, 1, 20-1, 74-6, 99, 102, 105-7, 206, 245-6, 257, 261, 267, 269, 297-8, 302, 306-9, 326, 385

L

Lightning Network, 294
liquidity, 184-5, 191, 195, 255, 258-9, 277
loan, 105, 261, 274-5, 277, 279-81, 283-6, 289, 290, 298-304, 306, 380
low time preference, 5, 58, 60, 107, 206-7, 253, 286, 288, 370, 376, 386

M

malinvestment, 305, 307, 312
marginal utility, 37-9, 41, 165, 185-6, 203, 215, 254-5, 260
market demand, 190-1, 198, 215-6, 219
markets, 5, 25, 71, 90, 100, 107, 123, 142-3, 177, 183-4, 189, 201, 209, 211, 221, 224, 230, 232-7, 244, 260, 265, 267, 269, 277, 311-2, 320, 324, 326-30, 336-9, 344-5, 347-8, 350-1, 354, 358, 361, 378, 380, 382-3, 388-89
meat, 166, 384
medium of exchange, 181, 183-7, 189, 191, 196-7, 199, 203, 238, 255-6, 265, 272, 291, 293-4, 383
Menger, Carl, 3, 12, 27-31, 36-9, 42, 80-1, 83, 89, 130, 141-2, 183-5, 198, 292-3
Mises, Ludwig von, 2, 5, 11-16, 23, 27, 29-30, 33, 37-8, 41, 45, 65-66, 68, 70, 79-82, 86-9, 92-4, 101-2, 104, 111, 113, 120, 129-31, 142, 161, 172-4, 181, 187, 196, 198, 201-2, 204-5, 209, 211, 226-8, 231-2, 234, 236, 238, 240-5, 266-8, 271, 273-4, 276, 282, 284, 286, 289, 291-6, 300, 302, 305, 307, 309, 317, 318-20, 322, 334, 342, 349, 350, 364, 367, 371, 373, 374, 382, 391
monetary demand, 190-1, 195, 198
monetary expansion, 5, 289-312

P

peer-to-peer, 268, 389
price, 16, 24-5, 31, 34-6, 40, 42, 46, 52, 54, 56-7, 69-70, 72-4, 101, 103-4, 123, 140-2, 166, 177, 184-6, 190-1, 193-5, 198, 201, 210-26, 228-30, 232, 239, 242, 248, 256, 258-9, 269, 280, 285, 296, 298-300, 302-5, 307-8, 310-1, 320-4, 330, 332-4, 347, 353, 384

R
recession, 20, 261, 307, 309
reserves, 48, 54-6, 58, 140-1, 154
risk, 86, 93, 96-7, 100, 102, 109, 112, 118, 122, 183, 185, 202, 225, 233, 237-8, 248, 257-61, 266, 268, 272, 284-6, 309, 321, 335, 382
Roman, 144, 322, 379
Rothbard, Murray, 12, 101, 104, 172, 187, 196, 201, 204-5, 232, 240, 276, 317, 322, 342, 350, 359

S
salability, 183-6, 188-91, 195-6, 198, 201-3, 256-60, 262, 310, 321, 383
savings, 60, 73, 102-3,105-7, 206-7, 229, 232, 237, 251, 254, 256-62, 264, 266-7, 269, 271-5, 277-8, 283, 286, 289, 301-2, 304, 306, 308, 311, 322, 324, 369, 382, 384
scarcity, 11, 14, 28-9, 36, 38, 43, 45-7, 52-4, 56-9, 65, 71, 74-5, 79-80, 83-5, 99, 114-5, 128, 130, 139-43, 239, 244, 252, 260, 268, 299, 342
silver, 55, 188-9, 192-4, 199, 256, 263, 295, 322
Simon, Julian, 45-6, 48, 52, 54
sound money, 73, 307, 311
the state, 5, 85, 128-9, 197-9, 229, 252, 312, 317-18, 338-9, 341-3, 347, 349-2, 354, 356, 358, 360, 362, 364-6, 382
store of value, 184, 190-1, 199, 263, 269
Switzerland, 72-3, 179, 380

T
time preference, 4-5, 58-60, 65-7, 85, 90, 92, 99, 103-4, 107, 109, 142, 201-2, 206-7, 237, 251-70

U
United States, 132, 236, 246, 310, 312, 343, 346, 357
unit of account, 199
unsound money, 307
U.S. dollar, 56, 196, 258, 383, 387

W
war, 281, 300, 317, 345, 358, 380-1, 383, 387, 189, 194, 235, 236, 244, 257, 261,
World War I, 189, 235, 380-1, 383

Printed in Great Britain
by Amazon

d0bd036a-0e2c-441d-acb0-0f795b50140fR01